ARTHUR RIMBAUD

Selected Poems and Letters

Translated and with an Introduction and Notes by
JEREMY HARDING *and* JOHN STURROCK

PENGUIN BOOKS

PENGUIN BOOKS

Published by the Penguin Group
Penguin Books Ltd, 80 Strand, London WC2R ORL, England
Penguin Group (USA) Inc., 375 Hudson Street, New York, New York 10014, USA
Penguin Books Australia Ltd, 250 Camberwell Road, Camberwell, Victoria 3124, Australia
Penguin Books Canada Ltd, 10 Alcorn Avenue, Toronto, Ontario, Canada M4V 3B2
Penguin Books India (P) Ltd, 11, Community Centre, Panchsheel Park, New Delhi – 110 017, India
Penguin Books (NZ) Ltd, Cnr Airborne and Rosedale Roads, Albany, Auckland 1310, New Zealand
Penguin Books (South Africa) (Pty) Ltd, 24 Sturdee Avenue, Rosebank 2196, South Africa

Penguin Books Ltd, Registered Offices: 80 Strand, London WC2R ORL, England

www.penguin.com

First published 2004
1

Translation, Introduction and Notes copyright © Jeremy Harding and John Sturrock, 2004
All rights reserved

The moral right of the translators has been asserted

Set in 10.25/12.25 pt PostScript Adobe Sabon
Typeset by Rowland Phototypesetting Ltd, Bury St Edmunds, Suffolk
Printed in England by Clays Ltd, St Ives plc

Contents

from *Album Zutique*

The Stupra

from *Last Poems*

from *Illuminations*

Acknowledgements

Jeremy Harding wishes to thank James Ozanne, Tim Curtis and Martin Thom for pointing the way to Rimbaud; Robert de Does, André Guyaux, Michel Murat and Lorna Scott Fox for their invaluable advice on some of the difficulties in the text; and Patrick and Geneviève Réal for their generous support. John Sturrock is grateful to André Guyaux for help on a number of points in the correspondence, and to Dr Richard Pankhurst, doyen of British Ethiopianists, who was able to explain numerous otherwise obscure references to local names, Amharic terms and events in Abyssinia in the 1880s.

Chronology

1854 Jean Nicolas Arthur Rimbaud born, 20 October, to Vitalie Cuif and Captain Frédéric Rimbaud in Charleville, a town in the Ardennes near the border with Belgium.

1860 Captain Rimbaud abandons his wife and family.

1865 Rimbaud starts to attend the Collège, or secondary school, at Charleville.

1869 Wins regional prize for Latin verse; writes 'The Orphans' New Year Gifts'.

1870 Georges Izambard takes a teaching post at the Collège. 'The Orphans' published in *La Revue pour tous*. Rimbaud sends work to the poet Théodore de Banville. France declares war on Prussia (19 July); Rimbaud leaves for Paris (end of August). During his detention at the Mazas prison (31 August–5 September), Napoleon III is defeated at the Battle of Sedan and surrenders to the Prussian Army; the Third Republic replaces the Second Empire on 4 September, and a Government of National Defence is formed to prosecute the war. On his release from prison, Rimbaud stays with Izambard's 'aunts' in Douai, where he begins copying his verses into a notebook for the poet Paul Demeny. While Rimbaud is in Douai, the Prussians lay siege to Paris (19 September). He is sent home to Charleville, leaves again, travels through Belgium and comes back to Douai. Finishes the notebook and presents it to Demeny. Goes back to Charleville.

1871 Mézières, next to Charleville, falls to the Prussians (2 January). France signs an armistice with Prussia (28 January) and the Siege of Paris ends. A new National Assembly is elected (February) with Adolphe Thiers as President, to negotiate the peace. Rimbaud spends two weeks in Paris and returns on foot to Charleville (10 March). Paris defies the Government in Versailles by proclaiming a revolutionary Commune (18 March) and electing its own representatives (28 March). Rimbaud is most probably in Paris some time in April, briefly, or early May. According to his friend Ernest Delahaye, he joins an irregular Communard unit in the defence of Paris against Government troops. In Charleville, he writes the 'Seer Letter' to Demeny (15 May). The Commune is crushed in the 'Bloody Week' of 21–28 May. Still in Charleville (late September), Rimbaud writes 'Drunken Boat' and heads for Paris at the invitation of Paul Verlaine. Consorts with Verlaine and his acquaintances. Attends a dinner with the 'Vilains Bonshommes' – mostly Parnassians – and recites 'Drunken Boat'. Frequents the more radical circle known as the Zutistes.

1872 Leaves Paris (January) at the instigation of Verlaine, whose family life is in ruins, largely as a result of what is now a love-affair with Rimbaud. Heads for Charleville via Arras, in the north-east. A period of reading and writing (perhaps some early prose-poems). Returns to Paris (early May). Leaves with Verlaine for Brussels (July), where they stay, despite the efforts of Verlaine's wife and mother-in-law, for three months. They travel to London (September) and, on a recommendation from Eugène Vermesch, a journalist and Communard refugee, find lodgings at 34 Howland Street. In London they meet many former Communards. They fall into penury. At the instigation of his mother, Rimbaud returns to Charleville (December).

1873 Rejoins Verlaine in London (January). They work on their English, with a view to teaching; they frequent the British Library Reading Room. Rimbaud goes back to the family farm at Roche, outside Charleville (April). Speaks of his projected 'Pagan Book' or 'Negro Book' (*A Season in Hell*) to Delahaye (May); returns to London with Verlaine (May). They lodge at 8 Great College Street, Camden Town. They are ostracized by Communard refugee acquaintances because of their dissolute ways and their homosexuality. Verlaine leaves with a plan to appease his wife (July) and, from Brussels, broadcasts his impending suicide. Rimbaud arrives in Brussels (8 July) and, on announcing his departure two days later (10 July), is shot through the wrist by Verlaine. Returns to Roche. Verlaine is imprisoned; *A Season in Hell* is finished (August). The book is printed in Brussels (October): Rimbaud's mother puts up the advance to the printer; Rimbaud collects his author's copies; the rest remain undistributed. In Paris (November), Rimbaud meets the young poet Germain Nouveau. Winter in Charleville.

1874 Back to Paris (March); from there to London with Nouveau. They lodge at 178 Stamford Street, near Waterloo Station. Starts to copy out some of the *Illuminations*. Nouveau goes back to France (April). Rimbaud moves to rooms near Soho. His mother and sister come to London (July). He begins teaching in Reading. Returns to Charleville for the new year.

1875 Verlaine is released from prison (January). Rimbaud goes to Stuttgart (February), to learn German and prepare for a career in business or industry. Verlaine travels to Stuttgart (March), where Rimbaud gives him the manuscript of the *Illuminations*, which will not resurface for eleven years. Travels to Milan (May). Suffers sunstroke while walking through Liguria (June); repatriated to Marseille; announces intention to join Carlist troops in Spain. Travels to Paris (July); tutors in a private school; returns to Charleville (October). Writes his last known piece of verse ('Dream') in a letter to Delahaye.

1876 Leaves for Vienna (April), is robbed and returns to Charleville. To Brussels, then Rotterdam (May) to enlist in the Dutch Colonial Army. Takes ship for the East Indies (June); arrives (July); deserts in Java (early August); finds passage to Ireland (early December); and arrives in Charleville a few days later.

1877 Rest of the winter in Charleville or Roche. To Germany (May), first in Cologne, perhaps recruiting mercenaries, then Bremen, where he tries and fails to enlist in the US Navy, then Hamburg. Joins the Cirque Loisset, a French travelling circus, possibly as a cashier, and travels with them to Stockholm

(July), then Copenhagen. Returns to Charleville. To Marseille (September or October), walking for long stretches; embarks for Alexandria, falls ill and is put off the boat at Civitavecchia; returns to Charleville.

1878 Somewhere in Germany or Switzerland until late spring. Summer in Roche. On foot (October) through the Vosges and over the Alps by the Saint-Gothard pass. Sets sail from Genoa for Alexandria (November), where he signs up for a job in Cyprus as a quarry foreman (December).

1879 Tension with the workforce. Returns to France (May), to recover from typhoid. Summer in Roche. Tries to return to Alexandria in the autumn but, hit by fever in Marseille, returns to Roche for the winter.

1880 Arrives in Cyprus (March) and takes a new job, quits and takes another. Leaves for Aden via Alexandria (July). Later rumours suggest he was forced to leave Cyprus, after causing the death of a labourer on a works site by hitting him with a stone. Begins working for Alfred Bardey's import-export business in Aden and is sent to consolidate a branch of the business in Harar, a town under Egyptian control since 1875, lying at the western edge of the Ogaden. He arrives in December.

1881 Revolt, led by the Mahdi, against Anglo-Egyptian presence in nearby Sudan. Bardey and colleagues visit Rimbaud in Harar (April). Health problems. Rimbaud mounts expedition to Bubassa (May). Returns to Aden, where he continues working for Bardey.

1882 Boredom and discomfort in Aden.

1883 Sets out for Harar (March) and works, again, as Bardey's agent. Starts taking photographs. Organizes trading expeditions in the Ogaden. Completes a report on the Ogaden for the company, which Bardey sends on to the Société de Géographie in Paris. Verlaine publishes his study of Rimbaud in *Lutèce* (October, November), quoting generously from hitherto unpublished poems. The Mahdi inflicts major defeat on Hicks Pasha in Sudan (5 November).

1884 The report on the Ogaden is read out at the Société de Géographie (February). Mahdist revolt intensifies; Britain, now fully in charge of Egypt's affairs, resolves on an Egyptian withdrawal from the Red Sea coast and hinterlands, including Harar. Bardey closes the branch and Rimbaud decamps to Aden (April). Egypt evacuates Harar (September).

1885 Fall of Khartoum and death of General Gordon (January). Egyptian evacuation of Messawa: the Italians move in, consolidating their presence in the region (February). Rimbaud decides to leave Bardey's company. Signs contract for an arms-trading venture with Pierre Labatut, a dealer in Shewa (October). Rimbaud is to run a caravan of guns from the coast, near Djibouti, up into Abyssinia and deliver them to King Menilek of Shewa, who is arming for a confrontation with his Tigrean neighbour, Yohannes IV, Emperor of Abyssinia. Rimbaud crosses from Aden and prepares the caravan (November/December).

1886 Rimbaud is stuck on the coast for several months: the French authorities forbid the traffic of arms to Shewa; he obtains a special authorization, but Labatut falls ill (c. June) and later dies. Rimbaud hopes to proceed with another partner, Paul Soleillet, but he too dies (September). Rimbaud resolves to run arms up to Shewa on his own (October). In France, meanwhile, *La Vogue* publishes a sequence of *Illuminations* and some verse-poems (May, June).

1887 King Menilek captures the evacuated town of Harar (January) while Rimbaud is still en route from the coast to Shewa. Rimbaud arrives in the Shewan town of Ankober (February), only to discover that he must go on to Entotto, if he is to negotiate with Menilek. The King and his entourage force him to drop his price for the weapons, and invoke Labatut's debts – real and alleged – to lower it still further. Rimbaud leaves Shewa with the explorer Jules Borelli (May) and heads for Harar, where he will have to convert Menilek's promissory note into cash through the good offices of the King's new governor in Harar, his cousin Ras Mekonnen. Travels to Aden (July) and Cairo (August). Publishes a long article about his journey to Shewa in *Le Bosphore égyptien*; fails to secure backing from the Société de Géographie for an expeditionary project. Back to Aden (October).

1888 To Harar some time in the early part of the year; back to Aden and again to Harar (May), to trade on his own account and as a 'commission agent' for César Tian, another import-export entrepreneur in Aden.

1889 Rimbaud in Harar. Yohannes IV killed by Mahdists (March). Menilek becomes Emperor of Abyssinia.

1890 Rimbaud in Harar.

1891 Complains of pain in the right leg. Almost immobilized (March). Is carried down from Harar across the desert to Zeilah, a twelve-day journey (April). To Aden and then Marseille (May), where the leg is amputated. Leaves hospital in Marseille for Roche (July). Returns to Marseille as general paralysis sets in (August). Dies on 10 November at the age of thirty-seven.

Introduction

Arthur Rimbaud's demons allowed him very little rest. His life as a productive poet lasted five years and transformed him from a brilliant schoolboy with a gift for Latin verse into a major European poet. His first published poem in French, a deft piece of pilfering from the models of the day, was written in 1869, around the time of his sixteenth birthday. The last of his prose-poems, which recast the rules of composition as if from scratch, were probably written in 1874 or 1875. Between the beginning and the end of this brief career, there were several evolutions. In 1871, Rimbaud announced a 'visionary' poetics based on what he called a 'disordering of all the senses'. The results were spectacular. By the following year, he had stretched the rules of French prosody to breaking-point to produce the childlike lyric cadences of the *Last Poems*. Then, in 1873, he published *A Season in Hell*, a repudiation both of his life as a poet and of his project: to change the nature of poetry, as well as the world, by reinventing language itself. 'Now,' he wrote, 'I must bury my imagination and my memories.' He continued working on the prose-poems even so. In the end, however, *A Season in Hell* was as good as its word. At the age of twenty, Rimbaud had dealt with his unfinished business and abandoned literature for ever.

He has become a legendary figure on three counts: his extra-ordinary poetic achievement, the turbulence of his five years or so as a practising poet, and the rupture with poetry, followed by a new life as a colonial trader, in which he encountered some of the harshest conditions that Europeans had experienced in Africa. It is a legend of transformation and re-emergence, shadowed by fitful continuities between the errant poet and the errant trader. Legends often turn out to be shaky on close inspection, yet this one can be re-examined and demystified without losing its status, which has survived the debunking of many half-truths and lies about Rimbaud. Accordingly, the new Penguin Rimbaud aims to carry the reader beyond the period of *A Season in Hell* and the *Illuminations*, to the years in Africa. A generous selection of Rimbaud's work – around two-thirds of it – is presented here in French, with a parallel text translation. It is followed by more than a hundred of his letters, many of them written from Africa.

Poems, 1869–71

Rimbaud was born in the Ardennes, in the town of Charleville, not far from the Belgian border, on 20 October 1854. His father, Frédéric, was a Captain of Infantry in the French Army, who abandoned the family in 1860. His mother, Vitalie Cuif, was the daughter of well-to-do peasants with a farm near Charleville. She was a disciplinarian – a tendency reinforced by her husband's desertion – and a devout Catholic; Rimbaud's aggressive dislike of the Church and all its works is very much on display in the early poems. As a boy, he suffered both from his mother's pronounced sense of duty to her children and from the inertia of small-town provincial life. According to Enid Starkie (*Arthur Rimbaud*, 1938), Mme Rimbaud would punish her son and his brother Frédéric by making them memorize lines of Latin. 'Why learn Latin?' Rimbaud complained in a confident piece of prose, written when he was nine. 'No one speaks that language.' Yet in the regional examinations of 1869, his Latin verse submission earned him first prize – one of more than a dozen 'firsts' he racked up in two consecutive years.

A young teacher who arrived at the Collège in Charleville the following year was asked to keep an eye on its greatest asset. Georges Izambard, a liberal republican with radical tendencies, deeply at odds with the complacency of the Second Empire, gave Rimbaud the run of his library and was soon in trouble with the boy's mother. 'I am extremely grateful to you for all that you are doing for Arthur,' she wrote to him in 1870.

'. . . But there is one thing I cannot approve of and that is, for instance, the reading of the book you lent him the other day (Les Misérables, V. Hugot [sic]).' It was probably too late for parental censorship to make a difference, even if it had been enforceable. Beyond the dazzling achievements at school and the difficult scenes at home, a course of action was becoming clear to the young Rimbaud.

A few weeks later he sent three poems off to Théodore de Banville, a leading light of the Parnassian school. The Parnassians – the dominant poetic movement of the day – were a loosely defined group, whose first series of anthologies, *Le Parnasse contemporain* ('The Modern Parnassus') of 1866, were familiar to Rimbaud. By the 1870s the movement had become a major way-station between post-1830 Romanticism and Symbolism, which would not gain definition for another fifteen years or more. The work of the Parnassians was anti-inspirational. The movement's figurehead, Charles-Marie Leconte de Lisle, was a brilliant technician, whose followers came to see poetry as a highly methodical process, based on formal constraints which they welcomed. The political and social value of art – an outmoded Romantic idea – was rejected: the ideal was a burnished surface, depersonalized, detached and visibly skilful.

Banville was by all accounts a more approachable figure than Leconte de Lisle, but he did not help Rimbaud get his poems published. Rimbaud's ambition was undiminished. A penniless journey by train to Paris in August 1870, shortly after the outbreak of the Franco-Prussian War, gave notice of his intentions: whatever else poetry might be, it meant getting out of Charleville. With this founding escapade, he solemnized the bond between his calling as a poet and his urge to be on the move.

Having failed to pay his fare, Rimbaud was briefly imprisoned in Paris. Izambard negotiated his release in early September. He was brought to stay with a trio of sisters in Douai whom Izambard referred to as his adoptive 'aunts'. He returned to Charleville, only to take flight again, heading over the border to Belgium, in the vain hope of finding an opening in journalism,

and made his way back to Douai. By the time he left for Charleville, he had set out his stall: a fair copy of works to date, about
twenty poems altogether. He entered them in a notebook and
presented it to Paul Demeny, a teacher and poet, whom he'd
met through Izambard. The contents of the 'Douai notebook'
include a range of light-fingered prisings (from Victor Hugo and
Baudelaire, among others), recyclings (Villon, via Banville) and
satirical reworkings (Albert Glatigny), but there are also beautiful passages where the boy-impresario is auditioning the boy-
poet, out of earshot of any obvious masters. Parts of 'Nina Gets
Back to Him' and 'Popular Fiction' strike this vein. So do the
two superb sonnet-sketches, 'At the Green Inn' and 'Knowing
Way', which play with elements from Rimbaud's hike in Belgium. In both poems, a tricky adolescent with a good ear for
vernacular and a real skill with the standard twelve-syllable line,
or alexandrine, is trying out the breezy tone of the man's man –
food, beer, fancying the waitress – to see how it suits him. It's
the imperfect fit that works so well. The youth whose clothes
are a size too big is not a comic figure, but a little emperor, with
all the trappings of mastery billowing around him. His empire
is language.

At the beginning of November, Izambard again delivered
Rimbaud back to his mother. By now the Emperor proper,
Napoleon III, had capitulated to the Prussians at the Battle of
Sedan and France was struggling on under a Government of
National Defence. The Second Empire had ceased to exist, and
a Third Republic had been declared. Paris was under siege. It
held out until January 1871, when an armistice was signed.
Rimbaud, meanwhile, was confined to Charleville. He had
already conceived a loathing for Napoleon III and was now
honing a ferocious republican politics. As Bismarck bullied the
new Government into a humiliating peace, Rimbaud spent his
days in the Charleville library. 'Seat-People' is his revenge on
the librarian for his reluctance to supply the books Rimbaud
requested ('occult' and 'subversive' works, according to Enid
Starkie).

In February he headed off again for Paris, where he remained
for two miserable weeks, before returning on foot to Charleville

– more than 200 kilometres – to fester as popular sentiment in Paris turned against the Government for complying with the terms imposed by Prussia. The armistice had been signed over the heads of the city's inhabitants, already politicized by four months of hunger and isolation during the siege; now they shuddered to see a new National Assembly dominated by conservatives – and conservative liberals – including some 400 monarchist deputies. An insurrection began in Montmartre on 18 March, when the crowd, confronted by Government troops, persuaded them not to open fire. The Government withdrew to Versailles. It was the beginning of the Paris Commune. Municipal elections followed and, on 28 March, the Commune's representative leaders took office. The city embarked on a brief moment of self-rule and another bitter siege, complete with bombardment, directed not from Berlin this time but from Versailles.

Rimbaud naturally greeted the proclamation of the Commune with delight: he took to the streets of Charleville shouting, 'Order is vanquished!' It's likely that he was back in Paris again before the city was brutally subdued by Versaillais troops at the end of May. Yet his Communard credentials are obscure. Neither Graham Robb nor another recent biographer, Jean-Luc Steinmetz (*Arthur Rimbaud, une question de présence*, 1991), is in any doubt about this third trip to the city, some time in April 1871. Even so, there is no agreement as to its significance. Rimbaud was hardly a dedicated revolutionary. If anything, he was in search of a dedicated revolution. His idea was not to set his poetry manfully at the service of the Commune, but to steep the first in the second, partly as an act of solidarity, but more pertinently – on the business side – as an investment in the radicalized approach to writing that was now his priority: go to extremes (go to Paris), observe the effects.

A batch of so-called Communard poems, including 'The Hands of Jeanne-Marie', vouch for Rimbaud's partisan feelings about the Commune, if not his presence in Paris. But there is also the strange and beautiful 'Heart of a Clown', both an epiphany and the record of a sexual shaming, set in Paris and dated May 1871. We're to imagine a Communard barracks full of soldiers: irregulars as well as radicalized National Guardsmen (the military ballast of the Commune) and pro-Communard members of the 88th Regiment, who had disobeyed the order to shoot in Montmartre. They are off duty, drunk and up for an ugly scene. The 'I' of the poem is at once the victim of a degradation and a witness to it. 'Heart of a Clown' has been read as the poet's record of his rape by Communard militias, but it's clearly more – and less – than that. It speaks of a terrible disillusion in the face of human brutality. At the same time it is a perverse, vitalist tribute to the destructive force of an idealized revolutionary class, from which nothing, not even purity, is immune.

The Seer

If Rimbaud had indeed been in barracks in Paris, then it's quite possible that he was enrolled as a Communard irregular, but not for long: the likeliest dates are some time between mid-April and mid-May of 1871. The Commune was put down in a week of blood-letting at the end of May, by which time Rimbaud was back in the Ardennes. We know this because the two letters to Izambard and Paul Demeny in which he outlines a poetic 'method' are franked 13 and 15 May respectively, and written from Charleville. They are manifestos for a Commune-like shake-up of poetry – a revolution in the processes of production. What they show, above all, is Rimbaud's distaste for the idea that the poet's task might simply consist in a worka-day tinkering with the steady flow of information through the senses.

Rimbaud was by now much more than a young man with strong political opinions: he was busy demolishing and re-building on the site he knew best. As a poet he would henceforth be a militant advocate of the unforeseen: nothing less would do. The letters to Izambard and Demeny call the 'self' forcefully into play as the agent of a new visionary poetics. But it is not the integral, troubled, narcissistic self of Rimbaud's most obvious predecessor, Baudelaire, whose genius he admired (though he thought him diminished by his 'artistic' milieu). On the contrary, the Rimbaudian self is a harsh experiment in disfiguring. It is wilfully distended and distressed, offering the maximum surface area to which unusual information (the 'unknown') can adhere. The letter to Demeny speaks famously of the poet becoming 'a seer' by means of a 'long, immense and reasoned disordering of all the senses'. The word 'reasoned' is important, as John Sturrock explains in connection with Rimbaud's letters (see below). Alcohol and hashish had a role in this disordering, but the decisive factor was Rimbaud's intolerance of received wisdom and his hunger for experiment. 'Let us ask *poets* for the *new* – ideas and forms,' he says in the letter to Demeny.

The labours of the seer bore fruit in a handful of poems, including 'Seven-year-old Poets' and 'First Communion', composed during the summer of 1871. In August Rimbaud wrote to Banville again, enclosing 'To the Poet on the Matter of Flowers'. This long poem is a joke at the expense of the Parnassians, while remaining a homage to Banville (the Rimbaud scholar André Guyaux describes it perfectly as a study in 'insolence'). It is unmistakably a modern piece of writing, with its commotion of ironies, its plunges into obscurity and its modulating tones of voice: a tour de force – and probably Rimbaud's farewell to the Parnassian model. He nonetheless regarded Paul Verlaine – one of *Le Parnasse contemporain*'s younger contributors – as a great poet (a 'seer', indeed).

On the basis of the two letters and eight poems he received from Charleville, Verlaine felt much the same about the importunate Rimbaud, and duly invited him to Paris. Rimbaud's preparations for the visit included the composition of a big poem, something audacious to spring on the capital. Shortly before he was due to leave, in late September, he went for a walk with his loyal friend Ernest Delahaye. Graham Robb's account builds elegantly on Delahaye's recollections:

> It was a sunny autumn afternoon. They sat down at the edge of a wood and Rimbaud pulled out some sheets of paper. He had written a 100-line poem 'to show the people in Paris'. The verse was quite regular, but the content was extraordinary. Abruptly,

without any rhetorical introduction, a boat recounted its adventures since the massacre of its crew – its astounding visions and
gradual disintegration.[1]

Delahaye recalls Rimbaud reading 'without emphasis and with
no vocal flourishes, rather convulsively, like a child telling of
some great grief'.[2] And why not? 'Drunken Boat', after all, is a
poem that ends in defeat. It is also a spectacular literary success,
perhaps Rimbaud's most famous work, and a 'seer' poem *par
excellence*. Robb sees clear links between the poem and the
letter to Demeny, both of which envisage 'purification by dissol-
ution, the loosening of the rivets and tackle that bind the person-
ality, visions teetering on the brink of the incomprehensible,
and a strange nostalgia for the future'.[3]

Paris, Verlaine

In Paris, Verlaine was only a little quicker to show off his
boy-genius from the provinces than he was to fall in love with
him. That process nevertheless began under the nose of his
pregnant wife and the roof of his in-laws, the Mautés, who
provided Rimbaud with a room on his arrival. He proceeded to
make himself insufferable, calling for the removal of a picture
from one of the walls (he didn't like it) and apparently vandaliz-
ing an ivory Christ (religion was still an abomination to him).
Beyond the Mauté household, meanwhile, as Verlaine swished
Rimbaud hither and thither with growing excitement, the
condescending approval began to wane.

One of the reasons was that the homosexual character of their
relationship was becoming more ostentatious, and this was not
a state of affairs that many in Verlaine's circle, ankle-deep in
their nervous bohemianism, found easy to accept. But Rimbaud
had other, startling ways of giving offence. Early on, he told the
veteran Banville that it was time to dump the alexandrine,
the main joist in the edifice of French poetry dating back to the
twelfth century: not such a good idea, in view of the Parnassians'
high regard for the rules. In the garret Banville lent him, after
his eviction from the Mauté household, he went to the window,

stripped off in full view of the neighbours and threw his clothes on to the roof. (Banville told the journalist Rodolphe Darzens that he had also slept in his boots, smashed the china and sold the furniture.) Lodging with the bohemian poet and inventor Charles Cros, he broke a plaster bust and tore up back-issues of a journal containing his host's verses, which he used as lavatory paper. He cut Verlaine in a café during a game with a knife, and again in the street. He tried to stab the photographer Etienne Carjat with a sword-cane. He also claimed to have ejaculated into a glass of milk, destined to be drunk by the consumptive pianist Ernest Cabaner, while poor Cabaner was out of the room.

Many people who had never heard of his antics simply took an instant dislike to him. Everyone was impressed, for better or worse, by his looks. He reminded Mallarmé of 'a laundress, because of his great hands, red and chapped by the changes from warm to cold'. A few years later, the young poet Jean Richepin spoke of 'his gauche peasant appearance, his big hands and feet, his hair like thatch' but also of his 'angel's eyes'. He was in every way a striking figure, whose charm would merely have added to his awfulness. And of that charm there's little doubt. Delahaye speaks of him rubbing his eyes with his knuckles, like a sleepy child, and blushing if he were introduced to anyone new. A luminous innocence glimmered through the crust of monstrousness he had cultivated so assiduously.

The poetry from this period is sparse. 'The Seekers of Lice' perhaps – though it may have been written earlier, during the summer – and the untitled poem 'What are they to us . . .', a lament for the Commune in which the revolutionary ideal itself seems extinct beside the cosmic overhaul the poem has in mind. The hermetic sonnet 'Vowels', inspired by a synaesthetic game that Rimbaud and Cabaner used to play at the piano, or perhaps by an illustrated children's alphabet that Rimbaud recalled from the nursery, was also composed at this time. So too were the parodies and not-quite-parodies he wrote as a member of the Zutistes' circle – a fringe group of extravagantly bohemian poets, anarchists and survivor-Communards who convened for regular drinking sessions in a hotel overlooking the Boulevard

St Michel, with Rimbaud and Cabaner in charge of alcohol supplies. The *Album Zutique*, in which members wrote their entries – mocking, salacious, often spiced with images of pederasty – contains some twenty pieces by Rimbaud, among them, a duet with Verlaine, 'Idol. Arsehole Sonnet', and 'Reminiscence of an Aged Cretin'. Rimbaud's 'systematic disordering' was proceeding apace in all domains, including the senses.

The relationship between Rimbaud and Verlaine has been raked over and over. It was a hectic affair that asked much of Rimbaud and almost everything of Verlaine, including near ruin and a year and a half in Belgian prisons. Rimbaud himself was extremely demanding, though he could seem to want all and nothing by turns; he was loyal, even in his negligence, capricious in his utter single-mindedness, given to violence and provocation while capable of childlike remorse and tenderness. He hoped, perhaps, in taking up with Verlaine, to find a respite from the worst of his own solitude, and imagined that Verlaine – so incapable for so much of the time – would thrive under his supervision, itself a kind of charity he felt bound to bestow, without much sanctimony. On this basis, the two men would set about the great project of transforming poetry together. But Rimbaud's charity was his beneficiary's torment. He was a harsh taskmaster, for whom Verlaine was too often guilty of backsliding. In the end he reduced Verlaine to a state of agonized dependency, brutally evoked in *A Season in Hell* ('Delirium I').

Sooner or later, in connection with Verlaine, Rimbaud's sexuality comes up for discussion. If this was his only significant homosexual relationship, then how far was he 'really' homosexual? To the poet Yves Bonnefoy, Rimbaud's homosexuality began as 'no more than another element of his "reasoned disordering"'.[4] Graham Robb concurs: homosexuality was 'a blank space on the social map' and thus 'a powerful invitation'.[5] There is no reason why an icon of revolt and adolescent genius shouldn't become a gay icon too. Yet it's hard to keep him fast to any sexual identity: the problem lies not with his sexuality, but with his 'identity' as such – something of an experimental site between 1870 and 1875. That, no doubt, would have been part of his attraction, and part of what encouraged Verlaine to head off with him, abandoning his wife and child for a life of mesmerizing unpredictability. The affair ended in Brussels in July 1873, when Verlaine pulled a revolver and shot Rimbaud in the wrist. It was less than two years since they had met.

Last Poems, First Prose-poems

In the meantime there were important changes in Rimbaud's work. The first turning point came in the spring of 1872, when he left Paris for a brief stay in Charleville, allowing Verlaine to take stock of his unenviable family situation. The great poem sometimes associated with this period is 'Memory', a dramatic encryption of the brief Rimbaud–Cuif marriage – the fugitive male, the stern mother – in the symbolic world of an Ardennes landscape animated by the thoughts of a desperate young boy. Verse after verse, it reckons the weight that family history might exert on any childhood – and the haunting under-exposure of memory itself, as patches of shadow and grainy light give way to areas of unreadable darkness.

'Memory' is not an easy piece of writing, despite its use of familiar stagecraft: rhyming quatrains, alexandrines (though without the time-honoured rules that govern them), the dressing of a landscape, followed by the introduction of figures, and so on. But when Rimbaud set off again for Paris at the end of May, another development was under way. This time, the props – the twelve-syllable line certainly, but the vestiges of narrative, too – would be abandoned in favour of a sparse, declarative lyric which draws on the 'naive' forms of nursery-rhyme, popular song and comic opera. (The *Last Poems* in which these lyrics feature were also referred to as *Chansons* or 'Songs'; they include 'Comedy of Thirst', 'Song from the Highest Tower', 'Festivals of Hunger' and 'Happiness'.) Yet the declarations themselves, sometimes in lines of five or seven syllables, are closer to incantation than direct statement – charms, scraps of prophetic utterance, lamentations, records of unappeasable longing:

> Turn, my hungers! Hungers, graze
>   On fields of bran!
> Suck up the blithe poison
>   Of convolvulus . . .
>   ('Festivals of Hunger')

Even as these strange songs were being set down, another form had suggested itself to Rimbaud. *The Deserts of Love* is thought to have been written around this time, or even earlier, and may have been inspired by the prose-poems of Baudelaire. It is certainly a foretaste of Rimbaud's own, of which about forty would eventually surface as *Illuminations*. How likely is it that he was already experimenting with the prose-poem in the early part of 1872? Consider the following sequence of events: Rimbaud returned to Paris in May, spent about two months in the city and left with Verlaine for Belgium, where they stayed, despite the efforts of Verlaine's wife and mother-in-law, until September, when they took passage to England and found lodgings off the Tottenham Court Road; in November Verlaine wrote from London to a friend in Paris, asking him to recover some personal effects, including letters from Rimbaud which contained a number of 'verse and prose-poems'. It's thought that these were destroyed by Verlaine's wife, but the request in itself is evidence that the prose-poem was most likely a project in view before Rimbaud left Charleville for Paris, and that it may well have gained a preliminary shape.

The *Illuminations*, of which only three (or arguably two) are not in prose, present Rimbaud scholars, and the general reader, with several difficulties. In the first place, though they are among the most famous pieces of modern European literature, they lack the consistency, and the feel, of a thought-out sequence of work. They are not, in the words of André Guyaux, 'a single text with a beginning and an end'.[6] Indeed, the poems seem to stand as individual works, or pairs, or runs; there is no obvious over-arching design. A haze of conjecture surrounds the dating of the *Illuminations*. *A Season in Hell* always posed the biggest problem here: Rimbaud's passionate resignation from the world of letters encouraged the belief that none of the *Illuminations* could have been written after its publication in 1873. Yet the facts are otherwise, and a curious remark in the opening sequence of *A Season in Hell* – 'Since we're waiting for the last of my low little deeds' – is now thought to be a veiled admission that there was still a collection of prose-poems in the offing. Quite how the *Illuminations* divide on either side of *A Season in Hell* is uncertain. What matters is that they do, and that the various phases of poetic production overlap, so that the oracular lyrics of 1872 were probably being composed alongside early drafts of prose-poems; and then, as Rimbaud settled into London with Verlaine, a new idea began to infiltrate his thinking on the prose-poems: that of a work to end all work, or at any rate his own.

A Season in Hell

Rimbaud's time in London was marked by comings and goings: he made a brief visit to Charleville in December, another in the spring of 1873, and – after the saga with Verlaine in Brussels – a third in August. All the while, however, the city, with its intoxicating strangeness, kept the *Illuminations* in the mind's eye of the poet, most likely as a project in abeyance. For *A Season in Hell*, the old ground of the Ardennes was more fertile. The text is dated 'April–August 1873', and though it may have been started earlier, Rimbaud was 'at home' during both these months. The diary of his sister Vitalie records him at Roche in August, exempted from 'manual tasks' on the farm by his pressing work with 'the pen' ('The hand that guides the pen,' he writes in 'Bad Blood', 'is a match for the hand that guides the plough').

A Season in Hell is the seer's recantation. The achievement of the *Last Poems* is reviled ('outlandish and absurd'): actual verses are dragged, misshapen, before their disabused creator for judgment. The voice is sarcastic, harsh, sometimes desperate. Even more than the poems, the visionary scheme that informed them is rejected, along with the relationship with Verlaine, the vanity of the seer-project and everything it entailed.

The book – translated in its entirety here – is at the same time the record of a fresh search. An idiosyncratic search and, as Yves Bonnefoy has said, 'a private experience' full of 'difficult ellipses' and 'resolutely personal allusions'.[7] Earlier drafts show how stringently it was revised – almost assaulted – before it achieved its final density. The gist of *A Season in Hell* is clear, even so. As the ground is swept clean of earlier follies and affections, a different order of truth must be discovered; beauty must undergo redefinition; there must be a new idea of strength and wisdom. Long passages of *A Season in Hell* are attempts, sentence by sentence, blow by blow, to bring these 'unknowns' to light. 'Truth', 'beauty', 'strength' – big, cumbersome notions. But that is surely the point: the day of the clever boy, with his agile perversities, is over.

How, then, will the man be 'saved'? A double atheism frames this question: the prophetic 'alchemy of the word' has failed to divulge truth, beauty or wisdom; but there is no use believing that religion, and certainly not Christianity, which dogs this book from the outset, will ride to the rescue. Whence Rimbaud's working-title, confided to Delahaye in the spring of 1873: the 'Pagan Book' (also the 'Negro Book'). But paganism, it turns out, is a dead end too. Neither the 'Orient', which stands for a non-Christian, non-Islamic ideal of hardship and grace, nor a passionate identification with a nobly savage, pre-contact 'Africa' can offer solace. The protagonist of *A Season in Hell* is beyond religious faith, genealogy, race, political solidarity and the feeble consolations of his own creative past. The relationship with Verlaine, the 'Foolish Virgin' of 'Delirium I', has been aborted. There can be no turning back: 'One must be absolutely modern.'

Illuminations

A Season in Hell was printed in Brussels in October 1873. Rimbaud collected a handful of copies, distributed them to friends and, without the money to pay off the cost of production, left the rest to gather dust at the printer's (they were discovered in 1901). During a brief stop-over in Paris, he took up with Germain Nouveau, one of a group of young poets known as the 'Vivants', before returning to Charleville, where he would spend the winter. He found Nouveau again in Paris in March 1874, and the couple (as they probably were) left for England. Nouveau would head back to France some time in the early summer, leaving Rimbaud on his own. In the interim, Rimbaud began copying out his prose-poems with the help of his new accomplice. The manuscripts are the basis of the *Illuminations*. A few remixed snatches of pastoral and scrambled landscape – in 'Childhood', for instance, 'Fragments/12' and 'Historic Evening' – suggest the world of the Ardennes. Many more invoke the city. Not Paris or Brussels, but London: by now highly industrialized, exotic, glamorous yet filthy, seething with contradiction (spectacular feats of engineering and entrepreneurship on the one hand; extremes of deprivation on the other). A city awash with fog, in which the lamplight seemed to float like phosphorus.

If Rimbaud had been eager to get back to London after an absence of roughly nine months, it wasn't simply that he was in disgrace with almost everyone he'd known in Paris: there was still the important matter of the last 'low little deeds' to be accomplished. Yet the when and where of specific *Illuminations* are impossible to pinpoint. Some, whether or not they were committed to paper, would have germinated in Soho and Camden Town, when Verlaine and Rimbaud were still together. In 1874, Rimbaud was in a different part of London – Waterloo, to begin with – but his indefatigable walking habit would have taken him all over the place. The 'urban' *Illuminations* are indebted to the vast capital city which had intrigued him when he first arrived in September 1872 and which he saw for the last time at the end of 1874. Even so, it is hard to fix the city in the work for very long. It was the astonishing nature of London that held the mirror up to Rimbaud's art, and not the other way around.

The *Illuminations* are free-ranging. The writerly 'I' darts in and out of the material with no duty to coherence. The poems themselves (as we've seen already) are highly individuated. Some, like 'After the Flood', are modern – 'absolutely modern' even – in the manner of montage; others ('Workers', 'Dawn') resemble short stories; others dunk us in a torrent of idiom –

the parable, the letter to a friend or benefactor, the travelogue – which suddenly dries up: a habit that accounts for their lack of affect. Others still might be described as celebrations of anger or ecstasy ('Sale', 'Genie') were it not for a creeping anaesthesis which numbs them to the very states they propose. Two of the poems set as verse ('Seascape' and 'Movement') are entirely without metrical constraint, and have been hailed as the first 'free verse' in French. But are these liberties the result of some deep dissatisfaction with verse as such? There are no premonitory signs of crisis in the later verse. The prose-poem was the last form for Rimbaud, but surely not the last poetic resort.

Rimbaud travelled to Stuttgart at the beginning of 1875. He was learning German with a view to a career in business or industry. In any case, poetry was no longer in prospect. Verlaine, who had been imprisoned in Belgium after the shooting incident in Brussels, was released in January. Insofar as he could ever be wholly one thing – for he thrived, and foundered, on ambivalence – Verlaine was now a devout Catholic. He resolved to pay Rimbaud a visit. He would be reconciled with his old friend, and bring him the message of salvation in Christ. It was not a happy encounter. To Rimbaud, the great pedlar of obscenity, the spectacle of Verlaine's piety must have been truly obscene, though it was not without its comic side. He decided to ply the repentant sinner with drink and, with grim satisfaction, reported on the effects to Delahaye (see Letter 25): 'Verlaine arrived here the other day, with a rosary in his claws. Three hours later we'd renounced our god and made J. C.'s 98 wounds bleed.' For Rimbaud, Verlaine's conversion was probably the final piece of backsliding. He could see nothing for it but to kick down the fragile edifice of new-found faith and let Verlaine on his way to piece it back together. He did, however, retain an unscrupulous interest in Verlaine's money – it had been useful in London – and later, as Verlaine made a bid for respectability, he tried, unsuccessfully, to blackmail him. But after their encounter in Stuttgart, they never saw each other again. Verlaine, so often the injured party in all this, took Stuttgart badly. He was soon speaking bitterly of Rimbaud as a self-important charlatan. Yet he remained loyal to his earlier, idealized image of the boy-genius and, crucially, to Rimbaud's poetry, though in his unsteady posture as a Christian, he would tut-tut over 'First Communion'.

Verlaine left Stuttgart with an assortment of Rimbaud's papers, including most of the *Illuminations*. Rimbaud asked him to hand them on to Nouveau, who was in Belgium at the time: perhaps Nouveau would manage to have them printed. Or this is how Verlaine remembered it later. For many years the *Illuminations* were lost. In 1886 they were published along with a handful of the later verse in the literary review *La Vogue*, and then as a chapbook with an introduction by Verlaine, who explained that the title *Illuminations* was to be understood in the sense of 'coloured plates' – as in prints, or impressions. Elsewhere, in a letter to a friend, Verlaine played with the spelling, and wrote it as 'Illuminécheunes', the pseudo-English pronunciation stressing the link so many of the poems have with Rimbaud's time in London.

Modern editions tend to follow the order in which the poems appeared in *La Vogue*, spread across several issues. Félix Féneon, then a young editor at the review, received them in loose, unnumbered sheets, which he then numbered and prepared for the setter. Very likely they'd been pored over and shuffled more than once in the decade since the handover in Stuttgart. It's nonetheless been argued that the numbering may have been Rimbaud's own and that we have them in an approximation of the order he intended. While *La Vogue* was readying the first group for publication, there was no question of consulting the author. He was sweltering on the coast of Djibouti as he waited to run a shipment of guns up into the Abyssinian highlands. The break with poetry had been made a decade earlier, and it was total. Five further prose-poems, known as 'Other Illuminations', came to light in the 1890s. They appeared in 1895, in an edition of *Complete Poems*, with a preface by Verlaine. By then, Rimbaud had been dead for four years.

Obscurity

Verlaine's essay of 1886 and the appearance of the poems themselves were not Rimbaud's first formal presentation, in absentia, to the French poetry-reading public. Verlaine had already made the introductions in 1883, with an essay about Rimbaud in the literary journal *Lutèce*. Rimbaud was one of several poets he wrote about in the same journal, including Mallarmé and Tristan Corbière. The essays were published as a book, *Les Poètes maudits* ('The Cursed Poets'), the following year. It was the beginning of a rapid rise to fame. Yet that fame was already posthumous, if not in the strict sense, then in effect. For if Rimbaud the man was still alive, Rimbaud the poet was not. He had not written a poem for about ten years; he had severed almost every connection in Europe except with his family, and in the latter part of his life, it seems, he felt deeply uneasy about his earlier 'season' as a seer and a dissolute, and never spoke of it if he could avoid it.

What had happened in the interval? The adventure of the imagination had been decisively concluded. It had been replaced by something like adventure proper. For this, the old habits of vagrancy, now divorced from the processes of writing, remained useful. They persisted, only on a far grander scale. After Stuttgart, there were travels in Italy, a stint in Paris, an excursion to the Malay archipelago as a mercenary with the Dutch Colonial Army and work with a travelling circus in Denmark and Sweden. After some arduous walking in Europe, Rimbaud embarked for Alexandria at the end of 1878 and signed on for a job in Cyprus. In 1880, he arrived in Aden and found work with a trading company run by a Frenchman, Alfred Bardey. By the beginning of 1881 he was installed, under Bardey's aegis, in a trading post in Harar, between Abyssinia and the Ogaden in what is now Ethiopia. The rest of his life was spent largely in Harar and Aden as an unlikely avant-gardiste of commercial imperialism in North-east Africa. He was variously a trader in coffee and hides, an arms-dealer and a merchant-explorer, who set foot in places where very few Europeans had been before him.

However abrupt the divide between the first Rimbaud and

the second, the later part of his life refers us back irresistibly to his literary work, recasting parts of it as fantastic, tormented prophecy. 'My day is done,' he had written in 'Bad Blood' (*A Season in Hell*). 'I'm leaving Europe ... godforsaken climates will char my skin.' And again, 'I had to travel, to shake off the enchantments massing on my brain' ('Delirium II', ibid.). At moments we can hear the boy-poet intruding on the mundane or plaintive tones of the letters home – 'decisive letters', as Albert Camus called them in *L'Homme révolté* ('The Rebel: An Essay on Man in Revolt'), like this one from Aden: 'We're in our spring steamroom; skins stream, stomachs turn sour, brains are disturbed, business is lousy, the news is bad' – and, you might almost add, adapting a line from 'Song from the Highest Tower': 'a morbid thirst darkens our veins'. But to Abdoh Rinbo, as he became known in Harar, all that scintillating work was now a miserable indiscretion which, by and large, he succeeded in putting behind him, along with the life he'd led at the time.

Towards the end of 1883, returning to Aden after a stay in Europe, Alfred Bardey got wind of his Harar branch-manager's extraordinary past. Paul Bourde, a journalist who had been one of Rimbaud's fellow pupils at the Collège in Charleville, was on the boat to Aden with Bardey. By then Verlaine had already filled the columns of *Lutèce* with good words about the absentee ex-poet and steered some of his work into print. Bourde told Bardey everything he knew about Rimbaud's growing reputation. When Bardey next saw Rimbaud, he raised the subject. Rimbaud was obviously distressed. Bardey remembers him dismissing the poetry, or possibly the life he had led, but quite likely both, as 'absurd, ridiculous, disgusting, etc.'.[8] As for his relationship with Verlaine, it was an 'ivrognerie' – a jag.[9]

The Pedestrian

For most of his life, Rimbaud was a great walker, and much has been said about what he was walking away from, or heading towards. By the mid-1880s, he appears to be fleeing his growing reputation in Europe, and making for a thoroughgoing obscurity, although in his letters home there is talk of settling in France, and it's possible that he planned a new life as a writer of travel memoirs who would gradually process and publish the immense amounts of material he'd gathered in Harar and the highlands of Abyssinia. But this is conjecture, doubly unreliable because it's so tempting to imagine that the second Rimbaud, like the first, might have distinguished himself as a writer. There are far more obvious forms of kinship between the two, along with the many startling differences, though it seems pointless to attempt a psychological merger. Better to say simply that in youth and in manhood, Rimbaud was a wilful person and a witty one (the Europeans in Harar remembered him as a great raconteur); that the schoolboy with the aptitude for Latin verse was quick to master Arabic and pick up indigenous African languages; that there was never any release from restlessness, either in mind (during the long stays in Harar) or in fact; above all, perhaps, that Rimbaud had an abiding taste for hardship, and that he had tremendous physical stamina. Of this, there is no better evidence than the compulsion to set one foot after another, for yard after yard and mile after mile. Though riding became a new and essential habit with him in Africa, the walking continued. Indeed, it only stopped with the onset of a terrible pain in his right leg that presaged his death.

Verlaine thought of Rimbaud as a fleet-footed trickster with 'soles of wind'.[10] A good image, but a touch too precious. As a young man, Rimbaud had a rougher and, in the end, more poetic sense of what it was to be on the move: 'I'm a pedestrian, nothing more' (see letter 9). A poet, he meant to suggest, needs legs, whether they're for pacing the same worn patch of carpet or trudging towards the evasions of wilderness, which was so often his preference. We find Rimbaud the walker relaxing ('At the Green Inn') after a long hike – 'For a week I've flayed my boots/On the stony roads' – and again in 'My Bohemia (Fantasy)', 'As I strummed the laces of my devastated boots/Like lyre-strings, one foot by my heart'. And we find him, fifteen years later, striding ahead of his caravans from the Somali coast into the interior. Wherever it took him, the walking was a kind of endurance test – perhaps even a self-administered punishment – and at the same time an argument with his own profound agitation that made for a measure of compromise; finally, too, for something like composure.

It's said that after he'd left the Bardey business and set off towards Shewa with a consignment of guns for King Menilek in 1887, he did much of the gruelling journey by foot. Yet the best description of Rimbaud on the move was given by Delahaye, probably around the time that the idea of the Dutch Colonial Army was beckoning, and certainly after the last poem had been written. The pair were on an outing together during one of Rimbaud's brief stop-overs in Charleville. 'He had the strong, supple look of a resolute and patient walker, who is always setting off,' Delahaye recalled, 'his long legs moving calmly and regularly, his body straight, his head straight, his beautiful eyes fixed in the distance, and his face entirely filled with a look of resigned defiance, an air of expectation.'[11]

J.H.

The Letters

To pass on from the poetry in this volume to the letters that follow is to be forced to ask oneself the great Rimbaud question: how could the *Wunderkind* who wrote verse of so bruising and exalted a kind in his adolescence have become within a few years the hard-headed man of business, writing letters about the prices coffee or ivory were trading at in Ethiopia? A psychological chasm seems to divide the boy from the adult. Nevertheless, we have the poems and we have the letters; put them together and we have Rimbaud, not as a coherent figure but as a fascinatingly divided one; and in as complete a form as his literary remains allow.

The letters have survived in a quantity that is itself surprising, when so many of them were written in East Africa in an age when one might suppose the mails were chancy. There are around 200, the great majority written after he left France once and for all in 1878, at the age of twenty-four. We have selected nearly 120 in whole or in part, shortening them here and there to avoid repetition. We have also included a small number of letters written to Rimbaud. In previous editions of Rimbaud in English, the rule has been to include only a handful of the letters he sent at the time when he was still writing poetry – and acting up. The slangy, conspiratorial exchanges he had with Verlaine, most notably, with whom he shared lodgings and escapades in both Brussels and London, and others which allude directly – and invaluably – to the vaultingly ambitious view he took of himself as a poet. The present selection, however, follows him right through to his death. They are letters written, first, as he made his way to the Middle East, then from Cyprus, then from British Aden, a town he detested and spent all too much time in, as a junior employee in Alfred Bardey's trading company, and finally, having gained the independence he craved, from Harar. The letters fall into two contrasting groups: those he wrote to his employers or fellow European traders, and those he wrote regularly to the family home in the Ardennes from which he had once been so urgently set on escaping.

Two of the early letters in particular count as significant documents in the formation of the 'Rimbaud myth'. The first is dated 13 May 1871, and was written to Georges Izambard. In it, the sixteen-year-old poet gives us a first summary of his extraordinary *art poétique*. Poor Izambard may have had to settle for a steady job in the public service but the insurgent Rimbaud certainly doesn't mean to; rather, he claims to be living as debauched a life as possible – 'encrapulating myself to the hilt', as he puts it – not simply for the pleasures which that brings, but with a higher purpose in view: 'Why? I want to be a poet and I'm working to make myself a *seer* . . . The thing is to arrive at the unknown by a disordering of *all the senses*.' And then, in a sentence that must have been quoted many thousands of times, though seldom in context, since he first wrote it, Rimbaud announces: *Je est un autre*, 'I is somebody else.' This robust if also elusive declaration has been variously interpreted over the years, but it appears to mean that the Cartesian Ego, the self supposedly fully open to introspection, is by no means the whole of a human being, psychically speaking: disorder all of the senses and we may encounter a dimension of the self we hadn't known existed – a pre-Freudian thought if ever there was one, and a seductive invitation to the poets of the future to let the subconscious off the leash.

Only two days later, on 15 May, Rimbaud wrote to Paul Demeny, enclosing three of his poems, and expanding passionately on the philosophy that he had just outlined to Izambard. On this occasion, he offers his correspondent 'some prose on the future of poetry', which amounts to a caustic, dismissive sweep through literary history declaring that since the Greek Golden Age there hasn't been a poet worthy of the name: 'Functionaries, writers: author, creator, poet, that man has never existed!' He goes on to restate the need for the poet to be 'a seer, by a long, immense and reasoned disordering of all the senses'. The word 'reasoned' is new: two days earlier the influence of reason seemed to have been outlawed, as that instrument of the human intelligence needing to be circumvented. Rimbaud has perhaps drawn back from advocating a willed state of mental chaos as the poet's ideal, since that would hardly be shareable with others through poetry or any other means. The true poet must invite a temporary dementia in himself nonetheless, by plunging uninhibitedly into the 'unknown' of his own being. These may not amount to practical recommendations for the working poet, but in its vigour and self-assurance the so-called 'letter of the seer' is all of a piece with the poems that Rimbaud was then writing.

In the correspondence that comes after this brief period of heroic extravagance, there isn't a single reference back to Rimbaud's ambitions or achievements as a poet. It's as if he never wanted to remind anyone or be reminded of the 'encrapulated' youth he had once been. Rather, he writes as an alert, sober and well-informed foreign trader in a little-known country. Indeed, quite apart from presenting us with a dramatically enhanced image of the poet, the African letters have much interest in themselves for the commentary they provide on what was going on in Ethiopia at a crucial period in its nineteenth-century history.

Ethiopia had long been an empire, but one in which the Emperor never had complete authority over the rulers of its component provinces. In Rimbaud's time, the nominal Emperor was Yohannes IV, whose base was in the north of the country, but the ruler with whom Rimbaud had mostly to deal was Menilek, the king of the province of Shewa, further south, with relatively easy access to the Red Sea, via the ports through which all foreign trade had to pass. When Rimbaud first arrived in Harar, it was not strictly speaking a part of the Abyssinian empire. The town itself and the Red Sea ports to the east were under Egyptian control. But Egypt began to withdraw to the north in 1884. The expansionist Menilek was meanwhile conquering more and more territory and in 1887 came into possession of Harar.

As the agent in Harar for a trading company with its head-quarters in Aden, Rimbaud was one of a number of Europeans – French, British and Italian for the most part – who were similarly engaged, contributing to the commercial invasion by European businesses that later became known as the 'scramble for Africa'. They traded in coffee, ivory, skins and many other items, but also in small arms, for which bellicose warlords like Menilek had a huge appetite. Menilek eventually became Emperor of Abyssinia, in succession to Yohannes, who was killed fighting supporters of the Mahdi. Menilek's chief adviser in this period was Alfred Ilg, a Swiss engineer whom Rimbaud knew, and to whom quite a number of the letters included here were written.

For all the seeming remoteness of his main bases, in Aden and Harar, Rimbaud keeps an intelligent, often cynical eye on the activities of the rival warlords and on the moves towards the unification and modernization of the region, much influenced as it now was by the intrusion of European powers eager for commercial and diplomatic advantage. He reports on the geography of an as yet inadequately mapped country, and keeps himself intellectually active, for a time at least, by forever sending back home or to Paris for books on a whole range of scientific or technological subjects. This voluntary exile didn't mean to vegetate.

At the same time, he is rarely other than profoundly dissatisfied and feeling sorry for himself. By his own account, business is constantly going badly, thanks to endemic incompetence or the failure of debtors to pay what they owe: his savings increase, but never to the point where he has enough money to think of leaving Ethiopia and returning to France, to find a wife, as he occasionally suggests he would like to. (Against this, Graham Robb calculates that Rimbaud was worth quite a bit at the time of his death: about £115,000 in today's terms – a great deal, you might say, for a poet.)

The last of the correspondence reflects the terrible end of Rimbaud's life. Early in 1891, while in Harar, he developed an agonizing inflammation of the right knee and within a few weeks was unable to walk. He designed a litter and had himself borne down to the Red Sea coast. The journey – about 300 kilometres – took twelve days, most of it spent in unbearable pain. He crossed to Aden, where a British doctor diagnosed synovitis, dangerously advanced, but the surgeons who amputated the leg in Marseille a few weeks later went on to conclude that he had cancer. The tone of Rimbaud's letters is now one of total despair about the way his life has turned out, when as a cripple his chances of returning to Harar or finding work of any kind have vanished. This final incapacitation of a man who had been doubly adventurous, first intellectually, as a young poet of stupendous gifts, and then physically, as an alien trading in the hazardous environment of East Africa, is painful to contemplate. Rimbaud spent a month at the family farm in Roche after the amputation, and returned to Marseille with his sister Isabelle in August. His health was now very much worse, but apparently he intended to find a boat to Aden. On their arrival in Marseille, Isabelle had her brother taken to the hospital, where paralysis set in. Rimbaud survived for another six weeks. His last letter, dictated to Isabelle, is addressed to a shipping company, the Messageries Maritimes. It begins with an inventory of tusks – as though he were still in Africa, or Aden – and goes on to inquire about the possibility of taking ship for Suez. Rimbaud died the following day, 10 November 1891, at the age of thirty-seven. He was buried in the family vault in Charleville.

J.S.

NOTES

1. Graham Robb, *Rimbaud* (London: Picador, 2001), p. 102.
2. Ernest Delahaye, *Rimbaud* (Reims/Paris, 1905), p. 86.
3. Robb, *Rimbaud*, p. 103.
4. Yves Bonnefoy, *Rimbaud* (Paris: Seuil, 1994), p. 95.
5. Robb, *Rimbaud*, p. 108.
6. André Guyaux, *Poétique du fragment* (Neuchâtel: Baconnière, 1985), p. 75.
7. Bonnefoy, *Rimbaud*, pp. 111–12.
8. Jean-Jacques Lefrère, *Arthur Rimbaud* (Paris: Fayard, 2001), p. 893.
9. Ibid., p. 539.
10. Enid Starkie, *Arthur Rimbaud* (London: Faber & Faber, 1973), p. 327.
11. Letter to Berrichon, 21 August 1896, reproduced in *Delahaye, Témoin de Rimbaud*, ed. F. Eigeldinger and A. Gendre (Neuchâtel: La Baconnière, 1974), p. 155.

Further Reading

EDITIONS OF RIMBAUD'S WORK

Collected Poems, a complete bilingual edition with translations by Martin Sorrell (Oxford: Oxford University Press, 2001).

A Season in Hell and *Illuminations*, a complete bilingual edition with translations by Mark Treharne (London: J. M. Dent, 1998).

Illuminations, ed. Nick Osmond, a complete edition of the French originals with detailed commentaries in English (London: Athlone, 1976).

CRITICAL STUDIES

Bonnefoy, Yves, *Rimbaud* (Paris: Seuil, 1961, reprinted 1994), trans. Paul Schmidt (New York: Harper & Row, 1973).

Fowlie, Wallace, *Rimbaud* (Chicago: University of Chicago Press, 1965).

Hackett, Cecil A., *Rimbaud: A Critical Introduction* (Cambridge: Cambridge University Press, 1981).

OTHER WORKS

Hampton, Christopher, *Total Eclipse* (London: Faber & Faber, 1969).

Nicholl, Charles, *Somebody Else: Arthur Rimbaud in Africa 1880–1891* (London: Jonathan Cape, 1997).

Rickword, Edgell, *Rimbaud: The Boy and the Poet* (London: Heinemann, 1924, reissued Daimon, 1963).

Robb, Graham, *Rimbaud* (London: Picador, 2000, paperback edition 2001).

Shaw, Mary Lewis, *The Cambridge Introduction to French Poetry* (Cambridge and New York: Cambridge University Press, 2003).

Starkie, Enid, *Arthur Rimbaud* (London: Faber & Faber, 1938, reissued 1973).

—, *Arthur Rimbaud in Abyssinia* (Oxford: Clarendon Press, 1937).

Steinmetz, Jean-Luc, *Rimbaud, une question de présence* (Paris: Tallandier, 1991).

BACKGROUND ON THE PARIS COMMUNE

Horne, Alistair, *The Fall of Paris: The Siege and the Commune 1870–1871* (London: Macmillan, 1965, reissued by Penguin, 1981).

Lissagaray, Prosper Olivier, *History of the Commune of 1871*, trans. Eleanor Marx (London, 1886); most recent edition, New Park, 1976.

Tombs, Robert, *The Paris Commune, 1871* (London: Longman, 1999).

FURTHER READING IN PENGUIN

Penguin Book of French Poetry, 1820–1950, selected and trans. William Rees (London and New York: Penguin, 1990).

A Note on the Translation

Translators of poetry owe a lot to their predecessors. Oliver Bernard brought Rimbaud to a wide English readership with his Penguin edition of 1962, which this one supersedes. There are a number of differences. It is now widely accepted that *A Season in Hell* predates many of the *Illuminations*, and so in this edition, *A Season in Hell* no longer appears at the end. I have also included *The Deserts of Love*, which was not in Bernard's volume. There have been other, lesser changes in ordering, and some of the poems have been retitled, or titled, in line with recent textual scholarship.

The parallel text has been adopted in preference to the prose translation at the foot of the page – a choice that could be said to cramp a translator's style rather more than a prose version does. But I am convinced it is more manageable for the reader. It's easier, after all, to run one's eye from version to original when the lines are juxtaposed in the verse, or more or less level in the prose-poems, than it is to move from a chunk of prose to a piece of verse, or to another piece of prose in a different type size.

This, in turn, makes it easier for readers to spot where a liberty has been taken in translation. To leave off a question mark in the French (as I've done with the last line of 'Memory') because something more desolate than a question seems to get the truth of the poem in English, and catch the right inflection, is to take a liberty. To update Rimbaud's idiomatic mode – assuredly not his only mode – by converting to current usage (as I've done with 'Knowing Way') is to take a greater liberty still. Often a loyal translation is nearer the mark than a faithful one. Not all readers will agree, but the parallel text format will help them to make their own judgements.

These translations do not attempt to track the syllable count of the French. Instead I've tried to work with rhythms that sound well on an English ear. Rhyme is also avoided, except in a handful of cases where it has insinuated itself into a version and gone on, through a number of drafts, to make itself at home. Here and there, an obscurity in the original has seemed to need an intrusion in the English. In a few of the explanatory notes, too, I've erred on the side of generosity. 'To the Poet on the Matter of Flowers', for example, requires rather more of translators and editors than an august silence.

The decision to select from Rimbaud's literary work was taken in order to make room for a good many of the letters he wrote after he had finished with poetry. But selecting cannot be done without a lot of head-shaking and hair-tearing. *A Season in Hell* stands entire – the only straightforward decision. Despite a dozen or more regrets, I'd like to think that this is a representative sample of the poetry.

The job of translating is made much easier by the existence of good editions in the original. The source for John Sturrock's translations is Antoine Adam's Pléiade edition of 1972, which remains authoritative with regard to the letters. The poems selected here were translated while André Guyaux was preparing a new edition of the Pléiade, and so the principal source for the poetry has been the Garnier *Œuvres* edited by Suzanne Bernard and André Guyaux. In the notes, I have drawn extensively on Bernard and Guyaux, and on the three-volume *Œuvres* edited by Jean-Luc Steinmetz (Flammarion), as well as volume I of the *Œuvres complètes* edited by Steve Murphy (Champion). I have used ideas from Guyaux's *Poétique du fragment* (Neuchâtel: La Baconnière, 1985) and *L'Art de Rimbaud* by Michel Murat (Paris: José Corti, 2002) in the Introduction and the notes, while the Chronology borrows liberally from Steinmetz.

J.H.

I have used underlinings to indicate words and phrases which were written by Rimbaud in English. In the case of the letters written in East Africa, I have, as far as possible, spelt place-names, titles and proper names etc. in the form used by Dr Richard Pankhurst in his book *The Ethiopians* (Oxford: Blackwell, 1998). Rimbaud's own spellings are often inconsistent, but I have standardized them; it seemed unnecessarily pedantic to imitate his understandably wayward practice.

J.S.

POEMS

from POEMES, 1869–71

Les Etrennes des orphelins

I

La chambre est pleine d'ombre; on entend vaguement
De deux enfants le triste et doux chuchotement.
Leur front se penche, encor, alourdi par le rêve,
Sous le long rideau blanc qui tremble et se soulève . . .
– Au dehors les oiseaux se rapprochent frileux;
Leur aile s'engourdit sous le ton gris des cieux;
Et la nouvelle Année, à la suite brumeuse,
Laissant traîner les plis de sa robe neigeuse,
Sourit avec des pleurs, et chante en grelottant . . .

II

Or les petits enfants, sous le rideau flottant,
Parlent bas comme on fait dans une nuit obscure.
Ils écoutent pensifs, comme un lointain murmure . . .
Ils tressaillent souvent à la claire voix d'or
Du timbre matinal, qui frappe et frappe encor
Son refrain métallique en son globe de verre . . .
– Puis, la chambre est glacée . . . on voit traîner à terre,
Epars autour des lits, des vêtements de deuil:
L'âpre bise d'hiver qui se lamente au seuil
Souffle dans le logis son haleine morose!
On sent, dans tout cela, qu'il manque quelque chose . . .

from POEMS, 1869–71

The Orphans' New Year Gifts

I

Shadows fill the room: you vaguely hear
The sad, low whispers of two children,
Heads inclined, still heavy with dreams.
The long, white curtain ripples and lifts . . .
Outside, the birds muster against the cold,
Wings drubbed by the grey of the sky;
The New Year, with its retinue of mist,
Trails its dress of snow across the ground.
Smiling through its tears, it shakes with cold and
      sings . . .

II

Beneath the drifting curtain the children
Speak quietly, as you would on a dark night.
They listen, braced, for any distant murmur;
Often they start at the clear gold voice
Of morning, beating its metallic refrain
Over and over in its glass world.
– The room, too, is icy.
Mourning clothes are scattered on the floor.
A bitter winter wind moans in the doorway,
Its morose breath gusts through the house.
Something is missing, you suspect . . .

– Il n'est donc point de mère à ces petits enfants,
De mère au frais sourire, aux regards triomphants?
Elle a donc oublié, le soir, seule et penchée,
D'exciter une flamme à la cendre arrachée,
D'amonceler sur eux la laine et l'édredon
Avant de les quitter en leur criant: pardon.
Elle n'a point prévu la froideur matinale,
Ni bien fermé le seuil à la bise hivernale? . . .
– Le rêve maternel, c'est le tiède tapis,
C'est le nid cotonneux où les enfants tapis,
Comme de beaux oiseaux que balancent les branches,
Dorment leur doux sommeil plein de visions blanches! . . .
– Et là, – c'est comme un nid sans plumes, sans chaleur,
Où les petits ont froid, ne dorment pas, ont peur;
Un nid que doit avoir glacé la bise amère . . .

III

Votre cœur l'a compris: – ces enfants sans mère.
Plus de mère au logis! – et le père est bien loin! . . .
– Une vieille servante, alors, en a pris soin:
Les petits sont tout seuls en la maison glacée;
Orphelins de quatre ans, voilà qu'en leur pensée
S'éveille, par degrés, un souvenir riant . . .
C'est comme un chapelet qu'on égrène en priant:
– Ah! quel beau matin, que ce matin des étrennes!
Chacun, pendant la nuit, avait rêvé des siennes
Dans quelque songe étrange où l'on voyait joujoux,
Bonbons habillés d'or, étincelants bijoux,
Tourbillonner, danser une danse sonore,
Puis fuir sous les rideaux, puis reparaître encore!
On s'éveillait matin, on se levait joyeux,
La lèvre affriandée, en se frottant les yeux . . .
On allait, les cheveux emmêlés sur la tête,
Les yeux tout rayonnants, comme aux grands jours de fête,

Don't these two children have a mother,
With a mother's smiles and proud demeanour?
Alone last night and stooping, did she forget
To coax a flame from the fire's embers
Or heap up the blankets and quilts
Before leaving – and calling 'Forgive me' on her way?
Hadn't she known the morning would be cold
And thought to bar the door against the winter wind?
Warm pile: every mother's dream,
The clotted nest where the young are snug
Like pretty birds on rocking branches,
Sleeping sweetly in their white vista.
But here the nest is featherless and cold,
The children in it sleepless, chilled and scared –
A nest that must have frozen in the bitter wind.

III

In your heart you know it: the children are motherless.
No mother at home and a father way off,
An old servant woman tending in their stead.
The little ones are alone in the icy house,
Orphaned four-year-olds, in whose thoughts,
By degrees, a benign memory stirs
Like a rosary told during prayer.
What a morning that was – on New Year's Day,
The night before spent dreaming of what lay ahead:
Strange dreams to do with toys,
Sweets wrapped in gold, and sparkling gems,
Spinning in a sonorous dance,
Slipping beneath curtains, reappearing once more.
When morning came they were out of bed,
Mouths watering, rubbing their eyelids.
Now the dash – with hair dishevelled
And the brightness of a feast-day in their eyes,

Et les petits pieds nus effleurant le plancher,
Aux portes des parents tout doucement toucher . . .
On entrait! . . . Puis alors les souhaits, . . . en chemise,
Les baisers répétés, et la gaîté permise!

IV

Ah! c'était si charmant, ces mots dit tant de fois!
– Mais comme il est changé, le logis d'autrefois:
Un grand feu pétillait, clair, dans la cheminée,
Toute la vieille chambre était illuminée;
Et les reflets vermeils, sortis du grand foyer,
Sur les meubles vernis aimaient à tournoyer . . .
– L'armoire était sans clefs! . . . sans clefs, la grande
　　armoire!
On regardait souvent sa porte brune et noire . . .
Sans clefs! . . . c'était étrange! . . . on rêvait bien des fois
Aux mystères dormant entre ses flancs de bois,
Et l'on croyait ouïr, au fond de la serrure
Béante, un bruit lointain, vague et joyeux murmure . . .
– La chambre des parents est bien vide, aujourd'hui:
Aucun reflet vermeil sous la porte n'a lui;
Il n'est point de parents, de foyer, de clefs prises:
Partant, point de baisers, point de douces surprises!
Oh! que le jour de l'an sera triste pour eux!
– Et, tout pensifs, tandis que de leurs grands yeux bleus
Silencieusement tombe une larme amère,
Ils murmurent: «Quand donc reviendra notre mère?»
. . . .

V

Maintenant, les petits sommeillent tristement:
Vous diriez, à les voir, qu'ils pleurent en dormant,
Tant leurs yeux sont gonflés et leur souffle pénible!
Les tout petits enfants ont le cœur si sensible!
– Mais l'ange des berceaux vient essuyer leurs yeux,
Et dans ce lourd sommeil met un rêve joyeux,

Their small bare feet scarcely grazing the floor –
To see their parents; hesitation at the door,
Then in! The New Year greetings, nightshirts,
Kiss upon kiss, high spirits tolerated!

IV

The charm of words spoken so many times!
But how remote that home now seems:
A great fire crackled gaily in the hearth,
The whole room glowed
And glints of crimson from the fireplace
Played across the varnished furniture.
There were no keys in the cupboard! . . . the big
    one,
With the brown and lacquer door they used to scrutinize.
No keys . . . Quite strange! . . . they would review
The mysteries incubating in its panels,
And think they heard a vague, distant sound,
An amenable murmur from deep in the gaping lock.
That room, their parents' room, is empty now:
No glint of red beneath the door,
Their parents gone, no hearth and no sequestered keys,
And so, no kisses, not a single sweet surprise.
How sad their New Year's Day will be,
These thoughtful ones. In the great blue eyes
There are silent, bitter tears. The murmured question:
'When will our mother return?'
. . . .

V

Two unhappy children, slumbering now.
They look as though they're crying in their sleep,
Their eyes are so swollen, their breath is so laboured.
The very young are fragile creatures.
But the angel of the cradle wipes their tears away
And slips a good dream into their heavy sleep –

Un rêve si joyeux, que leur lèvre mi-close,
Souriante, semblait murmurer quelque chose . . .
– Ils rêvent que, penchés sur leur petit bras rond,
Doux geste du réveil, ils avancent le front,
Et leur vague regard tout autour d'eux se pose . . .
Ils se croient endormis dans un paradis rose . . .
Au foyer plein d'éclairs chante gaîment le feu . . .
Par la fenêtre on voit là-bas un beau ciel bleu;
La nature s'éveille et de rayons s'enivre . . .
La terre, demi-nue, heureuse de revivre,
A des frissons de joie aux baisers du soleil . . .
Et dans les vieux logis tout est tiède et vermeil:
Les sombres vêtements ne jonchent plus la terre,
La bise sous le seuil a fini par se taire . . .
On dirait qu'une fée a passé dans cela! . . .
– Les enfants, tout joyeux, ont jeté deux cris . . . Là,
Près du lit maternel, sous un beau rayon rose,
Là, sur le grand tapis, resplendit quelque chose . . .
Ce sont des médaillons argentés, noirs et blancs,
De la nacre et du jais aux reflets scintillants;
Des petits cadres noirs, des couronnes de verre,
Ayant trois mots gravés en or: «A NOTRE MERE!»
. . . .

Première soirée

– Elle était fort déshabillée
Et de grands arbres indiscrets
Aux vitres jetaient leur feuillée
Malinement, tout près, tout près.

Assise sur ma grande chaise,
Mi-nue, elle joignait les mains.
Sur le plancher frissonnaient d'aise
Ses petits pieds si fins, si fins.

So good their half-closed lips
Appear to smile and mutter something . . .
In the dream, they're leaning on their small, chubby arms;
Raising their heads in the sweet gesture of coming to,
And casting about with bleary eyes . . .
Thinking they've drifted into a rosy paradise.
The hearth is lit up and the fire sings.
The sky beyond the window – blue.
Nature stirs, intoxicated by the light.
The earth, half-naked, gratefully revives,
Rippling with pleasure in the sun's embrace . . .
And in the old house everything is warm and colourful,
The floor no longer strewn with mourning clothes,
The wind no longer wailing at the door . . .
All this as if a wand had just been flourished . . .
The children shout ecstatically – two cries. Here,
By their mother's bed, in a shaft of pinkish light,
On the big rug, something shines.
A pair of plaques, silver, black and white,
In mother-of-pearl and scintillating jet
With small black frames and glassware wreaths;
And three words – 'TO OUR MOTHER' – cut in gold.[1]

. . . .

First Attempt

She was pretty much undressed
And big brazen trees
Thrust their leaves against the panes,
To snoop – so close, that close.

She sat in my big chair,
Half-naked now, and clasped her hands;
Her little feet – so fine, that fine –
All astir on the floor: pure pleasure.

– Je regardai, couleur de cire
Un petit rayon buissonnier
Papillonner dans son sourire
Et sur son sein, – mouche au rosier.

– Je baisai ses fines chevilles.
Elle eut un doux rire brutal
Qui s'égrenait en claires trilles,
Un joli rire de cristal.

Les petits pieds sous la chemise
Se sauvèrent: «Veux-tu finir!»
– La première audace permise,
Le rire feignait de punir!

– Pauvrets palpitants sous ma lèvre,
Je baisai doucement ses yeux:
– Elle jeta sa tête mièvre
En arrière: «Oh! c'est encor mieux!…

«Monsieur, j'ai deux mots à te dire…»
– Je lui jetai le reste au sein
Dans un baiser, qui la fit rire
D'un bon rire qui voulait bien…

– Elle était fort déshabillée
Et de grands arbres indiscrets
Aux vitres jetaient leur feuillée
Malinement, tout près, tout près.

Sensation

Par les soirs bleus d'été, j'irai dans les sentiers,
Picoté par les blés, fouler l'herbe menue:
Rêveur, j'en sentirai la fraîcheur à mes pieds.
Je laisserai le vent baigner ma tête nue.

A shaft of light, the colour
Of wax, played truant
On her smiling mouth (I watched)
And then on her breast – a midge on a rose.

I kissed her pretty ankles.
She gave a sudden laugh, pealing
And sweet, in bright trills.
A laugh like faceted glass.

The little feet took cover
In her skirts. 'That's far enough.'
– But even so, she'd let it go –
Her laughter made a poor reproach.

Her helpless eyes beat under my kisses
– A gentle application of the lips.
She threw back that hopeless head
Of hers: 'Well, honestly, Monsieur!'

And then: 'You really have a nerve . . .'
A kiss on her breast was how I handled
That. Which raised a laugh –
The kind that says, I'm on for it.

She was pretty much undressed
And big brazen trees
Thrust their leaves against the panes,
Snooping – so close, that close.

Sensation

On blue summer evenings I'll take to the paths.
Prickled by the corn, I'll tread the young grass,
I'll dream of its coolness under my feet.
My bare head will bask in the wind.

Je ne parlerai pas, je ne penserai rien:
Mais l'amour infini me montera dans l'âme,
Et j'irai loin, bien loin, comme un bohémien,
Par la Nature, – heureux comme avec une femme.

Mars 1870

Le Forgeron

Palais des Tuileries,
vers le 10 août 92

Le bras sur un marteau gigantesque, effrayant
D'ivresse et de grandeur, le front vaste, riant
Comme un clairon d'airain, avec toute sa bouche,
Et prenant ce gros-là dans son regard farouche,
Le Forgeron parlait à Louis Seize, un jour
Que le Peuple était là, se tordant tout autour,
Et sur les lambris d'or traînant sa veste sale.
Or le bon roi, debout sur son ventre, était pâle,
Pâle comme un vaincu qu'on prend pour le gibet,
Et, soumis comme un chien, jamais ne regimbait
Car ce maraud de forge aux énormes épaules
Lui disait de vieux mots et de choses si drôles,
Que cela l'empoignait au front, comme cela!

«Or, tu sais bien, Monsieur, nous chantions tra la la
Et nous piquions les bœufs vers les sillons des autres:
Le Chanoine au soleil filait des patenôtres
Sur des chapelets clairs grenés de pièces d'or.
Le Seigneur, à cheval, passait, sonnant du cor
Et l'un avec la hart, l'autre avec la cravache
Nous fouaillaient. – Hébétés comme des yeux de vache,
Nos yeux ne pleuraient plus; nous allions, nous allions,
Et quand nous avions mis le pays en sillons,

I shan't speak; I shan't even think,
But a love without limits will fill up my soul.
I'll go far, very far, a vagrant in the countryside
– Happy, like a man with a woman.

March 1870

Blacksmith

Palais des Tuileries,
circa 10 August 1792[1]

One arm on a massive hammer, terrifying,
Drunk, gigantic; vast forehead; laughter ringing
Like a brazen trumpet from his mouth in its entirety,
Fixing the fat man with a withering gaze,
A Blacksmith spoke to Louis XVI one day
Before the People, thronging round,
Trailing grubby coats across the gilded panelling.
The good King, joisted on his belly, was as pale
As a condemned man headed for the gibbet.
He offered no defence – cowered like a dog.
Ransacker Blacksmith with his towering shoulders
Gave him hell: strange utterances in old idioms
That had him rooted to the spot, just so!

'You'll recall, Sire, our touching folk-songs, hey nonny-no,
As we drove our teams down other men's furrows;
How the Canon churned out Paternosters in the sun,
Working bright rosaries strung with gold coin.
How My Lord So-and-So rode by, sounding his horn,
How a minion with a lash and another with a riding crop
Bent to the business. Cow-eyed and dazed,
We no longer wept; we went on and on ploughing,
Until the land was pure furrow –

Quand nous avions laissé dans cette terre noire
Un peu de notre chair . . . nous avions un pourboire.
On nous faisait flamber nos taudis dans la nuit,
Nos petits y faisaient un gâteau fort bien cuit.

«Oh! je ne me plains pas. Je te dis mes bêtises,
C'est entre nous. J'admets que tu me contredises.
Or, n'est-ce pas joyeux de voir, au mois de juin
Dans les granges entrer des voitures de foin
Enormes? De sentir l'odeur de ce qui pousse,
Des vergers quand il pleut un peu, de l'herbe rousse?
De voir des blés, des blés, des épis pleins de grain,
De penser que cela prépare bien du pain? . . .
Oh! plus fort, on irait, au fourneau qui s'allume,
Chanter joyeusement en martelant l'enclume,
Si l'on était certain de pouvoir prendre un peu,
Etant homme, à la fin!, de ce que donne Dieu!
– Mais voilà, c'est toujours la même vieille histoire!

«Mais je sais, maintenant! Moi, je ne peux plus croire,
Quand j'ai deux bonnes mains, mon front et mon marteau,
Qu'un homme vienne là, dague sur le manteau,
Et me dise: Mon gars, ensemence ma terre;
Que l'on arrive encor, quand ce serait la guerre,
Me prendre mon garçon comme cela, chez moi!
– Moi, je serais un homme, et toi, tu serais roi,
Tu me dirais: Je veux! . . . – Tu vois bien, c'est stupide.
Tu crois que j'aime voir ta baraque splendide,
Tes officiers dorés, tes mille chenapans,
Tes palsembleu bâtards tournant comme des paons:
Ils ont rempli ton nid de l'odeur de nos filles
Et des petits billets pour nous mettre aux Bastilles
Et nous dirons: C'est bien: les pauvres à genoux!
Nous dorerons ton Louvre en donnant nos gros sous!
Et tu te soûleras, tu feras belle fête.
– Et ces Messieurs riront, les reins sur notre tête!

Bits of our flesh consigned to that blackened soil –
And then we drew our modest pay:
Our hovels torched in the dead of night,
Our children inside them, done to a turn.

'I'm not complaining. Take what I say
With a pinch of salt. Between ourselves. No doubt
You know better. But isn't it something,
To see the huge haycarts roll into the barns
In June? Or to smell new growth –
Orchards under drizzle, fields of tawny grass?
Or survey the endless wheat, ears full of grain,
And all the bread they bode?
A man goes happier to the heat of the forge
To sing and beat the anvil
If he rests assured that a small proportion
– We're human beings after all – of what God gives
Is his. But it's the same old story.

'Only, now I'm wise to it. I've got two good hands,
A head on my shoulders and a hammer.
So why should a man with a dagger in his coat
Come and tell me: You, boy! Sow my land!
Or another drag my children
From their home to fight a war?
Very well – so I'm a man and you're a king
And you can order me about . . . but it's nonsense really.
D'you think I'm impressed by the splendour of your pile,
Or your gilded flunkeys, your droves of spongers,
Your "Zounds, man!" strutting peacock upstarts
Who've lined your nest with the smell of our daughters
And paper writs to have us slung in your Bastilles?
And we're supposed to say: That's right, the poor man's place
Is on his knees, our last pennies will gild your Louvre,
You'll binge, you'll have a good time –
And these courtiers will smirk, as they squat on our faces.

«Non. Ces saletés-là datent de nos papas!
Oh! Le Peuple n'est plus une putain. Trois pas
Et, tous, nous avons mis ta Bastille en poussière.
Cette bête suait du sang à chaque pierre
Et c'était dégoûtant, la Bastille debout
Avec ses murs lépreux qui nous racontaient tout
Et toujours, nous tenaient enfermés dans leur ombre!
– Citoyen! citoyen! c'était le passé sombre
Qui croulait, qui râlait, quand nous prîmes la tour!
Nous avions quelque chose au cœur comme l'amour.
Nous avions embrassé nos fils sur nos poitrines.
Et, comme des chevaux, en soufflant des narines
Nous allions, fiers et forts, et ça nous battait là . . .
Nous marchions au soleil, front haut, – comme cela –,
Dans Paris! On venait devant nos vestes sales.
Enfin! Nous nous sentions Hommes! Nous étions pâles,
Sire, nous étions soûls de terribles espoirs:
Et quand nous fûmes là, devant les donjons noirs,
Agitant nos clairons et nos feuilles de chêne,
Les piques à la main; nous n'eûmes pas de haine,
– Nous nous sentions si forts, nous voulions être doux!

....
....

«Et depuis ce jour-là, nous sommes comme fous!
Le tas des ouvriers a monté dans la rue,
Et ces maudits s'en vont, foule toujours accrue
De sombres revenants, aux portes des richards.
Moi, je cours avec eux assommer les mouchards:
Et je vais dans Paris, noir, marteau sur l'épaule,
Farouche, à chaque coin balayant quelque drôle,
Et si tu me riais au nez, je te tuerais!
– Puis, tu peux y compter, tu te feras des frais
Avec tes hommes noirs, qui prennent nos requêtes
Pour se les renvoyer comme sur des raquettes
Et, tout bas, les malins! se disent: «Qu'ils sont sots!»
Pour mitonner des lois, coller des petits pots

'No. That was the bullshit our fathers were raised on.
The People are no longer whores. Together,
We reduced your Bastille to rubble in a trice –
Blood seeped from every stone,
An abomination while it stood,
With its leprous walls, it said all that needed saying,
And us in their shadow, under lock and key.
Citizen! Citizen! A dark past groaned
And crumbled when we trashed that Tower.
It was a feeling a bit like love.
We lifted up our sons and kissed them.
With our nostrils flared, we advanced like horses
Resolute and proud – hearts thumping *here*, in our chests;
We strode through Paris in the sunshine, heads up
Like so! We were welcomed, in our filthy clothes.
We felt like men, at last. We were pale,
Sire, drunk on terrific hope.
And when we reached that gloomy keep,
Brandishing our bugles and our sprigs of oak,[2]
Pikes at our sides, we'd gone beyond hatred.
In our very strength, we aspired to calm.

....
....

'Since then we've been like men possessed.
The ranks of workers on the streets have grown;
The poor wretches – numbers swelled by dark spectres –
Take off en masse to haunt the porches of the rich.
And I go with them, flattening your spies,
Roaming Paris, shouldering my hammer,
Dark, implacable, flushing out jokers from every recess;
And if you laugh at me, I'll kill you.
You can be sure your men in office
Will cost you dear – the way they treat our petitions,
Batting them back and forth like tennis balls,
Sneering at us on the sly: "How dim they are!"
Dreaming up laws, posting their little bills

Pleins de jolis décrets roses et de droguailles,
S'amuser à couper proprement quelques tailles,
Puis se boucher le nez quand nous marchons près d'eux,
– Nos doux réprentants qui nous trouvent crasseux! –
Pour ne rien redouter, rien, que les baïonnettes . . .,
C'est très bien. Foin de leur tabatière à sornettes!
Nous en avons assez, là, de ces cerveaux plats
Et de ces ventres-dieux. Ah! ce sont là les plats
Que tu nous sers, bourgeois, quand nous sommes féroces,
Quand nous brisons déjà les sceptres et les crosses! . . .»
....

Il le prend par le bras, arrache le velours
Des rideaux, et lui montre en bas les larges cours
Où fourmille, où fourmille, où se lève la foule,
La foule épouvantable avec des bruits de houle,
Hurlant comme une chienne, hurlant comme une mer,
Avec ses bâtons forts et ses piques de fer,
Ses tambours, ses grands cris de halles et de bouges,
Tas sombre de haillons saignant de bonnets rouges:
L'Homme, par la fenêtre ouverte, montre tout
Au roi pâle et suant qui chancelle debout,
Malade à regarder cela!
                              «C'est la Crapule,
Sire. Ça bave aux murs, ça monte, ça pullule:
– Puisqu'ils ne mangent pas, Sire, ce sont des gueux!
Je suis un forgeron: ma femme est avec eux,
Folle! Elle croit trouver du pain aux Tuileries!
– On ne veut pas de nous dans les boulangeries.
J'ai trois petits. Je suis crapule. – Je connais
Des vieilles qui s'en vont pleurant sous leurs bonnets
Parce qu'on leur a pris leur garçon ou leur fille:
C'est la Crapule. – Un homme était à la Bastille,
Un autre était forçat: et tous deux, citoyens
Honnêtes. Libérés, ils sont comme des chiens:
On les insulte! Alors, ils ont là quelque chose
Qui leur fait mal, allez! C'est terrible, et c'est cause

With pretty pink decrees, sweet blandishments,
Trimming the tithes by a smidgin here and there,
Then holding their noses when we get too close –
Our distinguished representatives find us dirty –
Till they've nothing to fear, bar the bayonet . . .
Very well! To Hell with their facetious speeches.
Enough of these thickheads, these deified
Paunches. This is how you treat us,
You bourgeois, when our blood is up
And we're already smashing croziers and sceptres.'

. . . .

He takes him by the arm and jerks the velvet
Curtains down. Below in the courtyard
The mob is teeming; teeming and surging –
The chastening mob with its tidal roar,
Howling like a bitch, howling like an ocean,
With its staves, its metal pikes
And drums, its clamouring of shanty-towns and markets,
A shadowy, tattered mass, flecked with blood-red
Liberty caps. At the open window, the Man
Shows it all to the pale, reeling King
– His stomach turns.

                      'And that, Your Majesty,
Is scum! It slobbers on the walls, it swarms
And multiplies – and, Sire, it doesn't eat, it has to beg.
I'm a blacksmith. My wife down there,
Poor fool, she thinks she'll find bread in the Tuileries!
The bakeries have barred the door to us.
I've got three children. I'm scum. I know
Of old women weeping under their bonnets
Because a son or daughter – also scum – has been
Marched off. Then there was a man in the Bastille,
And another in the galleys, both honest
Citizens. We've freed them now, but they've become dogs.
People abuse them. Something hurts them
That they can't shake off – surely you see that. They feel

Que se sentant brisés, que, se sentant damnés,
Ils sont là, maintenant, hurlant sous votre nez!
Crapule! – Là-dedans sont des filles, infâmes
Parce que, – vous saviez que c'est faible, les femmes, –
Messeigneurs de la cour, – que ça veut toujours bien, –
Vous leur avez craché sur l'âme, comme rien!
Vos belles, aujourd'hui, sont là. C'est la Crapule.

....

«Oh! tous les Malheureux, tous ceux dont le dos brûle
Sous le soleil féroce, et qui vont, et qui vont,
Qui dans ce travail-là sentent crever leur front,
Chapeau bas, mes bourgeois! Oh! ceux-là, sont les Hommes!
Nous sommes Ouvriers, Sire! Ouvriers! Nous sommes
Pour les grands temps nouveaux ou l'on voudra savoir,
Où l'Homme forgera du matin jusqu'au soir,
Chasseur de grands effets, chasseur de grandes causes;
Où, lentement vainqueur, il domptera les choses
Et montera sur Tout, comme sur un cheval!
Oh! splendides lueurs des forges! Plus de mal,
Plus! – Ce qu'on ne sait pas, c'est peut-être terrible:
Nous saurons! – Nos marteaux en main, passons au crible
Tout ce que nous savons: puis, Frères, en avant!
Nous faisons quelquefois ce grand rêve émouvant
De vivre simplement, ardemment, sans rien dire
De mauvais, travaillant sous l'auguste sourire
D'une femme qu'on aime avec un noble amour:
Et l'on travaillerait fièrement tout le jour,
Ecoutant le devoir comme un clairon qui sonne:
Et l'on se sentirait très heureux; et personne,
Oh! personne, surtout, ne vous ferait ployer!
On aurait un fusil au-dessus du foyer . . .

....

«Oh! mais l'air est tout plein d'une odeur de bataille.
Que te disais-je donc? Je suis de la canaille!
Il reste des mouchards et des accapareurs.
Nous sommes libres, nous! nous avons des terreurs

Horribly broken; they feel cursed, which is why
They're down there now, howling at you.
Scum. There are women down there, dishonoured
Because . . . well you knew their weakness,
You gentlemen of the court, and their willingness.
You spat on their souls, for sport.
Your girlfriends are out there now. Scum, too.

....

'Oh the dispossessed, all of them, backs
Blistering in the pitiless sun, toiling on,
Heads throbbing with exertion –
Now bourgeois, doff your hat to them. They're Men!
Your Majesty, we're workers. Workers hungry
For the brave new world of knowledge,
When the furnace will glow from dawn till dusk
And men will quarry for great causes, great effects,
And gradually prevail – dominate the realm of things,
Saddle Nature like a horse!
Here's to the glare of the forge! And the end of pain –
Done with pain! What's unknown may well be terrifying.
But it will be known. Let's redraft what we know so far,
Hammers in hand. And Brothers, on from there!
Sometimes we're lost in the great and moving dream
Of living well, exactingly: not an ill word spoken,
Our work done in the smiling ambit
Of a woman loved with intelligible love.
A long day's work proudly performed,
Our obligations ringing in our ears.
Happiness! And no one, absolutely no one,
To rub our noses in the dirt!
In the dream, a rifle, hanging by the mantelshelf.

....

'The air is thick with the smell of battle!
Didn't I say I was bona fide riffraff?
There are still some sneaks and racketeers to deal with.
But us, we're free! We have chilling intimations

Où nous nous sentons grands, oh! si grands! Tout à l'heure
Je parlais de devoir calme, d'une demeure . . .
Regarde donc le ciel! – C'est trop petit pour nous,
Nous crèverions de chaud, nous serions à genoux!
Regarde donc le ciel! – Je rentre dans la foule,
Dans la grande canaille effroyable, qui roule,
Sire, tes vieux canons sur les sales pavés:
– Oh! quand nous serons morts, nous les aurons lavés!
– Et si, devant nos cris, devant notre vengeance,
Les pattes des vieux rois mordorés, sur la France
Poussent leurs régiments en habits de gala,
Eh bien, n'est-ce pas, vous tous? Merde à ces chiens-là!»
....

– Il reprit son marteau sur l'épaule.
                                             La foule
Près de cet homme-là se sentait l'âme soûle,
Et, dans la grande cour, dans les appartements,
Où Paris haletait avec des hurlements,
Un frisson secoua l'immense populace.
Alors, de sa main large et superbe de crasse,
Bien que le roi ventru suât, le Forgeron,
Terrible, lui jeta le bonnet rouge au front!

Ophélie

I

Sur l'onde calme et noire où dorment les étoiles
La blanche Ophélia flotte comme un grand lys,
Flotte très lentement, couchée en ses longs voiles . . .
– On entend dans les bois lointains des hallalis.

Voici plus de mille ans que la triste Ophélie
Passe, fantôme blanc, sur le long fleuve noir,
Voici plus de mille ans que sa douce folie
Murmure sa romance à la brise du soir.

Of our own strength. Such strength! But wasn't I on
Just now about moderation, duty, home?
Look at the sky! It's too small for us,
The heat would stifle us, we'd be down on our knees!
The sky! I'm going back to the crowd,
That great, monstrous rabble, rolling Your Majesty's
Venerable ordnance over the filthy cobbles.
Our deaths, I suppose, will wash them clean.
And if, to silence our avengers' chanting,
The paws of rusty kings should push
Their full-dress regiments the length of France,
Then – am I wrong? – we'll shit on them. Curs!'

....

He shouldered his hammer.
                                    The crowd
Felt drunk to its soul, to be near that man.
And in the great courtyard, in the royal apartments,
Where Paris heaved and bellowed,
A shiver ran through the enormous gathering.
Then, raising his broad hand superb with grime,
That terrifying Blacksmith crowned the portly,
Sweating monarch with the red cap of the Revolution!

Ophelia

I

On the calm, black waters where the stars sleep,
White Ophelia drifts, like a great lily,
Very slowly, laid out in her long veils.
In the woods, way off, the mort sounds.

Sad Ophelia – a white spectre carried down
The long, black river for a thousand years.
For a thousand years her song of madness
Has bewitched the evening breeze.

Le vent baise ses seins et déploie en corolle
Ses grands voiles bercés mollement par les eaux;
Les saules frissonnants pleurent sur son épaule,
Sur son grand front rêveur s'inclinent les roseaux.

Les nénuphars froissés soupirent autour d'elle;
Elle éveille parfois, dans un aune qui dort,
Quelque nid, d'où s'échappe un petit frisson d'aile:
– Un chant mystérieux tombe des astres d'or.

II

O pâle Ophélia! belle comme la neige!
Oui tu mourus, enfant, par un fleuve emporté!
– C'est que les vents tombant des grands monts de
            Norwège
T'avaient parlé tout bas de l'âpre liberté;

C'est qu'un souffle, tordant ta grande chevelure,
A ton esprit rêveur portait d'étranges bruits;
Que ton cœur écoutait le chant de la Nature
Dans les plaintes de l'arbre et les soupirs des nuits;

C'est que la voix des mers folles, immense
            râle,
Brisait ton sein d'enfant, trop humain et trop doux;
C'est qu'un matin d'avril, un beau cavalier pâle,
Un pauvre fou, s'assit muet à tes genoux!

Ciel! Amour! Liberté! Quel rêve, ô pauvre
            Folle!
Tu te fondais à lui comme une neige au feu:
Tes grandes visions étranglaient ta parole
– Et l'Infini terrible effara ton œil bleu!

Her long veils rise and fall with the water.
They flare in the wind, which kisses her breasts.
Shivering willows weep on her shoulder,
Rushes stoop over her wide, dreamer's face.

Sighing water lilies furrow round her.
Sometimes in a sleeping alder she disturbs
A nest, and wings beat briskly on the air.
Eerie plainsong falls from the golden stars.

II

O pale Ophelia, beautiful as snow!
Yes, child, the current took you to your death.
– Because the winds swooped from the great
        Norwegian ranges,
And you heard their talk of harsh freedom;

Because a gust that twisted your thick hair
Put strange sounds in your dreaming head,
And your heart heard Nature's song
In the wailing trees and sighing nights;

Because the voice of maddened seas – an immense
        moaning –
Broke your child's heart, too human and too kind;
Because a sallow, courtly prince[1] who'd lost his mind
Sat by your knees in silence on an April morning.

Heaven, Love, Freedom! What a dream, you poor,
        crazed seer!
You were snow in its fire, melting into it.
Your soaring visions choked your power of speech
– A terrible Infinity scared your blue eyes!

III

– Et le Poète dit qu'aux rayons des étoiles
Tu viens chercher, la nuit, les fleurs que tu cueillis;
Et qu'il a vu sur l'eau, couchée en ses longs voiles,
La blanche Ophélia flotter, comme un grand lys.

Bal des pendus

Au gibet noir, manchot aimable,
Dansent, dansent les paladins
Les maigres paladins du diable
Les squelettes de Saladins.

Messire Belzébuth tire par la cravate
Ses petits pantins noirs grimaçant sur le ciel,
Et, leur claquant au front un revers de savate,
Les fait danser, danser aux sons d'un vieux Noël!

Et les pantins choqués enlacent leurs bras grêles:
Comme des orgues noirs, les poitrines à jour
Que serraient autrefois les gentes damoiselles,
Se heurtent longuement dans un hideux amour.

Hurrah! les gais danseurs, qui n'avez plus de panse!
On peut cabrioler, les tréteaux sont si longs!
Hop! qu'on ne sache plus si c'est bataille ou danse!
Belzébuth enragé racle ses violons!

O durs talons, jamais on n'use sa sandale!
Presque tous ont quitté la chemise de peau;
Le reste est peu gênant et se voit sans scandale.
Sur les crânes, la neige applique un blanc chapeau:

III

And when the stars are bright, the poet says,
You take to looking for the flowers you picked. He says
He's studied white Ophelia, laid out in her long veils,
Floating like a lily, there on the water.

Dance of the Hanged Men

The gibbet only has one arm
To dance its partners up and down –
The devil's skinny paladins,
And skeletons of Saladins.

Our good lord Beelzebub hoiks small black puppets
By their hempen neckties. They grimace at the sky.
He lays into them – slippers them about the head –
And shortly has them dancing to a Christmas carol!

The battered puppets interlock their bony arms.
Like tarnished organ pipes, the slatted ribs –
Which ladies of distinction used to press against their own –
Jangle together in long and hideous fornication.

Keep at it, you fine dancers with your guts long gone.
Cavort! Why not! You've got a sturdy wooden dais.
Beelzebub raves and scrapes on his fiddle.
Fighting or dancing – never mind which!

These bone-hard heels put cobblers out of business!
Almost everyone has taken off his shirt of skin,
And stripped for comfort – not that you'll blush.
Each skull sports a white cap, courtesy of the snow,

Le corbeau fait panache à ces têtes fêlées,
Un morceau de chair tremble à leur maigre menton:
On dirait, tournoyant dans les sombres mêlées,
Des preux, raides, heurtant armures de carton.

Hurrah! la bise siffle au grand bal des squelettes!
Le gibet noir mugit comme un orgue de fer!
Les loups vont répondant des forêts violettes:
A l'horizon le ciel est d'un rouge d'enfer . . .

Holà, secouez-moi ces capitans funèbres
Qui défilent, sournois, de leurs gros doigts cassés
Un chapelet d'amour sur leurs pâles vertèbres:
Ce n'est pas un moustier ici, les trépassés!

Oh! voilà qu'au milieu de la danse macabre
Bondit dans le ciel rouge un grand squelette fou
Emporté par l'élan, comme un cheval se cabre:
Et, se sentant encor la corde raide au cou,

Crispe ses petits doigts sur son fémur qui craque
Avec des cris pareils à des ricanements,
Et comme un baladin rentre dans la baraque,
Rebondit dans le bal au chant des ossements.

            Au gibet noir, manchot aimable,
            Dansent, dansent les paladins
            Les maigres paladins du diable
            Les squelettes de Saladins.

Le Châtiment de Tartufe

Tisonnant, tisonnant son cœur amoureux sous
Sa chaste robe noire, heureux, la main gantée,
Un jour qu'il s'en allait, effroyablement doux,
Jaune, bavant la foi de sa bouche édentée,

And for a plume, a perching crow, on every fissured head.
Remnants of flesh chatter on lean chins.
They revolve in their dark tournament
Like brittle knights, to the clash of pasteboard armour.

The wind whistles at the skeleton-ball,
The black gibbet bellows like an iron organ.
Wolves answer from the purple forests.
The sky at the horizon turns the red of Hell . . .

Somebody cut them down! – these sinister show-offs
Whose broken fingers tell their sexual conquests
On rosaries of pale vertebrae.
Hey you – the dear departed! It's not a seminary!

Now from the depths of the Danse Macabre,
A giant of frenzied bone rears like a horse
Catapulted into the red sky.
He feels the rope go tight around his neck,

He clasps his thighbone in his shrunken fingers
Till it cracks – his shriek becomes a cackle –
Then, like a clown resuming a routine,
Falls back into the dance, to the dirge of bones.

> The gibbet only has one arm
> To swing its partners up and down –
> The devil's skinny paladins,
> And skeletons of Saladins.

Tartufe Punished

Stoking the engine of his lusts beneath
His chaste black cassock, hand in glove,
He oozed along one day, so unspeakably meek
And yellow – piety dripping from his toothless mouth,

Un jour qu'il s'en allait, «Oremus», – un Méchant
Le prît rudement par son oreille benoîte
Et lui jeta des mots affreux, en arrachant
Sa chaste robe noire autour de sa peau moite!

Chatîment! . . . Ses habits étaient déboutonnés,
Et le long chapelet des péchés pardonnés
S'égrenant dans son cœur, Saint Tartufe était pâle! . . .

Donc, il se confessait, priait, avec un râle!
L'homme se contenta d'emporter ses rabats . . .
– Peuh! Tartufe était nu du haut jusques en bas!

Vénus Anadyomène

Comme d'un cercueil vert en fer blanc, une tête
De femme à cheveux bruns fortement
     pommadés
D'une vieille baignoire émerge, lente et bête,
Avec des déficits assez mal ravaudés;

Puis le col gras et gris, les larges omoplates
Qui saillent; le dos court qui rentre et qui ressort;
Puis les rondeurs des reins semblent prendre l'essor;
La graisse sous la peau paraît en feuilles plates;

L'échine est un peu rouge, et le tout sent un goût
Horrible étrangement; on remarque surtout
Des singularités qu'il faut voir à la loupe . . .

Les reins portent deux mots gravés: Clara
     Vénus;
– Et tout ce corps remue et tend sa large croupe
Belle hideusement d'un ulcère à l'anus.

Oozing along with all that 'Let us pray' until
A brutal Unbeliever grabbed him by his holy ear,
Cursed him horribly, and tore
The chaste black cassock from his dank skin.

Quite a come-uppance! His clothes were all unbuttoned
To reveal the long chaplet of his pardoned sins,
Told in some intimacy. Our saint went pale . . .

Nothing for it but confession now – bronchitic prayer!
His nemesis relieved him of his bands . . . And so:
The great Tartufe, naked from head to toe.

Venus Rising from the Water[1]

Slow and stupefied, a woman's head emerges
From a green tinplate coffin – actually an ancient
     bath-tub;
Her brown hair is plastered with pomade,
The bald bits nonetheless quite ill-concealed.

Sequel: a fatty, greying neck, wide, protruding
Shoulder blades; short, corrugated back.
Then aloft with the puckered bottom,
Cellulite in flattened plates beneath the skin.

The spine is a touch red; the entire business
Does not smell good. A number of particulars
Would merit further study with a magnifying glass . . .

Two words – Illustrious Venus – inscribed on the
     buttocks.
Now the whole contraption shifts, to show the hideous
Adornment on its massive croup – an anal ulcer.

Les Reparties de Nina

....

LUI – Ta poitrine sur ma poitrine,
     Hein? Nous irions,
Ayant de l'air plein la narine,
     Aux frais rayons

Du bon matin bleu, qui vous baigne
     Du vin de jour? . . .
Quand tout le bois frissonnant saigne
     Muet d'amour

De chaque branche, gouttes vertes,
     Des bourgeons clairs,
On sent dans les choses ouvertes
     Frémir des chairs:

Tu plongerais dans la luzerne
     Ton blanc peignoir,
Rosant à l'air ce bleu qui cerne
     Ton grand œil noir,

Amoureuse de la campagne,
     Semant partout,
Comme une mousse de champagne,
     Ton rire fou:

Riant à moi, brutal d'ivresse
     Qui te prendrais
Comme cela, – la belle tresse,
     Oh! – qui boirais

Nina Gets Back to Him[1]

....

HIM: Your breasts on my breast,
              For instance? Air in
       Our flaring nostrils, as we step
              Into the sun's cool rays,

       A fine, blue morning – you,
              Bathed in the wine of daylight . . .
       The whole wood shivering and bleeding,
              Speechless with love,

       Green drops on the branches,
              Pale buds;
       A quiver of flesh
              Where they've opened.

       You'd steep your white gown
              In the tall grass,
       Those blue rings round
              Your black eyes would fade.

       Infatuated with the great outdoors
              You'd scatter
       Your wild laughter everywhere
              Like the head on champagne.

       You'd tease me; I'd catch hold of you
              In drunken earnest
       Like so – your pretty hair –
              I'd get to taste

Ton goût de framboise et de fraise
　　O chair de fleur!
Riant au vent vif qui te baise
　　Comme un voleur,

Au rose églantier qui t'embête
　　Aimablement:
Riant surtout, ô folle tête,
　　A ton amant! . . .

. . . .

[Dix-sept ans! Tu seras heureuse!
　　– Oh! les grands prés,
La grande campagne amoureuse!
　　– Dis, viens plus près! . . .]

– Ta poitrine sur ma poitrine,
　　Mêlant nos voix,
Lents, nous gagnerions la ravine,
　　Puis les grands bois! . . .

Puis, comme une petite morte,
　　Le cœur pâmé,
Tu me dirais que je te porte,
　　L'œil mi-fermé . . .

Je te porterais, palpitante,
　　Dans le sentier:
L'oiseau filerait son andante:
　　Au Noisetier . . .

Je te parlerais dans ta bouche;
　　J'irais, pressant
Ton corps, comme un enfant qu'on couche,
　　Ivre du sang

You (raspberries and strawberries),
    Relishing your flower-flesh;
You, laughing at the agile wind,
    As it kisses you like a thief,

At the wild rose that snags
    You so agreeably,
Laughing, most of all, at me,
    Your lover – a madcap laugh.

· ·

[Seventeen! You'll like it
    In the open fields,
The sprawling, amorous countryside –
    Here, come closer . . .]

Your breasts on my breast,
    Our voices the same . . .
Slowly we'd reach the gully
    And then the great wood . . .

Then, like a little dead thing,
    Your strength quite drained,
You'd ask me to carry you,
    Your eyes half-closed.

I'd bear you, trembling,
    Along the track,
A bird's andante spinning
    Out: 'Beside the Hazel Tree . . .'

I'd speak into your mouth
    And walk on, taking you
Up like a child to bed,
    Drunk on the blood

Qui coule, bleu, sous ta peau blanche
      Aux tons rosés:
Et te parlant la langue franche . . .
      Tiens! . . . – que tu sais . . .

Nos grands bois sentiraient la sève
      Et le soleil
Sablerait d'or fin leur grand rêve
      Vert et vermeil.

. . . .

Le soir? . . . Nous reprendrons la route
      Blanche qui court
Flânant, comme un troupeau qui broute,
      Tout à l'entour

Les bons vergers à l'herbe bleue,
      Aux pommiers tors!
Comme on les sent toute une lieue
      Leurs parfums forts!

Nous regagnerons le village
      Au ciel mi-noir;
Et ça sentira le laitage
      Dans l'air du soir;

Ça sentira l'étable, pleine
      De fumiers chauds,
Pleine d'un lent rhythme d'haleine,
      Et de grands dos

Blanchissant sous quelque lumière;
      Et, tout là-bas,
Une vache fientera, fière,
      A chaque pas . . .

Running blue beneath your pale skin,
    Tinted pink,
And I'd speak in a candid language
    That I see you know.

The forests would smell of sap
    And the sun
Would dust their dream
    Of green and red with gold.

· ·

In the evening? The white
    Aimless road
That seems to idle
    Like a grazing fold.

Fine orchards with blue grass
    And gnarled apple trees,
Their fragrance carrying
    For a mile or more.

We'll get back to the village
    In the half-light
And recognize the smell of milking
    On the evening air,

The reek of cowsheds, carpeted
    With warm manure,
Filled with the slow rhythm of breath,
    Great backs

Glistening under a storm lamp,
    And at the far end
An ambling cow, dung flopping down
    With every ostentatious step.

– Les lunettes de la grand'mère
      Et son nez long
Dans son missel: le pot de bière
      Cerclé de plomb,

Moussant entre les larges pipes
      Qui, crânement,
Fument: les effroyables lippes
      Qui, tout fumant,

Happent le jambon aux fourchettes
      Tant, tant et plus:
Le feu qui claire les couchettes
      Et les bahuts:

Les fesses luisantes et grasses
      Du gros enfant
Qui fourre, à genoux, dans les tasses,
      Son museau blanc

Frôlé par un mufle qui gronde
      D'un ton gentil,
Et pourlèche la face ronde
      Du cher petit . . .

[Noire, rogue, au bord de sa chaise,
      Affreux profil,
Une vieille devant la braise
      Qui fait du fil;]

Que de choses verrons-nous, chère,
      Dans ces taudis,
Quand la flamme illumine, claire,
      Les carreaux gris! . . .

Grandmother with her reading glasses,
    And her long nose
In her missal; the beer-jug
    Chased in pewter,

Foaming between the stout tobacco
    Pipes, gallantly
Smoking – and the awful lips
    Still puffing

As they snaffle up ham by the forkful:
    More – and more to follow.
Bunks and sideboards glow
    In the firelight.

Then the fat, lustrous bottom
    Of a bulky baby,
On all fours
    Snout-first in the crockery,

Nudged by a muzzle
    – Soft lowing noises –
Which licks the little darling's
    Oval face.

[Black with disdain at the edge of her chair
    An old crone
In atrocious profile
    Sits by the embers and spins.]

All that to see, and more, my Nina,
    In these hovels,
When the firelight burnishes
    The ashen window panes.

> – Puis, petite et toute nichée
>   Dans les lilas
> Noirs et frais: la vitre cachée,
>   Qui rit là-bas . . .
>
> Tu viendras, tu viendras, je t'aime!
>   Ce sera beau.
> Tu viendras, n'est-ce pas, et même . . .

ELLE –   Et mon bureau?

A la musique

> Place de la Gare, à Charleville.

Sur la place taillée en mesquines pelouses,
Square où tout est correct, les arbres et les fleurs,
Tous les bourgeois poussifs qu'étranglent les chaleurs
Portent, les jeudis soirs, leurs bêtises jalouses.

– L'orchestre militaire, au milieu du jardin,
Balance ses schakos dans la Valse des fifres:
– Autour, aux premiers rangs, parade le gandin;
Le notaire pend à ses breloques à chiffres:

Des rentiers à lorgnons soulignent tous les couacs:
Les gros bureaux bouffis traînent leurs grosses dames
Auprès desquelles vont, officieux cornacs,
Celles dont les volants ont des airs de réclames;

Sur les bancs verts, des clubs d'épiciers retraités
Qui tisonnent le sable avec leur canne à pomme,
Fort sérieusement discutent les traités,
Puis prisent en argent, et reprennent: «En somme! . . .»

Then there's that other window,
    Nestling in dark, cool lilac –
That small, occluded window
    With its beckoning smile.

You'll come. You must. I love you.
    It'll be good.
You'll think it over, yes? And even . . .

HER: Even skive off work?

Set to Music

Place de la Gare, Charleville

In the square, cropped into mean little lawns,
Flowers and trees and everything just so,
Wheezing burghers stifled by the evening heat
Parade on Thursdays, envious stupidities in tow.

The bandsmen in the gardens strike up
Waltz of the Fife, their shakos nod to the refrain.
The local dandy lolls by the front seats
And the notary swings by his own watch chain.

Gilt-edge investors with pince-nez deplore the duff notes.
Puffy bureaucrats heave along their puffy spouses.
And hard by, like officious elephant handlers, other ladies
Raise the advertising panels of their flounces.

On green benches the Association of Retired Grocers
Work the gravel with their pommelled canes,
Mull over trade agreements, snap the silver snuffbox
Open and resume: 'The bottom line, it's plain . . .'

Epatant sur son banc les rondeurs de ses reins,
Un bourgeois à boutons clairs, bedaine flamande,
Savoure son onnaing d'où le tabac par brins
Déborde – vous savez, c'est de la contrebande; –

Le long des gazons verts ricanent les voyous;
Et, rendus amoureux par le chant des trombones,
Très naïfs, et fumant des roses, les pioupious
Caressent les bébés pour enjôler les bonnes . . .

– Moi, je suis débraillé comme un étudiant,
Sous les marronniers verts les alertes fillettes:
Elles le savent bien; et tournent en riant,
Vers moi, leurs yeux tout pleins de choses indiscrètes.

Je ne dis pas un mot: je regarde toujours
La chair de leurs cous blancs brodés de mèches folles:
Je suis, sous le corsage et les frêles atours,
Le dos divin après la courbe des épaules.

J'ai bientôt déniché la bottine, le bas . . .
– Je reconstruis les corps, brûlé de belles fièvres.
Elles me trouvent drôle et se parlent tout bas . . .
– Et mes désirs brutaux s'accrochent à leurs lèvres . . .

Roman

I

On n'est pas sérieux, quand on a dix-sept ans.
– Un beau soir, foin des bocks et de la limonade,
Des cafés tapageurs aux lustres éclatants!
– On va sous les tilleuls verts de la promenade.

Flattening his ample bum across a bench,
And savouring a pipe – tobacco dangling off in strands –
A shiny-buttoned bourgeois with a Flemish paunch
Brags of his smoke: 'Of course, it's contraband.'

Sneering town lads dawdle on the lawns.
Pulling at a cheap cigarette,[1] a fresh-faced soldier
Turned on by the slithering trombones,
Hopes to pull a nanny by cooing at her toddler.

Me, I'm a kind of student scruff,
Eyeing brash little girls beneath the chestnut trees.
They know the story, turn and face me, laugh –
I read the improprieties in their eyes.

I don't say a word, just gaze on, at the white skin
Of their necks, the stray curls; I make tracks
From the curving shoulders, down the flimsy
Dresses, in at the bodices – along the divine backs.

Soon I'm uncovering an ankle-boot, a stocking –
Reinventing each one's body; burning fever grips
Me as I go. They find me funny; they whisper
Low – and my abrupt desires batten on their lips.

Popular Fiction

I

Nobody of seventeen is all that serious.
One fine evening you decide you're done with pint pots
And lemonades, chic cafés and gleaming lights.
You take to the promenade, under the green lime trees.

Les tilleuls sentent bon dans les bons soirs de juin!
L'air est parfois si doux, qu'on ferme la paupière;
Le vent chargé de bruits, – la ville n'est pas loin, –
A des parfums de vigne et des parfums de bière . . .

II

– Voilà qu'on aperçoit un tout petit chiffon
D'azur sombre, encadré d'une petite branche,
Piqué d'une mauvaise étoile, qui se fond
Avec de doux frissons, petite et toute blanche . . .

Nuit de juin! Dix-sept ans! – On se laisse griser.
La sève est du champagne et vous monte à la tête . . .
On divague; on se sent aux lèvres un baiser
Qui palpite là, comme une petite bête . . .

III

Le cœur fou Robinsonne à travers les romans,
– Lorsque, dans la clarté d'un pâle réverbère,
Passe une demoiselle aux petits airs charmants,
Sous l'ombre du faux-col effrayant de son père . . .

Et, comme elle vous trouve immensément naïf,
Tout en faisant trotter ses petites bottines,
Elle se tourne, alerte et d'un mouvement vif . . .
– Sur vos lèvres alors meurent les cavatines . . .

IV

Vous êtes amoureux. Loué jusqu'au mois d'août.
Vous êtes amoureux. – Vos sonnets La font rire.
Tous vos amis s'en vont, vous êtes mauvais goût.
– Puis l'adorée, un soir, a daigné vous écrire . . . !

The smell of those trees on fine June nights!
Sometimes the air's so sweet you close your eyes.
The wind is thick with noise – the town's not far –
Rich with the scent of vines, and beer.

II

That's when you notice a flimsy patch of blue,
Framed by a small branch
And punctured by a desolate star, quite white
But fading now, in little fits and starts.

A night in June. You're seventeen. And drunk on it.
Sap makes your head spin – like champagne . . .
You're losing the plot; you think you feel a kiss,
Still whirring on your mouth like an insect.

III

You Crusoe madly through the pulp romances.
And then a fetching girl with pretty airs
Crosses the pool of light beneath a feeble streetlamp,
Face half-hidden by her father's monstrous collar.

She clacks along in that nice pair of ankle-boots
And clearly finds you terribly naive. You can tell
By the way she turns her head, so quick and critical.
Your cavatinas die a death upon your lips.

IV

You're smitten. Spoken for till August at the least.
Smitten. Your sonnets reduce Her to tears of laughter.
Your friends evaporate. You're deeply unfashionable.
Then, one night, the Object of Devotion deigns to write.

– Ce soir-là, . . . – vous rentrez aux cafés éclatants,
Vous demandez des bocks ou de la limonade . . .
– On n'est pas sérieux, quand on a dix-sept ans
Et qu'on a des tilleuls verts sur la promenade.

29 septembre 70

Au Cabaret-Vert
cinq heures du soir

Depuis huit jours, j'avais déchiré mes bottines
Aux cailloux des chemins. J'entrais à Charleroi.
– Au Cabaret-Vert: je demandai des tartines
De beurre et du jambon qui fût à moitié froid.

Bienheureux, j'allongeai les jambes sous la table
Verte: je contemplai les sujets très naïfs
De la tapisserie. – Et ce fut adorable,
Quand la fille aux tétons énormes, aux yeux vifs,

– Celle-là, ce n'est pas un baiser qui l'épeure!
Rieuse, m'apporta des tartines de beurre,
De jambon tiède, dans un plat colorié,

Du jambon rose et blanc parfumé d'une gousse
D'ail, – et m'emplit la chope immense, avec sa mousse
Que dorait un rayon de soleil arriéré.

Octobre 70

La Maline

Dans la salle à manger brune, que parfumait
Une odeur de vernis et de fruits, à mon aise
Je ramassais un plat de je ne sais quel mets
Belge, et je m'épatais dans mon immense chaise.

And that's the night you hit the dazzling café scene again.
You order up large beers, or lemonade . . .
Nobody of seventeen is all that serious –
Not with the limes on the promenade in leaf.

                                        29 September '70

At the Green Inn
Five p.m.

For a week I've flayed my boots
On the stony roads. I swing into Charleroi.
– The Green Inn. I ask for buttered bread
And a plate of half-cold ham.

I feel superb – legs at full stretch under the green
Table. I study the wallpaper, check the repeat.
Bright eyes and an enormous cleavage
Earn the barmaid ten out of ten –

Definitely not a shrinking violet. Service
With a smile: in comes my warmish ham
On a garish plate, and yes, the buttered bread;

The ham's pink and white, frisked with a garlic clove.
She pours me out a massive mug of beer –
A ray of Indian summer gilds the head.

                                        October '70

Knowing Way

There's a smell of fruit and wood-polish
In the brown dining-room; I feel good,
Help myself to a dollop of some Belgian dish
Or other, sprawl in my enormous chair.

En mangeant, j'écoutais l'horloge, – heureux et coi.
La cuisine s'ouvrit avec une bouffée,
– Et la servante vint, je ne sais pas pourquoi,
Fichu moitié défait, malinement coiffée

Et, tout en promenant son petit doigt tremblant
Sur sa joue, un velours de pêche rose et blanc,
En faisant, de sa lèvre enfantine, une moue,

Elle arrangeait les plats, près de moi, pour m'aiser;
– Puis, comme ça, – bien sûr pour avoir un baiser, –
Tout bas: «Sens donc, j'ai pris une froid sur la joue . . .»

Charleroi, octobre 70

Ma Bohème (fantaisie)

Je m'en allais, les poings dans mes poches crevées;
Mon paletot aussi devenait idéal;
J'allais sous le ciel, Muse! et j'étais ton féal;
Oh! là! là! que d'amours splendides j'ai rêvés!

Mon unique culotte avait un large trou.
– Petit-Poucet rêveur, j'égrenais dans ma course
Des rimes. Mon auberge était à la Grande-Ourse.
– Mes étoiles au ciel avaient un doux frou-frou

Et je les écoutais, assis au bord des routes,
Ces bons soirs de septembre où je sentais des gouttes
De rosée à mon front, comme un vin de vigueur;

Où, rimant au milieu des ombres fantastiques,
Comme des lyres, je tirais les élastiques
De mes souliers blessés, un pied près de mon cœur!

Between mouthfuls, I'm happy monitoring the clock.
I'm lying low. Then the kitchen door gusts open;
In comes the servant girl – why, I can't think –
Bonnet loose; knowing way with the hair.

She puts a vibrant little finger out,
Touches her cheek – peach-skin velvet, pink
On white – and sets the babe-lips to 'pout';

She eases close – quite nice – adjusts my place,
And just like so, prospecting for a kiss,
'I've catched a chill,' she murmurs. 'Feel my face.'

                                    Charleroi, October '70

My Bohemia (Fantasy)

I lit off with my hands in my torn pockets,
My overcoat worn down to a notion;
Walking beneath the sky, Muse! I was all yours.
And – oh my! – what fabulous loves I dreamed of!

My only trousers had a major hole.
A dreamy Tom Thumb, I scattered verses in my path
Like seed. I lodged under the Great Bear,
My stars rustled gently in the sky.

Sat on the road's edge, I listened out for them
On fine September evenings, sampling the dew
On my face like a heady wine,

And rhyming in the thick of unfamiliar shadows,
As I strummed the laces of my devastated boots
Like lyre-strings, one foot by my heart.

Les Assis

Noirs de loupes, grêlés, les yeux cerclés de bagues
Vertes, leurs doigts boulus crispés à leurs fémurs,
Le sinciput plaqué de hargnosités vagues
Comme les floraisons lépreuses de vieux murs;

Ils ont greffé dans des amours épileptiques
Leur fantasque ossature aux grands squelettes noirs
De leurs chaises: leurs pieds aux barreaux rachitiques
S'entrelacent pour les matins et pour les soirs!

Ces vieillards ont toujours fait tresse avec leurs sièges,
Sentant les soleils vifs percaliser leur peau,
Ou, les yeux à la vitre où se fanent les neiges,
Tremblant du tremblement douloureux du crapaud

Et les Sièges leur ont des bontés: culottée
De brun, la paille cède aux angles de leurs reins;
L'âme des vieux soleils s'allume emmaillotée
Dans ces tresses d'épis où fermentaient les grains.

Et les Assis, genoux aux dents, verts pianistes
Les dix doigts sous leur siège aux rumeurs de tambour,
S'écoutent clapoter des barcarolles tristes,
Et leurs caboches vont dans des roulis d'amour.

– Oh! ne les faites pas lever! C'est le naufrage . . .
Ils surgissent, grondant comme des chats giflés,
Ouvrant lentement leurs omoplates, ô rage!
Tout leur pantalon bouffe à leurs reins boursouflés.

Et vous les écoutez, cognant leurs têtes chauves
Aux murs sombres, plaquant et plaquant leurs pieds tors,
Et leurs boutons d'habit sont des prunelles fauves
Qui vous accrochent l'œil du fond des corridors!

Seat-People

Wart-clotted, pox-pitted; green rings
Around their eyes; distended fingers clenched on thighs;
Scalps pitted with blurred, angry scabs
Like leprous excrescences on ageing walls;

In seizures of passion, they have fused
Their own fantastic skeletons to the black
Bone structure of their chairs, day upon day,
Their feet now grafted to the creaking leg-rests.

These old buffers have always been woven
Into their chairs, feeling the sun polish their skin
To glazed calico, or watching the snow on the windows
Turn to slush, as they shudder and wince like toads.

Their chairs return the courtesy – straw seats
Browned with age yield to the contours of their backsides;
The spirit of ancient, glowing suns is swaddled
In those braided stalks that once held ripening corn.

Seat-people, teeth against knees, green piano
Players, all ten fingers drumming at the chair's edge,
Rippling out sad barcaroles,[1] one to another,
Heads bobbing in the swells of love.

Don't make them get up! It's catastrophic!
They loom to attention, snarling like wounded cats,
Rabidly, intently, easing apart their shoulder blades.
Their trousers bulge around their swollen haunches.

You can hear the thud of balding heads
On obscure walls and the stamping of arthritic feet.
You're transfixed by the buttons on their coats,
Like wild eyes gleaming at the far end of a corridor.

Puis ils ont une main invisible qui tue:
Au retour, leur regard filtre ce venin noir
Qui charge l'œil souffrant de la chienne battue
Et vous suez pris dans un atroce entonnoir.

Rassis, les poings noyés dans des manchettes sales
Ils songent à ceux-là qui les ont fait lever
Et, de l'aurore au soir, des grappes d'amygdales
Sous leurs mentons chétifs s'agitent à crever.

Quand l'austère sommeil a baissé leurs visières
Ils rêvent sur leur bras de sièges fécondés,
De vrais petits amours de chaises en lisières
Par lesquelles de fiers bureaux seront bordés;

Des fleurs d'encre crachant des pollens en virgules
Les bercent, le long des calices accroupis
Tels qu'au fil des glaïeuls le vol des libellules
– Et leur membre s'agace à des barbes d'épis.

Le Cœur du pitre

    Mon triste cœur bave à la poupe,
    Mon cœur est plein de caporal:
    Ils y lancent des jets de soupe,
    Mon triste cœur bave à la poupe:
    Sous les quolibets de la troupe
    Qui pousse un rire général,
    Mon triste cœur bave à la poupe,
    Mon cœur couvert de caporal!

    Ithyphalliques et pioupiesques,
    Leur insultes l'ont dépravé!
    A la vesprée, ils font des fresques
    Ithyphalliques et pioupiesques.
    O flots abracadabrantesques

They have a hidden hand that does for you:
As they return, their look secretes black venom
Like the abject gaze of a whipped bitch.
You're sweating; you're being poured down a horrific funnel.

Seated again, fists knotted in their filthy sleeves,
Their thoughts turn on whoever forced them to their feet
And so from dawn till dusk the polyps clustering
Beneath their paltry chins quiver in frenzy.

Then stringent slumber drags their eyeshades down;
Their heads droop on their arms. They dream
Of chair insemination – and a progeny of toddler chairs
Chairs gracing the edges of some stately desk.

Ink-flowers spitting commas of seed
Entrance them, as they crouch above the blooms
Like dragonflies along a line of yellow flag –
Their pricks stirred by the harsh proximity of straw.

Heart of a Clown

My poor heart drools in the stern.
Quid-spit spatters my heart:
They stain it with chewed tobacco,
My poor heart drools in the stern.
To the gibes of the crew
And belly laughs all round,
My poor heart drools in the stern,
Quid-spit spatters my heart!

It's been sullied by their
Cock-stiff, squaddy taunts –
And their cock-stiff, squaddy
Scrawlings on the walls at dusk.
You abracadabral waves,

Prenez mon cœur, qu'il soit sauvé:
Ithyphalliques et pioupiesques
Leurs quolibets l'ont dépravé!

Quand ils auront tari leurs chiques
Comment agir, ô cœur volé?
Ce seront des refrains bachiques
Quand ils auront tari leurs chiques
J'aurai des sursauts stomachiques
Si mon cœur triste est ravalé:
Quand ils auront tari leurs chiques
Comment agir, ô cœur volé?

Mai 1871

Les Mains de Jeanne-Marie

Jeanne-Marie a des mains fortes,
Mains sombres que l'été tanna,
Mains pâles comme des mains mortes.
– Sont-ce des mains de Juana?

Ont-elles pris les crèmes brunes
Sur les mares des voluptés?
Ont-elles trempé dans les lunes
Aux étangs de sérénités?

Ont-elles bu des cieux barbares,
Calmes sur les genoux charmants?
Ont-elles roulé des cigares
Ou trafiqué des diamants?

Sur les pieds ardents des Madones
Ont-elles fané des fleurs d'or?
C'est le sang noir des belladones
Qui dans leur paume éclate et dort.

Save this heart – carry it off:
It's been sullied by their
Cock-stiff, squaddy gibes.

And what, my ripped-off heart,
When their quids are chewed out?
There'll be carnival songs to come
When their quids are chewed out –
My stomach will heave
As my sad heart is defiled:
And what, my ripped-off heart,
When their quids are chewed out?

May 1871

The Hands of Jeanne-Marie[1]

Her hands – the hands of Jeanne-Marie –
Are strong, tanned by summer,
Pale as the hands of the dead.
Are these the hands of Juana?[2]

Were they stained in the waters
Of concupiscence, or steeped
In lunar craters, flooded with serenity,
To turn so creamy dark?

Poised on those charming knees, perhaps,
They drank the fervour of savage skies?
Or rolled cigars?
Or smuggled diamonds?

Did they wilt the gilded flowers
At the smouldering feet of Madonnas?
Or is the black blood of belladonna
Surging and sleeping in their palms?

Mains chasseresses des diptères
Dont bombinent les bleuisons
Aurorales, vers les nectaires?
Mains décanteuses de poisons?

Oh! quel Rêve les a saisies
Dans les pandiculations?
Un rêve inouï des Asies,
Des Khenghavars ou des Sions?

– Ces mains n'ont pas vendu d'oranges,
Ni bruni sur les pieds des dieux:
Ces mains n'ont pas lavé les langes
Des lourds petits enfants sans yeux.

Ce ne sont pas mains de cousine
Ni d'ouvrières aux gros fronts
Que brûle, aux bois puant l'usine,
Un soleil ivre de goudrons.

Ce sont des ployeuses d'échines,
Des mains qui ne font jamais mal,
Plus fatales que des machines,
Plus fortes que tout un cheval!

Remuant comme des fournaises,
Et secouant tous ses frissons,
Leur chair chante des Marseillaises
Et jamais les Eleisons!

Ça serrerait vos cous, ô femmes
Mauvaises, ça broierait vos mains,
Femmes nobles, vos mains infâmes
Pleines de blancs et de carmins.

Hands that chase the diptera
Buzzing in the blues of dawn
Towards the nectaries?
Hands that measure out poisons?

What dream has fixed them
In pandiculation?
Outlandish dreams of Asia,
Zion, Khenghavar?[3]

– These hands have not sold oranges
Or darkened at the feet of gods,
Or washed the wraps
Of heavy infants with no eyes.

They're not the hands of prostitutes[4]
Or women with swollen foreheads – workers –
Scorched by a tar-blind sun
In woods that stink of factories.

They are benders of backbones,
Hands that do no harm,
More inexorable than machines,
Stronger than a horse.

Stoked like furnaces,
Immune to their own tremblings,
Their flesh shouts down the Kyrie Eleison[5]
With verses from the Marseillaise.

These hands would wring your necks,
You dire women; and crush your own,
You rustling ladies – your infamous hands
Awash with noble whites and carmines.

L'éclat de ces mains amoureuses
Tourne le crâne des brebis!
Dans leurs phalanges savoureuses
Le grand soleil met un rubis!

Une tache de populace
Les brunit comme un sein d'hier;
Le dos de ces Mains est la place
Qu'en baisa tout Révolté fier!

Elles ont pâli, merveilleuses,
Au grand soleil d'amour chargé
Sur le bronze des mitrailleuses
A travers Paris insurgé!

Ah! quelquefois, ô Mains sacrées,
A vos poings, Mains où tremblent nos
Lèvres jamais désenivrées,
Crie une chaîne aux clairs anneaux!

Et c'est un soubresaut étrange
Dans nos êtres, quand, quelquefois,
On veut vous déhâler, Mains d'ange,
En vous faisant saigner les doigts!

Les Poètes de sept ans

Et la Mère, fermant le livre du devoir,
S'en allait satisfaite et très-fière, sans voir,
Dans les yeux bleus et sous le front plein d'éminences,
L'âme de son enfant livrée aux répugnances.

Tout le jour il suait d'obéissance; très
Intelligent: pourtant des tics noirs, quelques traits,
Semblaient prouver en lui d'âcres hypocrisies.
Dans l'ombre des couloirs aux tentures moisies,

Adroit in love, these lustrous hands
Have turned the mutton-heads at every rally.
Over the spicy knuckle of each finger
The great sun has slipped a ruby.

The stain of the masses darkens them
Like a breast with no prospects.
They've been raised and kissed
By every Insurrectionary who's worth the name!

These magnificent hands have grown pale
In the great sun filled with love,
On the bronze of the machine guns,
Across insurgent Paris!

Sometimes, Sacred Hands – Hands
That day and night inebriate our trembling lips,
The bright links of a chain
Rattle in protest on your wrists.

And sometimes we're jolted, at our very core,
Imagining the urge to mutilate
These angel's hands, and turn them white,
By making your fingers bleed!

Seven-year-old Poets

And the Mother, folding up his homework,
Went her way, satisfied and proud, not seeing
In those blue eyes, or the precocious forehead,
That the soul of her boy was full of dark disgust.

All day he sweated obedience; so very
Bright; given nonetheless to sombre nervous tics
And tell-tale defects that betrayed a bitter fakery.
As he passed the mildewed hangings in the gloomy
    corridors,

En passant il tirait la langue, les deux poings
A l'aine, et dans ses yeux fermés voyait des points.
Une porte s'ouvrait sur le soir: à la lampe
On le voyait, là-haut, qui râlait sur la rampe,
Sous un golfe du jour pendant du toit. L'été
Surtout, vaincu, stupide, il était entêté
A se renfermer dans la fraîcheur des latrines:
Il pensait là, tranquille, et livrant ses narines.
Quand, lavé des odeurs du jour, le jardinet
Derrière la maison, en hiver, s'illunait,
Gisant au pied d'un mur, enterré dans la marne
Et pour des visions écrasant son œil darne,
Il écoutait grouiller les galeux espaliers.
Pitié! ces enfants seuls étaient ses familiers
Qui, chétifs, fronts nus, œil déteignant sur la joue,
Cachant de maigres doigts jaunes et noirs de boue
Sous des habits puant la foire et tout vieillots,
Conversaient avec la douceur des idiots!
Et si, l'ayant surpris à des pitiés immondes,
Sa mère s'effrayait; les tendresses, profondes,
De l'enfant se jetaient sur cet étonnement.
C'était bon. Elle avait le bleu regard, qui ment!

A sept ans, il faisait des romans, sur la vie
Du grand désert, où luit la Liberté ravie,
Forêts, soleils, rios, savanes! – Il s'aidait
Des journaux illustrés où, rouge, il regardait
Des Espagnoles rire et des Italiennes.
Quand venait, l'œil brun, folle, en robes d'indiennes,
– Huit ans, – la fille des ouvriers d'à côté,
La petite brutale, et qu'elle avait sauté,
Dans un coin, sur son dos, en secouant ses tresses,
Et qu'il était sous elle, il lui mordait les fesses,
Car elle ne portait jamais de pantalons;
– Et, par elle meurtri des poings et des talons,
Remportait les saveurs de sa peau dans sa chambre.

He'd stick his tongue out, fists stuffed in his crotch;
Or inspect the mottled world behind his eyelids.
A door would swing open on to the evening. By the lamp
You'd see him fulminating on the stairs, caught
In a span of daylight thrust from the roof. Summers
Especially – done for, stupefied – he beat an obstinate
Retreat to the cool of the latrines:
Locked in, nostrils flared, he set to thinking, undisturbed.
Or at the back of the house in the little garden
Cleansed of daytime smells by a winter moon,
He'd lie at the foot of a wall, buried in marl
And squeeze his dazzled eyes to induce visions
As he listened to the seethings of the mangy espaliers.
Pity! . . . the only friends he made were scrawny kids
With shaven heads, and rheumy tears on their cheeks,
Who hid their skinny yellow fingers, dark with mud,
In hand-me-downs smelling of shit
And spoke with the kindness of halfwits.
And if, when she caught him in some lamentable act,
The Mother seemed fraught, the boy's affections
– deep affections – seized on her amazement. It was good.
She'd got the blue gaze – the gaze that lies.[1]

At seven, he was writing romances about life
In the great desert, where kidnapped Freedom shone,
Forests, suns, river banks, savannas. He borrowed
From the illustrated magazines – Spanish and Italian
Girls smiled out at him; he blushed.
And when the wayward brown-eyed eight-year-old –
the daughter of the working couple up the road –
Came by in a calico frock, and jumped him, in a corner,
Riding his back and tossing her hair, and him below,
He bit the buttocks of that little savage.
Underwear was not her thing.
Pummelled blue by her fists and feet,
He made off to his bedroom with the taste of her skin.

Il craignait les blafards dimanches de décembre,
Où, pommadé, sur un guéridon d'acajou,
Il lisait une Bible à la tranche vert-chou;
Des rêves l'oppressaient chaque nuit dans l'alcôve.
Il n'aimait pas Dieu; mais les hommes, qu'au soir fauve,
Noirs, en blouse, il voyait rentrer dans le faubourg
Où les crieurs, en trois roulements de tambour,
Font autour des édits rire et gronder les foules.
– Il rêvait la prairie amoureuse, où des houles
Lumineuses, parfums sains, pubescences d'or,
Font leur remuement calme et prennent leur essor!

Et comme il savourait surtout les sombres choses,
Quand, dans la chambre nue aux persiennes closes,
Haute et bleue, âcrement prise d'humidité,
Il lisait son roman sans cesse médité,
Plein de lourds ciels ocreux et de forêts noyées,
De fleurs de chair aux bois sidérals déployées,
Vertige, écroulements, déroutes et pitié!
– Tandis que se faisait la rumeur du quartier,
En bas, – seul, et couché sur des pièces de toile
Ecrue, et pressentant violemment la voile!

                                        26 mai 1871

A Monsieur Théodore de Banville:

Ce qu'on dit au poète à propos de fleurs

I

Ainsi toujours, vers l'azur noir
Où tremble la mer des topazes,
Fonctionneront dans ton soir
Les Lys, ces clystères d'extases!

He dreaded the anaemic Sundays in December –
Hair-oil; readings from a Bible
With cabbage-green edging; a mahogany pedestal table.
Oppressive dreams every night in the little chamber.
He didn't care for God: better the silhouettes of working-men
In smocks going home through the brazen evening
To the faubourgs, where the crowds jeer or grumble
At the town-crier's edicts, between triple drumrolls.
He dreamed of fields of love, where billowing brightness,
Wholesome smells, and pubescent, gilded down
Were calmly wafted upwards through the air.

He was drawn above all to dark things.
With the shutters closed in the bare room,
Lofty and blue, besieged by bitter damp,
He read his endlessly absorbing romance
Full of heavy ochre skies and flooded forests,
Flowers of flesh unfurling in star-pitted woods,
Vertigo, collapse, disaster and dismay!
– And all the while the noises rose from the street
Below. He lay in his coarse canvas sheets
Gripped by a premonition of setting sail.

26 May 1871

For M. Théodore de Banville

To the Poet on the Matter of Flowers[1]

I

And so to Lilies! Pessaries of ecstasy,
Forever tending to an azure black
Where topaz seas vibrate, serving
Their purposes in your night!

A notre époque de sagous,
Quand les Plantes sont travailleuses,
Le Lys boira les bleus dégoûts
Dans tes Proses religieuses!

– Le lys de monsieur Kerdrel,
Le Sonnet de mil huit cent trente,
Le Lys qu'on donne au Ménestrel
Avec l'œillet et l'amarante!

Des lys! Des lys! On n'en voit pas!
Et dans tons Vers, tel que les manches
Des Pécheresses aux doux pas,
Toujours frissonnent ces fleurs blanches!

Toujours, Cher, quand tu prends un bain,
Ta chemise aux aisselles blondes
Se gonfle aux brises du matin
Sur les myosotis immondes!

L'amour ne passe à tes octrois
Que les Lilas – ô balançoires!
Et les Violettes du Bois,
Crachats sucrés des Nymphes noires! . . .

II

O Poètes, quand vous auriez
Les Roses, les Roses soufflées,
Rouges sur tiges de lauriers,
Et de mille octaves enflées!

Quand BANVILLE en ferait neiger,
Sanguinolentes, tournoyantes,
Pochant l'œil fou de l'étranger
Aux lectures mal bienveillantes!

This is the age of tapioca.
The vegetation is no longer work-shy.
The lily soaks up blue antipathies
From your religious prose.

– Kerdrel's[2] monarchist fleur-de-lys,
The Sonnet of 1830,[3]
The lily, the pink and the amaranth,[4]
Conferred upon the Bard.

Lilies! Lilies! Not that one finds them,
Except in your verse, where
Their white heads stir like the sleeves
Of Fallen Women treading softly.

Always, Dear Master, when you take a bath,
That shirt of yours with yellow armpits
Billows in the morning breeze
Above the gross forget-me-nots.

Love can only carry lilacs – quite
Ludicrous – down your Customs ramp.
And woodland violets,
Sugary hawkings of blackened larvae.

II

Poets, what would you say
To Roses – blown roses,
Red on laurel stems, inflated
By quires of octosyllables!

BANVILLE snows his roses down
In blood-flecked eddies:
A jab in the rough, untutored eye
With all its dim misreadings.

De vos forêts et de vos prés,
O très-paisibles photographes!
La Flore est diverse à peu près
Comme des bouchons de carafes!

Toujours les végétaux Français,
Hargneux, phtisiques, ridicules,
Où le ventre des chiens bassets
Navigue en paix, aux crépuscules;

Toujours, après d'affreux dessins
De Lotos bleus ou d'Hélianthes,
Estampes roses, sujets saints,
Pour de jeunes communiantes!

L'Ode Açoka cadre avec la
Strophe en fenêtre de lorette;
Et de lourds papillons d'éclat
Fientent sur la Pâquerette.

Vieilles verdures, vieux galons!
O croquignoles végétales!
Fleurs fantasques des vieux Salons!
– Aux hannetons, pas aux crotales,

Ces poupards végétaux en pleurs
Que Grandville eût mis aux lisières,
Et qu'allaitèrent de couleurs
De méchants astres à visières!

Oui, vos bavures de pipeaux
Font de précieuses glucoses!
– Tas d'œufs frits dans de vieux chapeaux,
Lys, Açokas, Lilas et Roses! . . .

In your fields and forests,
You tranquillized photographers,
The Flora is about as various
As a pile of wine-corks!

The great French vegetable,
Ill-natured, shrivelled and absurd!
Skimmed by the bellies of basset hounds
Waddling through the uneventful dusk!

Always, after frightful drawings
Of a blue lotus or a sunflower
Come the pink prints, on pious themes
For the young girls' First Communion!

Odes to the Asoka[5] tree work well
As verses shaped like a courtesan's window.
Heavy, startling butterflies
Defecate on the daisies.

Old greenery, old bits of braid!
Vegetable savouries!
Exotic flowers of the old salons!
– Those Grandville[6] marginalia,

The snivelling vegetable-babies
That suck their colours from the dugs
Of evil stars with vizors on their eyes
Are snacks for beetles, not for rattlesnakes!

The droolings of your shepherds' flutes
Make priceless saccharine, it's true –
Fried eggs heaped up in addled hats:
Lilies, Asokas, Lilacs, Roses.

III

O blanc Chasseur, qui cours sans bas
A travers le Pâtis panique,
Ne peux-tu pas, ne dois-tu pas,
Connaître un peu ta botanique?

Tu ferais succéder, je crains,
Aux Grillons roux les Cantharides,
L'or des Rios au bleu des Rhins –
Bref, aux Norwèges les Florides:

Mais, Cher, l'Art n'est plus, maintenant,
– C'est la vérité, – de permettre
A l'Eucalyptus étonnant
Des constrictors d'un hexamètre;

Là! . . . Comme si les Acajous
Ne servaient, même en nos Guyanes,
Qu'aux cascades des sapajous,
Au lourd délire des lianes!

– En somme, une Fleur, Romarin
Ou Lys, vive ou morte, vaut-elle
Un excrément d'oiseau marin?
Vaut-elle un seul pleur de chandelle?

– Et j'ai dit ce que je voulais!
Toi, même assis là-bas, dans une
Cabane de bambous, – volets
Clos, tentures de perse brune, –

Tu torcherais des floraisons
Dignes d'Oises extravagantes! . . .
– Poète! ce sont des raisons
Non moins risibles qu'arrogantes! . . .

III

O Spotless Hunter, stockings off
And running through the meads of Pan,
You really might – you ought to – know
Your botany a little better.

I fear you'd kick the russet cricket out
In favour of the Spanish fly,
Replace our Rhineland blues with Rio golds,
Turn Norways into Floridas.

But art, good Sir, has ceased
To be a case of wrapping anacondas,
One hexameter in length,
Around flamboyant gumtrees.

A forest of mahogany has many uses,
Even in our very own Guyanas.
It isn't just a climbing-frame for monkeys,
Crashing through deliriums of thick lianas.

I mean, is a flower, dead or alive,
Lily or rosemary, worth more in the end
Than one specimen of gull-shit
Or a teardrop of wax on a candle?

There. I've spoken my mind.
Even sitting stranded in
Some bamboo hut – shutters tight,
Plenty of Oriental hangings –

You'd churn out flower-poems that might
As well have come from a warmed-up
Wiltshire.[7] Poet, your methods are worse
Than arrogant: they're laughable!

IV

Dis, non les pampas printaniers
Noirs d'épouvantables révoltes,
Mais les tabacs, les cotonniers!
Dis les exotiques récoltes!

Dis, front blanc que Phébus tanna,
De combien de dollars se rente
Pedro Velasquez, Habana;
Incague la mer de Sorrente

Où vont les Cygnes par milliers;
Que tes strophes soient des réclames
Pour l'abattis des mangliers
Fouillés des hydres et des lames!

Ton quatrain plonge aux bois sanglants
Et revient proposer aux Hommes
Divers sujets de sucres blancs,
De pectoraires et de gommes!

Sachons par Toi si les blondeurs
Des Pics neigeux, vers les Tropiques,
Sont ou des insectes pondeurs
Ou des lichens microscopiques!

Trouve, ô Chasseur, nous le voulons,
Quelques garances parfumées
Que la Nature en pantalons
Fasse éclore! – Pour nos Armées!

Trouve, aux abords du Bois qui dort,
Les fleurs pareilles à des mufles,
D'où bavent des pommades d'or
Sur les cheveux sombres des Buffles!

IV

Say less about the pampas in spring,
Darkened by dreadful revolt
And more about tobacco, cotton plants,
Exotic harvests!

Tell us, man of pallor
Tanned by Phoebus, what Pedro Velasquez
Of Havana[8] would be worth in dollars;
Fill the Sea of Sorrento,[9]

Where swans light in their thousands,
With sewage. Turn your verses
Into billboards for the clearing of mangrove
Swamps infested by hydras and choppy tides!

Your quatrain plunges into bloody forests
And comes back to edify us
With a range of subjects: refined sugar,
Cough sweets and varieties of rubber!

Tell us, O Great One, whether it is
Insects laying eggs or microscopic
Lichens that produce a yellow haze
On snowcaps near the Tropics.

O Hunter, we insist that you retrieve
The red of perfumed madders
So that Nature herself may dye
The trousers of our Army.[10]

At the edges of the Dormant Wood,
Discover flowers like snouts
That slobber gold pomade
Across the dark manes of buffaloes.

Trouve, aux prés fous, où sur le Bleu
Tremble l'argent des pubescences,
Des calices pleins d'œufs de feu
Qui cuisent parmi les essences!

Trouve des Chardons cotonneux
Dont dix ânes aux yeux de braises
Travaillent à filer les nœuds!
Trouve des Fleurs qui soient des chaises!

Oui, trouve au cœur des noirs filons
Des fleurs presque pierres, – fameuses! –
Qui vers leurs durs ovaires blonds
Aient des amygdales gemmeuses!

Sers-nous, ô Farceur, tu le peux,
Sur un plat de vermeil splendide
Des ragoûts de Lys sirupeux
Mordant nos cuillers Alfénide!

V

Quelqu'un dira le grand Amour,
Voleur des sombres Indulgences:
Mais ni Renan, ni le chat Murr
N'ont vu les Bleus Thyrses immenses!

Toi, fais jouer dans nos torpeurs,
Par les parfums les hystéries;
Exalte-nous vers les candeurs
Plus candides que les Maries . . .

Commerçant! colon! médium!
Ta Rime sourdra, rose ou blanche,
Comme un rayon de sodium,
Comme un caoutchouc qui s'épanche!

And in the mad fields where a silvery
Pubescence flickers on Blue,
Find Calyxes containing fiery eggs
Basted with essential oils.

Find knots of down-smothered thistle
That ten asses with searing eyes
Are struggling to work loose.
Find flowers that are chairs!

And buried in obscure seams
Find flowers like stones – extraordinary
stones – with diamantine tonsils
Growing by the hard, pale ovaries.

In your inimitable style, you joker,
Bring in a splendid, ruby-coloured platter
And dish up a syrupy stew of lilies
To strip the nickel from our spoons.

V

Someone will speak of the Great Love,
Cutpurse of dark Indulgences,
But who has seen the huge blue Thyrsuses?[11]
– Not Renan;[12] not Kater Murr.[13]

Quicken our lassitude – yes, you –
With hysterias induced by perfume;
Loft us into realms of candour
Whiter than the Marys . . .

Tradesman! Settler! Table turner!
Your rhymes will surge forth, pink or white,
Like a streak of sodium,
Like the oozings of the rubber plant.

De tes noirs Poèmes, – Jongleur!
Blancs, verts, et rouges dioptriques,
Que s'évadent d'étranges fleurs
Et des papillons électriques!

Voilà! c'est le Siècle d'enfer!
Et les poteaux télégraphiques
Vont orner, – lyre aux chants de fer,
Tes omoplates magnifiques!

Surtout, rime une version
Sur le mal des pommes de terre!
– Et, pour la composition
De poèmes pleins de mystère

Qu'on doive lire de Tréguier
A Paramaribo, rachète
Des Tomes de Monsieur Figuier,
– Illustrés! – chez Monsieur Hachette!

14 juillet 1871

Alcide Bava
A.R.

Les Premières Communions

I

Vraiment, c'est bête, ces églises des villages
Où quinze laids marmots encrassant les piliers
Ecoutent, grasseyant les divins babillages,
Un noir grotesque dont fermentent les souliers:
Mais le soleil éveille, à travers les feuillages
Les vieilles couleurs des vitraux irréguliers.

Mountebank! Let strange flowers
And electric butterflies,
Refracted whites, greens and reds,
Stream from your black Poems!

It's the Century of Hell! Absolutely.
Telegraph poles like humming
Iron lyres will adorn
Your splendid shoulder blades.

Grace us, above all, with a rhyming
Exposition of potato-blight!
And if you wish to work up
Poems full of mystery

– Destined to be read from Tréguier[14]
To Paramaribo[15] – you should get
Yourself a few of Monsieur Figuier's[16]
Volumes – 'illustrated' – from Hachette!

14 July 1871

Alcide Bava[17]
A.R.

First Communion

I

Too stupid, these village churches
Where fifteen ugly little scruffs smear dirt on the pillars
And lap up the heavenly prattle gargled
By a pervert in black whose boots are fermenting.
Yet through the leaves the sun revives
The faded colours of the crude stained glass.

La pierre sent toujours la terre maternelle,
Vous verrez des monceaux de ces cailloux terreux
Dans la campagne en rut qui frémit solennelle
Portant près des blés lourds, dans les sentiers ocreux,
Ces arbrisseaux brûlés où bleuit la prunelle,
Des nœuds de mûriers noirs et de rosiers fuireux.

Tous les cent ans on rend ces granges respectables
Par un badigeon d'eau bleue et de lait caillé:
Si des mysticités grotesques sont notables
Près de la Notre-Dame ou du Saint empaillé,
Des mouches sentant bon l'auberge et les étables
Se gorgent de cire au plancher ensoleillé.

L'enfant se doit surtout à la maison, famille
Des soins naïfs, des bons travaux abrutissants;
Ils sortent, oubliant que la peau leur fourmille
Où le Prêtre du Christ plaqua ses doigts puissants.
On paie au Prêtre un toit ombré d'une charmille
Pour qu'il laisse au soleil tous ces fronts brunissants.

Le premier habit noir, le plus beau jour de tartes
Sous le Napoléon ou le Petit Tambour
Quelque enluminure où les Josephs et les Marthes
Tirent la langue avec un excessif amour
Et que joindront, au jour de science, deux cartes,
Ces seuls doux souvenirs lui restent du grand Jour.

Les filles vont toujours à l'église, contentes
De s'entendre appeler garces par les garçons
Qui font du genre après Messe ou vêpres chantantes.
Eux qui sont destinés au chic des garnisons
Ils narguent au café les maisons importantes
Blousés neuf, et gueulant d'effroyables chansons.

Always the stone, with its smell of mother earth.
You'll see platforms of this earthy rock
In the rutting countryside, which trembles with solemnity.
They're set in the ochre footpaths, close to the heavy corn.
Here the sloe turns blue on parched bushes
Beside entanglements of blackberry and dog-rose.

Every hundred years the barns get a once-over –
A whitewash of curdled milk and watery blue pigment.
The grotesque devotions near the statue
Of Our Lady, or the stuffed saint, are remarkable,
And bring the flies, smelling nicely of inns and stables,
To feast off wax on the sunlit floor.

Home is chiefly where the child's duty lies. Family, too,
Its simple comforts and its honest, stupefying toil.
The children leave; their goose-bumps, where
The Man of God had pressed his powerful fingers,
Disappear. His arbour-shaded roof is a vocational perk.
No sweat, for him, if little faces pucker in the sun.

The first black suit, the day of special cakes.
Some aquatint with a Joseph and a Martha –
Tongues at the ready, in an excess of love – is hung
Beneath 'Napoleon' or a 'Little Drummer Boy'.
Two framed maps will follow on the day of knowledge.
Beyond these souvenirs of the Great Day, nothing.

The girls never miss a service, thrilled
As they come out of Mass or Sung Vespers to be told
They're sluts by boys who think themselves quite stylish –
Destined for nothing more chic than the barracks.
For now, they taunt the better families in the café,
Dressed in new shirts and bawling out ghastly songs.

Cependant le Curé choisit pour les enfances
Des dessins; dans son clos, les vêpres dites, quand
L'air s'emplit du lointain nasillement des danses,
Ils se sent, en dépit des célestes défenses,
Les doigts de pied ravis et le mollet marquant.

– La Nuit vient, noir pirate aux cieux d'or débarquant.

II

Le Prêtre a distingué parmi les catéchistes,
Congrégés des Faubourgs ou des riches Quartiers,
Cette petite fille inconnue, aux yeux tristes,
Front jaune. Les parents semblent de doux portiers.
«Au grand Jour, le marquant parmi les Catéchistes,
Dieu fera sur ce front neiger ses bénitiers.»

III

La veille du grand Jour, l'enfant se fait malade.
Mieux qu'à l'Eglise haute aux funèbres
         rumeurs,
D'abord le frisson vient, – le lit n'étant pas
         fade –
Un frisson surhumain qui retourne: «Je meurs . . .»

Et, comme un vol d'amour fait à ses sœurs stupides,
Elle compte, abattue et les mains sur son cœur,
Les Anges, les Jésus et ses Vierges nitides
Et, calmement, son âme a bu tout son vainqueur.

Adonaï! . . . – Dans les terminaisons latines,
Des cieux moirés de vert baignent les Fronts vermeils
Et tachés du sang pur des célestes poitrines
De grands linges neigeux tombent sur les soleils!

The priest, meanwhile, chooses pictures
For the young. In his garden, after Vespers,
As the distant twang of dance-tunes fills the air,
He feels his toes bewitched; in breach of Heaven's
Admonitions, his calves start flexing to the beat.

Night steps ashore – black pirate on a golden sky.

II

From the faubourgs and the smarter neighbourhoods,
The communicants-to-be have gathered. The priest is struck
By an obscure little girl with mournful eyes
And a sallow face (her parents might be simple caretakers).
'On the Great Day, singling her out among all the rest,
God will snow down His blessings on her head.'

III

On the eve of the Great Day she is taken ill.
First the shivers, even better than her frissons in the tall
      church
Full of gloomy mutterings – bed, in its way, can be quite
      exalting –
A persistent, barely human shiver. 'I am dying.'

Exhausted, with her hands across her heart, she counts
Angels, Jesuses and radiant Virgins, like takings:
The heavenly love she's stolen from her yokel sisters.
Calmly, her soul has swallowed her Lord and Master whole.

Adonai!¹ In the Latin endings, crimson Brows
Are assuaged by shimmering green skies.
And snowy robes, spotted with pure blood
From the divine body, veil the firmament!

– Pour ses virginités présentes et futures
Elle mord aux fraîcheurs de ta Rémission,
Mais plus que les lys d'eau, plus que les confitures
Tes pardons sont glacés, ô Reine de Sion!

IV

Puis la Vierge n'est plus que la vierge du livre.
Les mystiques élans se cassent quelquefois . . .
Et vient la pauvreté des images, que cuivre
L'ennui, l'enluminure atroce et les vieux bois;

Des curiosités vaguement impudiques
Epouvantent le rêve aux chastes bleuités
Qui s'est surpris autour des célestes tuniques,
Du linge dont Jésus voile ses nudités.

Elle veut, elle veut, pourtant, l'âme en détresse,
Le front dans l'oreiller creusé par les cris sourds,
Prolonger les éclairs suprêmes de tendresse,
Et bave . . . – L'ombre emplit les maisons et les cours.

Et l'enfant ne peut plus. Elle s'agite, cambre
Les reins et d'une main ouvre le rideau bleu
Pour amener un peu la fraîcheur de la chambre
Sous le drap, vers son ventre et sa poitrine en feu . . .

V

A son réveil, – minuit – la fenêtre était blanche.
Devant le sommeil bleu des rideaux illunés,
La vision la prit des candeurs du dimanche;
Elle avait rêvé rouge. Elle saigna du nez.

Et se sentant bien chaste et pleine de faiblesse
Pour savourer en Dieu son amour revenant
Elle eut soif de la nuit où s'exalte et s'abaisse
Le cœur, sous l'œil des cieux doux, en les devinant,

For her virginity, now and in the future,
She bites on the cold of Your Remission.
But more than water-lilies, more than sweetmeats,
Your pardons, Queen of Zion,[2] are like ice.

IV

Yet soon enough, the Virgin's just 'the virgin' of the book.
The mystical urge can sometimes crumble . . .
The images seem trite, behind the patina
Of tedium: the dire aquatint, the old woodcuts.

Vaguely indecent interests have begun
To fray her dream of chaste blueness, which
Catches itself in Our Redeemer's celestial wardrobe,
Straying through his intimate linen.

Deep in anguish, her face in the pillow,
Racked by muffled cries, she yearns for
That high and tender radiance not to wane –
She dribbles. Shadows invest the blocks and courtyards.

And then the girl can bear no more. She stirs, arches,
One hand drawing back the poster-curtain – blue –
To take the coolness of the room beneath the sheet
And down along her fevered breasts and belly.

V

When she woke, at midnight, the casement was white.
Beyond the blue repose of moonlit curtains
She could already see it, in a vision – that pure Sunday;
She had dreamed in red, her nose was bleeding;

Chaste and enfeebled, wanting now
To taste in God her resurrecting love, she hungered
For darkness, when the heart soars and plummets
Sensing the clement gaze of the sky;

De la nuit, Vierge-Mère impalpable, qui baigne
Tous les jeunes émois de ses silences gris;
Elle eut soif de la nuit forte où le cœur qui saigne
Ecoule sans témoin sa révolte sans cris.

Et faisant la victime et la petite épouse,
Son étoile la vit, une chandelle aux doigts
Descendre dans la cour où séchait une blouse,
Spectre blanc, et lever les spectres noirs des toits . . .

VI

Elle passa sa nuit sainte dans les latrines.
Vers la chandelle, aux trous du toit coulait l'air blanc,
Et quelque vigne folle aux noirceurs purpurines,
En deçà d'une cour voisine s'écroulant.

La lucarne faisait un cœur de lueur vive
Dans la cour où les cieux bas plaquaient d'ors vermeils
Les vitres; les pavés puant l'eau de lessive
Soufraient l'ombre des murs bondés de noirs sommeils.

....

VII

Qui dira ces langueurs et ces pitiés immondes,
Et ce qu'il lui viendra de haine, ô sales fous,
Dont le travail divin déforme encor les mondes,
Quand la lèpre à la fin mangera ce corps doux?

....

VIII

Et quand, ayant rentré tous ses nœuds d'hystéries
Elle verra, sous les tristesses du bonheur,
L'amant rêver au blanc million des Maries,
Au matin de la nuit d'amour, avec douleur:

For darkness, impalpable Virgin Mother, who steeps
The ardours of youth in her grey silences.
She thirsted for the hardiness of night, when rebellion
Streams unseen, in silence, from a bleeding heart.

Doubling as Martyr and little bride, she trod the stairs,
Candle in hand, watched by her guiding star.
A smock hung on a line, a pale spectre
Raising flocks of darker spectres from the roofs.

VI

She spent her holy night in the lavatories.
White air flowed towards the candle through gaps
In the roof, where a lavish creeper, goitred black and purple,
Burrowed from the neighbour's crumbling wall.

Low skies slid a gilt and crimson lamina across the windows.
In the courtyard, her window shone like a living heart.
Awash with stale laundry slops, the flagstones gave
A sulphur cast to the shadows of the sleep-stashed walls.
....

VII

Your holy work contaminates the spheres, you filthy
Perverts. When a leprous death devours her sweet body,
Who'll record the languor, the obscene compassion,
Or the hatred that lay there, biding its time?
....

VIII

Then, when she's suppressed her clenched hysterias,
In the painful morning after love, through the misery
Of happiness, she'll notice the mind's eye of her lover
Ogling a million Marys of the driven snow.

«Sais-tu que je t'ai fait mourir? J'ai pris ta bouche,
Ton cœur, tout ce qu'on a, tout ce que vous avez;
Et moi, je suis malade: oh! je veux qu'on me couche
Parmi les Morts des eaux nocturnes abreuvés.

«J'étais bien jeune, et Christ a souillé mes haleines.
Il me bonda jusqu'à la gorge de dégoûts!
Tu baisais mes cheveux profonds comme les laines,
Et je me laissais faire . . . ah! va, c'est bon pour vous,

«Hommes! qui songez peu que la plus amoureuse
Est, sous sa conscience aux ignobles terreurs,
La plus prostituée et la plus douloureuse,
Et que tous nos élans vers vous sont des erreurs!

«Car ma Communion première est bien passée.
Tes baisers, je ne puis jamais les avoir sus:
Et mon cœur et ma chair par ta chair embrassée
Fourmillent du baiser putride de Jésus!»

IX

Alors l'âme pourrie et l'âme désolée
Sentiront ruisseler tes malédictions.
– Ils auront couché sur ta Haine inviolée,
Echappés, pour la mort, des justes passions.

Christ! ô Christ, éternel voleur des énergies,
Dieu qui pour deux mille ans vouas à ta pâleur,
Cloués au sol, de honte et de céphalalgies
Ou renversés les fronts des femmes de douleur.

                                                        Juillet 1871

'D'you understand I've killed you off?' she'll say.
'I've had your mouth, your heart, everything on offer –
And now I'm a casualty. I want to be laid out beside the dead
And cooled, like them, in the waters of the night.

'I was very young. Christ sullied my breath,
Force-fed me with dark disinclinations . . .
You kissed my hair, as thick as lambs' wool
And I let you do it . . . It's easy enough

'For men. The deeper women's love, the more mortified
We are, in the ugly nightmare of our conscience, and the more
We think of ourselves as whores. None of this crosses
Your mind. Our every urge towards you is fatal.

'My First Communion is long since gone.
My spirit and flesh – embraced in your flesh –
Are seething with the rancid kiss of Christ;
And so I never really tasted yours.'

IX

And now two souls, one rotten, one quite desolate,
Must feel Your curses raining down. Your hate
Inviolate is the bed they'll lie in: fugitives
From honest passions, who preferred a living death.

Christ, eternal thief of vigour! Christ . . .
Two thousand years of godhead – the cult of your pallor!
It has nailed the brows of abject women to the ground
With shame and head pains – jammed them down.

                                                July 1871

Le Bateau ivre

Comme je descendais des Fleuves impassibles
Je ne me sentis plus guidé par les haleurs:
Des Peaux-rouges criards les avaient pris pour cibles
Les ayant cloués nus aux poteaux de couleurs.

J'étais insoucieux de tous les équipages,
Porteur de blés flamands ou de cotons anglais.
Quand avec mes haleurs ont fini ces tapages
Les Fleuves m'ont laissé descendre où je voulais.

Dans les clapotements furieux des marées,
Moi, l'autre hiver, plus sourd que les cerveaux d'enfants,
Je courus! Et les Péninsules démarrées
N'ont pas subi tohu-bohus plus triomphants.

La tempête a béni mes éveils maritimes.
Plus léger qu'un bouchon j'ai dansé sur les flots
Qu'on appelle rouleurs éternels de victimes,
Dix nuits, sans regretter l'œil niais des falots!

Plus douce qu'aux enfants la chair des pommes sures,
L'eau verte pénétra ma coque de sapin
Et des taches de vins bleus et des vomissures
Me lava, dispersant gouvernail et grappin.

Et dès lors, je me suis baigné dans le Poème
De la Mer, infusé d'astres, et lactescent,
Dévorant les azurs verts; où, flottaison blême
Et ravie, un noyé pensif parfois descend;

Où, teignant tout à coup les bleuités, délires
Et rhythmes lents sous les rutilements du jour,
Plus fortes que l'alcool, plus vastes que nos lyres,
Fermentent les rousseurs amères de l'amour!

Drunken Boat

On my way down inscrutable Rivers
My haulers seemed to slacken off the ropes –
Yelping redskins had taken good aim,
Stripped them and nailed them to painted poles.

The crews and cargo meant nothing to me
– Flemish wheat or English cottons.
The clamour was done with, and so were the haulers.
The Rivers took me downstream as I pleased.

A winter ago, fast like a child in its own head,
I ran with the wild lapping
Of the tide-rips. Drifting peninsulas
Were never prey to such formidable commotion!

My awakenings at sea were graced by storms.
Lighter than a cork, I danced on the waves –
Eternal breakers of men, some say. Ten nights
Without the imbecile blink of harbour beacons.

Sweeter than the flesh of sour apples to a child,
Green water surged through my pine-plank hull,
Washing out the stains of vomit and bluish wine –
It bore off my rudder, and my grapnel too.

From that time on, I basked in the Poem of the Sea,
A milk-white suspension of stars that devours
Raw azures. Through it drowned men
Fall like bleached driftwood, heavy with trance.

In that Poem, slow deliriums in shifting light
– Stronger than liquor, more enormous than lyres –
Infiltrate the bluenesses with bitter, drastically
Fermented rednesses of love.

Je sais les cieux crevant en éclairs, et les trombes
Et les ressacs et les courants: je sais le soir,
L'aube exaltée ainsi qu'un peuple de colombes
Et j'ai vu quelquefois ce que l'homme a cru voir!

J'ai vu le soleil bas, taché d'horreurs mystiques,
Illuminant de long figements violets,
Pareils à des acteurs de drames très-antiques
Les flots roulant au loin leurs frissons de volets!

J'ai rêvé la nuit verte aux neiges éblouies,
Baiser montant aux yeux des mers avec lenteurs,
La circulation des sèves inouïes,
Et l'éveil jaune et bleu des phosphores chanteurs!

J'ai suivi, des mois pleins, pareille aux vacheries
Hystériques, la houle à l'assaut des récifs,
Sans songer que les pieds lumineux des Maries
Pussent forcer le mufle aux Océans poussifs!

J'ai heurté, savez-vous, d'incroyables Florides
Mêlant aux fleurs des yeux de panthères à peaux
D'hommes! Des arcs-en-ciel tendus comme des brides
Sous l'horizon des mers, à de glauques troupeaux!

J'ai vu fermenter les marais énormes, nasses
Où pourrit dans les joncs tout un Léviathan!
Des écroulements d'eaux au milieu des bonaces
Et les lointains vers les gouffres cataractant!

Glaciers, soleils d'argent, flots nacreux, cieux de
        braises!
Echouages hideux au fond des golfes bruns
Où les serpents géants dévorés des punaises
Choient, des arbres tordus, avec de noirs parfums!

I know skies fissured by lightning, water-spouts,
Breakers, undertows. I know dusk
And dawn, rising like a multitude of doves.
What men have only thought they'd seen, I've seen.

I've seen the low sun, flecked with mystic horrors,
Cast its monumental, violet welts of light,
Like figures in an antique drama,
On the distant, louvred surface of the rolling sea.

In the green night, I dreamed of snow-dazzle,
A slow kiss rising to the eyes of the ocean,
The circulation of bizarre sap,
Siren phosphorus, dawning blue and yellow.

For months at a stretch I've pursued the swells
That stampede on the reefs like maddened steer.
I never did believe in Marys-of-the-Sea[1] who stifle
Wheezing oceans with their shining feet.

I've struck amazing Floridas, you know.
In the thick of their flora, panther eyes stare
From the hides of men. Rainbows crouch harness-taut
On glaucous wave-herds under the horizon of the seas.

I've seen vast, seething swamps, fish traps
In the rushes where entire Leviathans fester;
Downpours of water in the midst of calm;
Perspective hurtling over the abyss;

Glaciers, silver suns, reaches like mother-of-pearl, furnace
     skies!
Hideous wrecks at the bottom of deep, brown sumps
Where gigantic snakes, maddened by vermin and stinking
Of blackness, plummet from twisted trees.

J'aurais voulu montrer aux enfants ces dorades
Du flot bleu, ces poissons d'or, ces poissons chantants.
– Des écumes de fleurs ont bercé mes dérades
Et d'ineffables vents m'ont ailé par instants.

Parfois, martyr lassé des pôles et des zones,
La mer dont le sanglot faisait mon roulis doux
Montait vers moi ses fleurs d'ombre aux ventouses jaunes
Et je restais, ainsi qu'une femme à genoux . . .

Presque île, ballottant sur mes bords les querelles
Et les fientes d'oiseaux clabaudeurs aux yeux blonds,
Et je voguais, lorsqu'à travers mes liens frêles
Des noyés descendaient dormir, à reculons!

Or moi, bateau perdu sous les cheveux des anses,
Jeté par l'ouragan dans l'éther sans oiseau,
Moi dont les Monitors et les voiliers des Hanses
N'auraient pas repêché la carcasse ivre d'eau;

Libre, fumant, monté de brumes violettes,
Moi qui trouais le ciel rougeoyant comme un mur,
Qui porte, confiture exquise aux bons poètes,
Des lichens de soleil et des morves d'azur,

Qui courais, taché de lunules électriques,
Planche folle, escorté des hippocampes noirs,
Quand les juillets faisaient crouler à coups de triques
Les cieux ultramarins aux ardents entonnoirs;

Moi qui tremblais, sentant geindre à cinquante lieues
Le rut des Béhémots et les Maelstroms épais,
Fileur éternel des immobilités bleues,
Je regrette l'Europe aux anciens parapets!

I might have shown children the dorados[2]
In the blue waters – and golden fish, and fish that sing.
Flower-strewn foam rocked me adrift
And ineffable winds supplied me with wings.

Sometimes I grew tired – a martyr of the latitudes and poles –
Then the sobbing ocean rolled me gently,
Made me offerings of shadow-flowers with yellow suckers,
And I hung there, like a kneeling woman.

I had become a floating island; the shit and bickerings
Of rowdy, pale-eyed birds slid down my flanks.
I sailed on, while drowned men toppled
Backwards through my frayed ropes and slept.

And now, a lost ship tangled in the hair of coves, I who am
Flung by hurricanes into the birdless ether,
I whose salvage – so much drunken, waterlogged debris –
Would not detain an ironclad or an escort;

Billowing smoke, and free, and garlanded in violet fog,
I who stove in the sky, which smouldered like a wall
Pocked with solar lichen and azure snot –
Sweetmeats prized by poets –

Who hurtled like a bedlam timber, flecked
With small electric moons, and flanked
By black sea-horses under skies of lapis lazuli
Hammered by the solstice into raging cyclones;

I who trembled as I heard the creak of rutting
Behemoths and stacked thunderheads at fifty leagues,
Eternal weaver of the blue quiescence,
I now ache for Europe and its ancient parapets.

J'ai vu des archipels sidéraux! et des îles
Dont les cieux délirants sont ouverts au
     vogueur:
Est-ce en ces nuits sans fonds que tu dors et t'exiles,
Million d'oiseaux d'or, ô future Vigueur? –

Mais vrai, j'ai trop pleuré! Les Aubes sont navrantes.
Toute lune est atroce et tout soleil amer:
L'âcre amour m'a gonflé de torpeurs enivrantes.
O que ma quille éclate! O que j'aille à la mer!

Si je désire une eau d'Europe, c'est la flache
Noire et froide où vers le crépuscule embaumé
Un enfant accroupi plein de tristesses, lâche
Un bateau frêle comme un papillon de mai.

Je ne puis plus, baigné de vos langueurs, ô lames,
Enlever leur sillage aux porteurs de cotons,
Ni traverser l'orgueil des drapeaux et des flammes,
Ni nager sous les yeux horribles des pontons.

Les Chercheuses de poux

Quand le front de l'enfant, plein de rouges tourmentes,
Implore l'essaim blanc des rêves indistincts,
Il vient près de son lit deux grandes sœurs charmantes
Avec de frêles doigts aux ongles argentins.

Elles assoient l'enfant devant une croisée
Grande ouverte où l'air bleu baigne un fouillis de fleurs
Et dans ses lourds cheveux où tombe la rosée
Promènent leurs doigts fins, terribles et charmeurs.

I've seen archipelagos of stars; islands whose feverish
Skies are spread above the mariner – are these the
        boundless
Nights in which you sleep out exile in your millions,
Golden birds, you prophets of our restitution?

I've cried too much, though. Dawns destroy me.
All moons are atrocious, all suns are a grievance:
An acrid passion has warped my sluggish keel.
Let it split! Let me sink without trace!

Do I long for European waters? Only a sullen pond
Where a small, demoralized boy, crouching
In the musk of a provincial evening
Launches his unsteady boat: a butterfly in May.

The languor of the waves has finally reclaimed me.
I can no longer ride in the wake of cotton freighters,
Or tack along the braggart lines of flags and pennants,
Or slink beneath the frightful eyes of prison ships.[3]

The Seekers of Lice

When the boy's head, full of raw torment,
Longs for hazy dreams to swarm in white,
Two charming older sisters come to his bed
With slender fingers and silvery nails.

They sit him at a casement window, thrown
Open on a mass of flowers basking in blue air,
And run the fine, intimidating witchcraft
Of their fingers through his dew-dank hair.

Il écoute chanter leurs haleines craintives
Qui fleurent de longs miels végétaux et rosés
Et qu'interrompt parfois un sifflement, salives
Reprises sur la lèvre ou désirs de baisers.

Il entend leurs cils noirs battant sous les silences
Parfumés; et leurs doigts électriques et doux
Font crépiter parmi ses grises indolences
Sous leurs ongles royaux la mort des petits poux.

Voilà que monte en lui le vin de la Paresse,
Soupir d'harmonica qui pourrait délirer;
L'enfant se sent, selon la lenteur des caresses,
Sourdre et mourir sans cesse un désir de pleurer.

Voyelles

A noir, E blanc, I rouge, U vert, O bleu: voyelles,
Je dirai quelque jour vos naissances latentes:
A, noir corset velu des mouches éclatantes
Qui bombinent autour des puanteurs cruelles,

Golfes d'ombre; E, candeurs des vapeurs et des tentes,
Lances des glaciers fiers, rois blancs, frissons d'ombelles;
I, pourpres, sang craché, rire des lèvres belles
Dans la colère ou les ivresses pénitentes;

U, cycles, vibrements divins des mers virides,
Paix des pâtis semés d'animaux, paix des rides
Que l'alchimie imprime aux grands fronts studieux;

O, suprême Clairon plein des strideurs étranges,
Silences traversés des Mondes et des Anges:
– O l'Oméga, rayon violet de Ses Yeux!

He listens to their diffident, sing-song breath,
Smelling of elongated honey off the rose,
Broken now and then by a hiss: saliva sucked
Back from the lip, or a longing to be kissed.

He hears their dark eyelashes start in the sweet-
Smelling silence and, through his grey listlessness,
The crackle of small lice dying, beneath
The imperious nails of their soft, electric fingers.

The wine of Torpor wells up in him then
– Near on trance, a harmonica-sigh –
And in their slow caress he feels
The endless ebb and flow of a desire to cry.

Vowels

A black, E white, I red, U green, O blue: vowels,
I shall speak one day of your hidden origins:
A, black fur-corset of the dazzling flies
Buzzing round every cruel stink,

Gulfs of darkness. E, candour of vapour and tents,
Proud glacier shards; white kings; flicker of umbel;
I, purples; spat blood; full lips laughing
In anger or bouts of contrite ecstasy;

U, gyrations, divine shiver of viridian seas,
Peace of cattle-studded pastures, peace of the wrinkles
Carved by alchemy on a broad, studious forehead;

O, the Last Trumpet with its strange clangour,
Silent wastes of Worlds and Angels – traversed;
O: Omega, the violet gleam of Those Eyes![1]

from L'ALBUM ZUTIQUE

L'Idole. Sonnet du trou du cul

Obscur et froncé comme un œillet violet
Il respire, humblement tapi parmi la mousse
Humide encor d'amour qui suit la fuite douce
Des Fesses blanches jusqu'au cœur de son ourlet.

Des filaments pareils à des larmes de lait
Ont pleuré, sous le vent cruel qui les repousse,
A travers de petits caillots de marne rousse
Pour s'aller perdre où la pente les appelait.

Mon Rêve s'aboucha souvent à sa ventouse;
Mon âme, du coït matériel jalouse,
En fit son larmier fauve et son nid de sanglots.

C'est l'olive pâmée, et la flûte câline,
C'est le tube où descend la céleste praline:
Chanaan féminin dans les moiteurs enclos!

ALBERT MERAT.
P.V.-A.R.

from ALBUM ZUTIQUE

Idol. Arsehole Sonnet[1]

Dark and puckered like a purple carnation
It breathes, meekly nestling in the moss –
Still damp from sex – which spreads along
The slow, pale incline of the buttocks to its rim.

Filaments like tears of milk,
Wept in the cruel South Wind that beats
Them back over little clots of reddened marl,
Lose themselves where the slope beckons.

Often my dream was spellbound by its suction;
Jealous of real intercourse, my soul construed it
As a wild, wet eye's edge, a nest for my tears.

It is the swooning olive, the seductive flute,
The shaft that yields the heavenly praline,
The Promised Land of the damp and feminine.

ALBERT MERAT.
P.V.-A.R.

I. *Cocher ivre* (*'Conneries 2e série'*)

Pouacre
Boit:
Nacre
Voit:

Acre
Loi,
Fiacre
Choit!

Femme
Tombe:
Lombe

Saigne:
– Clame!
Geigne.

A.R.

Etat de siège?

Le pauvre postillon, sous le dais de fer blanc,
Chauffant une engelure énorme sous son gant,
Suit son lourd omnibus parmi la rive gauche,
Et de son aine en flamme écarte la sacoche.
Et tandis que, douce ombre où des gendarmes sont,
L'honnête intérieur regarde au ciel profond
La lune se bercer parmi la verte ouate,
Malgré l'édit et l'heure encore délicate,
Et que l'omnibus rentre à l'Odéon, impur
Le débauché glapit au carrefour obscur!

FRANÇOIS COPPÉE.
A.R.

I. *Drunken Coachman (from 'Imbecilities 2nd Series')*

Drunken
Tosser
Seeing
Double,

Bitter
Outcome:
Coach in
Trouble,

Headlong
Woman,
Much

Distress –
Alarums,
Nasty mess.

A.R.

State of Siege?[1]

On the back platform, trundling along the Left Bank
Behind his heavy omnibus, the poor conductor
Warms a stupendous chilblain beneath his glove.
He shifts his satchel to one side
Of his blazing boner. Inside the bus, a shadowy
Haven seething with police, the worthy passengers
Gaze out at a deep sky – moon cocooned
In green cotton wool – and head towards the Odéon;
Despite the curfew and the edgy hour, the moanings
Of that seedy wanton echo in the darkened square.

FRANÇOIS COPPE.
A.R.

Vieux de la vieille!

Aux paysans de l'empereur!
A l'empereur des paysans!
Au fils de Mars,
Au glorieux 18 Mars!
Où le ciel d'Eugénie a béni les entrailles!

Les Remembrances du vieillard idiot

Pardon, mon père!
                    Jeune, aux foires de campagne,
Je cherchais, non le tir banal où tout coup gagne,
Mais l'endroit plein de cris où les ânes, le flanc
Fatigué, déployaient ce long tube sanglant
– Que je ne comprends pas encore! . . .
                                        Et puis ma mère,
Dont la chemise avait une senteur amère
Quoique fripée au bas et jaune comme un fruit,
Ma mère, qui montait au lit avec un bruit
– Fils du travail pourtant, – ma mère, avec sa cuisse
De femme mûre, avec ses reins très gros où plisse
Le linge, me donna ces chaleurs que l'on tait! . . .

Une honte plus crue et plus calme, c'était
Quand ma petite sœur, au retour de la classe,
Ayant usé longtemps ses sabots sur la glace,
Pissait, et regardait s'échapper de sa lèvre
D'en bas, serrée et rose, un fil d'urine mièvre! . . .

O pardon!
              Je songeais à mon père parfois:
Le soir, le jeu de cartes et les mots plus grivois,
Le voisin, et moi qu'on écartait, choses vues . . .

Very Old Guard[1]

To the emperor's[2] peasants!
To the peasants' emperor!
To the progeny of Mars![3]
And the glorious 18 March![4]
When Heaven's gift spilled from Eugénie's[5]
        belly!

Reminiscence of an Aged Cretin

Forgive me, Father!
                        At country fairs
When I was young, the shooting gallery where nobody
Can miss seemed dull. I headed for the paddock
Where the worn-out donkeys bray and put that long,
Bloodshot tube on display
– I still don't really understand it . . .
                                And then my mother:
That sour smell on her blouse,
Frayed at the hem and yellow like a fruit,
The din of my mother going upstairs to bed
– Yes, child of toil – my mother whose ripening
Thighs and huge buttocks rucking her skirts
Inflamed me in ways one keeps to oneself . . .

I felt a cruder shame, and calmer, when
My little sister, getting back from school
– Her clogs were ruined on the icy roads –
Pissed and watched the thin thread of urine
Leak from her tight, pink lower lip! . . .

Forgive me!
            I had thoughts sometimes of my father:
The evening card game, the dirty talk,
The neighbour; me wide-eyed, having to clear off . . .

– Car un père est troublant! – et les choses conçues! . . .
Son genou, câlineur parfois; son pantalon
Dont mon doigt désirait ouvrir la fente, . . . – oh! non! –
Pour avoir le bout, gros, noir et dur, de mon père,
Dont la pileuse main me berçait! . . .

                              Je veux taire
Le pot, l'assiette à manche, entrevue au grenier,
Les almanachs couverts en rouge, et le panier
De charpie, et la Bible, et les lieux, et la bonne,
La Sainte-Vierge et le crucifix . . .

                              Oh! personne
Ne fut si fréquemment troublé, comme étonné!
Et maintenant, que le pardon me soit donné:
Puisque les sens infects m'ont mis de leurs victimes.
Je me confesse de l'aveu des jeunes crimes! . . .
. . . .
Puis! – qu'il me soit permis de parler au Seigneur!
Pourquoi la puberté tardive et le malheur
Du gland tenace et trop consulté? Pourquoi l'ombre
Si lente au bas du ventre? et ces terreurs sans nombre
Comblant toujours la joie ainsi qu'un gravier noir?

Moi, j'ai toujours était stupéfait! Quoi savoir?
. . . .
Pardonné? . . .

                  Reprenez la chancelière bleue,
Mon père.

              O cette enfance! . . . .
. . . .
. . . .– et tirons-nous la queue!

                          FRANÇOIS COPPE.
                              A.R.

– A father can be unsettling – the strange stirrings
I had on his knee, which could be so inviting, his trousers,
And my fingers itching to undo his fly – no! –
And get at the big, dark, hard bit of my father,
As he rocked me with his hairy hand! . . .

                                          I'll say nothing
Of the chamber-pot, the dish with handles glimpsed
In the attic, the almanacs with red covers and the basket
Of patches, the Bible, the lavatory, the maid,
The Blessed Virgin and the crucifix . . .

                                     No one
Could have been so constantly vexed, so taken by surprise!
May I be forgiven now.
I was the victim of my wicked senses,
And I confess my youthful crimes! . . .
. . . .

And then – let me speak directly to our Lord!
Why the sluggish puberty and the misery
Of the obstinate glans, too often deferred to? Why
That creeping darkness in the crotch? The countless fears
Which follow pleasure like a deluge of black gravel?

It's always dumbfounded me! What should I know?
. . . .
Forgiven? . . .
                  Here's your blue footwarmer,
Father.
          What a childhood! . . . .
. . . .
. . . . Let us now jerk off!

                                FRANÇOIS COPPE.
                                A.R.

LES STUPRA

'Les anciens animaux saillissaient . . .'

Les anciens animaux saillissaient, même en course,
Avec des glands bardés de sang et d'excrément.
Nos pères étalaient leur membre fièrement
Par le pli de la gaine et le grain de la bourse.

Au Moyen Age pour la femelle, ange ou pource,
Il fallait un gaillard de solide grément;
Même un Kléber, d'après culotte qui ment
Peut-être un peu, n'a pas dû manquer de ressource.

D'ailleurs l'homme au plus fier mammifère est égal;
L'énormité de leur membre à tort nous étonne;
Mais une heure stérile a sonné: le cheval

Et le bœuf ont bridé leurs ardeurs, et personne
N'osera plus dresser son orgueil génital
Dans les bosquets où grouille une enfance bouffonne.

'Nos fesses ne sont pas les leurs . . .'

Nos fesses ne sont pas les leurs. Souvent j'ai vu
Des gens déboutonnés derrière quelque haie,
Et, dans ces bains sans gêne où l'enfance s'égaie,
J'observais le plan et l'effet de notre cul.

THE STUPRA

'Animals in former times . . .'

Animals in former times ejaculated on the hoof,
Their glans caked in blood and excrement.
Our fathers bore their members up with pride,
The fold of the sheath and the scrotum's swell.

Angel or sow, the female in the Middle Ages
Needed a beau with solid tackle.
Even a general of Kléber's[1] stature – his breeches a trifle
Over the top – would nonetheless have had it in him.

Man, as it happens, can match the proudest mammals,
Whose massiveness should come as no surprise.
And yet a sterile hour has struck; the horse

And the ox have doused their ardours; no one
Dares to flaunt his genital credentials
In the thickets where giggling children teem.

'Our buttocks are not like theirs . . .'

Our buttocks are not like theirs. Often I've seen
Men with their trousers lowered behind a hedge,
Or bath-time with its sploshing, child-like innocence
And I'd inspect the structure of the human arse.

Plus ferme, blême en bien des cas, il est pourvu
De méplats évidents que tapisse la claie
Des poils; pour elles, c'est seulement dans la raie
Charmante que fleurit le long satin touffu.

Une ingéniosité touchante et merveilleuse
Comme l'on ne voit qu'aux anges des saints tableaux
Imite la joue où le sourire se creuse.

Oh! de même être nus, chercher joie et repos,
Le front tourné vers sa portion glorieuse,
Et libres tous les deux murmurer des sanglots?

Leaner, often quite anaemic, the male arse
Is endowed with form beneath the lattice-work
Of hairs; in the female arse the charming crack
Alone is where the lengthy tufts of satin grow.

A marvellous and touching ingenuity – you'll find it
Only on the angels' faces in religious works –
Mimics the dimple on a smiling cheek.

We, too, might be naked – happy and resolved –
Face to face with one another's glory,
Freely giving vent to a two-part dirge.

from DERNIERS VERS

'Qu'est-ce pour nous . . .'

Qu'est-ce pour nous, mon cœur, que les nappes de sang
Et de braise, et mille meurtres, et les longs cris
De rage, sanglots de tout enfer renversant
Tout ordre; et l'Aquilon encor sur les débris

Et toute vengeance? Rien! . . . – Mais si, toute encor,
Nous la voulons! Industriels, princes, sénats,
Périssez! puissance, justice, histoire, à bas!
Ça nous est dû. Le sang! le sang! la flamme d'or!

Tout à la guerre, à la vengeance, à la terreur,
Mon Esprit! Tournons dans la morsure: Ah! passez,
Républiques de ce monde! Des empereurs,
Des régiments, des colons, des peuples, assez!

Qui remuerait les tourbillons de feu furieux,
Que nous et ceux que nous nous imaginons frères?
A nous! Romanesques amis: ça va nous plaire.
Jamais nous ne travaillerons, ô flots de feux!

Europe, Asie, Amérique, disparaissez.
Notre marche vengeresse a tout occupé,
Cités et campagnes! – Nous serons écrasés!
Les volcans sauteront! et l'Océan frappé . . .

from LAST POEMS

'What are they to us . . .'[1]

What are they to us, my heart, the sheets of blood
And embers, the thousand murders, and the long cries
Of rage, the sobs from every hell, bringing down
Every order – and still the North Wind, over the
    wreckage,

And total vengeance? Nothing! . . . Even so,
We want it! Industrialists, princes, senates,
Die! Down with power, justice, history!
This is our due. Blood! Blood! The golden flame!

Throw everything into war, vengeance, terror,
My soul! We must spin in those jaws! Republics
Of the known world, wither! Emperors
Out! Regiments, settlers, nations, out! out! out!

Who'll stir up the whirlwinds of frenzied fire
If not us and those we call our brothers? Partners
In Romance, our turn has come, we'll revel in it.
We shall never toil, O waves of fire!

Europe, Asia, America, disappear!
Everything has fallen to our march of revenge –
Cities and hinterlands! – We will be crushed!
Volcanoes will explode! And the ocean stricken . . .

Oh! mes amis! – Mon cœur, c'est sûr, ils sont des frères:
Noirs inconnus, si nous allions! allons! allons!
O malheur! je me sens frémir, la vieille terre,
Sur moi de plus en plus à vous! la terre fond,

Ce n'est rien! j'y suis! j'y suis toujours.

Mémoire

I

L'eau claire; comme le sel des larmes d'enfance;
l'assaut au soleil des blancheurs des corps de femmes;
la soie, en foule et de lys pur, des oriflammes
sous les murs dont quelque pucelle eut la défense;

l'ébat des anges; – non . . . le courant d'or en marche,
meut ses bras, noirs, et lourds, et frais surtout, d'herbe.
    Elle
sombre, ayant le Ciel bleu pour ciel-de-lit, appelle
pour rideaux l'ombre de la colline et de l'arche.

II

Eh! l'humide carreau tend ses bouillons limpides!
L'eau meuble d'or pâle et sans fond les couches
    prêtes.
Les robes vertes et déteintes des fillettes
font les saules, d'où sautent les oiseaux sans brides.

Plus pure qu'un louis, jaune et chaude paupière
le souci d'eau – ta foi conjugale, ô l'Epouse! –
au midi prompt, de son terne miroir, jalouse
au ciel gris de chaleur la Sphère rose et chère.

Oh, my friends! My heart, I know they're brothers:
Dark strangers, if we once got started! Let's go! Go!
I can't! I'm beginning to tremble, the old earth
Is on me – I am more and more yours – the earth melts.

It's an illusion. I'm here. I'm still here.

Memory[1]

I

Clear water. Like the salt of childhood tears,
The shocking whiteness of women's bodies in the sun.
Massed banners, silk and pure as the lily,
Under battlements defended by a Maid.

Dalliance of angels; – No. The flowing golden current
Moves its arms, black and heavy with weeds. Cool, above
   all.
It slips away,[2] beneath its canopy of blue sky, curtained
In the shade of the hill and the bridge's arch.

II

Clear bubbles streaming in the tiled surface
Of the water – look! – decking these fresh beds with pale
   gold.
The young girls' dresses are faded green, like studies
Of willows, where the birds swoop freely.

On the stroke of noon, that warm, yellow eyelid,
The water lily – your marriage vows, Wife! – purer
Than a gold sovereign on the dull mirror of the current,
Envies the fine, rosy Sun in a heat-wrung sky.

III

Madame se tient trop debout dans la prairie
prochaine où neigent les fils du travail; l'ombrelle
aux doigts; foulant l'ombelle; trop fière pour elle;
des enfants lisant dans la verdure fleurie

leur livre de maroquin rouge! Hélas, Lui, comme
mille anges blancs qui se séparent sur la route,
s'éloigne par delà la montagne! Elle, toute
froide, et noire, court! après le départ de l'homme!

IV

Regret des bras épais et jeunes d'herbe pure!
Or des lunes d'avril au cœur du saint lit! Joie
des chantiers riverains à l'abandon, en proie
aux soirs d'août qui faisaient germer ces pourritures!

Qu'elle pleure à présent sous les remparts! l'haleine
des peupliers d'en haut est pour la seule brise.
Puis, c'est la nappe, sans reflets, sans source, grise:
un vieux, dragueur, dans sa barque immobile, peine.

V

Jouet de cet œil d'eau morne, je n'y puis prendre,
ô canot immobile! oh! bras trop courts! ni l'une
ni l'autre fleur: ni la jaune qui m'importune,
là; ni la bleue, amie à l'eau couleur de cendre.

Ah! la poudre des saules qu'une aile secoue!
Les roses des roseaux dès longtemps dévorées!
Mon canot, toujours fixe; et sa chaîne tirée
au fond de cet œil d'eau sans bords, – à quelle boue?

III

The filaments of toil[3] snow down on the nearby field,
Where Madame's posture is too stiff, fingering her parasol
And stamping the cow-parsley – too proud for her liking;
Children, in the flower-studded pasture, read

A book bound in red leather. And HE, alas,
Is making off beyond the mountains, like a thousand
White angels scattering on the road. Chilled
And black, SHE is running in his wake!

IV

Longings for thick arms, young with pure grass!
Gold of April moonlight deep in the sacred bed! Joy
Of the ruined boatyards, enslaved
By the August nights that hastened this decay!

Let her weep now below the ramparts. The breath
Of the poplars overhead, spent on the winds.
Then it's the dull grey tract of the surface, no source
And no reflections. An old boy dredging from a moored
    barge.

V

I'm the plaything of this lugubrious eye of water.
My arms are too short! A boat becalmed! I can reach
Neither one flower nor the other – not this taunting,
Yellow one; not that blue one in league with the ashen
    surface.

Wingbeats shaking the dust from the willows!
The flowers long since eaten off the rushes!
My boat still fast, the chain drawn taut,
Down through this rimless eye of water – into what mud.

Larme

Loin des oiseaux, des troupeaux, des villageoises,
Je buvais, accroupi dans quelque bruyère
Entourée de tendres bois de noisetiers,
Par un brouillard d'après-midi tiède et vert.

Que pouvais-je boire dans cette jeune Oise,
Ormeaux sans voix, gazon sans fleurs, ciel couvert.
Que tirais-je à la gourde de colocase?
Quelque liqueur d'or, fade et qui fait suer.

Tel, j'eusse été mauvaise enseigne d'auberge.
Puis l'orage changea le ciel, jusqu'au soir.
Ce furent des pays noirs, des lacs, des perches,
Des colonnades sous la nuit bleue, des gares.

L'eau des bois se perdait sur des sables vierges,
Le vent, du ciel, jetait des glaçons aux mares . . .
Or! tel qu'un pêcheur d'or ou de coquillages,
Dire que je n'ai pas eu souci de boire!

                                        Mai 1872

La Rivière de Cassis

La Rivière de Cassis roule ignorée
            En des vaux étranges:
La voix de cent corbeaux l'accompagne, vraie
            Et bonne voix d'anges:
Avec les grands mouvements des sapinaies
            Quand plusieurs vents plongent.

Tear

Far from the birds and cattle, the village girls,
I drank, kneeling in heather,
Ringed by copses of budding hazel,
In the warm, green mist of afternoon.

What could I be drinking from that young Oise
– Voiceless elms, flowerless grass, grey sky –
What was I sucking from the arum's gourd?
An insipid golden brew that bathes you in sweat.

I'd have made a lousy inn-sign, as I was.
– Then the storm changed the sky until evening.
It was all black lands, and lakes and poles,
Colonnades beneath blue night, railway stations.

The woodland water spent itself in virgin sand,
The wind flung ice from the sky into the ponds . . .
But like a fisher of gold or precious shells,
– Strange thing – I hadn't thought to drink!

                                        May 1872

River of Cassis

The River of Cassis rolls unremarked
            Through strange valleys,
Mobbed by a hundred noisy crows – benign,
            Authentic voice of angels –
And the great stirrings of the forest pines
            When the winds drive down.

Tout roule avec des mystères révoltants
    De campagnes d'anciens temps;
De donjons visités, de parcs importants:
    C'est en ces bords qu'on entend
Les passions mortes des chevaliers errants:
    Mais que salubre est le vent!

Que le piéton regarde à ces claires-voies:
    Il ira plus courageux.
Soldats des forêts que le Seigneur envoie,
    Chers corbeaux délicieux!
Faites fuir d'ici le paysan matois
    Qui trinque d'un moignon vieux.

                       Mai 1872

Comédie de la soif

1. Les Parents

Nous sommes tes Grands-Parents,
    Les Grands!
Couverts des froides sueurs
De la lune et des verdures.
Nos vins secs avaient du cœur!
Au soleil sans imposture
Que faut-il à l'homme? Boire.

MOI – Mourir aux fleuves barbares.

Nous sommes tes Grands-Parents
    Des champs.
L'eau est au fond des osiers:
Vois le courant du fossé
Autour du Château mouillé.
Descendons en nos celliers;
Après, le cidre et le lait.

Everything rolls with the loathsome mysteries
      Of archaic ground;
Dungeons surveyed, sizeable estates:
      Along the banks you hear
The dead passions of knights errant –
      Yet how good the wind feels!

Let the traveller look through this fence-work:
      He'll go a little bolder on his way.
And you, soldiers of the forests, sent by the Lord,
      Dear, ravishing crows,
Drive out the wily peasant with the full glass
      Raised in his aged stump!

                        May 1872

Comedy of Thirst

1. Parents

We are your grandparents,
      Elders!
Bathed in the cold sweats
Of the moon and green pasture.
Our dry wines had guts!
Beneath the ingenuous sun
What must man do? Drink.

ME – Die in barbarous rivers.

We are your grandparents,
      Tillers!
Below the osier lies the water:
See it flowing in the moat
Around the dank Castle.
Let's go down to our store-rooms;
Afterwards, cider or milk.

MOI – Aller où boivent les vaches.

Nous sommes tes Grands-Parents
            Tiens, prends
Les liqueurs dans nos armoires;
Le Thé, le Café, si rares,
Frémissent dans les bouilloires
– Vois les images, les fleurs.
Nous rentrons du cimetière.

MOI – Ah! tarir toutes les urnes!

2. L'Esprit

Eternelles Ondines,
        Divisez l'eau fine.
Vénus, sœur de l'azur,
        Emeus le flot pur.
Juifs errants de Norwège
        Dites-moi la neige.
Anciens exilés chers
        Dites-moi la mer.

MOI – Non, plus ces boissons pures,
        Ces fleurs d'eau pour verres;
Légendes ni figures
        Ne me désaltèrent;
Chansonnier, ta filleule
        C'est ma soif si folle
Hydre intime sans gueules
        Qui mine et désole.

3. Les Amis

Viens, les Vins vont aux plages,
Et les flots par millions!
Vois le Bitter sauvage
Rouler du haut des monts!

ME – Or drink with the cows.

We are your grandparents,
          Hoarders
Of liqueur in cupboards. Try it!
Teas and Coffees, hard to come by,
Simmer in our kettles.
– Look at the pictures, the flowers.
We're back from the cemetery.

ME – Ah, drain the urns dry!

2. *Spirit*

Eternal water-spirits
   Divide the slender waters.
Venus, sister of azure,
   Rouse the pure wave.
Wandering Jews of Norway,
   Tell me the snow.
Old, beloved exiles,
   Tell me the sea.

ME – No, enough of pure drinks –
   These decorative water-flowers;
No myth, no imagery
   Can quench my thirst;
Song-maker, your godchild
   Is my crazed desire to drink –
My inside-Hydra, mouthless,
   Desolating, wasting.

3. *Friends*

Come, the Wines are running towards the shore,
And the waves in their millions!
See the Dutch gin, wild,
Pouring off the mountains!

Gagnons, pèlerins sages
L'Absinthe aux verts piliers . . .

MOI – Plus ces paysages.
          Qu'est l'ivresse, Amis?

          J'aime autant, mieux, même,
          Pourrir dans l'étang,
          Sous l'affreuse crème,
          Près des bois flottants.

4. *Le Pauvre Songe*

Peut-être un Soir m'attend
Où je boirai tranquille
En quelque vieille Ville,
Et mourrai plus content:
Puisque je suis patient!

Si mon mal se résigne,
Si j'ai jamais quelque or
Choisirai-je le Nord
Ou le Pays des vignes? . . .
– Ah songer est indigne

Puisque c'est pure perte!
Et si je redeviens
Le voyageur ancien
Jamais l'auberge verte
Ne peut bien m'être ouverte.

5. *Conclusion*

Les pigeons qui tremblent dans la prairie,
Le gibier, qui court et qui voit la nuit,
Les bêtes des eaux, la bête asservie,
Les derniers papillons! . . . ont soif aussi.

Good pilgrims, we must reach
The green portals of Absinthe! . . .

ME – Enough of these landscapes.
Friends, what is drunkenness?

I'd as soon – in fact I'd rather –
Rot among the pond-life
Under rank scum
Beside lumps of driftwood.

4. *The Poor Dreamer*

Perhaps there's an Evening in store
When I'll drink quietly
In some old City
And die the happier –
Patient as I am!

If my affliction lets up,
If I ever come by gold,
Will I choose the North
Or vineyard country? . . .
– Ah dreaming is shameful,

A perfect form of loss!
And if I become once more
The traveller I was,
The Green Inn[1]
Will have barred its door.

5. *Conclusion*

The pigeons trembling in the field,
Game in flight, seeing in the dark,
Water-creatures, beasts in thrall,
The last butterfly – thirst grips them all.

Mais fondre où fond ce nuage sans guide,
– Oh! favorisé de ce qui est frais!
Expirer en ces violettes humides
Dont les aurores chargent ces forêts?

Mai 1872

Bonne pensée du matin

A quatre heures du matin, l'été,
Le sommeil d'amour dure encore.
Sous les bosquets l'aube évapore
    L'odeur du soir fêté.

Mais là-bas dans l'immense chantier
Vers le soleil des Hespérides,
En bras de chemise, les charpentiers
    Déjà s'agitent.

Dans leur désert de mousse, tranquilles,
Ils préparent les lambris précieux
Où la richesse de la ville
    Rira sous de faux cieux.

Ah! pour ces Ouvriers charmants
Sujets d'un roi de Babylone,
Vénus! laisse un peu les Amants,
    Dont l'âme est en couronne.

    O Reine des Bergers!
Porte aux travailleurs l'eau-de-vie,
Pour que leurs forces soient en paix
En attendant le bain dans la mer, à midi.

Mai 1872

But to melt like the untended cloud,
– Chaperoned by coolness!
To expire among the moist violets
That daybreak strews in these woods?

                                                      May 1872

Good Thought for the Morning

Four in the morning, summertime
And love still dozing.
Dawn in the arbours lifts away
          The smell of last night's revels.

But down in the immense construction yards
Towards the Hesperidean sun,[1]
The carpenters in shirt-sleeves
          Are already at their work.

At ease in their desert of moss,
They trim the priceless panels
Where the wealth of the city
          Will laugh under artificial skies.

O Venus, leave the Lovers
And their souls in garlands, spare
A little time for these Workers,
          Charming subjects of a Babylonian king.

          O Queen of the Shepherds,[2]
Fetch these labourers eau-de-vie
To pacify their strength
Until they bathe at midday in the sea.

                                                      May 1872

Chanson de la plus haute tour
('Fêtes de la patience')

Oisive jeunesse
A tout asservie,
Par délicatesse
J'ai perdu ma vie.
Ah! Que le temps vienne
Où les cœurs s'éprennent.

Je me suis dit: laisse,
Et qu'on ne te voie:
Et sans la promesse
De plus hautes joies.
Que rien ne t'arrête,
Auguste retraite.

J'ai tant fait patience
Qu'à jamais j'oublie;
Craintes et souffrances
Aux cieux sont parties.
Et la soif malsaine
Obscurcit mes veines.

Ainsi la Prairie
A l'oubli livrée,
Grandie, et fleurie
D'encens et d'ivraies
Au bourdon farouche
De cent sales mouches.

Ah! Mille veuvages
De la si pauvre âme
Qui n'a que l'image

Song from the Highest Tower
(from 'Festivals of Patience')

Idleness of youth,
In thrall to everything –
I've wasted my life
In endless discretion.
Ah! Let the time come
When all hearts are smitten.

I told myself: leave it
And stay out of sight.
Abandon the promise
Of deeper delight.
Let nothing delay
Your august retreat.

I've waited so long
I've forgotten everything.
Pain and fear
Have vanished in thin air
And a morbid thirst
Darkens my veins.

Whence the wide meadow
Left untended –
Flowering high
With rosemary and rye,
The brutal hum
Of congregating flies.

A soul that is widowed
A thousand ways
Will cling to the holy

De la Notre-Dame!
Est-ce que l'on prie
La Vierge Marie?

Oisive jeunesse
A tout asservie,
Par délicatesse
J'ai perdu ma vie.
Ah! Que le temps vienne
Où les cœurs s'éprennent!

Mai 1872

Fêtes de la faim

Ma faim, Anne, Anne,
Fuis sur ton âne.

Si j'ai du *goût*, ce n'est guères
Que pour la terre et les pierres
Dinn! dinn! dinn! dinn! Mangeons l'air,
Le roc, les terres, le fer.

Tournez, les faims! Paissez, faims,
Le pré des sons!
Attirez le gai venin
Des liserons;

Les cailloux qu'un pauvre brise,
Les vieilles pierres d'églises,
Les galets, fils des déluges,
Pains couchés aux vallées grises!

Mes faims, c'est les bouts d'air noir;
L'azur sonneur;
– C'est l'estomac qui me tire.
C'est le malheur.

Image of Our Lady.
Are we really to pray
To the Mother of God?

Idleness of youth,
In thrall to everything –
I've wasted my life
In endless discretion.
Let the time come
When all hearts are smitten!

May 1872

Festivals of Hunger

Anne, Anne,[1] my hunger,
Ride out on your donkey.

What *taste* I have is for little
More than earth and stones.
Dinn! dinn! dinn! dinn! We will eat air,
Rock, earth, iron.

Turn, my hungers! Hungers, graze
        On fields of bran!
Suck up the blithe poison
        Of convolvulus;

Stones broken by a poor man,
Old masonry from churches,
Pebbles – flood-progenies,
Loaves slumped in the grey valleys!

My hungers, leavings of black air;
        Resounding azure,
The tugging of my guts.
        Despair.

Sur terre ont paru les feuilles:
Je vais aux chairs de fruit blettes.
Au sein du sillon je cueille
La doucette et la violette.

Ma faim, Anne, Anne!
Fuis sur ton âne.

[Bonheur]

O saisons, ô châteaux,
Quelle âme est sans défauts?

O saisons, ô châteaux!

J'ai fait la magique étude
Du Bonheur, que nul n'élude.

O vive lui, chaque fois
Que chante son coq gaulois.

Mais! je n'aurai plus d'envie,
Il s'est chargé de ma vie.

Ce Charme! il prit âme et corps,
Et dispersa tous efforts.

Que comprendre à ma parole?
Il fait qu'elle fuie et vole!

O saisons, ô châteaux!

[Et, si le malheur m'entraîne,
Sa disgrace m'est certaine.

Now on earth, leaves have appeared,
I'm eager for the flesh of pulpy fruit.
Deep in the furrow I root
for violets and corn-salad.

> Anne, Anne, my hunger,
> Ride out on your donkey.

[Happiness]¹

O seasons, O châteaux
Show me the soul as pure as snow.

O seasons, O châteaux,

I've learned the magic spell
Of happiness, which no one withstands.

So here's to happiness, with every crow
Of the Gallic cockerel.

But! I'll forget what it was to want:
It's taken my life in hand.

Body and soul are in its Sway
And all my efforts spent.

What do my words mean, after all?
It lifts them clean away.

O seasons, O châteaux!

[I'm sure it will relent
When bad luck comes my way

Il faut que son dédain, las!
Me livre au plus prompt trépas!

– O Saisons, ô Châteaux!
Quelle âme est sans défauts?]

Honte

Tant que la lame n'aura
Pas coupé cette cervelle,
Ce paquet blanc vert et gras
A vapeur jamais nouvelle,

(Ah, Lui, devrait couper son
Nez, sa lèvre, ses oreilles,
Son ventre! et faire abandon
De ses jambes! ô merveille!)

Mais, non, vrai, je crois que tant
Que pour sa tête la lame,
Que les cailloux pour son flanc,
Que pour ses boyaux la flamme

N'auront pas agi, l'enfant
Gêneur, la si sotte bête,
Ne doit cesser un instant
De ruser et d'être traître

Comme un chat des Monts-Rocheux;
D'empuantir toutes sphères!
Qu'à sa mort pourtant, ô mon Dieu!
S'élève quelque prière!

And kill me with contempt,
– The kindest blow.

– O seasons, O châteaux!
Show me the soul as pure as snow.]

Shame[1]

So long as the steel
Hasn't sliced up that brain,
That green-white wad of fat
Full of spent steam,

(Ah, but He's the one
Who should sever his nose,
Lips, ears, stomach! Jettison
His legs! Imagine that!)

But no, I honestly think
That so long as the steel
Hasn't sorted his head,
the stones his ribs, the flame

His tripes, that wearisome
Child, that creature of such
Foolishness, will never desist
From his guile and treachery

Like a Rocky-Mountain cat[2]
Stinking up everything!
Yet at his death, please God,
Let someone venture a prayer.

LES DESERTS DE L'AMOUR

Avertissement

Ces écritures-ci sont d'un jeune, tout jeune *homme*, dont la vie s'est développée n'importe où; sans mère, sans pays, insoucieux de tout ce qu'on connaît, fuyant toute force morale, comme furent déjà plusieurs pitoyables jeunes hommes. Mais, lui, si ennuyé et si troublé, qu'il ne fit que s'amener à la mort comme à une pudeur terrible et fatale. N'ayant pas aimé de femmes, – quoique plein de sang! – il eut son âme et son cœur, toute sa force, élevés en des erreurs étranges et tristes. Des rêves suivants, – ses amours! – qui lui vinrent dans ses lits ou dans les rues, et de leur suite et de leur fin, de douces considérations religieuses se dégagent. Peut-être se rappellera-t-on le sommeil continu des Mahométans légendaires, – braves pourtant et circoncis! Mais, cette bizarre souffrance possédant une autorité inquiétante, il faut sincèrement désirer que cette Ame, égarée parmi nous tous, et qui veut la mort, ce semble, rencontre en cet instant-là des consolations sérieuses et soit digne!

A. Rimbaud.

I

C'est certes la même campagne. La même maison rustique de mes parents: la salle même où les dessus de porte sont des bergeries roussies, avec des armes et des lions. Au dîner, il y a un salon, avec des bougies et des vins et des boiseries rustiques.

THE DESERTS OF LOVE

Foreword

These are the writings of a young man, a very young *man*,[1] whose life has unfolded in no fixed place; no mother, no country, careless of the things one should care about; like many wretched young men, evading moral laws. He was aimless and troubled to such a degree that he could only trudge towards death as though towards a terrible and fatal propriety. He had never loved women – though full of passion! – and so his heart, his soul and all his strength were prey to a strange, sad waywardness. From a succession of dreams – their evolution and their endings – which came to him in his bed or on the street, delicate religious notions took shape. Perhaps you recall the uninterrupted sleep of the legendary Mohamedans[2] – good men and circumcised. Yet his strange suffering has a disquieting ring of truth, and we must hope in all earnest that this Soul, lost in our very midst, apparently longing to die, will find true consolation at the moment of death, and prove worthy of it!

A. Rimbaud

I

It's the same countryside all right. The same old farmhouse belonging to my parents; the same living-room with the discoloured pastoral scenes above the doorways, the lions and coats-of-arms. At dinner a room with candles and wines and

La table à manger est très grande. Les servantes! Elles étaient plusieurs, autant que je m'en suis souvenu. – Il y avait là un de mes jeunes amis anciens, prêtre et vêtu en prêtre, maintenant: c'était pour être plus libre. Je me souviens de sa chambre de pourpre, à vitres de papier jaune; et ses livres, cachés, qui avaient trempé dans l'océan!

Moi j'étais abandonné, dans cette maison de campagne sans fin: lisant dans la cuisine, séchant la boue de mes habits devant les hôtes, aux conversations du salon: ému jusqu'à la mort par le murmure du lait du matin et de la nuit du siècle dernier.

J'étais dans une chambre très sombre: que faisais-je? Une servante vint près de moi: je puis dire que c'était un petit chien: quoiqu'elle fût belle, et d'une noblesse maternelle inexprimable pour moi: pure, connue, toute charmante! Elle me pinça le bras.

Je ne me rappelle même plus bien sa figure: ce n'est pas pour me rappeler son bras, dont je roulai la peau dans mes deux doigts; ni sa bouche, que la mienne saisit comme une petite vague désespérée, minant sans fin quelque chose. Je la renversai dans une corbeille de coussins et de toiles de navire, en un coin noir. Je ne me rappelle plus que son pantalon à dentelles blanches. – Puis, ô désespoir, la cloison devint vaguement l'ombre des arbres, et je me suis abîmé sous la tristesse amoureuse de la nuit.

II

Cette fois, c'est la Femme que j'ai vue dans la ville, et à qui j'ai parlé et qui me parle.

J'étais dans une chambre sans lumière. On vint me dire qu'elle était chez moi: et je la vis dans mon lit, toute à moi, sans lumière: je fus très ému, et beaucoup parce que c'était la maison de famille; aussi une détresse me prit: j'étais en haillons, moi, et elle, mondaine, qui se donnait, il lui fallait s'en aller! Une détresse sans nom: je la pris, et la laissai tomber hors du lit, presque nue; et, dans ma faiblesse indicible, je tombai sur elle et me traînai avec elle parmi les tapis sans lumière. La lampe de la famille rougissait

rustic woodwork. The dining table is huge. The maids! – plenty of them; as many as I'd thought. One of my young friends was there – an old friend really, a priest in what was now priest's raiment: this in the interests of greater latitude. I remember his purple bedroom and its yellow-paper window panes, his secret stash of books pickled in sea brine!

I was left to my own devices in that endless house in the country: reading in the kitchen, drying the mud off my clothes in front of the guests as they chatted in the drawing-room; moved to the point of death by the murmur of morning milk, the murmur of a night from the last century.

I was in a very dark room. Doing . . . ? A servant girl approached me – somehow also a small dog, though beautiful, with a maternal nobility I can't describe: pure, familiar, utterly charming! She pinched my arm.

I don't even recall her face that clearly. I can't see her arm, whose skin I rolled between my fingers, or her mouth, on which my own now battened like a desperate little wave, endlessly hammering away at something. I toppled her into a basket of cushions and sailcloth in a dark corner. All I remember now are her white lace knickers. – Then despair! The walls changed hazily into the shadows of trees, and I sank into the tender sadness of the night.

II

This time it's the Woman I've seen in the City – I've spoken to her; she speaks to me.

I was in an unlit bedroom. I was told she'd arrived. And I saw her in my bed, all mine, no lights on. I was very much aroused – it was the family home – but then an anguish came over me. I was in rags and she, a woman of the world, had offered herself to me. But she'd have to leave! Anguish beyond words! I took her and let her fall from the bed, almost naked; and in my unspeakable weakness I fell on her and dragged her over the rugs, in the dark. The family light burnished the adjoining

l'une après l'autre les chambres voisines. Alors la femme dispa-
rut. Je versai plus de larmes que Dieu n'en a pu jamais demander.

Je sortis dans la ville sans fin. O Fatigue! Noyé dans la nuit
sourde et dans la fuite du bonheur. C'était comme une nuit
d'hiver, avec une neige pour étouffer le monde décidément. Les
amis auxquels je criais: où reste-t-elle, répondaient faussement.
Je fus devant les vitrages de là où elle va tous les soirs: je
courais dans un jardin enseveli. On m'a repoussé. Je pleurais
énormément, à tout cela. Enfin je suis descendu dans un lieu
plein de poussière, et assis sur des charpentes, j'ai laissé finir
toutes les larmes de mon corps avec cette nuit. Et mon épuise-
ment me revenait pourtant toujours.

J'ai compris qu'elle était à sa vie de tous les jours, et que le
tour de bonté serait plus long à se reproduire qu'une étoile. Elle
n'est pas revenue, et ne reviendra jamais, l'Adorable qui s'était
rendue chez moi, – ce que je n'aurais jamais présumé. – Vrai,
cette fois j'ai pleuré plus que tous les enfants du monde.

rooms, one by one. Then the woman disappeared. I shed more tears than God has ever asked for.

I went out into the endless city. Exhaustion! Foundering in the hollow night and the loss of happiness. It was like a winter's night, with enough snow to smother the world for good. I shouted, 'Where has she gone?' to friends; they answered with lies. Then I was in front of the windows, in that spot she goes to every evening. I ran through a sepulchral garden. I was turned away. I began to cry uncontrollably. Finally, I went down to a place full of dust and in the course of that night, sitting on the timber-frames, I shed every tear in my body – and still my exhaustion rolled back over me.

I've realized that she must have gone back to everyday normality, that this benediction would take longer than a planet to come around again. She has not returned. She will never return, the Adorable One who came to me in my house – I never would have thought it possible. This time, it's true, I have wept more than all the children in the world.

UNE SAISON EN ENFER

«Jadis, si je me souviens bien, ma vie était un festin où s'ouvrai-
ent tous les cœurs, où tous les vins coulaient.

Un soir, j'ai assis la Beauté sur mes genoux. – Et je l'ai trouvée
amère. – Et je l'ai injuriée.

Je me suis armé contre la justice.

Je me suis enfui. O sorcières, ô misère, ô haine, c'est à vous
que mon trésor a été confié!

Je parvins à faire s'évanouir dans mon esprit toute l'espérance
humaine. Sur toute joie pour l'étrangler j'ai fait le bond sourd
de la bête féroce.

J'ai appelé les bourreaux pour, en périssant, mordre la crosse
de leurs fusils. J'ai appelé les fléaux, pour m'étouffer avec le
sable, le sang. Le malheur a été mon dieu. Je me suis allongé
dans la boue. Je me suis séché à l'air du crime. Et j'ai joué de
bons tours à la folie.

Et le printemps m'a apporté l'affreux rire de l'idiot.

Or, tout dernièrement m'étant trouvé sur le point de faire le
dernier *couac!* j'ai songé à rechercher la clef du festin ancien, où
je reprendrais peut-être appétit.

La charité est cette clef. – Cette inspiration prouve que j'ai
rêvé!

«Tu resteras hyène, etc...,» se récrie le démon qui me
couronna de si aimables pavots. «Gagne la mort avec tous tes
appétits, et ton égoïsme et tous les péchés capitaux.»

Ah! j'en ai trop pris: – Mais, cher Satan, je vous en conjure,
une prunelle moins irritée! et en attendant les quelques petites
lâchetés en retard, vous qui aimez dans l'écrivain l'absence des

A SEASON IN HELL

Once, if I recall correctly, my life was a banquet. Every wine flowed, all hearts were open.

One night I settled Beauty on my knee and found her bitter. – And I insulted her.

I armed myself against justice.

I fled. You, Sorcerers! And you, Misery and Hatred! I placed my treasure in your hands!

I succeeded in driving all hope from my mind. With the stealth of beasts, I leapt on every happiness and wrung its neck.

I summoned executioners, so I could bite on the butts of their rifles in my death throes. I invoked plagues, to choke myself on sand, on blood. Despair has been my God. I've lain head to toe in the mud. I've dried out in the crime-ridden air. I've run rings around madness.

And Spring has brought me the hideous laugh of the idiot.

But lately, on the point of uttering my last *squawk*, I thought of searching for the key to that long-gone banquet. Maybe my appetite would be restored.

That key is charity. (Which only suggests how deeply I've been dreaming!)

'Once a hyena, always a hyena, etc. . . .' yells the demon who once crowned my head with the loveliest poppies. 'Go to your death with all your appetites, your selfishness, with every deadly sin.'

No shortage of those. But, kind Satan, I beg you, a touch less tetchiness in your look! Since we're waiting for the last of my low little deeds, and since you admire the absence of

facultés descriptives ou instructives, je vous détache ces quelques hideux feuillets de mon carnet de damné.

Mauvais sang

J'ai de mes ancêtres gaulois l'œil bleu blanc, la cervelle étroite, et la maladresse dans la lutte. Je trouve mon habillement aussi barbare que le leur. Mais je ne beurre pas ma chevelure.

Les Gaulois étaient les écorcheurs de bêtes, les brûleurs d'herbes les plus ineptes de leur temps.

D'eux, j'ai: l'idolâtrie et l'amour du sacrilège; – oh! tous les vices, colère, luxure, – magnifique, la luxure; – surtout mensonge et paresse.

J'ai horreur de tous les métiers. Maîtres et ouvriers, tous paysans, ignobles. La main à plume vaut la main à charrue. – Quel siècle à mains! – Je n'aurai jamais ma main. Après, la domesticité même trop loin. L'honnêteté de la mendicité me navre. Les criminels dégoûtent comme des châtrés: moi, je suis intact, et ça m'est égal.

Mais! qui a fait ma langue perfide tellement, qu'elle ait guidé et sauvegardé jusqu'ici ma paresse? Sans me servir pour vivre même de mon corps, et plus oisif que le crapaud, j'ai vécu partout. Pas une famille d'Europe que je ne connaisse. – J'entends des familles comme la mienne, qui tiennent tout de la déclaration des Droits de l'Homme. – J'ai connu chaque fils de famille!

Si j'avais des antécédents à un point quelconque de l'histoire de France!

Mais non, rien.

Il m'est bien évident que j'ai toujours été [de] race inférieure. Je ne puis comprendre la révolte. Ma race ne se souleva jamais que pour piller: tels les loups à la bête qu'ils n'ont pas tuée.

Je me rappelle l'histoire de la France fille aînée de l'Eglise. J'aurais fait, manant, le voyage de terre sainte; j'ai dans la tête des routes dans les plaines souabes, des vues de Byzance, des remparts de Solyme; le culte de Marie, l'attendrissement sur le crucifié s'éveillent en moi parmi mille féeries profanes. – Je suis

descriptive or instructive power in a writer, I offer you a few
vile pages torn from the notebook of a damned soul.

Bad Blood

From my ancestors the Gauls I have inherited pale blue eyes, a
narrow skull, clumsiness in warfare. My clothes, I'd say, are as
barbaric as theirs. But I don't dress my hair with butter.

As flayers of beasts and burners of grass, the Gauls were the
most inept people of their age.

From them I get: idolatry and love of sacrilege – all the vices
really, quick temper, lust – a great thing, lust; lying and idleness
above all.

I abominate all trades. Professionals and workers, serfs to a
man! Despicable. The hand that guides the pen is a match for
the hand that guides the plough – What a century for hands! –
I'll never get my hand in. And besides, there's no end to 'service'.
The beggar's honesty distresses me. Criminals disgust me – men
without balls. Myself I'm intact; it's all the same to me.

But who made my tongue so treacherous that up till now it's
been the guide and guardian of my idleness? I've not even used
my body to pay my way; more otiose than the toad, I've dwelt
everywhere. Not a family in Europe but I know them. Families
like mine, I mean, who owe everything to the Declaration of the
Rights of Man.¹ I've known every young man of good family!

If only I had forebears at some point or other in the history of
France!

But no. Nothing.

It's quite clear to me that I've always belonged to a lesser race.
I fail to understand rebellion. My people only ever rose up in the
name of pillage, like wolves feasting on the prey they didn't kill.

I remember the history of France, eldest daughter of the
Church. I, a serf, would have made the journey to the Holy
Land; the routes through the Swabian plains are all in my head,
the views of Byzantium, the ramparts of Jerusalem; the cult of
the Virgin and compassion for the crucified Christ stir in me

assis, lépreux, sur les pots cassés et les orties, au pied d'un mur
rongé par le soleil. – Plus tard, reître, j'aurais bivaqué sous les
nuits d'Allemagne.

Ah! encore: je danse le sabbat dans une rouge clairière, avec
des vieilles et des enfants.

Je ne me souviens pas plus loin que cette terre-ci et le christianisme. Je n'en finirais pas de me revoir dans ce passé. Mais
toujours seul; sans famille; même, quelle langue parlais-je? Je ne
me vois jamais dans les conseils du Christ; ni dans les conseils
des Seigneurs, – représentants du Christ.

Qu'étais-je au siècle dernier: je ne me retrouve qu'aujourd'hui.
Plus de vagabonds, plus de guerres vagues. La race inférieure a
tout couvert – le peuple, comme on dit, la raison; la nation et la
science.

Oh! la science! On a tout repris. Pour le corps et pour l'âme,
– le viatique, – on a la médecine et la philosophie, – les remèdes
de bonnes femmes et les chansons populaires arrangés. Et les
divertissements des princes et les jeux qu'ils interdisaient! Géographie, cosmographie, mécanique, chimie! . . .

La science, la nouvelle noblesse! Le progrès. Le monde
marche! Pourquoi ne tournerait-il pas?

C'est la vision des nombres. Nous allons à l'*Esprit*. C'est
très-certain, c'est oracle, ce que je dis. Je comprends, et ne
sachant m'expliquer sans paroles païennes, je voudrais me
taire.

Le sang païen revient! L'Esprit est proche, pourquoi Christ ne
m'aide-t-il pas, en donnant à mon âme noblesse et liberté. Hélas!
L'Evangile a passé! l'Evangile! l'Evangile.

J'attends Dieu avec gourmandise. Je suis de race inférieure de
toute éternité.

Me voici sur la plage armoricaine. Que les villes s'allument
dans le soir. Ma journée est faite; je quitte l'Europe. L'air marin
brûlera mes poumons; les climats perdus me tanneront. Nager,
broyer l'herbe, chasser, fumer surtout; boire des liqueurs fortes
comme du métal bouillant, – comme faisaient ces chers ancêtres
autour des feux.

amid a thousand profane enchantments. I sit, stricken with leprosy, on broken pots and nettles at the foot of a wall gnawed by the sun. Later, as a mercenary, I would have camped out under the stars in Germany.

And more: I'm dancing at a witches' sabbath, in a firelit clearing, with crones and children.

I can remember nothing beyond this country, and Christianity. I never cease to see myself in that past. Always alone, though; no family; come to think of it, what language did I speak? I could hardly have called myself a follower of Christ; or of his representatives, the Nobility.

What was I in the last century? I can only see myself as I am right now. No more wanderers, no more random wars. The inferior race has spread to every corner – the people, as they're known; reason, the nation, science.

Ah yes, science! Everything's been reassigned. For the body and the soul, – the Eucharist, – we now have medicine and philosophy: old wives' tales and rearranged folk songs. And instead of the diversions of royalty? The entertainments forbidden by princes? Geography, cosmography, mechanics, chemistry.

Science, the new aristocracy! Progress. The world marches forward! It could just as easily be turning, too.

Numbers – that's the mission now. We're moving towards the *Spirit*. What I'm saying is prophetic and entirely true. I've grasped it. Yet I'm incapable of explaining myself in anything but paganisms; I'd sooner hold my peace.

Pagan blood returns! The Spirit is near. Why will Christ not come to my aid, covering my soul with nobility and freedom? Too bad. The Gospel's over and done with! The Gospel! The Gospel.

I'm avid for God. Since the beginning of time I've belonged to a lesser race.

And here I am on the shoreline of Brittany. Let the lights go on in the cities at dusk. My day is done; I'm leaving Europe. The sea air will burn my lungs; godforsaken climates will char my skin. I'll swim, trudge the grass underfoot; I'll hunt. Above all, I'll smoke; drink liquors as fierce as molten metal, like my dear ancestors around their fires.

Je reviendrai, avec des membres de fer, la peau sombre, l'œil furieux; sur mon masque, on me jugera d'une race forte. J'aurai de l'or: je serai oisif et brutal. Les femmes soignent ces féroces infirmes retour des pays chauds. Je serai mêlé aux affaires politiques. Sauvé.

Maintenant je suis maudit, j'ai horreur de la patrie. Le meilleur, c'est un sommeil bien ivre, sur la grève.

On ne part pas. – Reprenons les chemins d'ici, chargé de mon vice, le vice qui a poussé ses racines de souffrance à mon côté, dès l'âge de raison – qui monte au ciel, me bat, me renverse, me traîne.

La dernière innocence et la dernière timidité. C'est dit. Ne pas porter au monde mes dégoûts et mes trahisons.

Allons! La marche, le fardeau, le désert, l'ennui et la colère.

A qui me louer? Quelle bête faut-il adorer? Quelle sainte image attaque-t-on? Quels cœurs briserai-je? Quel mensonge dois-je tenir? – Dans quel sang marcher?

Plutôt, se garder de la justice. – La vie dure, l'abrutissement simple, – soulever, le poing desséché, le couvercle du cercueil, s'asseoir, s'étouffer. Ainsi point de vieillesse, ni de dangers: la terreur n'est pas française.

– Ah! je suis tellement délaissé que j'offre à n'importe quelle divine image des élans vers la perfection.

O mon abnégation, ô ma charité merveilleuse! ici-bas, pourtant!

De profundis Domine, suis-je bête!

Encore tout enfant, j'admirais le forçat intraitable sur qui se referme toujours le bagne; je visitais les auberges et les garnis qu'il aurait sacrés par son séjour; je voyais *avec son idée* le ciel bleu et le travail fleuri de la campagne; je flairais sa fatalité dans les villes. Il avait plus de force qu'un saint, plus de bon sens qu'un voyageur – et lui, lui seul! pour témoin de sa gloire et de sa raison.

I shall return with limbs of iron, dark skin, a furious aspect. From my mask I'll be thought to belong to a mighty race. I shall have gold: I shall be slothful and brutal – the ferocious invalid back from the tropics, fussed around by women. I'll be embroiled in politics. Saved.

Right now, I'm damned. My country appals me. The best course of action: drink myself comatose and sleep it off on the beach.

Foreign parts are out. I'll head for the roads round here again, saddled with my vice – the vice that took painful root in my side when I grew up . . . it rakes the sky, batters me, flattens me, drags me on.

The dregs of innocence, the last scrap of reticence. It's on record. I refuse to carry my loathings and betrayals into the world.

All right then. The slog, the backpack, the desert, tedium and anger.

Who shall I sign up with? Which brute shall I worship? What holy image shall I desecrate? Whose hearts shall I break? What lie shall I espouse? Whose blood shall I trample?

Better to steer clear of the law. – The hard life; pure, mindless drudgery – raise the coffin lid with a shrivelled hand, settle in and expire. That way no growing old, no risks run: terror is unknown to the French.

– Ah but I'm so desolate, I'll dedicate my drive for perfection to the first divine image that happens along.

What self-denial! What consummate charity! Still stuck here, even so!

De profundis Domine,[2] how foolish can you get?

When I was still a small boy, I admired the unrepentant convict on whom the prison gates would always close; I'd visit the bars and boarding houses he would have consecrated with his presence. *With his eyes*, I saw the blue sky, the flourishing business of the countryside; I was on the trail of his fate in the city. He had more strength than a saint, a traveller's instincts, better even – he, and only he, had the measure of his pride and his integrity.

Sur les routes, par des nuits d'hiver, sans gîte, sans habits, sans pain, une voix étreignait mon cœur gelé: «Faiblesse ou force: te voilà, c'est la force. Tu ne sais ni où tu vas ni pourquoi tu vas, entre partout, réponds à tout. On ne te tuera pas plus que si tu étais cadavre.» Au matin j'avais le regard si perdu et la contenance si morte, que ceux que j'ai rencontrés *ne m'ont peut-être pas vu.*

Dans les villes la boue m'apparaissait soudainement rouge et noire, comme une glace quand la lampe circule dans la chambre voisine, comme un trésor dans la forêt! Bonne chance, criais-je, et je voyais une mer de flammes et de fumée au ciel; et, à gauche, à droite, toutes les richesses flambant comme un milliard de tonnerres.

Mais l'orgie et la camaraderie des femmes m'étaient interdites. Pas même un compagnon. Je me voyais devant une foule exaspérée, en face du peloton d'exécution, pleurant du malheur qu'ils n'aient pu comprendre, et pardonnant! – Comme Jeanne d'Arc! «Prêtres, professeurs, maîtres, vous vous trompez en me livrant à la justice. Je n'ai jamais été de ce peuple-ci; je n'ai jamais été chrétien; je suis de la race qui chantait dans le supplice; je ne comprends pas les lois; je n'ai pas le sens moral, je suis une brute: vous vous trompez . . .»

Oui, j'ai les yeux fermés à votre lumière. Je suis une bête, un nègre. Mais je puis être sauvé. Vous êtes de faux nègres, vous maniaques, féroces, avares. Marchand, tu es nègre; magistrat, tu es nègre; général, tu es nègre; empereur, vieille démangeaison, tu es nègre: tu as bu d'une liqueur non taxée, de la fabrique de Satan. – Ce peuple est inspiré par la fièvre et le cancer. Infirmes et vieillards sont tellement respectables qu'ils demandent à être bouillis. – Le plus malin est de quitter ce continent, où la folie rôde pour pourvoir d'otages ces misérables. J'entre au vrai royaume des enfants de Cham.

Connais-je encore la nature? me connais-je? – *Plus de mots.* J'ensevelis les morts dans mon ventre. Cris, tambour, danse, danse, danse, danse! Je ne vois même pas l'heure où, les blancs débarquant, je tomberai au néant.

On the road, on winter nights, no shelter, no clothes, no food, a voice would fasten on my heart: 'Weakness and strength: the fact is you are here – that much is strength. You don't know where you're going or why. Go everywhere, answer every greeting. You're no more likely to get yourself killed than if you were already a corpse.' In the morning, my eyes would be so blank, my expression so dead, that the people I encountered *may not even have seen me*.

The mud in the towns would seem to turn suddenly red and black, like a mirror when a lamp is carried about in the next-door room, like treasure in the forest. I'd call out, Good luck, and I'd visualize the sky as a reach of fire and smoke; to left and right, all known wealth was flaming like a billion thunderbolts.

But orgies and the fellowship of women were denied me. Not so much as a companion! I saw myself in front of an angry crowd, before a firing squad, weeping in my misery because they hadn't understood, and then forgiving them! Like Joan of Arc! – 'Priests, teachers, masters, handing me over to justice is a mistake. I was never one of you; I was never a Christian; I belong to a race that sang at the gallows. I've no grasp of the laws; no moral sense; I'm an animal; you're making a mistake . . .'

Yes, my eyes are shut against your light. I'm an animal, a nigger. But I can be saved. You people are all covert niggers, maniacs, savages, misers. Tradesman, you're a nigger; Judge, you're a nigger; General, you're a nigger; Emperor, you old pus ball, you're a nigger: you've slugged down contraband liquor from Satan's still. – This nation runs on ague and cancer. The sick and the elderly fawn and beg to be boiled alive. – On a continent where madness prowls in search of hostages for all these woeful characters, the smartest way is out. I shall enter the true kingdom of the sons of Ham.[3]

Have I begun to understand nature? Do I know myself? – *No more words*. I shall wall up the dead in my stomach. Whooping and drumming, dance, dance, dance, dance! I haven't yet foreseen the moment when the whites come ashore and I'm pitched into nothingness.

Faim, soif, cris, danse, danse, danse, danse!

Les blancs débarquent. Le canon! Il faut se soumettre au baptême, s'habiller, travailler.

J'ai reçu au cœur le coup de la grâce. Ah! je ne l'avais pas prévu!

Je n'ai point fait le mal. Les jours vont m'être légers, le repentir me sera épargné. Je n'aurai pas eu les tourments de l'âme presque morte au bien, où remonte la lumière sévère comme les cierges funéraires. Le sort du fils de famille, cercueil prématuré couvert de limpides larmes. Sans doute la débauche est bête, le vice est bête; il faut jeter la pourriture à l'écart. Mais l'horloge ne sera pas arrivée à ne plus sonner que l'heure de la pure douleur! Vais-je être enlevé comme un enfant, pour jouer au paradis dans l'oubli de tout le malheur!

Vite! est-il d'autres vies? – Le sommeil dans la richesse est impossible. La richesse a toujours été bien public. L'amour divin seul octroie les clefs de la science. Je vois que la nature n'est qu'un spectacle de bonté. Adieu chimères, idéals, erreurs.

Le chant raisonnable des anges s'élève du navire sauveur: c'est l'amour divin. – Deux amours! je puis mourir de l'amour terrestre, mourir de dévouement. J'ai laissé des âmes dont la peine s'accroîtra de mon départ! Vous me choisissez parmi les naufragés; ceux qui restent sont-ils pas mes amis?

Sauvez-les!

La raison m'est née. Le monde est bon. Je bénirai la vie. J'aimerai mes frères. Ce ne sont plus des promesses d'enfance. Ni l'espoir d'échapper à la vieillesse et à la mort. Dieu fait ma force, et je loue Dieu.

L'ennui n'est plus mon amour. Les rages, les débauches, la folie, dont je sais tous les élans et les désastres, – tout mon fardeau est déposé. Apprécions sans vertige l'étendue de mon innocence.

Je ne serais plus capable de demander le réconfort d'une bastonnade. Je ne me crois pas embarqué pour une noce avec Jésus-Christ pour beau-père.

Hunger, thirst, whooping and ... dance, dance, dance, dance!

The whites are landing. Cannon rounds! Next stop baptism, shirts and trousers, work.

A *coup de grâce* – through the heart. I hadn't reckoned on that.

I've done no wrong. My days will be easy. I'll be spared repentance. I shan't have had the torment of a soul almost dead to goodness, the grim light rising like funeral tapers. The fate of the son of good family – a premature coffin watered with limpid tears. Debauchery is stupid, of course, vice is stupid; corruption has to be cast out. But the clock has yet to reach the point when it can only strike the hour of pure pain! Shall I be carried away like a child, to revel in paradise, oblivious of all unhappiness?

Quick! Are there other lives to be led? The rich man – wealth has always been common property – sleeps fitfully. Divine love alone is the keeper of the key to knowledge. Nature, I can tell, is merely a show of goodness. Farewell to chimeras, ideals, errors.

The reasonable song of angels rises from the rescue ship; it is divine love. – Two loves! I can die of earthly love or die of devotion. I've left behind souls whose sorrow will grow in the wake of my departure. Among the castaways, you choose me; but those who remain, are they not my friends?

Save them!

Reason dawns on me. The world is good. I shall bless life! I shall love my neighbour. These are no longer childhood vows. Nor a trick to escape old age and death. God is my strength and God I praise.

I no longer go courting trouble. Fits of temper, debauchery, or madness, whose transports and disasters I know in full, – I lay down my burden, all of it. Now for a clear-headed reckoning of my innocence.

I can't any longer petition for the solace of a hiding. I don't delude myself that I'm lined up for a wedding feast with Jesus for a father-in-law.

Je ne suis pas prisonnier de ma raison. J'ai dit: Dieu. Je veux la liberté dans le salut: comment la poursuivre? Les goûts frivoles m'ont quitté. Plus besoin de dévouement ni d'amour divin. Je ne regrette pas le siècle des cœurs sensibles. Chacun a sa raison, mépris et charité: je retiens ma place au sommet de cette angélique échelle de bon sens.

Quant au bonheur établi, domestique ou non . . . non, je ne peux pas. Je suis trop dissipé, trop faible. La vie fleurit par le travail, vieille vérité: moi, ma vie n'est pas assez pesante, elle s'envole et flotte loin au-dessus de l'action, ce cher point du monde.

Comme je deviens vieille fille, à manquer du courage d'aimer la mort!

Si Dieu m'accordait le calme céleste, aérien, la prière, – comme les anciens saints. – Les saints! des forts! les anachorètes, des artistes comme il n'en faut plus!

Farce continuelle! Mon innocence me ferait pleurer. La vie est la farce à mener par tous.

Assez! voici la punition. – *En marche!*

Ah! les poumons brûlent, les tempes grondent! la nuit roule dans mes yeux, par ce soleil! le cœur . . . les membres . . .

Où va-t-on? au combat? Je suis faible! les autres avancent. Les outils, les armes . . . le temps! . . .

Feu! feu sur moi! Là! ou je me rends. – Lâches! – Je me tue! Je me jette aux pieds des chevaux!

Ah! . . .

– Je m'y habituerai.

Ce serait la vie française, le sentier de l'honneur!

Nuit de l'enfer

J'ai avalé une fameuse gorgée de poison. – Trois fois béni soit le conseil qui m'est arrivé! – Les entrailles me brûlent. La violence du venin tord mes membres, me rend difforme, me terrasse. Je meurs de soif, j'étouffe, je ne puis crier. C'est l'enfer, l'éternelle

I'm not a prisoner of my reason. I've said the word: God. I want freedom through salvation. How shall I attain it? I've lost the taste for frivolity. No need any more for devotion or divine love. I harbour no longings for the age of the sensitive soul. Contempt and charity – each is proper in its way; I cling to my place at the top, on the angelic ladder of good sense.

As for bedrock happiness, domestic or otherwise . . . No. I couldn't. I'm too far gone, too feeble. Life flourishes through work – an old truth: but my own life lacks weight, it's adrift, floating high above the focus of the world's admiration: action.

What an old woman I'm becoming: I haven't the guts to befriend death!

If God would grant me celestial, aethereal calm, and prayer – like the early saints – the saints! Those were people! Anchorites, artists of the kind we no longer require!

The farce goes on! I could weep at my gullibility. Living is a farce: we all play a part.

Enough! Now for the punishment: *Forward march!*

Ah! My lungs are burning, my temples throb! Darkness reels in my eyes, in spite of this sun! Heart! . . . limbs!

Where are we going? To battle? I'm weak! The others push onward. Tools, weapons . . . time! . . .

Fire! fire at me! Now! or I'll surrender. – Cowards! – I'll kill myself! Fling myself under the horses' hoofs.

Agh!

I'll get used to it.

That would be the French thing, the path of honour!

Night in Hell

I've swallowed a tremendous dose of poison. – Thrice blessed be the counsel I received! – My tripes are on fire. The strength of the poison racks my limbs, deforms me, knocks me flat. I'm dying of thirst, suffocating, I can't cry out. It's hell, eternal

peine! Voyez comme le feu se relève! Je brûle comme il faut. Va, démon!

J'avais entrevu la conversion au bien et au bonheur, le salut. Puis-je décrire la vision, l'air de l'enfer ne souffre pas les hymnes! C'était des millions de créatures charmantes, un suave concert spirituel, la force et la paix, les nobles ambitions, que sais-je?

Les nobles ambitions!

Et c'est encore la vie! – Si la damnation est éternelle! Un homme qui veut se mutiler est bien damné, n'est-ce pas? Je me crois en enfer, donc j'y suis. C'est l'exécution du catéchisme. Je suis esclave de mon baptême. Parents, vous avez fait mon malheur et vous avez fait le vôtre. Pauvre innocent! – L'enfer ne peut attaquer les païens. – C'est la vie encore! Plus tard, les délices de la damnation seront plus profondes. Un crime, vite, que je tombe au néant, de par la loi humaine.

Tais-toi, mais tais-toi! . . . C'est la honte, le reproche, ici: Satan qui dit que le feu est ignoble, que ma colère est affreusement sotte. – Assez! . . . Des erreurs qu'on me souffle, magies, parfums faux, musiques puériles. – Et dire que je tiens la vérité, que je vois la justice: j'ai un jugement sain et arrêté, je suis prêt pour la perfection . . . Orgueil. – La peau de ma tête se dessèche. Pitié! Seigneur, j'ai peur. J'ai soif, si soif! Ah! l'enfance, l'herbe, la pluie, le lac sur les pierres, *le clair de lune quand le clocher sonnait douze* . . . le diable est au clocher, à cette heure. Marie! Sainte-Vierge! . . . – Horreur de ma bêtise.

Là-bas, ne sont-ce pas des âmes honnêtes, qui me veulent du bien . . . Venez . . . J'ai un oreiller sur la bouche, elles ne m'entendent pas, ce sont des fantômes. Puis, jamais personne ne pense à autrui. Qu'on n'approche pas. Je sens le roussi, c'est certain.

Les hallucinations sont innombrables. C'est bien ce que j'ai toujours eu: plus de foi en l'histoire, l'oubli des principes. Je m'en tairai: poëtes et visionnaires seraient jaloux. Je suis mille fois le plus riche, soyons avare comme la mer.

Ah ça! l'horloge de la vie s'est arrêtée tout à l'heure. Je ne suis plus au monde. – La théologie est sérieuse, l'enfer est certainement *en bas* – et le ciel en haut. Extase, cauchemar, sommeil dans un nid de flammes.

torment! See the flames rise! I'm seared to perfection. Come on, demon!

I'd glimpsed the prospect of conversion – to goodness and happiness. How should I describe that vision? Hymns don't carry on the air of hell! There were millions of graceful creatures in elegant spiritual concert, strength and peace, noble ambitions, and I don't know what besides.

Noble ambitions!

All the same, still alive! – What if damnation is everlasting? A man who wants to mutilate himself is truly damned, isn't he? I think I'm in hell, therefore I am. That's the catechism for you. I'm the slave of my baptism. You, my parents – you've brought ruin on me, and yourselves. Poor innocent! – Hell spares heathens. – I am still alive! Later the delights of damnation will increase. Quick – a crime: that way I can be pitched into nothingness, in accordance with the laws of men.

Just shut up! Shame and reproach are the business here: Satan informs me that hellfire is undignified and my anger quite ridiculous – Stop! . . . The confidential rubbish I'm told; spells, false perfumes, nursery rhymes. – And to think I hold the truth, or understand justice: my judgement is sane and sound, I'm on the threshold of perfection . . . Pride. – The skin on my head is drying up. Mercy, I beg you. I'm afraid. So thirsty! Ah childhood, grass, rain, the stones in the lake, *the moonlight when the church clock sounded twelve* . . . the devil's in the belfry even now. Mary! Holy Virgin! . . . – The horror of my stupidity.

Over there, are those not honest souls, wishing me well? . . . Come . . . There's a pillow over my mouth, they can't hear me, they're phantoms. Anyway, no one cares about anyone else. Keep your distance. I reek of charred flesh, I'm sure I do.

Countless hallucinations! It's the story of my life: no more faith in history, principles abandoned. That's all I'll say: the poets and seers would be jealous. I'm a thousand times richer than them: I aim to hoard it all, like the sea.

Look! – Here. The clock of life has just stopped ticking. I'm no longer of the world. Theology's in earnest: Hell really is *down below*, and Heaven up there. – Ecstasy, nightmare, sleep in a nest of flames.

Que de malices dans l'attention dans la campagne . . . Satan, Ferdinand, court avec les graines sauvages . . . Jésus marche sur les ronces purpurines, sans les courber . . . Jésus marchait sur les eaux irritées. La lanterne nous le montra debout, blanc et des tresses brunes, au flanc d'une vague d'émeraude . . .

Je vais dévoiler tous les mystères: mystères religieux ou naturels, mort, naissance, avenir, passé, cosmogonie, néant. Je suis maître en fantasmagories.

Ecoutez! . . .

J'ai tous les talents! – Il n'y a personne ici et il y a quelqu'un: je ne voudrais pas répandre mon trésor. – Veut-on des chants nègres, des danses de houris? Veut-on que je disparaisse, que je plonge à la recherche de l'*anneau*? Veut-on? Je ferai de l'or, des remèdes.

Fiez-vous donc à moi, la foi soulage, guide, guérit. Tous, venez, – même les petits enfants, – que je vous console, qu'on répande pour vous son cœur, – le cœur merveilleux! – Pauvres hommes, travailleurs! Je ne demande pas de prières; avec votre confiance seulement, je serai heureux.

– Et pensons à moi. Ceci me fait peu regretter le monde. J'ai de la chance de ne pas souffrir plus. Ma vie ne fut que folies douces, c'est regrettable.

Bah! faisons toutes les grimaces imaginables.

Décidément, nous sommes hors du monde. Plus aucun son. Mon tact a disparu. Ah! mon château, ma Saxe, mon bois de saules. Les soirs, les matins, les nuits, les jours . . . Suis-je las!

Je devrais avoir mon enfer pour la colère, mon enfer pour l'orgueil, – et l'enfer de la caresse; un concert d'enfers.

Je meurs de lassitude. C'est le tombeau, je m'en vais aux vers, horreur de l'horreur! Satan, farceur, tu veux me dissoudre, avec tes charmes. Je réclame. Je réclame! un coup de fourche, une goutte de feu.

Ah! remonter à la vie! Jeter les yeux sur nos difformités. Et ce poison, ce baiser mille fois maudit! Ma faiblesse, la cruauté du monde! Mon Dieu, pitié, cachez-moi, je me tiens trop mal! – Je suis caché et je ne le suis pas.

C'est le feu qui se relève avec son damné.

Such tricks the mind plays, in the country ... Satan, Old Nick, swirling about with the wild pollen ... Jesus walking on the crimson brambles without bending them ... Jesus who walked on troubled waters. We saw him in the lamplight, all in white with long brown hair, on the flank of an emerald wave.

I shall now unveil all mysteries: religious or natural mysteries, death and life, the future, the past, cosmogony, nothingness. I'm a master of phantasmagoria.

Listen! ...

I have so many talents! There's no one here and there is someone: I'm not prepared to squander my treasure. – Are you after Negro chants? Oriental dancers? Want me to disappear, to dive in search of the *ring*? Shall I? I shall devise gold, and remedies.

Trust me, then. Faith is a balm, a guide, a healer. Come to me – even the little children – let me console you, let someone give his heart for you – the marvellous heart! – Poor men, who must work! I don't ask for your prayers; I shall be satisfied with your trust alone.

– And on the subject of myself. Few reasons in all this to mourn the world. I'm lucky my suffering is no worse. My life was so much sweet inanity – a shame.

Bah! Let's pull every horrifying face we can think of!

No doubt about it, we've left the world. Not a sound. My sense of touch is gone. Ah, my château, my Saxony, my willow groves! Evenings, mornings, nights, days ... so very tired!

I should have a hell for my anger, a hell for my pride – a hell for every caress; a proper symphony of hells.

I'm dying of fatigue. This is the grave, I'm off to the worms, horror of horrors! Satan, you scammer, you want to finish me off with your spells. I protest! I demand a stab of the pitchfork, a drop of fire.

Ah, to return to the living! To cast an eye over our deformity. And the poison, that kiss (damn it a thousand times)! My weakness, the cruelty of the world! God take pity on me, hide me, I'm not fit to be seen! – I'm hidden and I'm not hidden.

Look at the damned soul, feeding the flame.

Délires I. Vierge folle, l'époux infernal

Ecoutons la confession d'un compagnon d'enfer:

«O divin Epoux, mon Seigneur, ne refusez pas la confession de la plus triste de vos servantes. Je suis perdue. Je suis soûle. Je suis impure. Quelle vie!

«Pardon, divin Seigneur, pardon! Ah! pardon! Que de larmes! Et que de larmes encore plus tard, j'espère!

«Plus tard, je connaîtrai le divin Epoux! Je suis née soumise à Lui. – L'autre peut me battre maintenant!

«A présent, je suis au fond du monde! O mes amies! . . . non, pas mes amies . . . Jamais délires ni tortures semblables . . . Est-ce bête!

«Ah! je souffre, je crie. Je souffre vraiment. Tout pourtant m'est permis, chargée du mépris des plus méprisables cœurs.

«Enfin, faisons cette confidence, quitte à la répéter vingt autres fois, – aussi morne, aussi insignifiante!

«Je suis esclave de l'Epoux infernal, celui qui a perdu les vierges folles. C'est bien ce démon-là. Ce n'est pas un spectre, ce n'est pas un fantôme. Mais moi qui ai perdu la sagesse, qui suis damnée et morte au monde, – on ne me tuera pas! – Comment vous le décrire! Je ne sais même plus parler. Je suis en deuil, je pleure, j'ai peur. Un peu de fraîcheur. Seigneur, si vous voulez, si vous voulez bien!

«Je suis veuve . . . – J'étais veuve . . . – mais oui, j'ai été bien sérieuse jadis, et je ne suis pas née pour devenir squelette! . . . – Lui était presque un enfant . . . Ses délicatesses mystérieuses m'avaient séduite. J'ai oublié tout mon devoir humain pour le suivre. Quelle vie! La vraie vie est absente. Nous ne sommes pas au monde. Je vais où il va, il le faut. Et souvent il s'emporte contre moi, *moi, la pauvre âme*. Le Démon! – C'est un Démon, vous savez, *ce n'est pas un homme*.

«Il dit: «Je n'aime pas les femmes. L'amour est à réinventer, on le sait. Elles ne peuvent plus que vouloir une position assurée. La position gagnée, cœur et beauté sont mis de côté: il ne reste que froid dédain, l'aliment du mariage, aujourd'hui. Ou bien je vois des femmes, avec les signes du bonheur, dont, moi, j'aurais

Delirium I. Foolish Virgin, Infernal Groom[1]

Here follows the confession of an associate in hell:

'O Lord and heavenly Groom, do not spurn the confession of your most miserable handmaiden. I am lost. I am drunk. I'm impure. What a path!

'Forgive me, heavenly Lord, forgive me! Ah, forgive me! So much weeping! And so much weeping in store, I hope!

'Later I shall come to know the heavenly Groom! I was born to be His! – Meanwhile, this other groom can rain down blows on me!

'I've reached the lowest depths! You women friends! . . . Or rather, not-friends . . . There was never madness or torture like this . . . what folly!

'It hurts, and I cry out. It really hurts. Yet everything is permitted me, now that I'm despised by the most despicable of people.

'So, I venture this in confidence, even if I have to say it twenty times over – so dreary, so banal!

'I'm in thrall to the infernal Groom – the man who ruined all foolish virgins. That's the devil I'm talking about. Not a spectre or a ghost. But how can a woman like me, who has lost her reason, who is damned and dead to the world – nothing left in me to do away with – how should I describe him to you? Words fail me. I'm in mourning, I weep, I'm afraid. A breath of fresh air in here, Lord, if you wouldn't mind.

'I am a widow . . . I was a widow . . . oh yes, I was once a serious woman – I wasn't brought into the world to become a skeleton! . . . He, for his part, was little more than a child . . . His intriguing attentions had got the better of me. I forsook all my human obligations and followed him. What a path! The truth of life lies elsewhere. We are not in the realm of reality. I follow him wherever he goes; I have to. Often he has outbursts of anger – anger at me, *poor creature that I am*. Devil! – I mean, he's a Devil, *not a human being*.

'He says: "I don't like women. We must reinvent love, anyone knows that. Women want nothing nowadays but security. Once they have it, beauty and affection go by the board; there's only

pu faire de bonnes camarades, dévorées tout d'abord par des brutes sensibles comme des bûchers . . .»

«Je l'écoute faisant de l'infamie une gloire, de la cruauté un charme. «Je suis de race lointaine: mes pères étaient Scandinaves: ils se perçaient les côtes, buvaient leur sang. – Je me ferai des entailles partout le corps, je me tatouerai, je veux devenir hideux comme un Mongol: tu verras, je hurlerai dans les rues. Je veux devenir bien fou de rage. Ne me montre jamais de bijoux, je ramperais et me tordrais sur le tapis. Ma richesse, je la voudrais tachée de sang partout. Jamais je ne travaillerai . . .» Plusieurs nuits, son démon me saisissant, nous nous roulions, je luttais avec lui! – Les nuits, souvent, ivre, il se poste dans des rues ou dans des maisons, pour m'épouvanter mortellement. – «On me coupera vraiment le cou; ce sera dégoûtant.» Oh! ces jours où il veut marcher avec l'air du crime!

«Parfois il parle, en une façon de patois attendri, de la mort qui fait repentir, des malheureux qui existent certainement, des travaux pénibles, des départs qui déchirent les cœurs. Dans les bouges où nous nous enivrions, il pleurait en considérant ceux qui nous entouraient, bétail de la misère. Il relevait les ivrognes dans les rues noires. Il avait la pitié d'une mère méchante pour les petits enfants. – Il s'en allait avec des gentillesses de petite fille au catéchisme. – Il feignait d'être éclairé sur tout, commerce, art, médecine. – Je le suivais, il le faut!

«Je voyais tout le décor dont, en esprit, il s'entourait; vêtements, draps, meubles: je lui prêtais des armes, une autre figure. Je voyais tout ce qui le touchait, comme il aurait voulu le créer pour lui. Quand il me semblait avoir l'esprit inerte, je le suivais, moi, dans des actions étranges et compliquées, loin, bonnes ou mauvaises: j'étais sûre de ne jamais entrer dans son monde. A côté de son cher corps endormi, que d'heures des nuits j'ai veillé, cherchant pourquoi il voulait tant s'évader de la réalité. Jamais homme n'eut pareil vœu. Je reconnaissais, – sans craindre pour lui, – qu'il pouvait être un sérieux danger dans la société. – Il a peut-être des secrets pour *changer la vie*? Non, il ne fait qu'en chercher, me répliquais-je. Enfin sa charité

a cold disdain, the staple diet of marriage in our time. Or else I see women wearing the guise of happiness, with whom I could have forged real friendships, but they've already been guzzled by brutes with all the sensibility of a woodpile . . ."

'I hear him turn infamy into glory, cruelty into a magical attribute. "I belong to a distant race. My forefathers were Scandinavians; they pierced their sides and drank their own blood. – I shall cut grooves all over my body, tattoo it, I want to become as hideous as a Mongol: I'll run through the streets screaming, you'll see. I want to go quite mad with rage. Never let me see your jewels: I'll crawl and writhe on the carpet. I want my wealth thoroughly blood-stained. I shall never do an honest day's work . . ." On certain nights his spirit possessed me. We rolled about, locked in struggle! – Often at night he'll be drunk and hide somewhere in the street, or a house; he'll leap out at me, scare me witless. – "Someone's bound to slit my throat; it's going to be disgusting." God! the days he decides to prowl around with that look of criminal intent!

'Sometimes he speaks, in a touching patois, of death and repentance, the palpable existence of the wretched, miserable kinds of work, the heartbreak of parting. In the dens where we got drunk, he'd weep to observe the people around us, like long-suffering cattle. In dark streets he helped drunkards to their feet. His was the pity of the harsh mother for little children. – He would march off with the priggishness of a young girl attending catechism classes. – He affected a knowledge of everything, trade, art, medicine. – I followed him. I had to.

'I could see all the scenery with which he dressed his imagination: furniture, drapery, costumes: I decked him out with a coat of arms, a change of aspect. I could see everything that impressed him, just as he would have liked to create it. When I felt him succumb to lethargy, I'd follow him into strange, complicated undertakings, going all the way for good or ill. I knew I could never enter his world. How many nights, hour after hour, I've kept watch over his dear, sleeping body, trying to work out why he wanted so badly to escape from reality. No one ever had such a wish. I realized – without fearing for him – that he could be a

est ensorcelée, et j'en suis la prisonnière. Aucune autre âme
n'aurait assez de force, – force de désespoir! – pour la supporter,
– pour être protégée et aimée par lui. D'ailleurs, je ne me le
figurais pas avec une autre âme: on voit son Ange, jamais
l'Ange d'un autre, – je crois. J'étais dans son âme comme dans
un palais qu'on a vidé pour ne pas voir une personne si peu
noble que vous: voilà tout. Hélas! je dépendais bien de lui.
Mais que voulait-il avec mon existence terne et lâche? Il ne me
rendait pas meilleure, s'il ne me faisait pas mourir! Tristement
dépitée, je lui dis quelquefois: «Je te comprends.» Il haussait les
épaules.

«Ainsi, mon chagrin se renouvelant sans cesse, et me trouvant
plus égarée à mes yeux, – comme à tous les yeux qui auraient
voulu me fixer, si je n'eusse été condamnée pour jamais à l'oubli
de tous! – j'avais de plus en plus faim de sa bonté. Avec ses
baisers et ses étreintes amies, c'était bien un ciel, un sombre ciel,
où j'entrais, et où j'aurais voulu être laissée, pauvre, sourde,
muette, aveugle. Déjà j'en prenais l'habitude. Je nous voyais
comme deux bons enfants, libres de se promener dans le Paradis
de tristesse. Nous nous accordions. Bien émus, nous travaillions
ensemble. Mais, après une pénétrante caresse, il disait: «Comme
ça te paraîtra drôle, quand je n'y serai plus, ce par quoi tu as
passé. Quand tu n'auras plus mes bras sous ton cou, ni mon
cœur pour t'y reposer, ni cette bouche sur tes yeux. Parce qu'il
faudra que je m'en aille, très-loin, un jour. Puis il faut que
j'en aide d'autres: c'est mon devoir. Quoique ce ne soit guère
ragoûtant . . ., chère âme . . .» Tout de suite je me pressentais,
lui parti, en proie au vertige, précipitée dans l'ombre la plus
affreuse: la mort. Je lui faisais promettre qu'il ne me lâcherait
pas. Il l'a faite vingt fois, cette promesse d'amant. C'était aussi
frivole que moi lui disant: «Je te comprends.»

«Ah! je n'ai jamais été jalouse de lui. Il ne me quittera pas, je
crois. Que devenir? Il n'a pas une connaissance; il ne travaillera
jamais. Il veut vivre somnambule. Seules, sa bonté et sa charité
lui donneraient-elles droit dans le monde réel? Par instants,
j'oublie la pitié où je suis tombée: lui me rendra forte, nous
voyagerons, nous chasserons dans les déserts, nous dormirons

serious threat to society. – Perhaps he knows secrets that could *alter life itself*? No, I told myself, it's simply that he'd like to find them out. His charity is actually witchcraft and I am its prisoner. No other soul would have the strength – the strength of despair – to bear it, – to be favoured and loved by him. In any case I could never imagine him with anyone else: we can't see other people's Angels, only our own – or so I think. I lived in his soul as though in a palace which has been vacated in order to avoid the sight of just such inferior creatures as oneself. That's the essence of it. Damn it, I was so dependent on him. But what could he want with my lacklustre, spineless existence? He didn't make me any better, even if he failed to kill me! Sad and grudging, I'd say to him some-times: "I understand you." He would shrug his shoulders.

'So, with my unhappiness endlessly rekindled, and knowing myself more lost by the day – anybody could have seen it, had they thought to look at me closely, but I'd been consigned to oblivion by one and all – my hunger for his affection grew steadily worse. In his kisses, his tender embraces, I entered heaven, a dark heaven, and I'd willingly have stayed there, poor, deaf, dumb, blind. I was already getting used to it. I'd see us as a pair of happy children, wandering freely in our Paradise of sorrows. We were perfectly in tune. We worked as one, with deep emotion. But then, after a profoundly moving caress, he would say: "It'll seem very strange to you, when I'm no longer here, everything you've been through. You won't have my arms round your neck, or my heart to lay your head on, or my kisses on your eyes. And one of these days I will have to leave; I'll go miles away. Others need my help: it's my calling. Though I can't say I relish it, my dearest . . ." Right off I saw myself without him, seized by vertigo, pitched into the most terrifying darkness: death. I made him promise not to leave me. He must have made that lover's promise twenty times – as hollow as my own "I understand you."

'Not that I've ever been jealous of him. I don't believe he'll leave me. What would he do? He knows nobody; he'll never be able to work. He means to sleepwalk through life. Would his kindness and charity, on their own, assure him some kind of

sur les pavés des villes inconnues, sans soins, sans peines. Ou je me réveillerai, et les lois et les mœurs auront changé, – grâce à son pouvoir magique, – le monde, en restant le même, me laissera à mes désirs, joies, nonchalances. Oh! la vie d'aventures qui existe dans les livres des enfants, pour me récompenser, j'ai tant souffert, me la donneras-tu? Il ne peut pas. J'ignore son idéal. Il m'a dit avoir des regrets, des espoirs: cela ne doit pas me regarder. Parle-t-il à Dieu? Peut-être devrais-je m'adresser à Dieu. Je suis au plus profond de l'abîme, et je ne sais plus prier.

«S'il m'expliquait ses tristesses, les comprendrais-je plus que ses railleries? Il m'attaque, il passe des heures à me faire honte de tout ce qui m'a pu toucher au monde, et s'indigne si je pleure.

«– Tu vois cet élégant jeune homme, entrant dans la belle et calme maison: il s'appelle Duval, Dufour, Armand, Maurice, que sais-je? Une femme s'est dévouée à aimer ce méchant idiot: elle est morte, c'est certes une sainte au ciel, à présent. Tu me feras mourir comme il a fait mourir cette femme. C'est notre sort, à nous, cœurs charitables . . .» Hélas! il avait des jours où tous les hommes agissant lui paraissaient les jouets de délires grotesques; il riait affreusement, longtemps. – Puis, il reprenait ses manières de jeune mère, de sœur aimée. S'il était moins sauvage, nous serions sauvés! Mais sa douceur aussi est mortelle. Je lui suis soumise. – Ah! je suis folle!

«Un jour peut-être il disparaîtra merveilleusement; mais il faut que je sache, s'il doit remonter à un ciel, que je voie un peu l'assomption de mon petit ami!»

Drôle de ménage!

standing in the real world? There are times when I forget the
pathetic state I'm in: he'll fill me with strength, we'll travel, we'll
hunt in the wilderness, sleep on the pavements in unknown
cities, we'll be free and easy. Or I'll wake up to find that laws
and morals have changed – by virtue of his magical powers –
and the world, though still the same, will let me be, with my
desires, my joys, my strange indifference. Yes, the world of
adventure which only exists in children's books – can't you give
me that, by way of recompense? I've suffered so much. No. He
can't. And I can't conceive what his ideal world would be. He's
talked of his regrets and hopes, but I'm an irrelevance to both.
Does he speak to God? Perhaps I should appeal to God. I'm in the
deepest depths of the abyss . . . I no longer know how to pray.

'If he could explain what makes him sad, would I understand
it, any more than his jeering? He lays into me, he spends hours
making me ashamed of everything that's ever mattered to me.
Then he's shocked if I cry.

' "– See the chic young man going into that lovely, graceful
house? His name's Duval, or Dufour, or some such – an Armand
or a Maurice. Some woman once devoted herself to this worth-
less halfwit – to loving him – and now she's dead, undoubtedly
a saint in heaven. You'll be the death of me, just as he was the
death of her. That's our lot – those of us with selflessness in our
hearts." And then there were days when men and all their
business seemed to him the playthings of a grotesque delirium:
he would laugh long and terribly. – After which, he'd behave
once more like a young mother or a much-loved sister. If he
weren't so wild, we'd be saved! But his mildness is fatal, too. I
am in thrall to him. – I'm insane!

'One day, perhaps, there'll be a miracle and he'll disappear;
but I must have advance notice if he's being borne to heaven, so
I can get a glimpse of my boyfriend's assumption!'

Strange couple.

Délires II. Alchimie du verbe

A moi. L'histoire d'une de mes folies.

Depuis longtemps je me vantais de posséder tous les paysages possibles, et trouvais dérisoires les célébrités de la peinture et de la poésie moderne.

J'aimais les peintures idiotes, dessus de portes, décors, toiles de saltimbanques, enseignes, enluminures populaires; la littérature démodée, latin d'église, livres érotiques sans orthographe, romans de nos aïeules, contes de fées, petits livres de l'enfance, opéras vieux, refrains niais, rhythmes naïfs.

Je rêvais croisades, voyages de découvertes dont on n'a pas de relations, républiques sans histoires, guerres de religion étouffées, révolutions de mœurs, déplacements de races et de continents: je croyais à tous les enchantements.

J'inventai la couleur des voyelles! – *A* noir, *E* blanc, *I* rouge, *O* bleu, *U* vert. – Je réglai la forme et le mouvement de chaque consonne, et, avec des rhythmes instinctifs, je me flattai d'inventer un verbe poétique accessible, un jour ou l'autre, à tous les sens. Je réservais la traduction.

Ce fut d'abord une étude. J'écrivais des silences, des nuits, je notais l'inexprimable. Je fixais des vertiges.

*

Loin des oiseaux, des troupeaux, des villageoises,
Que buvais-je, à genoux dans cette bruyère
Entourée de tendres bois de noisetiers,
Dans un brouillard d'après-midi tiède et vert?

Que pouvais-je boire dans cette jeune Oise,
– Ormeaux sans voix, gazon sans fleurs, ciel couvert! –
Boire à ces gourdes jaunes, loin de ma case
Chérie? Quelque liqueur d'or qui fait suer.

Delirium II. Alchemy of the Word

My go. One of my insanities: an audit.

I had long boasted how the key to every conceivable scene was in my hands. I found the big names in modern painting and poetry quite laughable.

I liked idiotic paintings, motifs over doorways, stage sets, mummers' backdrops, inn-signs, popular colour prints; unfashionable literature, church Latin, erotic books with poor spelling, the novels our grandmothers read, fairy tales, small books for children, old operas, nonsensical refrains, galumphing rhythms.

I dreamed of crusades, voyages of discovery that were never recorded, republics with no history, suppressed wars of religion, revolutions in manners, a ferment of races and continents: I believed in each and every form of magic.

I invented colours for the vowels! – *A* black, *E* white, *I* red, *O* blue, *U* green. – I presided over the form and movement of every consonant and, making use of instinctive rhythms, I imagined I might invent a poetic language that would one day be accessible to all the senses. I would be the sole translator.

To begin with, I carried out a study. I committed silences and darknesses to paper, I recorded the inexpressible. I took the measure of vertigo.

*

Far from the birds and cattle, the village girls,
What was I drinking, as I knelt in that heather
Ringed by copses of budding hazel,
In the warm, green mist of afternoon?

What could I be drinking from that young Oise,
– Voiceless elms, flowerless grass, grey sky! –
From those yellow gourds, far from the lair
I loved? A golden brew that bathes you in sweat.

Je faisais une louche enseigne d'auberge.
– Un orage vint chasser le ciel. Au soir
L'eau des bois se perdait sur les sables vierges,
Le vent de Dieu jetait des glaçons aux mares;

Pleurant, je voyais de l'or – et ne pus boire. –

*

A quatre heures du matin, l'été,
Le sommeil d'amour dure encore.
Sous les bocages s'évapore
        L'odeur du soir fêté.

Là-bas, dans leur vaste chantier
Au soleil des Hespérides,
Déjà s'agitent – en bras de chemise –
        Les Charpentiers.

Dans leurs Déserts de mousse, tranquilles,
Ils préparent les lambris précieux
            Où la ville
        Peindra de faux cieux.

O, pour ces Ouvriers charmants
Sujets d'un roi de Babylone,
Vénus! quitte un instant les Amants
Dont l'âme est en couronne.

        O Reine des Bergers,
Porte aux travailleurs l'eau-de-vie,
Que leurs forces soient en paix
En attendant le bain dans la mer à midi.

*

La vieillerie poétique avait une bonne part dans mon alchimie
du verbe.

Je m'habituai à l'hallucination simple: je voyais très fran-
chement une mosquée à la place d'une usine, une école de

I had the air of a dubious inn-sign.
– A storm came on and swept out the sky. By evening
The woodland water had spent itself in virgin sand,
The wind of God flung ice into the ponds;

Through my tears I saw gold – and could not drink.

*

Four in the morning, summertime
And love still dozing.
In the groves the smell
          Of last night's revels fades away.

Down in the vast construction yards
Under the Hesperidean sun,
The Carpenters are already working,
          In their shirtsleeves.

At ease in their Deserts of moss,
They trim the priceless panels
                Which the city
                Will paint with artificial skies.

O Venus, leave the Lovers
And their souls in garlands, spare
A moment for these workers,
Charming subjects of a Babylonian king.

          O Queen of the Shepherds,
Fetch these labourers eau-de-vie
To pacify their strength
Until they bathe at midday in the sea.

*

Quaint poeticism played an important part in my alchemy of
the word.
   I grew used to basic hallucination: I would actually see a
mosque in place of a factory, a drummers' corps made up of

tambours faite par des anges, des calèches sur les routes du ciel, un salon au fond d'un lac; les monstres, les mystères; un titre de vaudeville dressait des épouvantes devant moi.

Puis j'expliquai mes sophismes magiques avec l'hallucination des mots!

Je finis par trouver sacré le désordre de mon esprit. J'étais oisif, en proie à une lourde fièvre: j'enviais la félicité des bêtes, – les chenilles, qui représentent l'innocence des limbes, les taupes, le sommeil de la virginité!

Mon caractère s'aigrissait. Je disais adieu au monde dans d'espèces de romances:

Chanson de la plus haute tour

Qu'il vienne, qu'il vienne,
Le temps dont on s'éprenne.

J'ai tant fait patience
Qu'à jamais j'oublie.
Craintes et souffrances
Aux cieux sont parties.
Et la soif malsaine
Obscurcit mes veines.

Qu'il vienne, qu'il vienne.
Le temps dont on s'éprenne.

Telle la prairie
A l'oubli livrée,
Grandie, et fleurie
D'encens et d'ivraies,
Au bourdon farouche
Des sales mouches.

Qu'il vienne, qu'il vienne,
Le temps dont on s'éprenne.

angels, coaches on the roads of the sky, a drawing-room at the bottom of a lake; monsters, mysteries; a vaudeville poster could conjure up a world of terrors.

And I divulged my magic sophisms by means of word-hallucination!

Finally I came to regard my mental disorder as something sacred. I grew idle, I succumbed to a leaden fever: I envied other creatures their happiness, – the caterpillar, symbol of the innocence of limbo, and the mole (the sleep of virginity)!

I became bitter. I took my leave of the world in unlikely ballads:

Song of the Highest Tower

Let it come, let it come,
The time we dote on.

I've waited so long
I've forgotten everything.
Pain and fear
Have vanished in thin air.
And a morbid thirst
Darkens my veins.

Let it come, let it come,
The time we dote on.

Like the wide meadow
Left untended,
Flowering high
With rosemary and rye,
And the brutal hum
Of blackening flies.

Let it come, let it come,
The time we dote on.

J'aimai le désert, les vergers brûlés, les boutiques fanées, les boissons tiédies. Je me traînais dans les ruelles puantes et, les yeux fermés, je m'offrais au soleil, dieu de feu.

«Général, s'il reste un vieux canon sur tes remparts en ruines, bombarde-nous avec des blocs de terre sèche. Aux glaces des magasins splendides! dans les salons! Fais manger sa poussière à la ville. Oxyde les gargouilles. Emplis les boudoirs de poudre de rubis brûlante . . .»

Oh! le moucheron enivré à la pissotière de l'auberge, amoureux de la bourrache, et que dissout un rayon!

Faim

Si j'ai du goût, ce n'est guère
Que pour la terre et les pierres.
Je déjeune toujours d'air,
De roc, de charbons, de fer.

Mes faims, tournez. Paissez, faims,
    Le pré des sons.
Attirez le gai venin
    Des liserons.

Mangez les cailloux qu'on brise,
Les vieilles pierres d'églises;
Les galets des vieux déluges,
Pains semés dans les vallées grises.

*

Le loup criait sous les feuilles
En crachant les belles plumes
De son repas de volailles:
Comme lui je me consume.

Les salades, les fruits
N'attendent que la cueillette;
Mais l'araignée de la haie
Ne mange que des violettes.

I loved emptiness and neglect, burned orchards, run-down shops, tepid drinks. I dragged myself through reeking alleyways, closed my eyes and offered myself up to the sun, the god of fire.

'General, if there's a decrepit cannon somewhere on your ruined ramparts, bombard us with clods of dried-up earth. Target the windows of sumptuous stores! Target drawing-rooms! Make the town eat its own dust. Make the drains rust. Fill the boudoirs with the smouldering powder of rubies . . .'

Oh! the gnat, a fool for borage, drunk in the piss-house of the village tavern, and dissolved in a ray of sunlight!

Hunger

What taste I have is for little
More than earth and stones.
I always dine on air,
Rock, coal and iron.

Turn, my hungers. Hungers, graze
      On fields of bran.
Suck up the blithe poison
      Of convolvulus.

Eat the broken flints,
Old masonry from churches,
Pebbles from ancient floods
Loaves slumped in the grey valleys.

*

The wolf howled in the cover
Spitting out bright feathers
From his feast of fowl.
Like him I consume myself.

Salad leaf and fruit –
There for the picking,
Yet the hedge-spider
Will only eat the violet.

Que je dorme! que je bouille
Aux autels de Salomon.
Le bouillon court sur la rouille,
Et se mêle au Cédron.

Enfin, ô bonheur, ô raison, j'écartai du ciel l'azur, qui est du
noir, et je vécus, étincelle d'or de la lumière *nature*. De joie, je
prenais une expression bouffonne et égarée au possible:

Elle est retrouvée!
Quoi? l'éternité.
C'est la mer mêlée
     Au soleil.

Mon âme éternelle,
Observe ton vœu
Malgré la nuit seule
Et le jour en feu.

Donc tu te dégages
Des humains suffrages,
Des communs élans!
Tu voles selon . . .

– Jamais l'espérance.
Pas d'*orietur*.
Science et patience,
Le supplice est sûr.

Plus de lendemain,
Braises de satin,
     Votre ardeur
     Est le devoir.

Elle est retrouvée!
– Quoi? – l'Eternité.
C'est la mer mêlée
     Au soleil.

> Let me sleep! Let me boil
> On the altars of Solomon.
> My stock seethes down the sides,
> Into the waters of the Kedron.[1]

Finally – O happiness and reason – I purged the sky of the blue which is blackness and lived as a golden spark of *natural* light. In my elation, I took on the most outlandish and absurd expression:

> Rediscovered!
> What? Eternity.
> The sun invaded
>   By the sea.
>
> Keep your vow,
> Eternal soul
> Through the bare night
> And fiery day . . .
>
> That way you're free
> Of public plaudits,
> Crass enthusiasms!
> Fly as you may . . .
>
> – No hope – not ever.
> No *orietur*.[2]
> Knowledge, patience,
> Torment certainly.
>
> No more tomorrow,
> Embers of silk,
>   Your heat
>   Is your only calling.
>
> Rediscovered!
> – What? – Eternity.
>   The sun invaded
>   By the sea.

*

Je devins un opéra fabuleux: je vis que tous les êtres ont une fatalité de bonheur: l'action n'est pas la vie, mais une façon de gâcher quelque force, un énervement. La morale est la faiblesse de la cervelle.

A chaque être, plusieurs *autres* vies me semblaient dues. Ce monsieur ne sait ce qu'il fait: il est un ange. Cette famille est une nichée de chiens. Devant plusieurs hommes, je causai tout haut avec un moment d'une de leurs autres vies. – Ainsi, j'ai aimé un porc.

Aucun des sophismes de la folie, – la folie qu'on enferme, – n'a été oublié par moi: je pourrais les redire tous, je tiens le système.

Ma santé fut menacée. La terreur venait. Je tombais dans des sommeils de plusieurs jours, et, levé, je continuais les rêves les plus tristes. J'étais mûr pour le trépas, et par une route de dangers ma faiblesse me menait aux confins du monde et de la Cimmérie, patrie de l'ombre et des tourbillons.

Je dus voyager, distraire les enchantements assemblés sur mon cerveau. Sur la mer, que j'aimais comme si elle eût dû me laver d'une souillure, je voyais se lever la croix consolatrice. J'avais été damné par l'arc-en-ciel. Le Bonheur était ma fatalité, mon remords, mon ver: ma vie serait toujours trop immense pour être dévouée à la force et à la beauté.

Le Bonheur! Sa dent, douce à la mort, m'avertissait au chant du coq, – *ad matutinum*, au *Christus venit*, – dans les plus sombres villes:

> O saisons, ô châteaux!
> Quelle âme est sans défauts?
>
> J'ai fait la magique étude
> Du bonheur, qu'aucun n'élude.
>
> Salut à lui, chaque fois
> Que chante le coq gaulois.

*

I became a fabulous opera: I saw that all creatures are driven to happiness: action isn't life but a way of running down one's strength, a strain on the nerves. Morality is a weakness of the brain.

To every being, it seemed to me, several *other* lives were due. Here's a gentleman who doesn't know what he's doing: he's an angel. Here's a family that's really a litter of dogs. In the company of several men, I conversed aloud with a moment of one of their other lives. – That's how I came to fall for a pig.

Not one of the sophistries of madness – the kind of madness that gets you put away – did I omit to study. I've got them all off, I could recite the lot.

My health was at risk. Terror was closing in. I fell into comas that lasted for days and when I woke, I continued dreaming the saddest dreams. I was fit for death; my weakness led along dangerous routes to the ends of the earth, to the marches of Cimmeria,[3] the home of shadows and whirlwinds.

I had to travel, to shake off the enchantments massing on my brain. Above the sea, which I loved as though it could cleanse me of some defilement, I saw the cross of consolations rise. I had been damned by the rainbow. Happiness was my lot, my remorse, my worm: my life would always be too vast to devote to strength and beauty.

Happiness! Its bite, so deathly sweet, alerted me at cockcrow – *ad matutinum*,[4] at the *Christus venit*[5] – in the darkest of cities:

> O seasons, O châteaux!
> Show me the soul as pure as snow.
>
> I've learned the magic spell
> Of happiness, which no one withstands.
>
> I toast it with every crow
> Of the Gallic cockerel.

Ah! je n'aurai plus d'envie:
Il s'est chargé de ma vie.

Ce charme a pris âme et corps
Et dispersé les efforts.

O saisons, ô châteaux!

L'heure de sa fuite, hélas!
Sera l'heure du trépas.

O saisons, ô châteaux!

*

Cela s'est passé. Je sais aujourd'hui saluer la beauté.

L'Impossible

Ah! cette vie de mon enfance, la grande route par tous les temps,
sobre surnaturellement, plus désintéressé que le meilleur des
mendiants, fier de n'avoir ni pays, ni amis, quelle sottise c'était.
– Et je m'en aperçois seulement!

– J'ai eu raison de mépriser ces bonshommes qui ne perdraient
pas l'occasion d'une caresse, parasites de la propreté et de la
santé de nos femmes, aujourd'hui qu'elles sont si peu d'accord
avec nous.

J'ai eu raison dans tous mes dédains: puisque je m'évade!

Je m'évade!

Je m'explique.

Hier encore, je soupirais: «Ciel! sommes-nous assez de
damnés ici-bas! Moi j'ai tant de temps déjà dans leur troupe! Je
les connais tous. Nous nous reconnaissons toujours; nous nous
dégoûtons. La charité nous est inconnue. Mais nous sommes
polis; nos relations avec le monde sont très-convenables.» Est-ce
étonnant? Le monde! les marchands, les naïfs! – Nous ne
sommes pas déshonorés. –

> Ah! I'll forget what it was to want.
> It's taken my life in hand.
>
> Body and soul are in its thrall –
> My efforts spent.
>
> O seasons, O châteaux!
>
> We die in the moment
> Of its dark farewell.
>
> O seasons, O châteaux!

*

But all that's finished. As for beauty, I know how to wish it a good day.

The Impossible

Ah! That life – the life of my childhood, the open road in all weathers, uncannily sober, more self-effacing than the finest beggar, proud to have no country, no friends. What junk it all was. And I've only just realized.

– I was right to scorn those simple souls who couldn't resist the chance of a fling, parasites on the cleanliness and health of our women, in these days when men and women are deeply at odds.

Right, too, to have scorned so much else – because I'm about to disappear!

To give you all the slip!

Allow me to explain.

Only yesterday, I was lamenting: 'God, we're a full house down here – us, the damned! I know everyone. There's no mistaking each other; we disgust each other. Charity is unheard of in our circles. But we're civil. Our dealings with people are perfectly proper.' Does it surprise you? 'People'! Boors and tradesmen! – We are not dishonoured. –

Mais les élus, comment nous recevraient-ils? Or il y a des gens hargneux et joyeux, de faux élus, puisqu'il nous faut de l'audace ou de l'humilité pour les aborder. Ce sont les seuls élus. Ce ne sont pas des bénisseurs!

M'étant retrouvé deux sous de raison – ça passe vite! – je vois que mes malaises viennent de ne m'être pas figuré assez tôt que nous sommes à l'Occident. Les marais occidentaux! Non que je croie la lumière altérée, la forme exténuée, le mouvement égaré ... Bon! voici que mon esprit veut absolument se charger de tous les développements cruels qu'a subis l'esprit depuis la fin de l'Orient ... Il en veut, mon esprit!

... Mes deux sous de raison sont finis! – L'esprit est autorité, il veut que je sois en Occident. Il faudrait le faire taire pour conclure comme je voulais.

J'envoyais au diable les palmes des martyrs, les rayons de l'art, l'orgueil des inventeurs, l'ardeur des pillards; je retournais à l'Orient et à la sagesse première et éternelle. – Il paraît que c'est un rêve de paresse grossière!

Pourtant, je ne songeais guère au plaisir d'échapper aux souffrances modernes. Je n'avais pas en vue la sagesse bâtarde du Coran. – Mais n'y a-t-il pas un supplice réel en ce que, depuis cette déclaration de la science, le christianisme, l'homme *se joue*, se prouve les évidences, se gonfle du plaisir de répéter ces preuves, et ne vit que comme cela! Torture subtile, niaise; source de mes divagations spirituelles. La nature pourrait s'ennuyer, peut-être! M. Prudhomme est né avec le Christ.

N'est-ce pas parce que nous cultivons la brume! Nous mangeons la fièvre avec nos légumes aqueux. Et l'ivrognerie! et le tabac! et l'ignorance! et les dévouements! – Tout cela est-il assez loin de la pensée de la sagesse de l'Orient, la patrie primitive? Pourquoi un monde moderne, si de pareils poisons s'inventent!

Les gens d'Eglise diront: C'est compris. Mais vous voulez parler de l'Eden. Rien pour vous dans l'histoire des peuples orientaux. – C'est vrai; c'est à l'Eden que je songeais! Qu'est-ce que c'est pour mon rêve, cette pureté des races antiques!

Les philosophes: Le monde n'a pas d'âge. L'humanité se déplace, simplement. Vous êtes en Occident, mais libre d'habiter

But the elect: now what sort of reception would we get from them? I mean, there are surly people and cheerful people, the phony elect, since you need audacity or humility to approach either. Yet they're the only elect. And they don't spread their blessings about!

Having recovered a modicum of sense – easily frittered away – I see how my troubles lie in a failure to realize sooner than I did that this is the West. That swampland! Not that I think the light's any worse, or the forms are superannuated, or the movement's wide of the mark ... Right! I'm resolved to take on all the cruel developments borne by the mind since the collapse of the East ... my insatiable mind!

... That's that for the modicum of sense. – The mind's in charge and it wants me in the West. For things to go the way I wished, it would have to be muzzled.

I used to think: to hell with martyrs' fronds, and the brilliance of art, the pride of the inventor, the frenzy of the plunderer; I turned to the East, to the fount of eternal wisdom. A woolly-minded, vulgar fantasy, it now transpires.

Still, I was hardly thinking of a pleasure-cruise away from modern suffering. Mongrel wisdoms from the Koran were not what I had in mind. – But there's real torment, surely, in the fact that ever since that great declaration of knowledge, Christianity, man has been *deluding himself*, bent on proving the self-evident, swelling with pride as he trots out the same proofs – the only life he knows! Insidious, mindless torture; the cause of my spiritual ramblings. Nature's bored stiff with it. Monsieur Prudhomme was born in the Manger.

It's all because we're in love with fog! We gulp down fevers with our soggy vegetables. And drink! Tobacco! Ignorance! Cults! – All of it far removed from the wisdom and thought of the Orient, our primal motherland. Why bother with a modern world, if it spawns so many poisons?

Men of the Church will say: Correct. But you're taking about Eden. There's nothing you can learn from the history of Oriental people. – Which is true. I *was* thinking of Eden! What does the purity of the ancient races have to do with my dream?

Philosophers will say: the world is ageless; humanity, simply,

dans votre Orient, quelque ancien qu'il vous le faille, – et d'y habiter bien. Ne soyez pas un vaincu. Philosophes, vous êtes de votre Occident.

Mon esprit, prends garde. Pas de partis de salut violents. Exerce-toi! – Ah! la science ne va pas assez vite pour nous!

– Mais je m'aperçois que mon esprit dort.

S'il était bien éveillé toujours à partir de ce moment, nous serions bientôt à la vérité, qui peut-être nous entoure avec ses anges pleurant! . . . – S'il avait été éveillé jusqu'à ce moment-ci, c'est que je n'aurais pas cédé aux instincts délétères, à une époque immémoriale! . . . – S'il avait toujours été bien éveillé, je voguerais en pleine sagesse! . . .

O pureté! pureté!

C'est cette minute d'éveil qui m'a donné la vision de la pureté! – Par l'esprit on va à Dieu!

Déchirante infortune!

L'Eclair

Le travail humain! c'est l'explosion qui éclaire mon abîme de temps en temps.

«Rien n'est vanité; à la science, et en avant!» crie l'Ecclésiaste moderne, c'est-à-dire *Tout le monde*. Et pourtant les cadavres des méchants et des fainéants tombent sur le cœur des autres . . . Ah! vite, vite un peu; là-bas, par delà la nuit, ces récompenses futures, éternelles . . . les échappons-nous? . . .

– Qu'y puis-je? Je connais le travail; et la science est trop lente. Que la prière galope et que la lumière gronde . . . je le vois bien. C'est trop simple, et il fait trop chaud; on se passera de moi. J'ai mon devoir, j'en serai fier à la façon de plusieurs, en le mettant de côté.

Ma vie est usée. Allons! feignons, fainéantons, ô pitié! Et nous existerons en nous amusant, en rêvant amours monstres et univers fantastiques, en nous plaignant et en querellant les apparences du monde, saltimbanque, mendiant, artiste, bandit, – prêtre! Sur mon lit d'hôpital, l'odeur de l'encens m'est

shifts its ground. You're in the West, yet you're free to invent your own Orient – it can be as ancient as you like – and live in it properly. Don't be so defeatist. Philosophers – your West is the place for you.

Mental caveat: no frantic dashes for salvation. Keep at it! – Science can't move quickly enough for us!

But I see my mind's asleep.

Were it to remain wide awake from this point on, we should quickly arrive at the truth, which may well be all around us now (its angels weeping)! Had it been alert a little earlier, I should not have yielded to debilitating instincts – to a time beyond all memory . . . Had it always been awake, I'd be running with the wind of full-blown wisdom!

Purity!

In this brief interval of waking, I've been granted the vision of purity! – We get to God by way of the mind!

An unbearable misfortune!

Lightning

Human labour! the explosion that lights up my abyss from time to time.

'Nothing is vanity; forward! – to knowledge,' cries the modern Ecclesiastes – *everyone*, in other words. Yet the bodies of the wicked and the idle still fall across the hearts of others . . . Come on. Hurry now! Over there, beyond the darkness, the eternal recompense that lies in store . . . are we to pass it up?

What can I do? I know about work; and science is too slow. That prayers gallop and the light rumbles on . . . I can see that. It's all too simple, and the weather's too warm; they'll have to do without me. I have my duty and like many others, I take pride in it, even as I set it to one side.

My life is threadbare. Come on then, let's fake it, let's be layabouts, for pity's sake! And we'll get by on a few diversions, on dreams of monstrous loves and fantastic universes, complaining, quarrelling with the world in all its guises: trickster, sponger, artist, bandit – priest! On my hospital bed, the smell revenue si puissante; gardien des aromates sacrés, confesseur, martyr . . .

Je reconnais là ma sale éducation d'enfance. Puis quoi! . . . Aller mes vingt ans, si les autres vont vingt ans . . .

Non! non! à présent je me révolte contre la mort! Le travail paraît trop léger à mon orgueil: ma trahison au monde serait un supplice trop court. Au dernier moment, j'attaquerais à droite, à gauche . . .

Alors, – oh! – chère pauvre âme, l'éternité serait-elle pas perdue pour nous!

Matin

N'eus-je pas *une fois* une jeunesse aimable, héroïque, fabuleuse, à écrire sur des feuilles d'or, – trop de chance! Par quel crime, par quelle erreur, ai-je mérité ma faiblesse actuelle? Vous qui prétendez que des bêtes poussent des sanglots de chagrin, que des malades désespèrent, que des morts rêvent mal, tâchez de raconter ma chute et mon sommeil. Moi, je ne puis pas plus m'expliquer que le mendiant avec ses continuels *Pater* et *Ave Maria. Je ne sais plus parler!*

Pourtant, aujourd'hui, je crois avoir fini la relation de mon enfer. C'était bien l'enfer; l'ancien, celui dont le fils de l'homme ouvrit les portes.

Du même désert, à la même nuit, toujours mes yeux las se réveillent à l'étoile d'argent, toujours, sans que s'émeuvent les Rois de la vie, les trois mages, le cœur, l'âme, l'esprit. Quand irons-nous, par-delà les grèves et les monts, saluer la naissance du travail nouveau, la sagesse nouvelle, la fuite des tyrans et des démons, la fin de la superstition, adorer – les premiers! – Noël sur la terre!

Le chant des cieux, la marche des peuples! Esclaves, ne maudissons pas la vie.

of incense returned to me with such power; keeper of the holy aromatics, confessor, martyr . . .

I recognize my foul upbringing at work there. Who cares? . . . I'll make it to twenty, if everyone else has the same plan . . .

No, no! Right now I'm up in arms against death! Work is too trifling for my kind of pride: the torture of betraying myself to the world would be too brief. At the last moment I'd lash out in all directions . . .

And then, my poor, sweet soul, we might have to do without eternity!

Morning

Did I not *once* have a pleasant youth, heroic, mythic, to be written on pages of gold – no such good fortune! What crime, what fault, condemned me to my present weakness? You who claim that animals sob with grief, that the sick despair, that the dead have bad dreams – try to tell the story of my fall, and my sleep. I can no more explain myself than the beggar, with his endless *Pater nosters* and *Ave Marias. I no longer know how to speak!*

And yet I think that today I've come to the end of my tale of hell. It was certainly hell; the old hell whose gates were opened by the Son of Man.

Out of the same desert, in the same darkness, always the silver star revives my weary eyes – and still no sign from the Kings of life, the three wise men, the heart, the soul, the mind. When shall we head beyond the shores and the mountains to greet the birth of the new work, the new wisdom, the rout of tyrants and demons, the end of superstition, and become the first worshippers to celebrate Christmas on earth!

The song of the heavens, the march of the nations! Slaves we remain, but let us not curse life.

Adieu

L'automne déjà! – Mais pourquoi regretter un éternel soleil, si nous sommes engagés à la découverte de la clarté divine, – loin des gens qui meurent sur les saisons.

L'automne. Notre barque élevée dans les brumes immobiles tourne vers le port de la misère, la cité énorme au ciel taché de feu et de boue. Ah! les haillons pourris, le pain trempé de pluie, l'ivresse, les mille amours qui m'ont crucifié! Elle ne finira donc point cette goule reine de millions d'âmes et de corps morts *et qui seront jugés!* Je me revois la peau rongée par la boue et la peste, des vers plein les cheveux et les aisselles et encore de plus gros vers dans le cœur, étendu parmi les inconnus sans âge, sans sentiment . . . J'aurais pu y mourir . . . L'affreuse évocation! J'exècre la misère.

Et je redoute l'hiver parce que c'est la saison du comfort!

– Quelquefois je vois au ciel des plages sans fin couvertes de blanches nations en joie. Un grand vaisseau d'or, au-dessus de moi, agite ses pavillons multicolores sous les brises du matin. J'ai créé toutes les fêtes, tous les triomphes, tous les drames. J'ai essayé d'inventer de nouvelles fleurs, de nouveaux astres, de nouvelles chairs, de nouvelles langues. J'ai cru acquérir des pouvoirs surnaturels. Eh bien! je dois enterrer mon imagination et mes souvenirs! Une belle gloire d'artiste et de conteur emportée!

Moi! moi qui me suis dit mage ou ange, dispensé de toute morale, je suis rendu au sol, avec un devoir à chercher, et la réalité rugueuse à étreindre! Paysan!

Suis-je trompé? la charité serait-elle sœur de la mort, pour moi?

Enfin, je demanderai pardon pour m'être nourri de mensonge. Et allons.

Mais pas une main amie! et où puiser le secours?

*

Oui, l'heure nouvelle est au moins très-sévère.

Car je puis dire que la victoire m'est acquise: les grincements de dents, les sifflements de feu, les soupirs empestés se modèrent.

Adieu

Autumn already! But why pine for an everlasting sun when we're embarked on the quest for divine light, far from those who die with the changing seasons.

Autumn. Our ship rises through the inert mists and swings towards the harbour of poverty, the enormous city with its fire-raked, filth-stained skies. The putrid rags, the bread soaked with rain, the drunkenness, the thousand loves that have crucified me! Will she never relent, this ghoul queen of a million dead in body and soul – *they will be judged!* I remember my skin gnawed by dirt and plague, worms seething in my hair and armpits, still bigger worms in my heart, laid out beside the nameless ones who have no age, no feeling . . . I could have died there . . . insufferable thought! I abhor poverty.

And I dread winter – season of snugness!

Sometimes, in the sky, I see endless beaches crowded with ecstatic white nations. Above me the multicoloured pennants of a great golden ship flutter in the morning breeze. I created every festival, every triumph, every drama. I tried to invent new flowers, new stars, new bodies, new tongues. I thought I had acquired supernatural powers. Well, now I must bury my imagination and my memories! So much for my fame as an artist and story-teller!

I – me! – who took myself for a magus or an angel, above morality! I'm firmly back on the ground, eager for tasks, for the rigours of the real! A peasant!

Or am I wrong? Could charity be the sister of death – in my case?

Anyhow, I'll beg forgiveness for my feast of lies. Let's go.

But there's no helping hand! And where will I turn?

*

The new era is nothing if not hard. Yes.

I consider I've won a victory: the gnashing of teeth, the hissing of flames, the pestilential sighs are dwindling. All the squalid

Tous les souvenirs immondes s'effacent. Mes derniers regrets détalent, – des jalousies pour les mendiants, les brigands, les amis de la mort, les arriérés de toutes sortes. – Damnés, si je me vengeais!

Il faut être absolument moderne.

Point de cantiques: tenir le pas gagné. Dure nuit! le sang séché fume sur ma face, et je n'ai rien derrière moi, que cet horrible arbrisseau! . . . Le combat spirituel est aussi brutal que la bataille d'hommes; mais la vision de la justice est le plaisir de Dieu seul.

Cependant c'est la veille. Recevons tous les influx de vigueur et de tendresse réelle. Et à l'aurore, armés d'une ardente patience, nous entrerons aux splendides villes.

Que parlais-je de main amie! Un bel avantage, c'est que je puis rire des vieilles amours mensongères, et frapper de honte ces couples menteurs, – j'ai vu l'enfer des femmes là-bas; – et il me sera loisible de *posséder la vérité dans une âme et un corps*.

avril–août, 1873

memories are fading. My last hankerings are disappearing fast
– my envy of beggars and bandits, lovers of death, backward
people of all kinds. – They'd be damned if I chose to take my
revenge.

One must be absolutely modern.

No hymn-singing: stand the hard-won ground. A testing
night! Dried blood smokes on my face and there's nothing at
my back but that horrible stunted tree![1] . . . The battle in the
mind is as ferocious as the battle of men; but the vision of justice
is for God's eyes only.

Yet this is the vigil. Accept every draught of strength and true
affection. Then at dawn, armed with a burning patience, we
shall enter the cities in all their splendour.

Why did I speak of a helping hand? My great advantage is
that I can laugh at the old infatuations – the lies – and put the
pretence of 'the couple' to shame: down in that place I saw the
hell of women. And now I shall be free *to possess the truth in
one soul and one body.*

April–August 1873

from ILLUMINATIONS

Après le Déluge

Aussitôt après que l'idée du Déluge se fut rassise,
   Un lièvre s'arrêta dans les sainfoins et les clochettes mouvantes et dit sa prière à l'arc-en-ciel à travers la toile de l'araignée.

Oh les pierres précieuses qui se cachaient, – les fleurs qui regardaient déjà.

Dans la grande rue sale les étals se dressèrent, et l'on tira les barques vers la mer étagée là-haut comme sur les gravures.

Le sang coula, chez Barbe-Bleue, – aux abattoirs, – dans les cirques, où le sceau de Dieu blêmit les fenêtres. Le sang et le lait coulèrent.

Les castors bâtirent. Les «mazagrans» fumèrent dans les estaminets.

Dans la grande maison de vitres encore ruisselante les enfants en deuil regardèrent les merveilleuses images.

Une porte claqua, et sur la place du hameau, l'enfant tourna ses bras, compris des girouettes et des coqs des clochers de partout, sous l'éclatante giboulée.

Madame *** établit un piano dans les Alpes. La messe et les premières communions se célébrèrent aux cent mille autels de la cathédrale.

Les caravanes partirent. Et le Splendide Hôtel fut bâti dans le chaos de glaces et de nuit du pôle.

Depuis lors, la Lune entendit les chacals piaulant par les déserts de thym, – et les églogues en sabots grognant dans le verger. Puis, dans la futaie violette, bourgeonnante, Eucharis me dit que c'était le printemps.

from ILLUMINATIONS

After the Flood

As soon as the idea of the Flood had abated,

A hare stopped in the clover and swaying flower-bells, and prayed to the rainbow, through the spider's web.

Oh! the precious stones that lay hidden – the flowers that began to open their eyes.

In the dirty high street, stalls were set up and boats were hauled to the sea, which rose like a staircase, as it does in old prints.

Blood flowed in Bluebeard's halls, – in the abattoirs – in circuses, where God's sign turned the windows cloudy. Blood and milk were flowing.

Beavers dammed. In the little bars, steam rose from liquor-laced coffees.

In the grand, glass-paned house, still awash with water, the children in mourning gazed at the marvellous pictures.

A door slammed and on the village square the child twirled his arms to general assent from weather-vanes and steeple-cocks, under a sudden, dazzling squall of rain.

Mme *** installed a piano in the Alps. Mass and first communion were celebrated at the hundred thousand altars of the cathedral.

The caravans moved off. And the Hotel Splendide was built in the chaos of ice and polar night.

From that time on, the Moon would hear jackals barking in the deserts of thyme – and flat-footed eclogues grunting in the orchard. Then, in the plum-coloured grove, all in bud, Eucharis[1] told me it was spring.

– Sourds, étang, – Ecume, roule sur le pont, et par dessus les bois; – draps noirs et orgues, – éclairs et tonnerre, – montez et roulez; – Eaux et tristesses, montez et relevez les Déluges.

Car depuis qu'ils se sont dissipés, – oh les pierres précieuses s'enfouissant, et les fleurs ouvertes! – c'est un ennui! et la Reine, la Sorcière qui allume sa braise dans le pot de terre, ne voudra jamais nous raconter ce qu'elle sait, et que nous ignorons.

Enfance

I

Cette idole, yeux noirs et crin jaune, sans parents ni cour, plus noble que la fable, mexicaine et flamande; son domaine, azur et verdure insolents, court sur des plages nommées, par des vagues sans vaisseaux, de noms férocement grecs, slaves, celtiques.

A la lisière de la forêt – les fleurs de rêve tintent, éclatent, éclairent, – la fille à lèvre d'orange, les genoux croisés dans le clair déluge qui sourd des prés, nudité qu'ombrent, traversent et habillent les arcs-en-ciel, la flore, la mer.

Dames qui tournoient sur les terrasses voisines de la mer; enfantes et géantes, superbes noires dans la mousse vert-de-gris, bijoux debout sur le sol gras des bosquets et des jardinets dégelés – jeunes mères et grandes sœurs aux regards pleins de pèlerinages, sultanes, princesses de démarche et de costume, tyranniques petites étrangères et personnes doucement malheureuses.

Quel ennui, l'heure du «cher corps» et «cher cœur».

II

C'est elle, la petite morte, derrière les rosiers. – La jeune maman trépassée descend le perron – La calèche du cousin crie sur le sable – Le petit frère – (il est aux Indes!) là, devant le couchant, sur le pré d'œillets. Les vieux qu'on a enterrés tout droits dans le rempart aux giroflées.

Pool, let your waters rise. Foam, roll over the bridge, over the woods – black palls and organs – lightnings, thunder – rise and roll – tides and sorrows, reinstate the Floods.

Since they've scattered – the precious stones digging their graves, the opened flowers! – life is dreary. And the Queen, the Witch who lights her fire in an earthen pot, will never consent to tell us what she knows – and we do not.

Childhood

I

That idol, black-eyed, yellow-maned, no kin, no court, nobler than fable, Mexican and Flemish: his domain – insolent green and azure – extends along beaches with fiercely Greek, or Slav, or Celtic names given them by unnavigable waves.

At the forest's edge – dream flowers jangle, split and flare – the girl with orange lips: her knees crossed in the clear spate pouring from the meadows, her nakedness shaded, traversed and clothed by rainbows, flora, sea.

Ladies circling on the terraces beside the sea; girls and giantesses, superbly black against the grey-green moss,[1] jewels set proud on the rich soil of the groves and little gardens after thaw – young mothers, older sisters, eyes brimming with pilgrimage, wives of Sultans, princesses of tyranny in their dress and their bearing, diminutive foreign women, people full of unpretentious sadness.

How trying when it comes, the moment for the routine kiss, the mechanical fondness.

II

That's her, the little dead girl behind the roses. – The youthful mamma, also dead, comes down the steps. – The cousin's carriage rasps on the sand. – There's the younger brother (away in the Indies!), with the sunset backdrop, on the field of pinks. – The old men buried upright in the rampart of wallflowers.

L'essaim des feuilles d'or entoure la maison du général. Ils sont dans le midi. – On suit la route rouge pour arriver à l'auberge vide. Le château est à vendre; les persiennes sont détachées. – Le curé aura emporté la clef de l'église. – Autour du parc, les loges des gardes sont inhabitées. Les palissades sont si hautes qu'on ne voit que les cimes bruissantes. D'ailleurs il n'y a rien à voir là-dedans.

Les prés remontent aux hameaux sans coqs, sans enclumes. L'écluse est levée. O les calvaires et les moulins du désert, les îles et les meules.

Des fleurs magiques bourdonnaient. Les talus *le* berçaient. Des bêtes d'une élégance fabuleuse circulaient. Les nuées s'amassaient sur la haute mer faite d'une éternité de chaudes larmes.

III

Au bois il y a un oiseau, son chant vous arrête et vous fait rougir.

Il y a une horloge qui ne sonne pas.

Il y a une fondrière avec un nid de bêtes blanches.

Il y a une cathédrale qui descend et un lac qui monte.

Il y a une petite voiture abandonnée dans le taillis, ou qui descend le sentier en courant, enrubannée.

Il y a une troupe de petits comédiens en costumes, aperçus sur la route à travers la lisière du bois.

Il y a enfin, quand l'on a faim et soif, quelqu'un qui vous chasse.

IV

Je suis le saint, en prière sur la terrasse, – comme les bêtes pacifiques paissent jusqu'à la mer de Palestine.

Je suis le savant au fauteuil sombre. Les branches et la pluie se jettent à la croisée de la bibliothèque.

Je suis le piéton de la grand'route par les bois nains; la rumeur des écluses couvre mes pas. Je vois longtemps la mélancolique lessive d'or du couchant.

Je serais bien l'enfant abandonné sur la jetée partie à la

The swarm of golden leaves encircles the general's quarters. They're down in the South. – You take the red road till you come to the disused inn. The grand house is for sale; its shutters are falling off. – The priest must have removed the key to the church. – The keepers' lodges on the estate are empty. The rustling treetops are all you glimpse over the tall fences. Nothing to be seen in there anyhow.

The fields slope up to villages without cockerels or anvils. The sluice gates are shut. Oh the Calvaries, the mills turning in the wilderness, the islands and hayricks!

A droning of magical flowers. And *him* – rocked by the slopes. Beasts on the prowl, fabulously suave. Clouds massing above the high sea, an eternity of warm tears.

III

In the wood there is a bird; you stop and blush at its song.

There is a clock which doesn't strike.

There is a dip in the ground with a nest of white animals.

There is a descending cathedral and a rising lake.

There is a little cart abandoned in the copse, or coming down the lane, covered in ribbons.

There is a troupe of little actors, in costume, spotted on the road through the edge of the wood.

There is someone, finally, to chase you away when you're tired and thirsty.

IV

I am the saint praying on the terrace – as the meek animals graze down to the Sea of Palestine.

I am the scholar in the dark armchair. Rain and foliage batter at the library window.

I am the traveller on the high road through the stunted trees; the sound of the lock-water drowns my footsteps. For a good while I watch the melancholy, golden wash of sunset.

I could well be the child abandoned on the jetty, torn away

haute mer, le petit valet, suivant l'allée dont le front touche le ciel.

Les sentiers sont âpres. Les monticules se couvrent de genêts. L'air est immobile. Que les oiseaux et les sources sont loin! Ce ne peut être que la fin du monde, en avançant.

V

Qu'on me loue enfin ce tombeau, blanchi à la chaux avec les lignes du ciment en relief – très loin sous terre.

Je m'accoude à la table, la lampe éclaire très vivement ces journaux que je suis idiot de relire, ces livres sans intérêt.

A une distance énorme au-dessus de mon salon souterrain, les maisons s'implantent, les brumes s'assemblent. La boue est rouge ou noire. Ville monstrueuse, nuit sans fin!

Moins haut, sont des égouts. Aux côtés, rien que l'épaisseur du globe. Peut-être des gouffres d'azur, des puits de feu. C'est peut-être sur ces plans que se rencontrent lunes et comètes, mers et fables.

Aux heures d'amertume je m'imagine des boules de saphir, de métal. Je suis maître du silence. Pourquoi une apparence de soupirail blêmirait-elle au coin de la voûte?

Vies

I

O les énormes avenues du pays saint, les terrasses du temple! Qu'a-t-on fait du brahmane qui m'expliqua les Proverbes? D'alors, de là-bas, je vois encore même les vieilles! Je me souviens des heures d'argent et de soleil vers les fleuves, la main de la campagne sur mon épaule, et de nos caresses debout dans les plaines poivrées. – Un envol de pigeons écarlates tonne autour de ma pensée – Exilé ici j'ai eu une scène où jouer les chefs-d'œuvre dramatiques de toutes les littératures. Je vous indiquerais les richesses inouïes. J'observe l'histoire des trésors que vous

and heading out to sea, the little servant boy following the lane which crests in the sky.

The paths are rough. Broom grows on the hillocks. The air is still. The birds seem so distant, and the springs! If you keep going, it can only be the end of the world.

V

They can rent me out this tomb, then, with cement lines picked out on whitewash – very deep in the ground.

I plant my elbows on the table, the lamplight glares on these newspapers which I'm an idiot to reread, and these mediocre books.

Way above my earth-walled sitting room, houses spread their roots, mists convene. The mud is red or black. Monstrous city, night without end!

Slightly nearer are the sewers. All around, only the thickness of the globe. Chasms of azure maybe, wells of fire. It's perhaps at these levels that moons clash with comets, or oceans with fables.

In more bitter moments, I imagine balls of sapphire, or metal. I'm master of the silence. What is that feeble gleam at the corner of the ceiling-vault, like light through a vent?

Lives

I

Oh the vast avenues of the holy land, the terraces of the temple! What became of the Brahmin who explained the Proverbs to me? I can even see the old women, from that time, in that place! I remember hours of silver and sunlight, near the river, the landscape with its arm around my shoulder, our caresses, as we stood on the spiced plains. – A flock of scarlet pigeons thunders around my thoughts. – Exiled now, I once had a stage on which to perform the great dramatic works of all literatures. I could show you unbelievable riches. I duly acknowledge the history

trouvâtes. Je vois la suite! Ma sagesse est aussi dédaignée que le chaos. Qu'est mon néant, auprès de la stupeur qui vous attend?

II

Je suis un inventeur bien autrement méritant que tous ceux qui m'ont précédé; un musicien même, qui ai trouvé quelque chose comme la clef de l'amour. A présent, gentilhomme d'une campagne aigre au ciel sobre, j'essaye de m'émouvoir au souvenir de l'enfance mendiante, de l'apprentissage ou de l'arrivée en sabots, des polémiques, des cinq ou six veuvages, et quelques noces où ma forte tête m'empêcha de monter au diapason des camarades. Je ne regrette pas ma vieille part de gaîté divine: l'air sobre de cette aigre campagne alimente fort activement mon atroce scepticisme. Mais comme ce scepticisme ne peut désormais être mis en œuvre, et que d'ailleurs je suis dévoué à un trouble nouveau, – j'attends de devenir un très méchant fou.

III

Dans un grenier où je fus enfermé à douze ans j'ai connu le monde, j'ai illustré la comédie humaine. Dans un cellier j'ai appris l'histoire. A quelque fête de nuit dans une cité du Nord j'ai rencontré toutes les femmes des anciens peintres. Dans un vieux passage à Paris on m'a enseigné les sciences classiques. Dans une magnifique demeure cernée par l'Orient entier j'ai accompli mon immense œuvre et passé mon illustre retraite. J'ai brassé mon sang. Mon devoir m'est remis. Il ne faut même plus songer à cela. Je suis réellement d'outre-tombe, et pas de commissions.

of the treasures you unearthed. I know what comes next! My wisdom is held in the same contempt as chaos. What is my nothingness, compared to the stupor that awaits you?

II

My merits as an inventor are quite different from those of my predecessors – a musician, you could venture, who has discovered something like the key of love. Presently a member of the landed gentry, in harsh countryside under sober skies, I should like to wax emotional about the memory of my pauper childhood, of an apprenticeship and turning up in clogs, of controversy, of five or six widowings and several wild sessions when a strong head kept me back from the fullness of pitch attained by my fellow drinkers. I don't regret my erstwhile share of divine high spirits: the sober air of this harsh landscape feeds my atrocious scepticism all too well. But since that scepticism no longer serves any purpose, and because I am now in the grip of a new uneasiness, I suspect my madness will be very ugly.

III

Shut up in an attic at the age of twelve, I came to know the world; I illustrated the human comedy. I learned my history in a store room. At some night-time festival in a Northern city, I met all the wives and women of the old painters. In a crumbling Paris backstreet, I was taught the classical sciences. In a magnificent dwelling surrounded by the entire Orient I completed my vast opus and sat out my illustrious retirement. I stirred my blood up. I have been relieved of my responsibilities. No point even thinking about them. I am really from beyond the grave; no debts outstanding.

Départ

Assez vu. La vision s'est rencontrée à tous les airs.

Assez eu. Rumeurs des villes, le soir, et au soleil, et toujours.

Assez connu. Les arrêts de la vie. – O Rumeurs et Visions!

Départ dans l'affection et le bruit neufs!

A une raison

Un coup de ton doigt sur le tambour décharge tous les sons et commence la nouvelle harmonie.

Un pas de toi, c'est la levée des nouveaux hommes et leur en-marche.

Ta tête se détourne: le nouvel amour! Ta tête se retourne, – le nouvel amour!

«Change nos lots, crible les fléaux, à commencer par le temps», te chantent ces enfants. «Elève n'importe où la substance de nos fortunes et de nos vœux» on t'en prie.

Arrivée de toujours, qui t'en iras partout.

Matinée d'ivresse

O mon Bien! ô mon Beau! Fanfare atroce où je ne trébuche point! chevalet féerique! Hourra pour l'œuvre inouïe et pour le corps merveilleux, pour la première fois! Cela commença sous les rires des enfants, cela finira par eux. Ce poison va rester dans toutes nos veines même quand, la fanfare tournant, nous serons rendu à l'ancienne inharmonie. O maintenant, nous si digne de ces tortures! rassemblons fervemment cette promesse surhumaine faite à notre corps et à notre âme créés: cette promesse, cette démence! L'élégance, la science, la violence! On nous a promis d'enterrer dans l'ombre l'arbre du bien et du mal, de déporter les honnêtetés tyranniques, afin que nous amenions

Departure

Seen enough. The vision was there in every light.

Had enough. City rumblings off in the distance, at dusk, in full-on sunlight, every which way.

Known enough. The strictures of life. O Rumblings and Visions!

Departure imminent, by way of new affection, new sounds.

To a Version of Reason

One tap of your finger on the drum releases every timbre and founds the new harmony.

You take a step and new men materialize; they march out.

You turn your head away: the new love! You turn back: the new love!

'Alter our destiny,' you hear these children sing. 'Stamp out plagues! Stamp out Time, for a start!' Everyone begs you: 'Raise the substance of our fortunes, our desires, wherever you can.'

You – fresh out of forever. Making for everywhere.

Morning of Intoxication

My Good! *My* Beauty! Atrocious fanfare – but I do not falter! Enchanted rack! Salute the undreamed-of work and the marvellous body, for the first time! It began with children laughing and so it will end. This poison will remain in all our veins even when the fanfare goes blowsy and we're back with the old dissonance. Let us now – we who deserve these tortures – passionately reaffirm the superhuman promise we made to our bodies and souls, as created: that promise, that madness! Elegance, knowledge, violence! We've been promised that the tree of good and evil will be buried in darkness, that tyrannical proprieties shall be banished, to make way for our love of the

notre très pur amour. Cela commença par quelques dégoûts et cela finit, – ne pouvant nous saisir sur-le-champ de cette éternité, – cela finit par une débandade de parfums.

Rire des enfants, discrétion des esclaves, austérité des vierges, horreur des figures et des objets d'ici, sacrés soyez-vous par le souvenir de cette veille. Cela commençait par toute la rustrerie, voici que cela finit par des anges de flamme et de glace.

Petite veille d'ivresse, sainte! quand ce ne serait que pour le masque dont tu nous as gratifié. Nous t'affirmons, méthode! Nous n'oublions pas que tu as glorifié hier chacun de nos âges. Nous avons foi au poison. Nous savons donner notre vie tout entière tous les jours.

Voici le temps des *Assassins*.

Fragments du feuillet 12

Une matinée couverte, en Juillet. Un goût de cendres vole dans l'air; – une odeur de bois suant dans l'âtre, – les fleurs rouies, – le saccage des promenades – la bruine des canaux par les champs – pourquoi pas déjà les joujoux et l'encens?

*

J'ai tendu des cordes de clocher à clocher; des guirlandes de fenêtre à fenêtre; des chaînes d'or d'étoile à étoile, et je danse.

*

Le haut étang fume continuellement. Quelle sorcière va se dresser sur le couchant blanc? Quelles violettes frondaisons vont descendre?

*

Pendant que les fonds publics s'écoulent en fêtes de fraternité, il sonne une cloche de feu rose dans les nuages.

*

Avivant un agréable goût d'encre de Chine une poudre noire pleut doucement sur ma veillée, – je baisse les feux du lustre, je

highest purity. It began with aversions and it ended – unable as we are to seize this eternity here and now – it ended in a riot of perfumes.

Laughter of children, discretion of slaves, austerity of virgins, horror of the faces and objects in this place, may you be hallowed by the memory of this vigil. It began in utter boorishness; see how it ends, in angels of fire and ice.

Little drunken vigil, holy! if only for the mask you've granted us. Method, we endorse you! We have not forgotten how you glorified our every age. We have faith in the poison. We know how to offer up our life, day after day, entire.

This is the time of the *Assassins*.[1]

Fragments/12[1]

An overcast morning in July. A taste of ashes drifts on the air – a smell of wood sweating in the hearth – flowers well drenched – the pillaged walkways – the drizzle of canals across the fields – why not baubles and incense, now!

*

I've hung ropes from belfry to belfry, garlands from window to window, golden chains from star to star, and I am dancing.

*

Endless steam off the highland pond. What witch will flare into view against the white sunset? What violet foliage will fall from the trees?

*

While public monies are lavished on festivals of brotherhood, a bell of crimson fire tolls in the clouds.

*

Exuding a pleasant flavour of Indian ink, a black powder rains softly down on my vigil. – I lower the gas-lamp, throw myself

me jette sur le lit, et tourné du côté de l'ombre, je vous vois, mes filles! mes reines!

Ouvriers

O cette chaude matinée de février. Le Sud inopportun vint relever nos souvenirs d'indigents absurdes, notre jeune misère.

Henrika avait une jupe de coton à carreau blanc et brun, qui a dû être portée au siècle dernier, un bonnet à rubans, et un foulard de soie. C'était bien plus triste qu'un deuil. Nous faisions un tour dans la banlieue. Le temps était couvert, et ce vent du Sud excitait toutes les vilaines odeurs des jardins ravagés et des prés desséchés.

Cela ne devait pas fatiguer ma femme au même point que moi. Dans une flache laissée par l'inondation du mois précédent à un sentier assez haut elle me fit remarquer de très petits poissons.

La ville, avec sa fumée et ses bruits de métiers, nous suivait très loin dans les chemins. O l'autre monde, l'habitation bénie par le ciel et les ombrages! Le sud me rappelait les misérables incidents de mon enfance, mes désespoirs d'été, l'horrible quant-ité de force et de science que le sort a toujours éloignée de moi. Non! nous ne passerons pas l'été dans cet avare pays où nous ne serons jamais que des orphelins fiancés. Je veux que ce bras durci ne traîne plus *une chère image*.

Les Ponts

Des ciels gris de cristal. Un bizarre dessin de ponts, ceux-ci droits, ceux-là bombés, d'autres descendant ou obliquant en angles sur les premiers, et ces figures se renouvelant dans les autres circuits éclairés du canal, mais tous tellement longs et légers que les rives chargées de dômes s'abaissent et s'amoin-drissent. Quelques-uns de ces ponts sont encore chargés de masures. D'autres soutiennent des mâts, des signaux, de frêles

on my bed and, with my face towards the shadows, I see you, my girls! my queens!

Workers

That warm February morning! An unseasonable South wind revived the memories of our ludicrous poverty, our youth of misery.

Henrika[1] wore a cotton skirt, brown and white check, no doubt from the previous century, a bonnet with ribbons and a silk scarf. It was sadder than a funeral. We were strolling on the outskirts of the town. It was overcast and that wind from the South whipped up the foul smells from the ravaged gardens and withered fields.

It can't have wearied my wife as much as it did me. In a slick of water left by the floods of the previous month, on a path quite high up, she drew my attention to some tiny fish.

The city – the smoke and hubbub of the workshops – went with us, far on our way. Oh the other world – a dwelling place blessed by sky and shaded trees! The South wind carried me back to the bleak episodes of childhood, my summers of despair, the horrifying reserves of strength and knowledge from which fate has always kept me at a distance. No! We shall not spend the summer in this mean place where we'll never be more than betrothed orphans. I won't have my work-hardened arm dragging round some *cherished fantasy*.

The Bridges

Grey crystal skies. A strange disposition of bridges, some straight, some convex, others slanting down, obliquely angled to the first, these patterns repeated in other, lamp-lit stretches of the canal, but each bridge so long and light that the banks, laden with domes, subside and shrink. Some of these bridges are still covered with hovels. Others support masts, signals, frail parapets. Minor chords cross over and fade; lengths of rope rise

parapets. Des accords mineurs se croisent, et filent, des cordes montent des berges. On distingue une veste rouge, peut-être d'autres costumes et des instruments de musique. Sont-ce des airs populaires, des bouts de concerts seigneuriaux, des restants d'hymnes publics? L'eau est grise et bleue, large comme un bras de mer. – Un rayon blanc, tombant du haut du ciel, anéantit cette comédie.

Ville

Je suis un éphémère et point trop mécontent citoyen d'une métropole crue moderne parce que tout goût connu a été éludé dans les ameublements et l'extérieur des maisons aussi bien que dans le plan de la ville. Ici vous ne signaleriez les traces d'aucun monument de superstition. La morale et la langue sont réduites à leur plus simple expression, enfin! Ces millions de gens qui n'ont pas besoin de se connaître amènent si pareillement l'éducation, le métier et la vieillesse, que ce cours de vie doit être plusieurs fois moins long que ce qu'une statistique folle trouve pour les peuples du continent. Aussi comme, de ma fenêtre, je vois des spectres nouveaux roulant à travers l'épaisse et éternelle fumée de charbon, – notre ombre des bois, notre nuit d'été! – des Erinnyes nouvelles, devant mon cottage qui est ma patrie et tout mon cœur puisque tout ici ressemble à ceci, – la Mort sans pleurs, notre active fille et servante, et un Amour désespéré, et un joli Crime piaulant dans la boue de la rue.

Villes (I)

L'acropole officielle outre les conceptions de la barbarie moderne les plus colossales. Impossible d'exprimer le jour mat produit par le ciel immuablement gris, l'éclat impérial des bâtisses, et la neige éternelle du sol. On a reproduit dans un goût d'énormité singulier toutes les merveilles classiques de l'architecture. J'assiste à des expositions de peinture dans des locaux vingt fois plus vastes qu'Hampton-Court. Quelle

from the banks. You can make out a red jacket, maybe other bits of clothing, and musical instruments. Are these popular tunes, snatches of a concert in the stately home, the tatters of public anthems? The water is grey and blue, wide as a stretch of sea. A ray of white light, falling from high in the sky, obliterates this dumbshow.

City

I am an ephemeral and none-too-disgruntled citizen of a metropolis reckoned to be modern because all standards of taste have been avoided in the decoration of the houses, and their exteriors, and indeed in the layout of the city. No trace here of any monuments to superstition. Morals and language have at last been reduced to their most basic expression! The millions of people who have no reason to know one another pursue their education, their work and their old age in such similar ways that their lifespan must be many times shorter than a lunatic set of statistics suggests about the peoples of the continent. And so from my window I see new spectres rolling through the dense eternity of coal smoke – our woodland shade, our summer night-sky – new Erinyes,[1] in front of my cottage, I mean my homeland and all my heart, because everything now looks much the same – dry-eyed Death, our assiduous daughter and servant, a desperate Love, and a juicy Crime cheeping in the filth-ridden streets.

Cities (I)[1]

The official acropolis surpasses the most colossal conceptions of modern barbarity. Impossible to describe the dull light produced by unchanging grey sky, the imperial glint of the buildings and the eternal snow on the ground. All the classical wonders of architecture have been reproduced in decidedly outrageous taste. I go to art exhibitions in places twenty times the size of Hampton Court. What paintings! A Norwegian

peinture! Un Nabuchodonosor norwégien a fait construire les escaliers des ministères; les subalternes que j'ai pu voir sont déjà plus fiers que des Brahmas et j'ai tremblé à l'aspect de colosses des gardiens et officiers de constructions. Par le groupement des bâtiments en squares, cours et terrasses fermées, on a évincé les cochers. Les parcs représentent la nature primitive travaillée par un art superbe. Le haut quartier a des parties inexplicables: un bras de mer, sans bateaux, roule sa nappe de grésil bleu entre des quais chargés de candélabres géants. Un pont court conduit à une poterne immédiatement sous le dôme de la Sainte-Chapelle. Ce dôme est une armature d'acier artistique de quinze mille pieds de diamètre environ.

Sur quelques points des passerelles de cuivre, des plates-formes, des escaliers qui contournent les halles et les piliers, j'ai cru pouvoir juger la profondeur de la ville! C'est le prodige dont je n'ai pu me rendre compte: quels sont les niveaux des autres quartiers sur ou sous l'acropole? Pour l'étranger de notre temps la reconnaissance est impossible. Le quartier commerçant est un circus d'un seul style, avec galeries à arcades. On ne voit pas de boutiques. Mais la neige de la chaussée est écrasée; quelques nababs aussi rares que les promeneurs d'un matin de dimanche à Londres, se dirigent vers une diligence de diamants. Quelques divans de velours rouge: on sert des boissons polaires dont le prix varie de huit cents à huit mille roupies. A l'idée de chercher des théâtres sur ce circus, je me réponds que les boutiques doivent contenir des drames assez sombres. Je pense qu'il y a une police, mais la loi doit être tellement étrange, que je renonce à me faire une idée des aventuriers d'ici.

Le faubourg aussi élégant qu'une belle rue de Paris est favorisé d'un air de lumière. L'élément démocratique compte quelques cents âmes. Là encore les maisons ne se suivent pas; le faubourg se perd bizarrement dans la campagne, le «Comté» qui remplit l'occident éternel des forêts et des plantations prodigieuses où les gentilshommes sauvages chassent leurs chroniques sous la lumière qu'on a créée.

Nebuchadnezzar[2] has commissioned the stairways in the Minis-
tries; the minor officials I was able to see are already prouder
than Brahmas,[3] while the look of the keepers beside the colossi,
and of the works officials, made me shudder. The arrangement
of buildings in squares, courtyards and closed-off terraces has
forced out the cabbies. The parks are models of primitive nature
shaped by a marvellous art. Parts of the better neighbourhoods
are inexplicable: a stretch of sea, without shipping, rolled out
like a bolt of blue sleet, between quays crammed with giant
candelabra. A small bridge leads to a postern immediately below
the dome of the Sainte-Chapelle.[4] This dome is an armature of
modelled steel some fifteen thousand feet across.

From certain points on the copper footbridges, the platforms
and staircases winding round the stalls and columns, I thought
I could judge the depth of the city! Here is the marvel I could
not elucidate: how far above or below the acropolis are the
other districts? The modern stranger cannot get his bearings.
The commercial district is built in a circle, all in one style, with
galleries of arcades. No stores to be seen, though the snow on
the streets is trudged down. A few nabobs, as rare as strollers
on a Sunday morning in London, make their way towards a
diamond coach. A few divans, in red velvet. Arctic drinks are
available for anything between eight hundred and eight thousand rupees. I might look for a theatre, somewhere in this circle,
but then, I decide, there'll be some pretty torrid dramas in the
shops. I think there's a police force, but the laws must be so
strange that I give up trying to imagine what the criminal classes
are like.

Towards the periphery, there is all the elegance of a fine street
in Paris, and a welcome impression of light. The democratic
element amounts to a few hundred souls. Here again, the houses
are not set in rows; the outskirts blur oddly into the countryside,
the 'County' that fills the everlasting west with forests and
massive plantations, where a savage gentry hunts through its
genealogies with the help of artificial light.

Vagabonds

Pitoyable frère! Que d'atroces veillées je lui dus! «Je ne me saisissais pas fervemment de cette entreprise. Je m'étais joué de son infirmité. Par ma faute nous retournerions en exil, en esclavage.» Il me supposait un guignon et une innocence très bizarres, et il ajoutait des raisons inquiétantes.

Je répondais en ricanant à ce satanique docteur, et finissais par gagner la fenêtre. Je créais, par delà la campagne traversée par des bandes de musique rare, les fantômes du futur luxe nocturne.

Après cette distraction vaguement hygiénique, je m'étendais sur une paillasse. Et, presque chaque nuit, aussitôt endormi, le pauvre frère se levait, la bouche pourrie, les yeux arrachés, – tel qu'il se rêvait! – et me tirait dans la salle en hurlant son songe de chagrin idiot.

J'avais en effet, en toute sincérité d'esprit, pris l'engagement de le rendre à son état primitif de fils du soleil, – et nous errions, nourris du vin des cavernes et du biscuit de la route, moi pressé de trouver le lieu et la formule.

Veillées

I

C'est le repos éclairé, ni fièvre ni langueur, sur le lit ou sur le pré.

C'est l'ami ni ardent ni faible. L'ami.

C'est l'aimée ni tourmentante ni tourmentée. L'aimée.

L'air et le monde point cherchés. La vie.

– Etait-ce donc ceci?

– Et le rêve fraîchit.

Tramps

Pitiful brother! What atrocious nights of sleeplessness he caused me! 'I was not all that wild to embark on this venture. I mocked his weakness. I'd be to blame if we went back into exile – into slavery.' He imagined I had the strangest ill-luck and innocence, and came up with disturbing explanations.

My reply was to sneer at this satanic scholar; in the end I would move to the window. Beyond the landscape traversed by lines of unearthly music, I would invoke the phantoms of the night-time luxury which lay ahead.

After this vaguely hygienic diversion, I would stretch out on a straw mattress. And almost every night, as soon as I was asleep, my poor brother would get up – stinking mouth and gouged eyes, exactly as he dreamt of himself – and drag me into the room, howling his dream of idiotic grief.

I'd actually undertaken, in all sincerity, to restore him to his original state as a child of the sun – and so we wandered, living on the wine of caverns and the crusts of travellers, as I stepped up my search for the place and the formula.

Vigils[1]

I

This is luminous repose, neither fever nor languor, in a bed or a meadow.

This is the friend, neither cool nor importunate. Friend.

This is the loved one, neither tormentor nor tormented. Loved one.

Air and world, in no way sought for. Life.

– So it was this?

– And the dream comes on.

II

L'éclairage revient à l'arbre de bâtisse. Des deux extrémités de la salle, décors quelconques, des élévations harmoniques se joignent. La muraille en face du veilleur est une succession psychologique de coupes de frises, de bandes atmosphériques et d'accidences géologiques. – Rêve intense et rapide de groupes sentimentaux avec des êtres de tous les caractères parmi toutes les apparences.

III

Les lampes et les tapis de la veillée font le bruit des vagues, la nuit, le long de la coque et autour du steerage.

La mer de la veillée, telle que les seins d'Amélie.

Les tapisseries, jusqu'à mi-hauteur, des taillis de dentelle, teinte d'émeraude, où se jettent les tourterelles de la veillée.

....

La plaque du foyer noir, de réels soleils des grèves: ah! puits des magies; seule vue d'aurore, cette fois.

Aube

J'ai embrassé l'aube d'été.

Rien ne bougeait encore au front des palais. L'eau était morte. Les camps d'ombres ne quittaient pas la route du bois. J'ai marché, réveillant les haleines vives et tièdes, et les pierreries regardèrent, et les ailes se levèrent sans bruit.

La première entreprise fut, dans le sentier déjà empli de frais et blêmes éclats, une fleur qui me dit son nom.

Je ris au wasserfall blond qui s'échevela à travers les sapins: à la cime argentée je reconnus la déesse.

Alors je levai un à un les voiles. Dans l'allée, en agitant les bras. Par la plaine, où je l'ai dénoncée au coq. A la grand'ville elle fuyait parmi les clochers et les dômes, et courant comme un mendiant sur les quais de marbre, je la chassais.

II

Light reverts, over the central joist. From the two ends of the
room, unremarkable motifs, harmonic elevations that meet. The
wall facing the observer is a psychological sequence of friezes in
cross-section, atmospheric seams, geological strata. – A vivid,
fleeting dream, with sentimental groups . . . beings of all kinds,
in every conceivable guise.

III

The lamps and hearthrugs of the vigil sound like waves along
the hull at night and deep below decks.

Sea of the vigil, like Amélie's breasts.

The wall-hangings, up to halfway, an undergrowth of
emerald-tinted lace where the doves of the vigil dart.

....

On the fireback in the blackened hearth, real suns on coastal
strands: ah! wells of magic; only the one glimpse of dawn this
time.

Dawn

I have embraced the summer dawn.

Nothing stirred on the palace façades. The water was dead.
The shadow-camps on the woodland road were not yet struck.
Warm living breaths were roused as I walked, and the precious
stones gazed on, the wings rose in silence.

The first engagement, on the path where cool, pale light
already played, was a flower that told me its name.

I laughed in front of the blond wasserfall,[1] its hair unkempt
in the pines: on its silver summit I recognized the goddess.

Then I lifted the veils, one by one. Down the footpath, arms
waving. Out on level ground, where I denounced her to the
cockerel. In the city she fled among the domes and bell-towers
and I ran like a beggar on the marble quays, in close pursuit.

En haut de la route, près d'un bois de lauriers, je l'ai entourée avec ses voiles amassés, et j'ai senti un peu son immense corps. L'aube et l'enfant tombèrent au bas du bois.

Au réveil il était midi.

Marine

Les chars d'argent et de cuivre –
Les proues d'acier et d'argent –
Battent l'écume, –
Soulèvent les souches des ronces.
Les courants de la lande,
Et les ornières immenses du reflux
Filent circulairement vers l'est,
Vers les piliers de la forêt, –
Vers les fûts de la jetée,
Dont l'angle est heurté par des tourbillons de
    lumière.

Barbare

Bien après les jours et les saisons, et les êtres et les pays,

Le pavillon en viande saignante sur la soie des mers et des fleurs arctiques; (elles n'existent pas.)

Remis des vieilles fanfares d'héroïsme – qui nous attaquent encore le cœur et la tête – loin des anciens assassins –

Oh! Le pavillon en viande saignante sur la soie des mers et des fleurs arctiques; (elles n'existent pas)

Douceurs!

Les brasiers pleuvant aux rafales de givre, – Douceurs! – les feux à la pluie du vent de diamants jetée par le cœur terrestre éternellement carbonisé pour nous. – O monde! –

(Loin des vieilles retraites et des vieilles flammes, qu'on entend, qu'on sent,)

At the top of the road, by a laurel grove, I wrapped myself around her, with her gathered veils, and had an intimation of her huge body. At the bottom of the grove, Dawn and the child fell to the ground.

When I woke it was noon.

Seascape

> Chariots of silver and copper –
> Prows of steel and silver –
> Pound the foam –
> Wrench the thorn-stumps out.
> The currents of this heath
> And the huge ruts of the ebb-tide
> Spiral away to the east,
> Towards the pillared forest
> And the piles of the jetty,
> Its corner pummelled by whirlwinds of light.

Barbaric

Long after the days and seasons, the creatures and countries,

The ensign of bleeding meat on the silk of the seas and the Arctic flowers; (they do not exist.)

Delivered from the old fanfares of heroism – which still assault our hearts and heads – far from the old assassins.

– Oh! The ensign of bleeding meat on the silk of the seas and the Arctic flowers; (they do not exist.)

Sweetness!

Fiery coals, raining down in volleys of frost, – Sweetness! – fires in the gusting rain of diamonds flung out of the earth's core, forever charring in our honour – World! –

(Far from the old haunts and old flames, which we hear and feel),

Les brasiers et les écumes. La musique, virement des gouffres et choc des glaçons aux astres.

O Douceurs, ô monde, ô musique! Et là, les formes, les sueurs, les chevelures et les yeux, flottant. Et les larmes blanches, bouillantes, – ô douceurs! – et la voix féminine arrivée au fond des volcans et des grottes arctiques.

Le pavillon . . .

Solde

A vendre ce que les Juifs n'ont pas vendu, ce que noblesse ni crime n'ont goûté, ce qu'ignorent l'amour maudit et la probité infernale des masses: ce que le temps ni la science n'ont pas à reconnaître:

Les Voix reconstituées; l'éveil fraternel de toutes les énergies chorales et orchestrales et leurs applications instantanées; l'occasion, unique, de dégager nos sens!

A vendre les Corps sans prix, hors de toute race, de tout monde, de tout sexe, de toute descendance! Les richesses jaillissant à chaque démarche! Solde de diamants sans contrôle!

A vendre l'anarchie pour les masses; la satisfaction irrépressible pour les amateurs supérieurs; la mort atroce pour les fidèles et les amants!

A vendre les habitations et les migrations, sports, féeries et comforts parfaits, et le bruit, le mouvement et l'avenir qu'ils font!

A vendre les applications de calcul et les sauts d'harmonie inouïs. Les trouvailles et les termes non soupçonnés, possession immédiate,

Elan insensé et infini aux splendeurs invisibles, aux délices insensibles, – et ses secrets affolants pour chaque vice – et sa gaîté effrayante pour la foule –

– A vendre les Corps, les voix, l'immense opulence inquestionable, ce qu'on ne vendra jamais. Les vendeurs ne sont pas à bout de solde! Les voyageurs n'ont pas à rendre leur commission de si tôt!

Blazing fire and foam. Music, spiralling gulfs, the smack of icicles against the stars.

Sweetness! World! Music! And there, the shapes, the sweatings, the heads of hair and the eyes, floating. And white tears, boiling – sweetness! – and the female voice that reaches to volcanic depths and Arctic caverns.

The ensign . . .

Sale

For sale: what the Jews have not sold, what nobility or crime has not tasted, what accursed love and the infernal propriety of the masses do not know; what time or knowledge doesn't need to bother with.

The Voices reconstituted; the fraternal awakening of every choral and orchestral energy and its immediate application; the opportunity – the only one – to liberate our senses!

For sale: priceless Bodies, unknown in any race or world or sex or lineage! Riches gushing at every step! Unregulated auctions of diamonds!

For sale: anarchy for the masses, irrepressible satisfaction for the aficionado, a terrible death for the faithful, and for lovers!

For sale: homelands and migrations, games, perfect comfort, perfect enchantments, and the noise, the movement, the future in which they conspire.

For sale: the uses of calculus; wild harmonic leaps; unsuspected terminologies; chance discoveries – ownership with immediate effect,

A senseless, incessant impulse (its secret maddens every vice; its gaiety strikes terror in the crowd) towards invisible splendours, insensible delights –

For sale: Bodies, voices, immense opulence beyond dispute, things that will never be sold. The vendors have plenty of stock to clear. No need for speculators to settle up this minute!

Jeunesse

I

DIMANCHE

Les calculs de côté, l'inévitable descente du ciel et la visite des souvenirs et la séance des rythmes occupent la demeure, la tête et le monde de l'esprit.

– Un cheval détale sur le turf suburbain, et le long des cultures et des boisements, percé par la peste carbonique. Une misérable femme de drame, quelque part dans le monde, soupire après des abandons improbables. Les desperadoes languissent après l'orage, l'ivresse et les blessures. De petits enfants étouffent des malédictions le long des rivières. –

Reprenons l'étude au bruit de l'œuvre dévorante qui se rassemble et remonte dans les masses.

II

SONNET

Homme de constitution ordinaire, la chair
n'était-elle pas un fruit pendu dans le verger; – ô
journées enfantes! – le corps un trésor à prodiguer; – ô
aimer, le péril ou la force de Psyché? La terre
avait des versants fertiles en princes et en artistes
et la descendance et la race vous poussaient aux
crimes et aux deuils: le monde votre fortune et votre
péril. Mais à présent, ce labeur comblé, – toi, tes calculs,
– toi, tes impatiences – ne sont plus que votre danse et
votre voix, non fixées et point forcées, quoique d'un double
événement d'invention et de succès + une raison,
– en l'humanité fraternelle et discrète par l'univers,
sans images; – la force et le droit réfléchissent la
danse et la voix à présent seulement appréciées.

Youth

I

SUNDAY

Set the sums to one side; the inevitable descent from the sky, the séance of memories and rhythms takes charge of the house, the head, and the life of the mind.

– A horse bolts on the suburban race-course, out past the fields and forests, stricken with carbonic plague. A miserable woman straight from some play, somewhere in the world, yearns for unlikely sexual abandon. Desperadoes languish after storms, drunkenness and wounds. Along the rivers little children stifle curses. –

Back to our studies and the thrum of the consuming project as it gathers and rises among the masses.

II

SONNET

Man of average constitution, was the flesh not
a fruit hanging in the orchard; – O
childhood days! – the body a treasure to squander; – O
loving, Psyche's[1] peril or her strength? The earth's
slopes were fat with princes and artists,
lineage and race drove you to
crime and mourning: the world is your fortune and your
jeopardy. But now your toil is over, you, your calculations
– you, your impatience – are no more than your dancing and
your voice, not fixed, not forced, though reason
enough for the double outcome of success + ingenuity
– in humanity, fraternal and discreet, throughout the
imageless universe; – might and justice mirror your
dancing and your voice, only now achieving recognition.

III

VINGT ANS

Les voix instructives exilées . . . L'ingénuité physique amèrement
rassise . . . – Adagio – Ah! l'égoïsme infini de l'adolescence,
l'optimisme studieux: que le monde était plein de fleurs cet été!
Les airs et les formes mourant . . . – Un chœur, pour calmer
l'impuissance et l'absence! Un chœur de verres, de mélodies
nocturnes . . . En effet les nerfs vont vite chasser.

IV

Tu en es encore à la tentation d'Antoine. L'ébat du zèle écourté,
les tics d'orgueil puéril, l'affaissement et l'effroi.

Mais tu te mettras à ce travail: toutes les possibilités
harmoniques et architecturales s'émouvront autour de ton siège.
Des êtres parfaits, imprévus, s'offriront à tes expériences. Dans
tes environs affluera rêveusement la curiosité d'anciennes foules
et de luxes oisifs. Ta mémoire et tes sens ne seront que la
nourriture de ton impulsion créatrice. Quant au monde, quand
tu sortiras, que sera-t-il devenu? En tout cas, rien des apparences
actuelles.

Promontoire

L'aube d'or et la soirée frissonnante trouvent notre brick en
large en face de cette villa et de ses dépendances, qui forment un
promontoire aussi étendu que l'Epire et le Péloponnèse, ou que
la grande île du Japon, ou que l'Arabie! Des fanums qu'éclaire
la rentrée des théories, d'immenses vues de la défense des côtes
modernes; des dunes illustrées de chaudes fleurs et de baccha-
nales; de grands canaux de Carthage et des Embankments d'une
Venise louche; de molles éruptions d'Etnas et des crevasses de
fleurs et d'eaux des glaciers; des lavoirs entourés de peupliers
d'Allemagne; des talus de parcs singuliers penchant des têtes

III

TWENTY YEARS OLD

The voices of instruction cast out . . . Physical innocence brought harshly to order . . . Adagio. Ah! the infinite egotism of adolescence, the diligence, the optimism: how full of flowers the world was that summer! Dying airs, dying forms . . . – A choir, to soothe helplessness and absence! A choir of glasses, of nocturnal melodies . . . Our nerves, of course, will soon be in tatters.

IV

You're still stuck at the temptation of St Anthony.[2] The wild enthusiasms waning, the grimaces of puerile pride, the fatigue and terror.

But you will not shirk this business: all harmonic and architectural possibilities will churn around you. Perfect, unenvisaged beings will volunteer for your experiments. The curiosity of ancient crowds and idle luxuries will hover dreamily about you. Your memory and senses will serve no other purpose than your impulse to create. And what will the world be like, when you venture out? Quite unlike the way it looks now.

Promontory

The golden dawn and the tremor of evening discover our brig near the coast, and this villa in prospect, with its outlying buildings, forming a promontory as long as Epirus[1] and the Peloponnese or the great island of Japan, or Arabia! Shrines lit up by returning processions; immense views of the well-defended modern coastline; dunes studded with torrid flowers and bacchanals; great Carthaginian waterways and louche Venetian embankments; Etnas erupting lamely, crevasses of flowers and glacial melt-water; wash-houses girdled with German poplars; Trees of Japan, their heads lolling on the slopes of

d'Arbre du Japon; les façades circulaires des «Royal» ou des «Grand» de Scarbro' ou de Brooklyn; et leurs railways flanquent, creusent, surplombent les dispositions de cet Hôtel, choisies dans l'histoire des plus élégantes et des plus colossales constructions de l'Italie, de l'Amérique et de l'Asie, dont les fenêtres et les terrasses à présent pleines d'éclairages, de boissons et de brises riches, sont ouvertes à l'esprit des voyageurs et des nobles – qui permettent, aux heures du jour, à toutes les tarentelles des côtes, – et même aux ritournelles des vallées illustres de l'art, de décorer merveilleusement les façades du Palais. Promontoire.

Soir historique

En quelque soir, par exemple, que se trouve le touriste naïf, retiré de nos horreurs économiques, la main d'un maître anime le clavecin des prés; on joue aux cartes au fond de l'étang, miroir évocateur des reines et des mignonnes, on a les saintes, les voiles, et les fils d'harmonie, et les chromatismes légendaires, sur le couchant.

Il frissonne au passage des chasses et des hordes. La comédie goutte sur les tréteaux de gazon. Et l'embarras des pauvres et des faibles sur ces plans stupides!

A sa vision esclave, – l'Allemagne s'échafaude vers des lunes; les déserts tartares s'éclairent – les révoltes anciennes grouillent dans le centre du Céleste Empire; par les escaliers et les fauteuils de rois, un petit monde blême et plat, Afrique et Occidents, va s'édifier. Puis un ballet de mers et de nuits connues, une chimie sans valeur, et des mélodies impossibles.

La même magie bourgeoise à tous les points où la malle nous déposera! Le plus élémentaire physicien sent qu'il n'est plus possible de se soumettre à cette atmosphère personnelle, brume de remords physiques, dont la constatation est déjà une affliction.

Non! – Le moment de l'étuve, des mers enlevées, des embrasements souterrains, de la planète emportée, et des exterminations conséquentes, certitudes si peu malignement indiquées dans la Bible et par les Nornes et qu'il sera donné à l'être sérieux de surveiller. – Cependant ce ne sera point un effet de légende!

strange parks; the sweeping front of a 'Royal' or a 'Grand',[2] in Scarborough or Brooklyn; their railways cut alongside or beneath or over the layout of this Hotel, based on the most elegant, the most colossal buildings in history, from Italy, America and Asia; its windows and terraces, now full of costly lights, of drinks and breezes, stand open to the spirit of the traveller, the nobleman – and during daylight hours they permit every tarantella of the coastline, even the ritornellos of art's illustrious valleys, to adorn the resplendent façades of the Palace. Promontory.

Historic Evening

On some evening, say, enjoyed by the innocent tourist, away from our economic woes, the harpsichord of the meadows responds to the touch of a master; a card game takes place at the bottom of the pool, the mirror which conjures queens and courtesans; there are the women saints, the veils, the threads of harmony, and the legendary chromatics against the sunset.

He shivers as the huntsmen and the hordes go past. The drama trickles on to the grass stage. The distress of the poor and the weak in these idiotic contexts!

Germany scaffolds up to the moons; the deserts of Tartary[1] are lit up – ancient revolts bubble in the heart of the Celestial Empire, on the stairways and in the armchairs of kings. In thrall to his vision, a small, flat, pale world, Africa and Occidents, will be built. Then the ballet of known seas and nights, a useless chemistry, impossible melodies.

It's the same bourgeois magic wherever the mailboat sets us ashore! The most elementary physicist will no longer submit to this intimate atmosphere, this fog of physical remorse which is already an affliction in its own right.

No! The hour of the cauldron, of the disappearing seas, of underground conflagrations, of the planet borne away, and with it all, extermination – certainties calmly announced by the Bible and the Norns,[2] which serious persons will be privileged to observe. – But it's scarcely the stuff of legend.

Mouvement

Le mouvement de lacet sur la berge des chutes du fleuve,
Le gouffre à l'étambot,
La célérité de la rampe,
L'énorme passade du courant,
Mènent par les lumières inouïes
Et la nouveauté chimique
Les voyageurs entourés des trombes du val
Et du strom.

Ce sont les conquérants du monde
Cherchant la fortune chimique personnelle;
Le sport et le comfort voyagent avec eux;
Ils emmènent l'éducation
Des races, des classes et des bêtes, sur ce Vaisseau.
Repos et vertige
A la lumière diluvienne,
Aux terribles soirs d'étude.

Car de la causerie parmi les appareils, – le sang, les fleurs,
      le feu, les bijoux –
Des comptes agités à ce bord fuyard,
– On voit, roulant comme une digue au-delà de la route
      hydraulique motrice,
Monstrueux, s'éclairant sans fin, – leur stock d'études; –
Eux chassés dans l'extase harmonique
Et l'héroïsme de la découverte.

Aux accidents atmosphériques les plus surprenants
Un couple de jeunesse s'isole sur l'arche,
– Est-ce ancienne sauvagerie qu'on pardonne? –
Et chante et se poste.

Movement

The swaying motion on the bank beside the falls,
The eddies at the sternpost,
The speed of the ramp,
The beaten track of the current, huge,
Past strange lights
And chemical surprise –
Bring the travellers through the vale
Of waterspouts and whirlpools.

These are the conquerors of the world,
Seeking their personal chemical fortunes;
Leisure and comfort travel with them;
They load this Vessel
With the education of races, classes, animals.
Repose and vertigo
In the diluvian light
During terrible evenings of study.

From the banter in the machinery – the blood and
      flowers, the fire and jewels –
From the nervous calculations on these fugitive decks,
You can make them out – driven to harmonic Ecstasy,
      the heroism of discovery –
And their wad of surveys, rolling like a dyke
Beyond the hydraulic pull of the channel,
Monstrous, and lit without end.

Surrounded by wild phenomena in the sky,
Two young people, isolated on the ark
– Earlier crimes excused? –
Sing as they take the watch.

Démocratie

«Le drapeau va au paysage immonde, et notre patois étouffe le tambour.

«Aux centres nous alimenterons la plus cynique prostitution. Nous massacrerons les révoltes logiques.

«Aux pays poivrés et détrempés! – au service des plus monstrueuses exploitations industrielles ou militaires.

«Au revoir ici, n'importe où. Conscrits du bon vouloir, nous aurons la philosophie féroce; ignorants pour la science, roués pour le confort; la crevaison pour le monde qui va. C'est la vraie marche. En avant, route!»

Génie

Il est l'affection et le présent puisqu'il a fait la maison ouverte à l'hiver écumeux et à la rumeur de l'été, lui qui a purifié les boissons et les aliments, lui qui est le charme des lieux fuyants et le délice surhumain des stations. Il est l'affection et l'avenir, la force et l'amour que nous, debout dans les rages et les ennuis, nous voyons passer dans le ciel de tempête et les drapeaux d'extase.

Il est l'amour, mesure parfaite et réinventée, raison merveilleuse et imprévue, et l'éternité: machine aimée des qualités fatales. Nous avons tous eu l'épouvante de sa concession et de la nôtre: ô jouissance de notre santé, élan de nos facultés, affection égoïste et passion pour lui, lui qui nous aime pour sa vie infinie ...

Et nous nous le rappelons et il voyage ... Et si l'Adoration s'en va, sonne, sa promesse sonne: «Arrière ces superstitions, ces anciens corps, ces ménages et ces âges. C'est cette époque-ci qui a sombré!»

Il ne s'en ira pas, il ne redescendra pas d'un ciel, il n'accomplira pas la rédemption des colères de femmes et des gaîtés des

Democracy

'The flag makes its way through filth-ridden lands, and our dialect muffles the pulse of the drums.

'In the interior, we shall feed the fires of cynical prostitution. We shall meet justifiable revolt with massacre.

'So – to the dark, dank lands of spices! In the name of the most craven industrial and military exploitation.

'Goodbye to this place, anywhere will do. We're willing conscripts. We take an implacable line. We know nothing of science but we're gluttons for rest and recreation. The world and its notions can crawl off and die. This is progress – the real thing. Forward, march!'

Genie

He is affection, he is here and now, because he has opened the house to the mullings of winter and the buzz of summer; he has purified our food and drink; he is the spell cast over elusive places, the superhuman delight of things in repose. He is affection and the future, the strength and love that we, mired in our fury and boredom, see overhead in the storm-filled sky, in banners of ecstasy.

He is love, his proportions perfect in the reinvention; he is reason, marvellous and unforeseen; he is eternity: cherished machine of whatever is fatal. We have all known the terror of his forbearance and our own: our health and pleasure, the vigour of our faculties, our selfish affection and passion for him – whose unending life is the love of us . . .

And we call him back to us, and he moves on . . . And if Adoration retreats, ringing, his promise also rings: 'Away with these superstitions, these antiquated bodies, all this playing house, these phases. They're part of a sunken era.'

He will not go away, he will not be returning to earth from any heaven, he will not bring about the redemption of women's

hommes et de tout ce péché: car c'est fait, lui étant, et étant aimé.

O ses souffles, ses têtes, ses courses; la terrible célérité de la perfection des formes et de l'action.

O fécondité de l'esprit et immensité de l'univers!

Son corps! Le dégagement rêvé, le brisement de la grâce croisée de violence nouvelle!

Sa vue, sa vue! tous les agenouillages anciens et les peines *relevés* à sa suite.

Son jour! l'abolition de toutes souffrances sonores et mouvantes dans la musique plus intense.

Son pas! les migrations plus énormes que les anciennes invasions.

O lui et nous! l'orgueil plus bienveillant que les charités perdues.

O monde! et le chant clair des malheurs nouveaux!

Il nous a connus tous et nous a tous aimés. Sachons, cette nuit d'hiver, de cap en cap, du pôle tumultueux au château, de la foule à la plage, de regards en regards, forces et sentiments las, le héler et le voir, et le renvoyer, et sous les marées et au haut des déserts de neige, suivre ses vues, ses souffles, son corps, son jour.

anger and men's nonchalance, or of all this sin: it is done, inasmuch as he exists and he is loved.

His every breath, his many-headedness, his fugues; the terrible, swift perfection of form and action!

Fecundity of the mind, immensity of the universe!

His body! The dream of release, the shattering of grace fused with a new violence!

The sight of him – the sight! All the punishment and the ancient genuflection, *lifted* as he passes.

His light! The abolition of all audible and active suffering in music far fiercer.

His tread! Migrations more enormous than the old invasions.

Him. Us. Pride more benign than any squandered charity.

World! And the clear song of new misfortunes!

He has known us all and loved us all. Let us hail him, this winter night, from cape to cape, from the tumult of the poles to the castle, from the throng to the shoreline, from one glance to another – with all strength and feeling spent – let us see him, acknowledge him and, deep beneath the tides or high in the deserts of snow, let us follow his image, his breath, his body, his light.

LETTERS

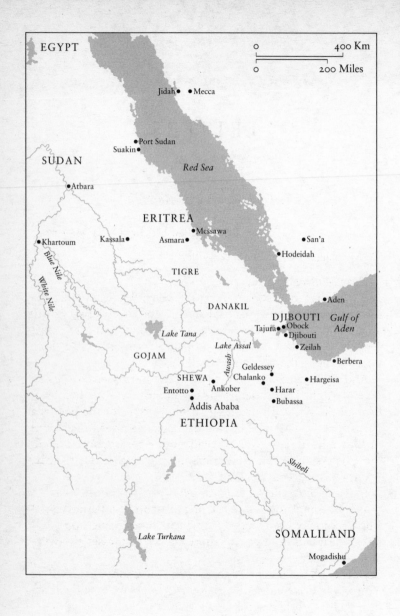

1. To Théodore de Banville[1]

Charleville (Ardennes), 24 May 1870

To Monsieur Théodore de Banville.

Dear *Maître*,

We are in the months of love; I'm seventeen years old.[2] The age of hopes and fancies, as they say, – and here I've sat down, a child touched by the finger of the Muse, – sorry if that's trite, – to tell of my fine beliefs, my hopes, my sensations, all those poet's things – the springtime I call this.

And if I'm sending you a few of these verses, – and this by way of Alph. Lemerre, the worthy publisher, – it's because I love all the poets, all the good Parnassians, – for the poet is a Parnassian, – enamoured of an ideal beauty; it's because I love in you, quite innocently, a descendant of Ronsard,[3] a brother of our masters of 1830, a true Romantic, a true poet. That's why. – Stupid, isn't it, but why not? . . .

In two years' time, in one year perhaps, I shall be in Paris.

– *Anch'io*,[4] gentlemen of the press, I shall be a Parnassian! – I don't know what I've got . . . which comes rising up . . . – I swear, dear *maître*, always to adore the two goddesses, the Muse and Liberty.

Don't pull too much of a face when you read these verses . . . You would drive me mad with joy and hope, were you willing, dear *Maître*, to find some small space for the *Credo in unam* item among the Parnassians . . . I'd come into the last series of the *Parnasse*: that would make the Credo of the poets! . . . Oh, the mad Ambition of it!

ARTHUR RIMBAUD

[Three poems were enclosed: 'Sensation'; 'Soleil et chair' ('Sun and Flesh') – here referred to as 'Credo in unam'; and 'Ophélie' ('Ophelia').]

Supposing these verses were to find a place in the *Parnasse contemporain*?
– Are they not the faith of poets?
– I'm not known; what does it matter? poets are brothers. These verses believe; they love; they hope; that's all.
– To me, dear *maître*; Raise me up a little; I am young; hold out your hand to me . . .

Monsieur Théodore de Banville,
Care of M. Alphonse Lemerre, publisher,
Passage Choiseul,
Paris.

2. *To Georges Izambard*[5]

Charleville, 25 August 70

Monsieur,
You're so lucky, not to be living in Charleville any more! – The town of my birth is the most supremely idiotic of all small provincial towns. I'm no longer under any illusions on that score, you know. Because it's next to Mézières, – a town you can't find, – because it sees two or three hundred squaddies ambling along the streets, this sanctimonious population gesticulates, like so many pontificating cut-throats, very different from those under siege in Metz and Strasbourg![6] It's frightening, the retired grocers putting their uniforms back on! They're so amazingly sexy, the lawyers, the glaziers, the tax-collectors, the carpenters, and all the fat bellies, rifles clutched to their hearts, who go patriotrolling[7] to the gates of Mézières; my country's

rising up! ... Myself, I'd rather see it sitting down; don't stir your boots! that's my principle.

I feel disoriented, sick, furious, stupid, upside down; I'd been hoping for some sunbathing, for endless walks, rest, journeys, adventures, to go gypsying in a word; I'd been hoping especially for newspapers, books ... Nothing! Nothing! The post no longer sends the booksellers a thing; Paris doesn't give two hoots for us: not a single new book! It's death! Here I am, reduced, where newspapers are concerned, to the honourable *Courrier des Ardennes*, – proprietor, managing director, editor-in-chief and sole editor: A. Pouillard! This paper sums up the aspirations, wishes and opinions of the population: so you can judge what things have come to! ... An exile in one's own homeland!!!

Luckily, I've got your room: – You remember the permission you gave me. – I've carried off half your books! I took *Le Diable à Paris*.[8] Tell me, will you, whether there's ever been anything more idiotic than Grandville's drawings?[9]

[...]

I've got Paul Verlaine's *Fêtes galantes*,[10] a nice 120 écu.[11] It's very weird, very funny; but adorable, truly. Big liberties at times. Thus one line from the book is 'Et la tigresse épou – vantable d'Hyrcanie'.[12] My advice is buy *La Bonne chanson*, a small volume of poetry by the same poet; it's just come out from Lemerre; I've not read it; nothing reaches here; but several newspapers have said lots of nice things about it.

Au revoir, send me a 25-page letter – poste restante – and very soon!

                                                        ARTHUR RIMBAUD

P.S. Coming next, revelations about the life I shall be leading after ... the holidays ...

Monsieur Georges Izambard,
29, rue de l'Abbaye-des-Près,
Douai (Nord).

In great haste.

3. To Georges Izambard

Paris, 5 September 1870

Dear Monsieur,

What you were advising me not to do, I've done: I've left the maternal home and gone to Paris! I performed this trick on 29 August.

Arrested getting off the train for not having a sou and owing the railway thirteen francs, I was taken to the prefecture, and today I'm waiting to be sentenced in Mazas![13] Oh! – *My hopes are in you* as in my mother; you've always been like a brother to me: I ask this instant for the help you offered me. I've written to my mother, to the imperial prosecutor, to the police commissioner in Charleville; if you've not heard anything more from me on Wednesday, before the train that goes from Douai to Paris, *catch that train, come here and ask to see me by letter, or by presenting yourself to the prosecutor*, imploring, *answering for me, paying my debt! Do everything you can* and, when you get this letter, you write, too, *I order you to*, yes, *write to my poor mother* (Quai de la Madeleine, 5, Charlev[ille]) *to comfort her. Write to me*, too; do everything! I love you like a brother, I shall love you like a father.

I shake you by the hand
Your poor

ARTHUR RIMBAUD
in Mazas.

(and if you succeed in getting me released, you can take me with [you] to Douai.)

Monsieur Georges Izambard,
Douai.

4. *To Georges Izambard*

Charleville, 2 November 1870

Monsieur,

– For your eyes only –

I came back home to Charleville one day after leaving you. My mother took me in, and I – am here . . . completely idle. My mother will send me to board only in January '71.

Well, I've kept my promise!

I'm dying, I'm rotting away in dreariness, badness, in grizzle. What do you expect, I'm horribly persistent in adoring free freedom, and . . . a whole stack of things so 'it's pitiful' is it not? – I ought to have left again this very day; I could have: I'd got new clothes on, I'd have sold my watch, and long live freedom! – So I stayed! I stayed! – and I shall want to leave again many more times. – Come on, hat, greatcoat, my two fists in my pockets, and out we go! – But I shall stay, I shall stay. I didn't promise that. But I shall do it to earn your affection: you told me so. I shall earn it.

I shan't be able to express the gratitude I feel towards you today any more than the other day. I'll prove it to you. It'll mean doing something for you, even if I die in the attempt, – I give you my word. – I still have a whole stack of things to say . . .

That 'heartless'

A. RIMBAUD

War: – No siege of Mézières.[14] When, then? People don't talk about it. – I ran your errand to M. Deverrière, and, if there's more to be done, I'll do it. Pot-shots here and there. – Abominable prurigo of idiocy, that's the state of mind of the population. You hear priceless things, I'll tell you. It fair breaks you up.

Monsieur Georges Izambard,
Douai.

5. To Georges Izambard

Charleville, [13] May 1871

Dear Monsieur,
So you're back being a schoolmaster. We owe ourselves to society, you told me; you form part of the teaching body; you're travelling down the right rut. – I, too, am following the principle; I'm having myself cynically *kept*; I unearth old imbeciles from college: I hand over to them everything I can invent that's stupid, dirty, wrong, in word and in deed: I'm paid in bocks and in girls.[15] *Sta[ba]t mater dolorosa, dum pendet filius*,[16] – I owe myself to society, that's right. – and I'm right. – You, too, you're right, for today. Deep down, you only see in your principle a subjective poetry: your insistence on getting back to the university feeding-trough – forgive me! – proves it. But you'll still end up a self-satisfied man who's done nothing, not having wanted to do anything. Not counting the fact that your subjective poetry will always be horribly cloying. One day, I hope, – a lot of others hope the same thing – I shall see the objective poetry in your principle, I shall see it more genuinely than you would! – I shall be a worker: that's the idea that holds me back, when my mad rages urge me towards the battle of Paris, – where so many workers are dying even as I write to you![17] To work now, never, never; I'm on strike.

Now, I'm encrapulating myself to the hilt. Why? I want to be a poet and I'm working to make myself a *seer*: you won't begin to understand, and I almost can't explain to you. The thing is to arrive at the unknown by a disordering of *all the senses*. The suffering is enormous, but you have to be strong, to be born a poet, and I've recognized I'm a poet. It's not at all my fault. It's false to say: I think; one ought to say I am thought. – Forgive the play on words.[18]

I is somebody else. Tough luck on the wood that finds it's a violin, and to hell with the people who don't think who quibble over things they know nothing at all about!

You're not a *Teacher* for me. I give you this: is it satire, as you would say? Is it poetry. It's imagination, anyway. – But I implore you, don't underline it, either with your pencil, or too much with your mind.

[Poem enclosed: 'Le Cœur supplicié' ('The Tortured Heart'), a version of 'Le Cœur du pitre' ('Heart of a Clown'), see p. 53.]

It doesn't mean nothing.[19] ANSWER: c/o M. Deverrière, for A.R.

Heartiest greetings,

AR. RIMBAUD

Monsieur Georges Izambard,
27, rue de l'Abbaye-des-Champs
Douai (Nord)

6. To Paul Demeny[20]

Charleville, 15 May 1871

I've resolved to give you an hour of new literature; I begin right away with a psalm about current events:

[Poem enclosed: 'Chant de guerre parisien' ('Parisian War-song').]

– Here's some prose on the future of poetry –

All ancient poetry leads up to Greek poetry. Harmonious Life. – From Greece to the romantic movement, – Middle Ages, – there are scholars, versifiers. From Ennius[21] to Théroldus,[22] from Théroldus to Casimir Delavigne,[23] it's all rhymed prose, a game, flabbiness and fame of countless generations of idiots: Racine is the pure, the strong, the great. – If they'd breathed on his rhymes, and jumbled his hemistiches, the Divine Fool would have been as unknown today as any old author of *Origins*.[24] – After Racine, the game goes mouldy. It's lasted two thousand years!

Neither a joke, nor a paradox. Reason fills me with more

certainties on the subject than a Jeune France[25] can ever have had rages. Besides, the *newcomers* are free to execrate their ancestors: we're at home and we have the time.

Romanticism has never been properly judged; who would have judged it? the Critics!! The Romantics, who prove so well that the song is so seldom the work, i.e., the thought sung and *understood by* the singer?

For I is somebody else. If brass wakes up as a bugle, it's in no way to blame. That I find obvious: I witness the flowering of my thought: I gaze at it, I listen to it: I set my bow moving: the symphony stirs into life in the depths, or comes leaping on to the stage.

If the old imbeciles hadn't found only the false significance of the self, we wouldn't have to sweep away those millions of skeletons who, since time immemorial, have been piling up the products of their one-eyed intelligence, loudly proclaiming to be their authors!

In Greece, as I've said, poetry and lyres *give rhythm to the Action*. Afterwards, music and rhymes are games, a relaxation. The study of that past charms the curious: several take delight in renewing these antiquities: – that's their affair. The universal intelligence has always thrown out its ideas, naturally; men gathered up one part of these fruits of the brain: they acted through, they wrote books out of them: so the process went, man not working on himself, not having yet woken up, or not yet in the fullness of the great dream. Functionaries, writers: author, creator, poet, that man has never existed!

The first study for the man who'd be a poet is knowledge of himself, entire; he seeks out his soul, he inspects it, tests it, learns it. As soon as he knows it, he must cultivate it; that seems simple: in every brain a natural development is fulfilled; so many *egotists* proclaim themselves to be authors; there are lots of others who attribute their intellectual progress to *themselves*! But the thing is to make the soul monstrous: you know, like the *comprachicos*![26] Imagine a man planting and cultivating warts on his face.

I say you must be a *seer*, make yourself a *seer*.

The Poet makes himself a *seer* by a long, immense and

reasoned *disordering* of *all the senses*. All the forms of love, of suffering, of madness; he seeks himself, he drains all the poisons in himself, so as to keep only the quintessences. Ineffable torture in which he has need of all the faith, all the superhuman strength, in which he becomes the sickest of the sick, the great criminal, the great accursed, – and the Supreme Knower! – For he arrives at the *unknown*! Since he has cultivated his already rich soul more than anyone! He arrives at the unknown, and even though he may be demented and lose the intelligence of his visions, he has seen them! So what if he dies as he bounds through unheard-of, unnameable things: other horrible toilers will come; they'll begin at the horizons where he has gone under!

– The rest in six minutes –

Here I insert a second psalm, an *illustration*: kindly lend an obliging ear, – and everyone will be charmed. – My bow's in my hand, I begin:

[Poem enclosed: 'Mes petites amoureuses'.]

A. R.

There. And take good note that, if I wasn't afraid of making you stump up more than 6oc. carriage, – I, a poor lost soul who hasn't owned one brass farthing these last seven months! – I'd be giving you my *Amants de Paris*, a hundred hexameters, Monsieur, and my *Mort de Paris*,[27] two hundred hexameters! – I resume:

Thus the poet is truly a stealer of fire.

He is entrusted with humankind, with the *animals* even; he must make his inventions so they can be felt, fingered, listened to; if what he brings back from *over there* has form, he gives form; if it's formless, he gives formlessness. To find a language;

– For the rest, every utterance being an idea, the day of a universal language will come! You need to be an academician, – deader than a fossil, – to complete a dictionary, of any language at all.[28] Weak minds would start *thinking* about the first letter of the alphabet, who could soon be careering off into madness! –

This language will be of the soul for the soul, summing up everything, perfumes, sounds, colours, thought latching on to thought and pulling. The poet would define the amount of the unknown awakening in his time in the universal soul: he would give more – than the formula of its thought, than the notation *of its march to Progress*! Enormity becoming the norm, absorbed by all, he would truly be a *multiplier of progress*!

That future will be materialist, you can see it. – Always full of *Number* and of *Harmony*, these poems will be made to remain. – Basically, it would be a bit like Greek poetry again.

Eternal art would have its functions, inasmuch as poets are citizens. Poetry will no longer give rhythm to the action; it will be *out ahead*.

These poets will be! Once the infinite servitude of woman is shattered, once she lives for herself and through herself, man – abominable up until now, – having given her her discharge, she too will be a poet! Woman will find the unknown! Will her worlds of ideas differ from our own? – She will find strange, unfathomable, repellent, delightful things: we shall take them, we shall understand them.

Meanwhile, let us ask *poets* for the *new* – ideas and forms. All the clever ones would quickly believe they had satisfied this demand. – That's not it!

[There follows a rapid and ruthless survey of French poetry of the nineteenth century, most of which, Baudelaire and Verlaine apart, is found very lacking.]

It would be execrable of you not to reply: quickly, for in a week's time, I shall be in Paris, perhaps.[29]

Au revoir,

A. RIMBAUD

Monsieur Paul Demeny
Douai.

7. To Paul Demeny

Charleville, 10 June 1871.

To M. P. Demeny

[Two poems enclosed: 'Les Poètes de sept ans' ('Seven-year-old Poets'); 'Les Pauvres à l'église' ('The Poor in Church').]

Here – don't be angry, – a motif of comic drawings: it's an antithesis to the sweet perennial vignettes of sporting cupids, where hearts are taking flight plumed with flames, green flowers, soaking-wet birds, Leucadian promontories, etc. . . . The triolets, too, what's more, will go

> Where the perennial vignettes,
> Where the sweet verses.

Here, – don't be angry:

[A third poem enclosed: 'Le Cœur du pitre' ('Heart of a Clown').]

A.R.

June 1871.

That's what I'm doing.

I've three requests to make to you

burn, *I want you to*, and I believe you'll respect my wishes like those of a dead man, burn *all the verses I was foolish enough* to give you at the time of my stay in Douai:[30] be so good as to send me, if it's possible and if you please, a copy of your *Glaneuses*,[31] which I would like to reread and which it's impossible for me to buy, my mother not having gratified me with a single brass farthing for six months, – have pity! finally, be so kind as to reply, whatever it may be, to this despatch and to the earlier one.

I wish you a good day, which is very kind of me.

Write to: M. Deverrière, 95, sous les Allées, for

A. Rimbaud.

Monsieur Paul Demeny,
Paris.

8. To Georges Izambard

Charleville, 12 July 1871.

Dear Monsieur,

You've been bathing in the sea, you've been in a boat . . . The boyars[32] are a long way away, you've done with them, I'm suffocating here and I'm jealous!

And then, I'm ineffably fed up and can't really get anything down on paper.

I want to ask you something, however: an enormous debt – at a bookseller's, – has come swooping down on me, who haven't the smallest of small change in my pocket. I need to sell off some books. Now you must recall that in September 1870, having come, – on my behalf, – to attempt to soften a mother's hardened heart, you took away, on my advice, several volumes, five or six, that in August, with you in mind, I had brought to your house.

Well, are you attached to Banville's *Florise*, to the same writer's *Exilés*? I who need to retrocede books to my bookseller would be very glad to have those two volumes back: I've got other Banvilles at home; joined with yours, they would make up a set, and sets are much more readily accepted than isolated volumes.

Do you not have *Les Couleuvres*? I could place that like new! – Are you attached to the *Nuits persanes*? A title that can entice, even among second-hand books. Are you attached to the Pontmartin volume? There exist book people round here who would buy such prose. Are you attached to the sky-blue of the *Glaneuses*? The schoolboys of the Ardennes might stump up three francs to potter about in it. I could demonstrate to my crocodile that the purchase of such a collection would bring portentous profits. I would cause titles that no one's noticed to flash fire. I guarantee I'll discover I'm so audacious at the second-hand trade you'll go weak at the knees.

If you knew the situation my mother can and will create for me with my debt of 35fr. 25c., you wouldn't hesitate to give these volumes up to me! You could send me the package care of M. Deverrière, 95 sous les Allées, who's been warned and is expecting it! I'll reimburse you for the costs of carriage, and would be fairly oozing gratitude!

If you've got any printed matter unsuitable for a schoolmaster's library, and have noticed, don't feel awkward. But quickly, I beg you, I'm hard pressed!

Cordially and many thanks in advance.

A. RIMBAUD.

P.S. I saw, in a letter from you to M. Deverrière, that you were worried about your boxes of books. He'll send them on to you as soon as he's received your instructions.

I shake you by the hand.

A. R.

Monsieur Georges Izambard,
Sixth-form master,
Collège de Cherbourg,
Cherbourg (Manche).

9. To Paul Demeny

Charleville (Ardennes), [28] August, 1871

Monsieur,

You make me start my entreaty again: so be it. Here is the full lament. I am looking to put it calmly: but my knowledge of the art is not very profound. Well, here goes:

Situation of the accused: I left normal life more than a year ago, for what you know. Endlessly shut off in this unspeakable landscape of the Ardennes, mixing with no one at all, absorbed in a labour that's vile, inept, obstinate, mysterious, replying to questions, to crude and malicious apostrophizings, only by my silence, displaying dignity in my extra-legal situation, I ended by provoking appalling resolutions in a mother as unyielding as sixty-three administrations in lead hats.

She wanted to impose work on me – perpetual, in Charleville (Ardennes)! A position for such and such a day, she said, or the door.

I rejected that life; without giving my reasons: it would have been pitiful. Up until today, I've been able to get round these ultimatums. She meanwhile has got to the point of forever hoping I'm going to go recklessly off, to flee! Penniless and inexperienced, I'd end up entering a house of correction. From which moment on, a curtain falls on me!

That's the handkerchief of disgust that's been stuffed into my mouth. It's very simple.

I'm not asking for anything, I'm asking for information. I want to work in freedom: but in Paris, which I love. Listen: I'm a pedestrian, nothing more; I arrive in the immense town without any material resources: but you told me: Anyone who wants to be a workman at fifteen sous a day applies there, does this, lives like so. I apply there, I do this, I live like so. I asked you to point out occupations that don't take too much out of you, because thought demands great stretches of time. They absolve the poet, these material hoaxes, and endear themselves to us. I'm in Paris: I need a positive *economy*! You don't find that genuine? I find it very strange having to protest how much I'm in earnest!

I'd had the above idea: the only one I found reasonable: I'm giving it you back in different words. I'm very willing, I do what I can, I speak as comprehensibly as the next unfortunate! Why scold the child who's not very well up in the principles of zoology and would like a bird with five wings? He'd be made to believe in birds with six tails, or three beaks! Lend him a family Buffon:[33] that would set him straight.

So, not knowing what you may write to me, I cut short the explanations and continue to trust in your experience, in your obligingness that I indeed blessed you for when I received your letter, and I'm rather committing you to start from my ideas, – please . . .

Would it put you out to receive some samples of my work?

A. RIMBAUD

Monsieur Paul Demeny,
15, place St-Jacques,
Douai (Nord)

10. To Paul Verlaine[34]

[Charleville, September 1871]

[. . .] I've had the idea of writing a big poem, and I can't work in Charleville. I'm prevented from coming to Paris, having no resources. My mother's a widow and extremely devout. She only gives me ten centimes every Sunday to pay for my chair in church. [. . .]

Monsieur Paul Verlaine,
Paris.

11. Verlaine to Rimbaud

Paris, 2 April 72.

From the Closerie des Lilas.[35]

Good friend,

The *Ariette oubliée*[36] is charming, words and music! I've had it deciphered and sung! Thank you for this thoughtful package! As for the things you speak of sending, send them *through the post*, still to Batignolles, r[ue] Lecluse. Find out about the cost of postage beforehand, and if you're short of the amount, warn me, and I'll send it you in stamps or postal orders (to Bretagne).[37] I'll really get down to selling things off and will make some money – sent to you, or kept for you till we meet – as you care to indicate.

And thank you for your kind letter! The '*little boy*' accepts the justified spanking, the '*toads' friend*' takes everything back

– and never having abandoned your martyrdom, thinks of it, if possible – with even greater *fervour* and joy, you know that, Rimbe.

That's right, love me, protect and give confidence. Being very weak, I have great need of kindnesses. And just as I won't plague you any more with my little boy act, so I won't get on the tits of our revered Priest[38] with it all – and promise him prontissimo a real letter, with drawings and other fun and games.

You must since have got my letter on pink onionskin anyway, and prob[ably] answered it. Tomorrow I shall go to my usual *poste restante* to fetch your probable missive and will answer it . . . But when on earth shall we begin that *way of the cross*,[39] – eh?

Gavroche[40] and I are busy today with your move. Your gear, engravings and smaller bits of furniture are safe. On top of which, you're a tenant in the rue Campe until the 8th. I've reserved – until your return – 2 lesbians in red chalk which I intend as a replacement for the doctor's *Camaïeu* in its black frame. In short, we're looking after you, you're wanted. Till then – for us – either here, or elsewhere.

And we're all yours.

P.V.
Still the same address.

Stuff Mérat – Chanal – Périn, Guérin! And Laure! May the late Carjat twine himself round you.[41]
Speak to me of Favart indeed.
Gavroche is going to write to you *ex imo*.

12. *To Paul Verlaine*

Charleville, April 1872

[. . .] Work is further away from me than my fingernail is from my eye. Shit for me! Shit for me! Shit for me! Shit for me? Shit for me! Shit for me! Shit for me! Shit for me!

Only when you see me positively eating shit will you no longer find that I'm expensive to feed! . . .

13. Verlaine to Rimbaud

[Paris, April 1872]

Rimbaud,

Thanks for your letter and *hosannah* for your '*prayer*'.

Certainly, we shall see one another again! When? – Wait a while! Stern necessities! Grudging opportunities! – So be it! And shit for one lot like shit for the other. And like shit for Me! – and for You!

But send me your 'bad' verses (!!!!), your prayers (!!!), – be sempiternally communicative in short, – while waiting for something better, once my *house's done up*. And write to me, *soon*, – via Bretagne, – either from Charleville, or from Nancy, *Meurthe. M. Auguste Bretagne, rue Ravinelle, No 11, eleven*.

And don't ever think you've been let go by me. <u>Remember</u>! <u>Memento</u>!

Your P.V.

And write to me soon! And send me your old verses and your new prayers. You will, won't you, Rimbaud?

14. Verlaine to Rimbaud

[Paris, May 1872]

Dear good kind Rimbe, I acknowledge receipt of the credit solicited and granted, with a thousand thanks, and (I'm wildly happy to be almost sure) this time *without any commission*. Till Saturday then, still around 7, yes? – To have a bit over, anyway, and me send sous at the opportune moment.

Meanwhile, all martyristic letters to my mother's, all letters concerning meeting again, precautions, etc. . . . care of *M. L. Forain, 17, quai d'Anjou, Hôtel Lauzun, Paris, Seine (for M. P. Verlaine)*.

Tomorrow, I hope to be able to tell you I finally have the Job (secretary in insurance).

No see Gavroche yesterday although rendez-vous. I'm writing this at the Cluny (3 o'clock), waiting for him. We're plotting joke *venjunce* on someone you'll know. As soon as you're back, in case it'll amuse you, *tigerish* things will take place. It involves a gentleman who hasn't been uninfluential during your 3 months in the Ardennes and my 6 months of shit. Well, you'll see!

At Gavroche's write to me and inform me of my duty, the life you intend we should lead, the joys, the heartaches, the hypocrisies, the cynicism we're going to need: me all yours, all you, – know it! – This at Gavroche's.

At my mother's your *martyristic* letters, no allusions to any seeing each other again.

Final bit of advice: as soon as you're back, grab me right away, so that no earthshakes, – you easily could, too!

Care:

for a time at least, try to look less terrifying than before: *clean clothes, boot polish, comb through hair, graceful expression*: this necessary if you join in tigerish projects: me moreover linen maid, brusher, etc. (if you want).

(The which projects by the by, you joining in, will be useful to *us*, because 'someone very big in Madrid's'[42] concerned, – whence security very good!).

Now, greetings, see you, joy, waiting for letters, waiting for You. – Me dreamt twice last night: *You, child martyrizer*, – *You all goldez.** Funny, isn't it, Rimbe!

Before closing this I'm waiting for Gavroche. Will he come? – or will he default? (– till in a few minutes! –)

                                                                            4 p.m.

Gavroche arrived, *will spk agn re gd safe lodgings*.[43] He'll write to you.

                                                                 Your old, P.V.

Write to me all the time from your Ardennes
write to you all this about my shit
Why not shit to H. Regnault?[44]

---

*In English, *doré*: I was forgetting you were as ignorant of that language as I am.

15. To Ernest Delahaye[45]

Parishit, Junphe[46] 72

My friend,

Yes, surprising is existence in the Arduan cosmorama. What [I] miss isn't the provinces, where you feed off starch and mud, where you drink rough wine and the local beer. So you're right to be forever running them down. But this place: distillation, composition, all constrictions; and the summer overwhelming: the heat isn't very consistent, but seeing that fine weather is in everyone's interest, and that everyone's a pig, I hate the summer, which kills me when it more or less shows itself. I've a thirst to make me fear gangrene; the Belgian and Ardennes rivers, the caves, that's what I miss.

There's one watering hole here I prefer. Long live the Academy of Absomphe, despite the malevolence of the waiters! It's the most delicate and most tremulous of garments, drunkenness thanks to that sage of the glaciers, absomphe. Only, afterwards, to go to bed in shit!

Forever the same lamentation, eh! What's certain, is shit to Perrin. And to the bar at the Univers, whether it's facing the square or not. I don't curse the Univers, though. – I very much wish the Ardennes would be occupied and squeezed till the pips squeak. But all this is still quite normal.

What's serious is that you must be tormenting yourself a lot, perhaps you'd be right to walk a lot and read. Right in any case not to be stuck in an office or family homes. One should go to the dogs far away from such places. I'm far from selling balm, but I don't think habits offer consolation, for the pitiful days.

Now it's at night that I labourify. From midnight till five in the morning. Last month, my room in the rue Monsieur-le-Prince looked out on a garden in the lycée Saint-Louis. There were enormous trees under my narrow window. At three in the morning, the candle goes pale: all the birds call out at once in the trees: it's over. No more work. I had to gaze at the trees, the sky, seized by that indescribable hour, the first of the morning.

I could see the school dormitories, absolutely dumb. And already the staccato, sonorous, delectable noise of the carts on the boulevards. – I was smoking my hammer-pipe, spitting on to the tiles, because my room was an attic. At five, I went down to buy some bread: that's the time. The workmen are on the move everywhere. For me, it's the hour to get drunk at the wine-shops. I came home to eat, and went to bed at seven in the morning, when the sun was bringing the wood-lice out from under the tiles. What's always enraptured me here is the early morning in summer, and the December evenings.

But at this moment, I have a pretty room, over a courtyard with no far end to it but three metres square. – The rue Victor-Cousin leads off the place de la Sorbonne by the Café du Bas-Rhin, and gives on to the rue Soufflot, at the far end. – Here, I drink water all night long, I don't see the morning, I don't sleep, I suffocate. And that's it.

Your demand will certainly be acceded to! Don't forget to shit on *La Renaissance*,[47] an artistic and literary journal, if you come across it. Up until now, I've avoided the pestilential émigrés from Carloshitville. And fuck the seasons. And *colrage*.
Courage.

A.R.
Rue Victor-Cousin, Hôtel de Cluny.

Monsieur Ernest Delahaye,
Charleville.

16. To Ernest Delahaye

(Roche) (Canton d'Attigny).
May '73

Dear friend, you can see my present existence in the water-colour below.
O Nature! O my mother!

[Drawing enclosed.]

What a shitheap! And what monsters of innocinch, these peasants. You have, in the evenings, to do six miles, and more, to get anything to drink. The <u>mother</u> has put me in a miserable hole.

[Another drawing.]

I don't know how to get out: I shall get out though. I miss the ghastly Charlestown, the Univers, the Libr. etc. . . . I'm working fairly regularly though, I'm doing little stories in prose, overall title: Pagan Book, or Negro Book.[48] It's stupid and innocent. O innocence! innocence; innocence, innoc . . . what a pain!

Verlaine will have given you the unhappy errand of parleying with Sire Devin, the printeur of the *Nôress*.[49] I fancy this Devin could do Verlaine's book fairly cheaply and almost properly. (If he doesn't use the shitty characters from the *Nôress*. He'd be capable of sticking in a plate, or an advertisement!)

I've nothing else to tell you, the contemplostate of Nature arseorbing me entirely. I'm yours, O Nature, O my mother!

I shake your hands, in the hope of a reunion that I'm working towards as hard as I can.

R.

I re-open my letter. Verlaine will have proposed a rendez-vol for Sunday the 18th in Boulion. I can't get there. If you go, he'll probably load you up with a few phragments of prose by me or by him, to give back to me.

Mother Rimb. will return to Charlestown in the course of June. That's certain, and I shall try to remain in this jolly town for a while.

The sun gets you down and it's freezing in the mornings. I went the day before yesterday to see the Prussmars in Vouziers, a sub-prefect[ur]e of 10,000 souls seven kilom. from here. It cheered me up.

I'm abominably hard up. Not a book, not a bar within range, not one incident in the streets. What a horror the French countryside is. My fate depends on this book, for which half a dozen horror stories have yet to be made up. How to make up horrors here! I'm not sending you any stories, although I've already got three, *and at what cost*! So there you are!

Au revoir, you'll see it.

RIMB.

I'll shortly be sending you stamps to buy me and send me Goethe's *Faust*, Bibliothèque Populaire. It should cost one sou to send.

Tell me if there aren't translat. of Shakespeare among the new books in that coll[ectio]n.

If you can even send me the latest catalogue, send.

Monsieur Ernest Delahaye,
Charleville.

17. *Verlaine to Rimbaud*

Boglione,[50] Sunday 18 [May 1873].

Dear friend, thank you for the English lesson, severe but just. You know, I 'sleep'. It's sheer somnambulism, the thine, the ours, the theirs; it's the sluggishness produced by Boredom, the choice of filthy auxiliary verbs, to do, to have, instead of more expressive analogues. I would defend my initial How for example. The line is:

Mais qu'est-ce qu'ils ont donc à dire que c'est laid . . .[51]

I can still only find How! (which anyway ranks as an exclamation of surprise) to render this. *Laid* seems to me rendered rather well by foul. Moreover, how to translate:

Ne ruissellent-ils pas de tendresse et de lait?

if not by:

Do not stream by fire and milk?[52]

Or so it seems to me, after ample contrition for my Sleeping Bloody Fool's garbage (Delatrichine[53] wouldn't have hit on that one!)

Got here at midday, teeming rain, on foot. No sign of Deléclanche. Shall leave again by mail-coach. – Dined with Frenchman from Sedan and a big schoolboy from the college in

Charleville. Gloomy banquet! Badingue[t][54] dragged through the shit, however, which is a treat in this land of vultures.

Brother of mine, I've lots of things to tell you, but now it's 2 o'clock and the mail's about to go. Tomorrow perhaps I'll write to you all the projects I have, literary and otherwise. You'll be pleased with your old sow (beaten, Delamorue!)

For the time being I embrace you and count on an interview very soon, hope of which you give me for this week. The moment you give the sign, I'll be there.

My brother (brother-plainly), I very much hope. It's going well. You'll be pleased.

See you soon, yes? Write quickly. *Send explanade*. You'll have your fragments soon.

I'm your old cunt ever open or opened, I don't have my irregular verbs here.

P.V.

Received letter from Lepelletier (business); he'll be responsible for the romances, – Claye and Lechevallier, Tomorrow I'll send him emmess.

And lock them away again for you for a second time.

P.V.

Forgive me for this stupid and *orde lette*.[55] A bit pissed. Plus I'm writing with a pen without a nib, while smoking a blocked pipe.

18. Verlaine to Rimbaud

At sea, [3 July 1873]

My friend,

I don't know if you'll still be in London when this gets to you. I have, however, to let you know that you must, *basically*, understand, *at last*, that I absolutely had to leave, that I couldn't fucking well take any more of that violent life of nothing but *scenes* based entirely on your own imaginings!

Only, since I was immensely fond of you (Honni soit qui mal

y pense) I'm anxious also to confirm that if, over the next three days, I'm not re- with my wife, in ideal conditions, I shall blow my brains out. 3 days in a hotel, a *revolvita*, that costs a bit: hence my 'stinginess' just now. You ought to forgive me. – If, as is only too likely, I need to commit this ultimate bloody foolishness, I'll be a brave bloody fool at least. – My last thought, my friend, will be for you, for you who called me from the <u>pier</u> just now, and whom I refused to rejoin *because I needed to kick the bucket*. FINALLY!

Do you want me to embrace you as I peg out?

Your poor
P. VERLAINE

We shan't see one another again in any case. If my wife comes, you'll have my address, and I hope you'll write to me. Meanwhile, over the next three days, *no more, no less*, poste restante Brussels, – in my name.

Give Barrère[56] back his three books.

ENGLAND

M. Arthur Rimbaud,
8 Great College Street,
Camden Town, N.W.
London.

Very Urgent.

<u>Or, in case of a departure</u>, Roche, canton d'Attigny, Ardennes, FRANCE (c/o Mme Rimbaud)

19. To Verlaine

London, Friday afternoon.
[4 July 1873]

Come back, come back, dear friend, one friend, come back. I swear I'll be good. If I was surly with you, it was a joke I persisted with, I'm sorrier for it than I can say. Come back, it'll soon be forgotten. How unfortunate that you should have believed in that joke. I haven't stopped crying for two days now.

Come back. Be brave, dear friend. Nothing's been lost. You
need only make the journey again. We'll live here again very
bravely, patiently. Oh, I implore you! It's for your own good,
moreover. Come back, you'll find all your things. I hope you
really know now that nothing was true in the argument we had.
What a ghastly moment! But when I signalled to you to get off
the boat, why didn't you come? We've been living together for
two years only to come to this! What are you going to do? If
you won't come back here, do you want me to come and find
you where you are?

Yes, it's I who was in the wrong.

Oh, say you won't forget me?

No, you can't forget me.

I still have you here.

Tell me, answer your friend, shouldn't we live together any
more?

Be brave. Answer me quickly.

I can't stay here any longer.

Listen only to your kind heart.

Quickly, say whether I'm to join you.

Yours for as long as I live.

RIMBAUD

Quickly, answer, I can't stay here any later than Monday
evening. I don't have a <u>penny</u> now, I can't put this in the post.
I've entrusted your books and manuscripts to *Vermersch*.[57]

If I'm not to see you again, I shall enlist in the navy or the
army.

Oh, come back, I weep again for you at all hours. Tell me to
meet you again, I'll come, tell me, wire me – I have to leave on
Monday evening, where are you going, what do you mean to
do?

20. *To Verlaine*

[London, 5 July 1873]

Dear friend, I have your letter dated 'at sea'. You're wrong, this time, and very wrong. First of all, nothing positive in your letter: your wife won't come or will come in three months' time, three years, how should I know? As for kicking the bucket, I know you. So, while you wait for your wife and your death, you'll be thrashing about, off wandering, annoying people. What, you still haven't recognized that the rages were as false on one side as on the other! But it's you who were in the wrong the last, since even after I called you back, you persisted in your false feelings. Do you think your life will be more agreeable with others than with me: *Think about it*! – It certainly won't be! –

With me alone you can be free, and, since I swear I'll be very nice in future, that I deplore all my share of the wrong, that my mind's clear at last, that I'm very fond of you, if you don't want to come back, or me to join you, you're committing a crime, and *you'll regret for LONG YEARS to come the loss of all freedom, and troubles more atrocious* perhaps than all those you've been through. After which, think back to what you were before you met me.

As for myself, I'm not going back to my mother's. I'm going to Paris, I'll try to be gone by Monday evening. You'll have forced me to sell all your clothes, I can't do otherwise. They're not yet sold: they'll only take them off me on Monday morning. If you want to address letters to me in Paris, send them to L. Forain, 289, rue St-Jacques, for A. Rimbaud. He'll know my address.

Certainly, if your wife comes back, I shan't compromise you by writing, – I shall never write.

The one true word is: come back, I want to be with you, I love you. If you heed that, you'll be showing courage and a sincere spirit.

Otherwise, I pity you.

But I love you, I embrace you and we shall see one another again.

                                                              RIMBAUD

8 Great Colle[ge] etc. . . . until Monday evening, or Tuesday midday, if you send for me.

21. To Verlaine

Monday midday. [London, 7 July 1873]

My dear friend,
I've seen the letter you sent to Mme Smith.[58]
It's too late unfortunately.

You want to come back to London! You don't know the welcome you'd get there! And the expression on the faces of Andrieu[59] and others if they saw me with you again. Nonetheless, I shall be very brave. Tell me quite sincerely what your idea is. Will you return to London for my sake? On which day? Is it my letter that's given you the idea? But there's no longer anything in the room. – Everything's sold, bar an overcoat. I got two pounds ten. But the linen's still with the laundrywoman, and I've kept a heap of things for myself: five waistcoats, all the shirts, pants, collars, gloves and all the shoes. All your books and ms are safe. In short, all that's been sold are your trousers, black and grey, an overcoat and one waistcoat, the bag and the hatbox. But why don't you write, to me?

Yes, *cher petit*, I'm going to stay for one more week. And you'll come, won't you? Tell me the truth. You'd have given a sign of courage. I hope it's true. You can be sure of me, I shall have a very good character.

Yours. I await you.

                                                              RIMB.

22. *Verlaine to Rimbaud*

Office of origin Brussels 8. 7
Handed in at 8.38
Sent out at 10.16
From Verlaine   To Rimbaud
                                            8 gt. College St.
                                                Camdentown
                                                  Lon[don].

Volunteer Spain come here Hôtel Liégois washerwoman manuscripts if possible.[60]

23. *Deposition by Rimbaud to the examining magistrate*

12 July 1873.

I made the acquaintance of Verlaine in Paris some two years
ago. Last year, following disagreements with his wife and the
latter's family, he proposed I go abroad with him; we were to
make a living by one means or another, for I have no fortune
of my own, and Verlaine has only the product of his work
and some money that his mother gives him. We came together
to Brussels in July of last year; we resided here for around
two months; seeing that there was nothing for us to do in the
town, we went to London. We lived there together until
recently, occupying the same lodgings and having everything in
common.

Following an argument which we had at the beginning of last
week, an argument arising out of the criticisms I had been
making of his indolence and his way of behaving towards
persons of our acquaintance, Verlaine left me almost without
warning, without even letting me know the place where he had
gone. I assumed, however, that he had gone to Brussels, or
would go by way of there, for he had taken the Antwerp boat.
I next received from him a letter dated 'at sea', which I will pass
on to you, in which he announced that he was going to appeal

to his wife to come back, and that if she did not answer his appeal within three days, he would kill himself; he told me also to write to him poste restante in Brussels. I next wrote to him two letters in which I asked him to come back to London or to agree to my going to rejoin him in Brussels. It was then that he sent me a telegram to come here, to Brussels. I wanted us to be reunited, because we had no reason to separate.

I therefore left London; I arrived in Brussels on Tuesday morning, and I rejoined Verlaine. His mother was with him. He had no set plans; he did not wish to remain in Brussels, because he was afraid there would be nothing to do in that town; I, for my part, would not agree to return to London, as he suggested, because our departure must have produced too unfortunate an effect in the minds of our friends, and I decided to return to Paris. At one moment Verlaine displayed an intention of accompanying me, to go and give the lie, as he put it, to his wife and parents-in-law; at another he refused to accompany me, because Paris brought back too many unhappy memories. He was in a very exalted state. However, he was very insistent in my presence that I should remain with him; at one moment he was in despair, the next he would fly into a rage. There was no continuity in his ideas. On Wednesday evening, he drank to excess and became drunk. On Thursday morning, he went out at six o'clock; he only returned around midday; he was once again in a drunken state, he showed me a pistol he had bought, and when I asked him what he was counting on doing with it, he replied, jokingly: 'It's for you, for me, for everyone!' He was greatly overexcited.

While we were together in our room, he went down several more times to drink liqueurs; he still wanted to stop me carrying out my plan of returning to Paris. I remained immovable. I even asked his mother for money for the journey. Then, at a given moment, he locked the door on to the landing and sat down on a chair against the door. I was standing up, with my back against the wall opposite. He then said to me: 'This is for you, since you're leaving!' or something of the sort; he directed his pistol at me and loosed off a shot which hit me on the left wrist; the first shot was followed almost instantly by a second, but this time the weapon was no longer directed at me, but lowered towards the floor.

Verlaine immediately expressed the keenest despair at what he had done; he dashed into the room adjoining occupied by his mother, and threw himself on to the bed. He was like a madman: he put the pistol into my hands and urged me to discharge it at his temple. His attitude was one of profound regret for what had happened to him.

Around five in the evening, he and his mother brought me here to have me bandaged. Once back in the hotel, Verlaine and his mother suggested I remain with them to be nursed, or to go back to the hospital until I was completely healed. The wound not seeming to me very serious, I made clear my intention of returning that same evening to France, to Charleville, to my mother's. This news once again cast Verlaine into despair. His mother handed me twenty francs for the journey, and they came out with me to go with me to the Gare du Midi. Verlaine was like a madman, he tried everything he could to detain me; moreover, he had his hand in his coat pocket all the time where his pistol was. Having got to the place Rouppe, he went a few paces ahead of us and then came back towards me; his attitude made me afraid he might give way to further excesses; I turned around and ran off. It was then that I begged a policeman to arrest him.

The bullet by which I was struck in the wrist hasn't yet been extracted, the doctor here told me it couldn't be done for two or three more days.

QUESTION: What were you living off in London?

ANSWER: Mainly off the money that Mme Verlaine sent to her son. We also had French lessons which we gave together, but the lessons didn't bring much in, a dozen francs a week, towards the end.

QUESTION: Do you know the source of the disagreements between Verlaine and his wife?

ANSWER: Verlaine didn't want his wife to continue living at her father's.

QUESTION: Did she not also invoke as a grievance your intimacy with Verlaine?

ANSWER: Yes, she even accuses us of immoral relations; but I don't wish to go to the trouble of denying such a calumny.

Read and certified:

A. RIMBAUD, TH. T'SERSTEVENS, C. LIGOUR.

24. Disclaimer

I the undersigned Arthur Rimbaud, 19 years old, man of letters, normally resident in Charleville (Ardennes, France), hereby declare, out of a respect for the truth, that on Thursday the 10th inst, around 2 o'clock, at the moment when M. Paul Verlaine, in his mother's room, fired a shot from a revolver at me which wounded me slightly in the left wrist, M. Verlaine was in a state of drunkenness such that he was quite unaware of his action.

That I am perfectly persuaded that, in buying this weapon, M. Verlaine had no hostile intention towards me, and that there was no criminal premeditation in the act of locking the door on us.

That the cause of M. Verlaine's drunkenness derived simply from the thought of his contretemps with Madame Verlaine, his wife.

I declare furthermore that I willingly make him this offer and consent purely and simply to renounce all criminal proceedings, before magistrates or in the civil court, and waive as from today the benefits of any prosecution that will or might be brought by the public authorities against M. Verlaine for the action in question.

A. RIMBAUD.
Saturday, 19 July 1873.

25. *To Ernest Delahaye*

[Stuttgart, 5 March 1875]

[Drawing, showing a figure labelled 'Wagner' hanging by the neck, with a wine-bottle inserted into his rectum.]

Verlaine arrived here the other day, with a rosary in his claws. Three hours later we'd renounced our god and made J. C.'s 98 wounds bleed. He stayed two and a half days, very reasonable and on my remonstrating went back to Paris, so as to go right away and finish studying *over there on the island*.

I've only one more week of Wagner[61] and I regret the money paid out for hatred, all this time spent on bugger all. On the 15th I shall have Ein freundliches Zimmer[62] somewhere or other, and I'm excavating the language like mad, so much so that I'll have finished in two months at the outside.

Everything's pretty inferior here, bar one thing: Riessling, a glarz of vich I trink to your imperpetual healt fazing ze slopes zat vitnessed itz birt. It sunshines and freezes, it's tanning.

(After the 15th, Poste restante Stuttgart.)
Yours.

RIMB.

[Drawing, showing bottles of Riesling and free-floating male genitalia.]

Monsieur Ernest Delahaye,
Charleville.

26. *To his family*

[Stuttgart] 17 March 1875

My dear relations,
I didn't want to write before having a new address. Today I acknowledge receipt of your last remittance, of 50 francs.

And here's the example of how letters to me should be addressed:

Wurtemberg,
   Monsieur Arthur Rimbaud
    2, Marien Strasse, 3 tr.
              STUTTGART.

'3 tr.' signifies 3rd floor.

I have a very large room here, very well furnished, in the centre of town, for ten florins, that's to say 21 francs 50 c[entimes], service included; and I'm being offered full board for 60 francs a month: I don't need it, however: those little arrangements are always a swindle and an imposition, however economical they look. So I shall attempt to keep going until April 15th with what I've got left (another 50 francs) as I shall need an advance again on that date: for, either I'll have to stay another month in order to get started properly, or I'll have advertised for placements going after which (the journey, e.g.) will take a bit of money. I hope you'll find that moderate and reasonable. I'm attempting to infiltrate the local ways by every means possible, I'm attempting to find things out; although the way they live's a real ordeal. I salute the army,[63] I hope that Vitalie and Isabelle are well, I ask that you alert me if there's anything you want from here, and am your devoted.

A. RIMBAUD

Charleville.

27. To Ernest Delahaye

[Charleville] 14 October '75.

Dear friend,
Received the <u>Postcard</u> and the letter from V. a week ago. To simplify things, I've told the Post Office to send his *restantes* to my place, so you can write here, if still nothing at the *restante*. I shan't comment on Loyola's[64] latest crudenesses, and shan't

be taking any more action in that direction at present, since it appears that the 2nd 'batch' of the 'contingent' of the class of '74 is going to be called up on the 3rd of November following or soon after: the barrackroom at night:

DREAM[65]

They're hungry in the barrackroom –
  It's true . . .
Emanations, explosions. An engineer:
  'I'm the gru[y]ère!' –
Lefèbvre:[66] 'Keller!'[67]
The engineer: 'I'm the Brie!' –
The soldiers cut into their bread:
  'C'est la vie!'
The engineer, – 'I'm the Roquefort!'
  'It'll be the death of us! . . .'
– 'I'm the gruère
And the Brie! . . . etc.

WALTZ

They joined us, Lefèbvre and I, etc.

Such preoccupations only allow one to become engrocered by them. Meanwhile kindly send back, when occajun arises, the 'Loyolas' that may turn up again.

A small favour: will you tell me precisely and concisely – what the current science '*bachot*'[68] consists of, classical part, and maths, etc. You could tell me the mark one has to get in each part: maths, phys., chem., etc., and then the titles, immed., (and the means of procuring them) of the books used in your school; e.g., for that '*Bachot*', unless it changes for different universities: at all events, make inquiries of teachers and competent pupils from the point of view I'm giving you. I'm keen above all on knowing precisely, as it would mean buying the books in the near future. Military training and '*bachot*', you see, would give me two or three agreeable seasons! To hell anyway with this 'gentle toil'. Simply be good enough to indicate in the bestest way possible how one goes about it.

Here absolutely nothing.

I like to think that Petdeloup[69] and the glue-pots full of haricot beans, patriotic or not, are not distracting you any more than you need. At least it's not sodding snowing, like here.

Yours 'to the best of my feeble ability'.

You write:

A. RIMBAUD.

31. rue St-Barthélémy,
Charleville (Ardennes), goes without saying.

[. . .]

28. Ernest Delahaye to Ernest Millot

Rethel, 28 January 1877

Dear Friend,

I've kept you waiting a while, and am ashamed even of having been warned, but as compensation I bring you a great piece of news:

He's back! . . .

From a brief voyage, nothing really. Here are the Stops: Brussels, Rotterdam, Le Helder, Southampton, Gibraltar, Naples, Suez, Aden, Sumatra, Java (two-month stay), the Cape, St Helena, Ascension, the Azores, Queenstown, Cork (in Ireland), Liverpool, Le Havre, Paris and still, to finish . . . in Charlestown.

[. . .]

He's been – what's depressing – [in] Charlest since the 9th of December: silence on that! It's not over, what's more, and (we) shall, it seems, see many more (adventures). That's all for the (moment). [. . .]

Till then,

YOUR OLD DELAHAYE.

29. To the United States Consul in Bremen[70]

Bremen the 14 mai 77

The untersigned Arthur Rimbaud – Born in Charleville (France) – Aged 23 – 5ft. 6 height – Good healthy, – Late a teacher of sciences and languages – Recently deserted from the 47e Regiment of the French army,[71] – Actually in Bremen without any means, the French Consul refusing any Relief.

Would like to know on which conditions he could conclude an immediate engagement in the American navy.

Speaks and writes English, German, French, Italian and Spanish.

Has been four months as a sailor in a Scotch bark, from Java to Queenstown, from August to December '76.

Would be very honoured and grateful to receive an answer.

JOHN ARTHUR RIMBAUD

30. To his family

Genoa, Sunday 17 November 78.

Dear friends,

I arrived in Genoa this morning and have got your letters. A passage to Egypt costs a fortune, so that there's no benefit. I leave on Monday the 19th at nine in the evening. We get there at the end of the month.

As for the manner in which I got here, it was eventful and refreshed from time to time by the season. On the straight line from the Ardennes to Switzerland, wishing to join, from Remiremont, the German conn[ection] at Wesserling, I had to go through the Vosges; first of all in a diligence, then on foot, no diligence being able to run any longer, in fifty centimetres of snow on average and with a storm forecast. But the anticipated exploit was crossing the Gothard, which you can no longer get over by carriage at this time of year, and that I couldn't get over by carriage.

[…]

The real ascent starts, at Hopital, I believe: at first, a scramble almost, taking the traverses, then plateaux or simply the carriage road. For you have very much to picture to yourselves that you can't follow this the whole time, it only goes up in zig-zags or very gentle terraces, which would take for ever, when vertically the elevation's only 4900, for each face, or even less than 4900, given the elevation round about. You don't climb vertically either, you follow the usual ways up even if they're not cleared. People unused to the spectacle of the mountains learn too that a mountain may have peaks, but that a peak isn't the mountain. Thus the summit of the Gothard covers a surface area of several kilometres.

The road, which is barely six metres across, is choked all the way along on the right by a fall of snow nearly two metres high, which is constantly stretching a barrier across the road a metre high that you have to push through under a frightful storm of hailstones. And here you are! Not a single shadow up above, below or round about, though we're surrounded by huge objects; no road any more, or precipices, or gorge or sky; nothing but white to dream about, to touch, to see or not see, for it's impossible to raise your eyes from the white unpleasantness you believe is the middle of the path. Impossible to raise your nose into such a biting north wind, your eyelashes and moustache forming stalactites, your ears torn, your neck swollen. But for the shadow which is you and but for the telegraph poles that follow the presumed road, you'd be as confused as a sparrow in an oven.

So there you are pushing through more than a metre high for a whole kilometre. It's a long time since you saw your knees. It warms you up. Out of breath, because in half an hour the storm could bury us without really trying, we shout encouragement to one another (you never go up singly, but in groups). Finally, here's a woman road-worker: you pay 1.50 for a cup of salty water. On you go. But the wind's starting to rage, you can see the road getting clogged. Here's a convoy of sledges, a fallen horse half buried. But the road's disappearing. Which side of the posts is it? (There are posts on one side only.) You stray off, you sink in up to your ribs, up under your arms ... A pale shadow behind a ditch: it's the Gothard hospice, a civilian hospital establishment, a sordid pinewood and stone building; a bell turret. You sound the bell and a shifty-looking young man greets you; you go up into a low-ceilinged, dirty room where you're treated by right to bread and cheese, soup and a dram. You see the beautiful big yellow dogs whose story everyone knows. Soon the laggards arrive half dead from the mountain. There are a good thirty of us in the evening, and after the soup, we're distributed amongst the hard palliasses and under inadequate blankets. In the night, you can hear the sacred chantings of your hosts as they breathe out their pleasure at robbing the governments that subsidize their shack for one more day.

In the morning, after the bread-cheese-dram, braced by this free hospitality that you can prolong for as long as the storm allows, you leave: this morning, in the sunshine, the mountain is wonderful: no more wind, all downhill, via the traverses, jumping, slithering down whole kilometres, which bring you to Airolo, on the other side of the tunnel, where the road resumes its Alpine character, going round in circles, in a gorge, but descending. This is Ticino.

The road's snow-covered until more than thirty kilometres from the Gothard. Only after thirty kilometres, at Giornico, does the valley open out a bit. A few vine arbours and a few bits of pasture that they manure carefully with leaves and other pine detritus that must have served as litter. Goats, oxen and grey cows, and black pigs file past on the road. In Bellinzona, there's a big market for these livestock. In Lugano, sixty miles from the Gothard, you catch the train and go from the pleasant Lake Lugano to the pleasant Lake Como. And then, the well-known route.

All the best to you, I thank you and in three weeks or so you'll have a letter.

Your friend.

31. To his family

Alexandria, [December] 1878

Dear friends,

I got here after a ten-day crossing and after sorting myself out for the past fortnight, only now are things beginning to look up! I am shortly to have a job; and I've already enough work to live on, meanly it's true. Either I shall be taken on at a large agricultural operation some thirty miles from here (I've already been there, but there wouldn't be anything for a few weeks); – or else I shall shortly enter the Anglo-Egyptian customs, at a good salary; – or else, I think rather I shall leave shortly for Cyprus, the English island, as an interpreter with a group of workmen. At all events, I've been promised something; and I'm dealing with a French engineer – an obliging and talented man. Only here is what I'm being asked for: a note from you, Mama, with the legal authority of the town hall and bearing as follows:

'I the undersigned, Mme Rimbaud, a householder in Roche, declare that my son Arthur Rimbaud has given up working on my property, that he left Roche of his own volition on 20 October 1878, that he conducted himself honourably both here and elsewhere, and that he is not currently subject to military law.

Signed: Mme R . . .'

And the town hall's stamp, which is essential.

Without this document I shan't be given a permanent position, though I think they would go on employing me casually. But be careful not to say that I only remained for a short time in Roche, because they'll want to know more, and there'll be no end to it; then it'll make the people in the agriculture company believe I'm capable of managing the work.

I ask as a favour that you send me word to this effect as soon as possible: it's a simple enough matter and will have good results, or at least that of giving me a good place for the whole winter.

I shall shortly send you details and descriptions of Alexandria and of life in Egypt. No time today. I bid you *au revoir*. Greetings to F[rédéric], if he's there. Here it's as hot as in summer at Roche.

News.

A. RIMBAUD.
Poste française, Alexandria, Egypt.

32. To his family

Larnaca (Cyprus),
15 February 1879

E. Jean and Thial fils,
Contractors
Larnaca (Cyprus)

Dear friends,

I haven't written to you before this, not knowing in which direction I'd be made to turn. However, you must have had a letter from Alexandria in which I spoke of being imminently taken on in Cyprus. Tomorrow, 16 February, it will be just two months since I was employed here. The bosses are in Larnaca, the principal port of Cyprus. I'm the overseer at a quarry in the desert, beside the sea: they're making a canal also. There's also the stone to be loaded on to the Company's five boats and one steamer. There's also a lime kiln, brickworks, etc. . . . The first village is an hour away on foot. Here there's only a chaos of rocks, the river and the sea. There's only one house. No earth, no gardens, not one tree. In summer, there are eighty degrees of heat. At the moment, we often get 50. It's the winter. It sometimes rains. We feed off game, chickens, etc. . . . All the Europeans have been ill, except me. We've been 20 Europeans here at the camp at most. The first ones arrived on 9 December. There have been 3 or 4 deaths. The Cypriot workmen come from the surrounding villages; they've taken on up to 60 a day. I manage them: I check off the hours worked, organize the equipment, send reports to the Company, keep accounts of the food and all the expenses; and I handle the pay; yesterday, I made a small payout of 500 francs to the Greek workmen.

I'm paid by the month, a hundred and fifty francs, I believe: as yet all I've received is twenty francs or so. But I'm soon going to be paid in full and I fancy even dismissed, as I believe a new company is coming to set up in our place and do the whole thing on piecework. It was this uncertainty that delayed me writing. At all events, my food only costing me 2.25 a day, and not owing anything very much to the boss, I'll always have enough left to wait for other work, and there'll always be some for me here in Cyprus. They're going to build railways, forts, barracks, hospitals, harbours, canals, etc. On 1 March they're going to give out land concessions, with no other costs except the registration fees.

What's happening at home? Would you rather I came back? How's business? Write to me very soon.

ARTHUR RIMBAUD.
Poste restante, Larnaca (Cyprus).

I'm writing this in the desert and don't know when to send it off.

33. To his family

Larnaca (Cyprus), 24 April 1879.

Only today can I get the power of attorney back from the chancellery; but I think it's going to miss the boat and to wait for next Thursday's sailing.[72]

I'm still the foreman at the Company's quarries, and I lay charges and blow up and cut the stone.

The heat is very severe. They're cutting the grain. The fleas are a frightful torment, at night and in the daytime. On top of which, the mosquitoes. You have to sleep beside the sea, in the desert. I've had set-tos with the workmen and have had to ask for weapons.

I'm spending a lot. 16 May will end my fifth month here.

I think I'm going to come back; but, before I do, I'd like you to give me some news.

Write to me, therefore.

I'm not giving you my address at the quarries, because the post never comes this way, but to the town, which is eighteen miles away.

A. RIMBAUD,
Poste restante, Larnaca (Cyprus).

34. To his family

[no date]

It's a fortnight since they announced from Paris that the tent and the dagger had been sent and I've still not received anything.

It's too bad.

35. To his family

Mont-Troodos (Cyprus), Sunday 23 May 1880

Forgive me for not having written sooner. You've perhaps felt a need to know where I was; but up until now it's truly been impossible for me to let you have my news.

I could find nothing to do in Egypt and I left for Cyprus nearly a month ago. On arrival, I found my old employers had gone bankrupt. After a week, however, I found the job I'm in at the moment. I'm an overseer at the palace they're building for the governor-general, on the summit of the Troodos, the highest mountain in Cyprus.

Up until now I've been alone with the engineer, in one of the wooden huts that form the camp. Yesterday some fifty workmen arrived and the work is going to get under way. I'm the only overseer, up until now I've only been getting two hundred francs a month. It's a fortnight since I was paid, but I have a lot of expenses: you have always to travel on horseback; transport is excessively difficult, the villages a long way off, food very expensive. What's more, whereas you get very hot on the plains, at this height it is, and will be for another month, unpleasantly cold; it rains, hails and blows enough to knock you over. I've had to buy a mattress, blankets, overcoat, boots, etc., etc.

On the summit of the mountain there's a camp where the English troops will arrive in a few weeks' time, as soon as it gets too hot on the plain and less cold on the mountain. Then the supply of provisions will be guaranteed.

Thus at present I'm in the employ of the English administration: I am reckoning on getting a rise shortly and on remaining employed until the work is done, which will probably finish around September. In this way I shall be able to earn a good certificate, so as to be employed on other works that will probably follow, and put aside a few hundred francs.

I'm not well; I have heart palpitations which trouble me a lot. But it's better that I shouldn't think about them. What can I do in any case? The air's very healthy here meanwhile. There are only pine trees and bracken on the mountain.

I'm writing this letter today, Sunday; but I shall have to post it thirty miles away, in a port called Limassol, and I don't know when I shall find an opportunity to go there or send it there. Probably not before the week's out.

[There follows a request for books on forestry and carpentry to be sent to him.]

Up until now, I've talked only about myself. Forgive me. The fact is I thought you must be in good health, and as well as could be in every other respect. You're certainly warmer than I am. And give me lots of news about the little train. And old Michel? And Cotaîche?[73]

I'm going to attempt shortly to get you sent a small consignment of the famous Commanderie wine.

Keep me in your thoughts.

Yours.

ARTHUR RIMBAUD.
Poste restante, Limassol (Cyprus).

Apropos, I was forgetting the record-book business.[74] I'll warn the French Consul here, and the matter will take its own course.

36. To his family

Aden, 17 August 1880.

Dear friends,

I left Cyprus with 400 francs, nearly two months ago, after arguments I had with the paymaster and my engineer. If I'd stayed, I'd have reached a good position within a few months. But I can go back there, however.

I've been looking for work in all the Red Sea ports, in Jidah, Suakin, Messawa, Hodeidah, etc. I came here after having tried to find work in Abyssinia. I was ill when I got here. I'm employed at a coffee merchant's, where I only get seven francs as yet. When I've got a few hundred francs, I shall leave for Zanzibar, where there's work to be had, so they say.

Give me your news.

RIMBAUD.
Aden-camp.

The postage is more than 25 centimes. Aden isn't in the Postal Union.

– By the way, did you send me those books, in Cyprus?

37. To his family

Aden, 25 August 1880.

Dear friends,

I fancy I recently posted a letter to you, telling how I unfortunately had to leave Cyprus and how I arrived here after having travelled down the Red Sea.

Here, I'm in a coffee merchant's office. The Company agent is a retired general. They do a fair amount of business, and are going to do much more. I don't earn much myself, it comes to no more than six francs a day; but if I stay here, and I certainly have to stay here, for it's too far away from everywhere for one not to stay for several months before earning a few hundred francs merely in order to go off in case of need, if I stay, I think I'll be given a position of trust, perhaps an agency in another town, and then I'd be able to make something a bit quicker.

Aden is a frightful rock, without a single blade of grass or drop of decent water: you drink distilled sea water. The heat is excessive, especially in June and September which are the two months of high summer. The constant temperature, night and day, in a very cool and well-ventilated office, is some 35 degrees. Everything's very expensive, and so on. But needs must: I'm like a prisoner here, and I shall assuredly have to stay at least three months before I'm more or less on my feet or get a better job.

And at home? Is the harvest in?

Tell me your news.

ARTHUR RIMBAUD.

38. To his family

Aden, 22 September 1880.

Dear friends,

I have received your letter of 9 Sept, and, as the mail leaves tomorrow for France, I am replying.

I'm as well as one can be here. The firm does several hundred thousand francs' worth a month. I'm the one employee and everything passes through my hands, I'm very much *au fait* with the coffee trade at present. The boss has complete confidence in me. Only, I'm badly paid: I get only five francs a day, fed, lodged, laundry etc., etc., etc., with horse and carriage, which represents a good dozen francs a day. But as I'm the one employee with a few brains in Aden, at the end of my second month here, that's to say on 16 October, if they don't give me two hundred francs a month, clear of all expenses, I shall be off. I'd rather leave than be exploited. I've got about two hundred francs in hand moreover. I should probably go to Zanzibar, where there's work to be had. Here, too, there's plenty of work. Several commercial companies are going to set up on the Abyssinian coast. The firm also has caravans into Africa; and it's still possible that I shall leave that way, where I'd make profits and be less bored than in Aden, which is, as everyone acknowledges, the most boring place in the world, after the one you live in, that is.

I have 40 degrees of heat here, in the house: you sweat litres of water a day. I only wish it was 60 degrees, like when I was staying in Messawa!

I see that you've had a good summer. So much the better. It's the revenge of the famous winter.

The books haven't reached me, because (I'm sure) someone will have appropriated them in my place, as soon as I left Troodos. I still need them, as well as other books, but I'm not asking you for anything, because I don't dare send money, until I'm sure I shan't need it, for example were I to leave at the end of the month.

I wish you every good fortune and a 50-year summer that never ends.

Reply to me still at the same address; if I go off, I'll have it forwarded.

RIMBAUD.
Maison Viannay,
Bardey and Co.
Aden.

– Get my address right, because there's a Rimbaud here, an agent for the Messageries Maritimes. They made me pay 10 centimes sup[plementary] post[age].

I don't believe Frédéric should be encouraged to come and settle down at Roche, if he has the least occupation elsewhere. He'd soon be bored, and you can't count on him staying. As for the idea of getting married, when you haven't a sou or any prospect or capacity of earning any, isn't that a miserable idea? As far as I'm concerned, anyone who condemned me to marriage in similar circs would do better to murder me straight off. But each to his own idea, what he thinks is no affair of mine, affects me not at all, and I wish him all possible happiness on earth and especially in the canton of Attigny (Ardennes).

Yours.

39. *To his family*

Aden, 2 November 1880

Dear friends,

I'm still here for a certain length of time, although I'm committed to another position that I must make my way to shortly. The firm has started an agency in Harar, a region you'll find on the map in the south-east of Abyssinia. From there they export coffee, hides, gum, etc., which they acquire in exchange for cottons and various other goods. The area is very healthy and cool thanks to its altitude. There are no roads and almost no communications. You go from Aden to Harar: by sea first of all, from Aden to Zeilah, a seaport on the African coast; from there to Harar, twenty days by caravan.

M. Bardey, one of the heads of the firm, made a first trip, set up an agency and brought back a lot of merchandise. He left a representative there, under whose orders I shall be. I've been taken on, as from the first of November, at a salary of 150 rupees a month, i.e., 330 francs, or 11 francs a day, plus food, all travelling expenses and 2 per cent of the profits. However, I shan't be leaving before a month or six weeks, because I have to take a large sum of money there which isn't yet available. It goes without saying that you can only go there armed and that there's a risk of leaving your bones in the hands of the Gallas – not that the danger is so very great.

[There follow detailed instructions about buying and sending out to him a long list of practical books and manuals, on metallurgy, hydraulics, naval architecture, mineralogy, etc.]

I'm really too busy today to write at greater length. I only hope you're well and that the winter won't be too hard on you. Give me your news in detail. As for myself, I'm hoping to be able to save something up.

[. . .]

RIMBAUD

40. To his family

Harar, 13 December 1880

Dear friends,

I have arrived in this region after twenty days on horseback across the Somali desert. Harar is a town colonized by the Egyptians and dependent on their government. The garrison is several thousand strong. Our agency and shops are here. The commercial produce of the region is coffee, ivory, hides, etc. The land is high up but not infertile. The climate is cool and not unhealthy. They import all merchandise from Europe here, by camel. There is, moreover, a lot of work to do in the region. We have no regular post here. We're obliged to send our mail to Aden, on rare occasions. This won't reach you for a long time therefore. I'm counting on your having received the *100 francs* that I had sent to you from the Lyon office, and that you've found a way of sending off the items I asked for. I don't, however, know when I shall get them.

I'm here in Galla country. I think I'll have to go further on shortly. I ask you to let me have your news as frequently as possible. I hope things are going well and that you're in good health. I shall find a way of writing to you again shortly. Address your letters or packages as follows: M. Dubar, agent general in Aden. For M. Rimbaud, Harar.

41. To his family

Harar, 15 January 1881.

Dear friends,

I wrote to you twice in December 1880, and naturally have not yet had any replies from you. I wrote in December that they are sending you a 2nd sum of 100 francs, which has perhaps already reached you and which you are to put to the use I said. I have great need of everything I asked you for, and I assume the first articles have already arrived in Aden. But it's another month from Aden to here. A mass of merchandise from Europe will be arriving for us, and we're really going to have to get down to it. I shall shortly be making a long round-trip in the desert, to buy camels. Naturally, we have horses, weapons and the rest of it. The country is not unpleasant: at the moment the weather is like May in France.

I got your two November letters; but I immediately lost them. Having had time to peruse them, however, I recall your acknowledging receipt of the first hundred francs I got sent to you. I'm having a hundred francs sent back to you in case I've involved you in any expense. This will be the 3rd consignment, and I shall stop at that until further notice; in any case, by the time I've had an answer to this, April will be here. I didn't tell you that I have signed on here for three years; which won't stop me leaving gloriously and with confidence, if they give me a bad time. My salary is some 300 francs a month, aside from expenses of every kind, and so much per cent on the profits.

We're going, in this town, to have a Catholic bishop who'll probably be the only Catholic in the region. We're in Galla country here.

We've got a camera coming and I shall send you views of the region and the people. We shall also be getting equipment for preparing natural history specimens, and I shall be able to send you birds and animals that haven't yet been seen in Europe. I already have a few curiosities here that I'm waiting for an opportunity to despatch.

I'm happy to hear that you think of me and that things are pretty good with you. I hope it will go on as well at home as possible. On my side, I shall try hard to make my work interesting and lucrative.

[Enclosed: further commissions in respect of books and precision instruments.]

RIMBAUD,
Maison Viannay, Bardey
Aden, Arabia.

42. *To his family*

Harar, 15 February 1881

Dear friends,

I have received your letter of 8 December, and think indeed I have written to you once since. I have, however, lost all memory of it up-country.

I remind you that I've had 300 francs sent to you: 1. from Aden; 2. from Harar on or around 10 December. 3. from Harar on or around January 10. I'm reckoning that at this moment you have already received these three consignments of a hundred francs and set in motion what I asked. I thank you as of now for the package you announce, but which I shan't receive for two months from now perhaps.

Send me Monge's *Constructions metalliques*, price 10 francs.

I'm not counting on staying here long; I shall know soon when I shall be leaving. I haven't found what I'd supposed; and I live in a very tedious fashion, without any profits. As soon as I've got 1,500 or 2,000 francs I shall leave, and will be very content to do so. I count on finding something better a bit further on. Write to me news of the building works in Panama:[75] as soon as it's open, I shall go. I'd even be happy to leave here, as of now. I've picked up an illness,[76] not so dangerous in itself; but the climate here is treacherous for any sort of illness. Injuries never heal. A cut in a finger one millimetre long suppurates for months and very easily turns gangrenous. Besides which, the Egyptian administration has only inadequate doctors and medicines. The climate is very humid in summer: it's unhealthy; I couldn't like it less, it's much too cold for me.

[. . .]

You mustn't think that the region is altogether uncivilized. We have the Egyptian army, artillery and cavalry, and their administration. Everything's just the same as what exists in Europe; only they're a heap of curs and bandits. The natives are Gallas, all farmers and shepherds: peaceful people, when you don't attack them. The country is excellent, though relatively cold and damp; but the agriculture is backward. Trade mainly comprises the hides of livestock, which are milked during their lifetime and then skinned; plus coffee, ivory, gold; perfumes, incense, musk, etc. The trouble is we're 180 miles from the sea and transport costs too much.

[. . .]

Tell F[rédéric] to look in the Arab papers for a notebook entitled *Jokes, Plays on words etc.* in Arabic; and there ought also to be a collection of *dialogues*, *songs* or I don't know what, useful for those learning the language. If there's a book in Arabic, send it; but all this as packing simply, because it's not worth the carriage.

I'm going to have you sent twenty kilos or so of mocha coffee at my own expense, if it doesn't cost too much in duty.

I'll say until next time!, in hopes of better weather and less stupid work; for if you suppose that I'm living like a prince, I'm certain for my part that I'm living in a very stupid and very tiresome fashion.

This is leaving with a caravan, and won't reach you before the end of March. That's one of the nice things about the situation. The worst of them indeed.

Yours,

RIMBAUD

43. *To his family*

Harar, 4 May 1881

Dear friends,

You're in summer and it's winter here, that's to say that it's quite hot, but it rains frequently. This will last several months.

The coffee harvest will take place in six months' time.

For my own part, I'm reckoning on leaving this town shortly to go and traffic or explore on my own account in the unknown. There's a big lake a few days' journey away, and it's in ivory country: I shall attempt to get there. But the country must be hostile.

I'm going to buy a horse and go off. In the event of it turning out badly, and I remain there, I advise you that I have a sum of 715 rupees belonging to me deposited at the agency in Aden, which you can claim, if it seems worth the bother.

Send me an issue of some public works newspaper or other, so I can know what's happening. Are they working in Panama?

[. . .]

Keep well. *Adieu*.

A. RIMBAUD.

44. *To his family*

Harar, 25 May 1881.

Dear friends,

Dear Mama, I have received your letter of 5 May. I'm glad to learn that your health has recovered and that you're able to continue to rest. At your age, it would be sad to be forced to work. I, alas, do not hold to life at all; and if I live, I'm used to living off fatigue; but if I'm forced to continue to tire myself out as I do at present, and to feed off disappointments that are as vehement as they're absurd in these atrocious climates, I fear I'll cut my existence short.

I'm still here in the same conditions, and, in three months' time, I'd be able to send you 5,000 francs of savings; but I think I shall hold on to them in order to start some small business on my own account in these parts, for I don't have any intention of spending my entire existence in slavery.

In short, may we enjoy a few years of true repose in this life; and happily this life is the only one, which is self-evident, since one can't imagine another life with a greater tedium than this one!

Yours,

RIMBAUD.

45. To his family

Harar, 2 July 1881

Dear friends,

I'm back from the interior, where I bought a considerable quantity of dried hides.

I've a bit of fever at present. I'm leaving again in a few days for a region totally unexplored by Europeans; and if I succeed in definitely setting out, it will be a journey of six weeks, hard and dangerous, but which could be profitable. – I have sole responsibility for this small expedition. I hope as few things will go wrong as possible. At all events, don't be concerned about me.

You must be very busy at present; and I hope the minor works turn out well.

Yours,

RIMBAUD.

P.S. – Am I in contravention of military law? I shall never know where I stand in the matter.

46. To his family

Harar, 22 September 1881

Dear friends,

Your news is late, it seems to me: I've received nothing here in a long time. They set little store by correspondence in this agency!

With you, the winter is about to start. Here, the rainy season is about to end and the summer to start.

I'm in sole charge of the business at the moment, in the agency, in the absence of the manager. I gave in my notice some three weeks ago, and am waiting for a replacement. Meanwhile, it's possible that I shall remain in the region.

[. . .]

Don't leave me too long without news, I wish you a pleasant autumn and every prosperity.

Yours,

RIMBAUD.

47. *To his family*

Aden, 18 January 1882.

Dear friends,

I have received your letter of 27 December 1881, containing a letter from Delahaye. You tell me you've written to me twice concerning the receipt for that sum of money. How come that your letters haven't reached me? And I've just telegraphed from Aden to Lyon, dated 5 January, calling on them to pay this amount! You haven't told me either what amount you have received, which I'm in a hurry to know meanwhile. In the end, it's lucky it should have arrived, after being held back for six months! I wonder also at what rate of exchange it may have been paid to you. In future, I shall choose another means for my consignments of money, for these people go about things in a very disagreeable manner. I have at this moment about 2000 francs free, but I shall have need of them shortly.

I have left Harar and returned to Aden, where I'm waiting to end my arrangement with the company. I shall easily find something else.

As for the military service business, you'll find enclosed a letter from the consul addressed to me, showing you what I've done and what documents are at the ministry. Show this letter to the army authorities, it'll reassure them. If it's possible to send me a duplicate of my lost record-book, I'd be obliged if you could do it soon, because the consul is asking me for it. In short, with what you have and what I've sent, I think the matter's going to be able to be sorted out.

Enclosed a letter for Delahaye,[77] make yourselves acquainted with it. If he has remained in Paris, that'll suit me very well: I need to have bought a few precision instruments. For I'm going to produce a book for the Société de Géographie, with maps and engravings, about Harar and the Galla regions. I'm getting a camera sent from Lyon at this moment; I shall transport it to Harar, and bring back views of those unknown parts. It's a very good proposition.

I also need instruments to make topographical surveys and fix latitudes. When this work's finished and been received by the Société de Géographie, I may be able to obtain funds from them for other journeys. It's a very simple matter.

I ask you therefore to see that the commission enclosed reaches Delahaye, who'll be responsible for the purchases and you will only have to pay for it all. It will run to several thousand francs, but will give me a good return. I shall be very grateful if you will send the whole lot on to me as soon as possible, *direct to* Aden. I implore you to carry out the commission in full; were you to make me go without any part of it, you would make it very awkward for me.

Fond regards,

RIMBAUD.

48. To M. Devisme

Aden, 22 January 1882

Monsieur,

I am travelling in Galla country (East Africa), and, being busy at the moment forming a troop of elephant hunters, I would be very truly grateful if you would kindly give me some information, as soon as possible, concerning the following subject:

Is there a special gun for hunting elephant?

Its description?

Advice on use?

Where is it to be found? Its cost?

The type of ammunition, poisonous, explosive?

I need to buy two trial guns – and possibly, after testing them, half a dozen.

Thanking you in advance for your reply, I remain your obedient servant,

                                                        RIMBAUD.
                                        Aden (English colonies).

Monsieur Devisme,
Paris.

49. To his family

                                        Aden, 10 May 1882

Dear friends,
I wrote twice during April, and my letters ought to have arrived. I have received yours of 23 April.

Don't be concerned on my account: there's nothing extraordinary about my situation. I'm still employed in the same outfit, and I slog away like a donkey in a country for which I feel an unconquerable horror. I am moving heaven and earth to try and get away from here and find more lucrative employment. I hope indeed that this existence will end before I've had time to become a complete idiot. What's more, I'm spending a lot here in Aden, and that gives me the advantage of tiring myself out much more than elsewhere. I shall shortly be sending you several hundred francs for purchases. At all events, if I leave here, I shall warn you. If I don't write more, it's because I'm very tired and because, with me, as with you, there's nothing new.

Good health, first and foremost.

                                                        RIMBAUD.

50. To his family

                                        Aden, 16 November 1882.

Dear friends,
I have received your letter of 24 October. I fancy that by now the cheque will have been paid, and that my stuff is on the way.
If I leave Aden, it will probably be on the Company's behalf.

All that will only be decided in a month or two; up until now, they've not let me see anything definite. As for coming back to France, what would I be doing there, at present? It's much better I should attempt to accumulate something here; then, I shall see. The important thing and the most urgent for me, is to be independent, no matter where.

The calendar tells me that the sun rises in France at a quarter past 7 and sets at 4.15 in November; here, it's always roughly from 6 to 6. I wish you a winter made to measure – and, in advance (for who knows where I shall be in a fortnight or a month), a good new year, what can be called a good new year, and everything as you would wish it, in 1883!

Once I've left again for Africa, with my photographic baggage, I'll be sending you some interesting things. Here, in Aden, there's nothing, not a single leaf (unless you bring it in), a place where one remains only out of necessity.

[. . .]

Forced to leave you. I thank you in advance.
Fond regards,

RIMBAUD.

51. To his mother

Aden, 8 December 1882

Dear Mama,

I have received your letter of 24 November informing me that the sum has been paid and that the shipment is in hand. Naturally, we didn't buy without knowing that the funds would be there to cover the purchase. That's the reason why the matter was decided on only on receipt of the 1850 francs.

You say I'm being robbed. I know very well what a camera alone costs: a few hundred francs. But there are the chemicals, a lot of them and very expensive, and amongst which there are compounds of gold and silver worth up to 250 francs the kilo, there are the plates, the maps, the developing dishes, the bottles, the very expensive packing, which put up the amount. I have requested all the ingredients for a two-year campaign. For myself, I reckon I've been served at a bargain price. My one fear is that the things may get broken en route, at sea. If it gets to me intact, I shall derive a large profit from it, and will send you some intriguing things.

Instead of getting angry, therefore, you need only rejoice, along with me. I know the price of money; and if I take a risk with it, it's in full knowledge.

I must ask you to be good enough to add whatever may be demanded of you on top for the costs of carriage and packing.

You have a sum of 2500 francs from me, from two years ago. Take over on to your own account the land you bought with it, up to the sums you'll be laying out on my behalf. It's a simple enough matter, nothing to put you out.

What's saddening above all is that you end your letter by declaring that you won't involve yourself in my affairs any further. That's not the right way to help a man three thousand miles from home, travelling among savage peoples and not having a single correspondent in his own country! I like to hope that you will modify that uncharitable intention. If I can't even apply to my own family any more for my commissions, who on earth can I apply to?

[. . .]

Regards,

RIMBAUD.

52. To M. de Gaspary

Aden, 28 January 1883.

Monsieur,
Forgive me for submitting the present circumstance to your verdict. Today, at 11 a.m., a man by the name of Ali Chemmak, a warehouseman at the firm where I am employed, having displayed great insolence towards me, I took the liberty of slapping him, not violently.

The coolies on duty and various Arab witnesses having then seized hold of me so as to leave him free to riposte, the said Ali Chemmak struck me in the face, tore my clothing and subsequently seized hold of a stick and threatened me with it.

The people present having intervened, Ali withdrew and shortly afterwards went out to lay charges against me with the municipal police for assault and set up several false witnesses to state that I had threatened to strike him with a dagger etc., etc., and other falsehoods designed to inflame the affair at my expense and arouse the hatred of the natives against me.

Presenting myself before the municipal police on the matter, I am taking the liberty of advising M. the French Consul concerning the violence and threats of which I was the object on the part of the natives, asking for his protection should the outcome of the affair seem to him to advise it.

I have the honour to be, Monsieur le Consul,
Your servant,

RIMBAUD.
Employee of the Maison Mazeran,
Viannay et Bardey,
in Aden.

Monsieur de Gaspary,
Vice-Consul of France,
In Aden.

53. To his family

Mazeran, Viannay et Bardey,
Lyon-Marseille-Aden

Harar, 6 May 1883

My dear friends,
On 30 April, I received your letter of 26 March in Harar.

You say you have sent me two boxes of books. I received one box only in Aden, the one for which Dubar[78] says he had put by twenty-five francs. The other has probably arrived in Aden by now, along with the graphometer. For I'd sent you, before leaving Aden, a cheque for 100 francs along with another list of books. You must have cashed that cheque; and you have probably bought the books. In short, at present, I'm no longer *au fait* with the dates. Before long, I'll be sending you another cheque for 200 francs, because I shall need to have some photographic plates brought back.

The commission has been well done; and if I want, I shall quickly recoup the 2000 francs it cost me. Everyone here wants to be photographed; they even offer a guinea a photograph. I'm not yet properly set up, nor *au fait*; but I soon will be, and I shall send you some interesting things.

Enclosed two photographs of me by me. I'm still better off here than in Aden. There's less work and much more air, greenery, etc. . . .

I have renewed my contract for three years here, but I think the establishment will close soon, the profits don't cover the costs. Anyway, the agreement is that the day I'm dismissed, they will give me three months' wages as an indemnity. At the end of this year, I shall have done three full years in this outfit.

Isabelle is very wrong not to get married if someone well educated and responsible offers himself, someone with a future. Life is like that, and solitude is a bad thing here below. For myself, I regret not being married and having a family. But at present, I am condemned to wander, tied to a distant enterprise, and every day I lose my liking for the climate and the way of life and even the language of Europe. Alas, what's the point of these comings and goings, the fatigue and the adventures among strange races, the languages one fills one's memory with, the nameless difficulties, if I'm not one day, after a few years, to be able to settle myself down in a place I more or less like and find a family, and have at least one son who I can spend the rest of my life raising according to my own ideas, decking him out and arming him with the most complete education that is to be attained in the present age, and who I see becoming a renowned engineer, a man made influential and rich by knowledge? But who knows how long my days in these mountains may last?

And I may die, in the midst of these peoples, without report of it ever getting out.

You speak to me of the political news. If only you knew how indifferent I am to it! I haven't touched a newspaper in more than two years. All those debates I now find incomprehensible. Like the Muslims, I know that what happens happens, and that's all.

The one thing that interests me is the news of home and I am always happy to comfort myself picturing your work in the fields. It's a pity it should be so cold and lugubrious with you, in winter! But you're in spring by this time, and your climate, in that season, corresponds to the one I have here, in Harar, at present.

The photographs show me, one, standing on a terrace of the house, the next, standing in the garden of a café; another, with arms folded in a banana garden. It's all gone white, because of the bad water I use to wash them. But I shall do better work later on. This is just to remind you of my face and give you an idea of the local landscapes.

Au revoir,

RIMBAUD.
Maison Mazeran, Viannay et Bardey,
Aden.

54. *To MM. Mazeran, Viannay et Bardey*

Harar, 25 August 1883.

Harar market's never been as dead as at this season of this year, that's the general view here.

– No coffee. What Bewin and Moussayas' agent[79] collects by the $^1/_4$ frasleh[80] is filth scraped off the floor of the Harari houses, they pay $5^1/_2$ talaris[81] for it.

– Hides prohibitive for us for the reasons already given; don't arrive anyway. 2600 government hides reached 70 paras[82] at auction; we're more or less counting on being able to buy them back next at P.1,50 and forming a caravan with them. They're the same quality as the last ones.

– Goatskins. Have 3000 in warehouse. The costs of purchase and the transporting of all the hides from the provinces put them at an average price of D.4. But we've organized their purchase, and we can collect 2500 to 3000 every month without their going beyond that price.

– Ivory. Looking to organize something but lack specialized men and specialized merchandise.

M. Sacconi,[83] who had pushed on into the Ogaden on a parallel expedition to ours, has been killed along with three servants in the Hammaden tribe adjoining the Wabi about 250 kilometres from Harar, on 11 August. The news reached us in Harar on the 23rd. The causes of this mishap were the poor make-up of the expedition's personnel, and the ignorance of the guides who also wrongly urged them on, on exceptionally dangerous routes, to challenge warlike populations.

Lastly, the wrong attitude of M. Sacconi himself, going against (out of ignorance) the manners, religious customs and rights of the natives. The massacre originated in a quarrel over abbans:[84] M. Sacconi maintained a guide of his own and tried to impose him, as he went, on the native abbans who offered themselves. And then M. Sacconi travelled dressed as a European, even clothed his Sebians[85] as *hostranis* (Christians), ate ham, drank spirits in the sheiks' councils, making them eat ham, and went on with his suspicious-looking geodesic activities, twiddling his sextants etc. at every bend in the road.

The natives who escaped the massacre are three Somali Sebians and the Indian cook Hadj-Sheiti, who took refuge with M. Sotiro[86] two days away, to the east.

M. Sacconi bought nothing and his one objective was to reach the Wabi, and then boast about it geographically. M. Sotiro halted at the first point where he thought he'd be able to get rid of his goods against others. Moreover, he followed a good route, very different from M. Sacconi's. He found a good abban and stopped in a good place. He travels, moreover, in Muslim dress and under the name Adji-Abdallah and accepts all the political and religious formalities of the natives. In the place where he stopped, he's become an object of pilgrimage as a *wodad* (a scholar) and a *sherif* (a descendant of the companions of the

Prophet). We get quite frequent reports of him, and expect him back at the end of the month.

– We're organizing other expeditions shortly. We shall return your funds via M. Sotiro, on his return from the Ogaden. The post, which was first of all due to transport our funds in consignments of 3000 talaris, refuses to do so at present. We regret sending our employees on these unproductive tours when we have great need of them here to work with the outside world.

Marseille imports have lost our orders.

We're now fed up with protesting about the situation we're being put in. We simply declare we are in no way responsible for the damage caused. However, we're advising yet again, for the last time, that all our orders for merchandise be manufactured in the quantity and quality requested. We advise on each order and demand it be carried out. But if no one is willing to get involved, it's unlikely to get done. The same goes for all the native merchandise from Aden, in future we shall go and buy it ourselves. Everything that arrives is very different in any case from what we've requested and doesn't suit us. Our sales this month won't reach 200 talaris, and consequently our costs are going to start swamping us. If they were able to do as we've requested, which is simple enough, we'd cover our costs by some distance, while we wait for better times. Others than ourselves are responsible for this, as well as the harm done to us *personally*.

– We're awaiting our new governor, who, it seems, has had some European education. The elephant hunter you sent us from Aden cavorts endlessly about in the Darimont gorges, and will emerge here once he's eaten his way through his dried pork and <u>preserved milk</u> among the Guerris and Bartris.[87]

Enclosed the July cash omitted from the contents of the last courier and a report on the merchandise for the Harar region.

RIMBAUD.

Messieurs Mazeran, Viannay et Bardey,
Aden.

55. To Mazeran, Viannay et Bardey

Harar, 23 September 1883.

Mazeran, Viannay et Bardey.
Lyon–Marseille–Aden.
Telegrams Mazeran–Lyon
          Maviba–Marseille.

Your letter of 9 September received. Confirm that of 9 September. We are despatching, this 23 September, with caravan no. 46: 42 camels ox-hides. We are preparing, with caravan no. 48, 5000 goatskins for 20 October. The same caravan will probably bring you feathers and ivory from the Ogaden, from where your expedition will return for good end September. We have tried a small expedition among the Itou Djardjar; it is carrying gifts for important chieftains and some merchandise; depending on the information brought back, we will look to set something up among these tribes on a serious footing. We augur well in that direction.

Our men for the Dankali and Awash expeditions have arrived from Zeilah, and we shall likewise set this profitable campaign in train.

Two other expeditions to the Wabi, one via the Ogaden, the other via the Ennya, are also in preparation. The rivers are going down at present and we're getting definitive information about all the business there is to be done in the great circle of Harar. A commercial and geographical report will follow all these researches and we shall address it to you in Marseille.

According to our particular information, we believe that the Itou will again be invaded and finally annexed to Menilek's empire at the beginning of 1884.[88] A residency could even be set up there. The frontiers of the Egyptian establishment and Abyssinia would thus be properly defined. And access for the Gallas, Itous and Arroussis would perhaps be easier. As for the city of Harar, it is off the Abyssinian map.

We are pleased to find your orders arriving bit by bit. We've never heard that the Aden agency was at fault or its delays. We don't have any need therefore for the documentary proof you're preparing. On other occasions, we shall go about it differently. We simply draw your kind attention to the few small orders that are behind, Guéset, Kéhas, Kasdir, Kahrab, Abbayas.[89]

Pearls among others; and add the following: 100 pieces Massachusetts Shirting A (30 yard) top quality (as in the last consignment). Try to get it at a few annas off per piece. – 100 pieces Vilayeti[90] Abou Raïa (Colabaland Smill and Co) over and above the 50 that are on the way.

Increase to 12 maunds[91] the small pearls of the last delivery, and to 12 maunds similarly the large white ones.

2 new maunds Asafoetida (actite).

2 corja largest aïtabanes (the *tobe*[92] blue and red stripes as per our order of 20 May).

Lastly, some ammunition that we have twice requested and the aforesaid Somali grammar.

Yours sincerely.

RIMBAUD.

MM. Mazeran, Viannay et Bardey,
In Aden.

56. Report on the Ogaden

By M. Arthur Rimbaud,
Agent of MM. Mazeran, Viannay et Bardey,
In Harar (East Africa).

Harar, 10 December 1883

Here is the information brought back by our first expedition into the Ogaden.

Ogaden is the name of a grouping of tribes of Somali origin, and of the country they occupy which is to be found generally delimited on the maps between the Somali tribes of the Habr-Gerhadjis, Doulbohantes, Midjertines and Hawïa to the north, east and south. To the west, the Ogaden borders the Gallas,

Ennya pastoralists, as far as the Wabi, and then the River Wabi divides it from the great Oromo tribe of the Oroussis.

[. . .]

The Egyptians appear to look on the Ogadens, like all the Somalis and Dankalis as it happens, as their subjects or rather natural allies by virtue of their being Muslims, and have no thought of invading their territory.

The Ogadens, those at least that we have seen, are tall in stature, more generally red than black; they keep their heads uncovered and their hair short, drape themselves in clean enough robes, carry their *sigadas* on their shoulders, a sabre and a gourd for washing at the hip, a stick in their hands, a large and a small spear, and walk in sandals.

Their daily occupation is to go and squat in groups under the trees, at some distance from the camp and, weapons in hand, deliberate endlessly on their various concerns as shepherds. Apart from these sessions, and also horseback patrols during watering and raids on their neighbours, they are wholly inactive. The children and women are left to look after the animals, to fashion the household utensils, to erect the huts, to get the caravans under way. The utensils are the milk jugs known from the Somal, and the plaited camelhair that is put up on sticks to form the houses in the temporary *gacias* (villages).

[. . .]

They are fanatical Muslims. Each camp has its imam who chants the prayer at the set times. *Wodads* (scholars) are to be found in every tribe; they know the Koran and Arab script and improvise poetry.

Ogaden families are very numerous. M. Sotiro's *abban* could count sixty sons and grandsons. When the wife of an Ogaden gives birth, the latter abstains from all commerce with her until the child is capable of walking unaided. Naturally, he marries one or several more in the meantime, but always with the same reservations.

Their herds consist of humped oxen, short-haired sheep, goats, an inferior breed of horses, milk camels and lastly ostriches, the rearing of which is a custom among all the Ogadens. Every village owns several dozen ostriches which graze apart, watched over by children, sleep by the fireside even in the huts and, both male and female, with their legs hobbled, walk in the caravans behind the camels they are almost as tall as.

They are plucked three or four times a year, and each time they pull out about half a pound of black feathers and sixty or so white feathers. The owners of ostriches value them highly.

There are numbers of wild ostriches. The hunter is covered by the skin of a female ostrich and fires arrows into the approaching male.

Dead feathers have less value than live ones. The tame ostriches were caught when young, the Ogadens not allowing the ostriches to reproduce in domesticity.

Elephants are neither very numerous nor of great size, in the centre of the Ogaden. They are hunted nonetheless on the Fafan, and their real meeting-place, the spot where they go to die, is all along the bank of the Wabi. There, they are hunted by the Dones, a Somali people mixed in with Galla and Swahili, agriculturalists settled on the river. They hunt on foot and kill with their huge spears. The Ogadens hunt on horseback: while fifteen or so horsemen occupy the animal from in front and along the flanks, an experienced hunter severs the animal's rear hocks with his sabre.

They also use poisoned arrows. The poison is called *ouabay* and is used throughout Somalia, and is made from the roots of a bush that have been ground up and boiled. We are sending you a fragment. According to the Somalis, the earth around the bush is always covered with the sloughed skins of snakes, and all the other trees wither around it. The poison only works rather slowly, however, since the natives wounded by the arrows (they are also weapons of war) save themselves by cutting away the injured part.

Dangerous animals are fairly uncommon in the Ogaden. The natives talk on the other hand about snakes, one species of which is horned, and whose breath even is fatal. The commonest wild animals are gazelles, antelopes, giraffes and rhinoceroses, whose skins are used for making shields. The Wabi has all the big river animals: elephants, hippopotamuses, crocodiles, etc.

[...]

Not in living memory had they seen in the Ogaden a quantity of merchandise as considerable as the few hundred dollars' worth we despatched there. It is true that the little we brought back from there works out very expensive, because one half of our merchandise went of necessity on presents to our guides, abbans, and hosts on every side and all along the way, and the Oughaz[93] personally received from us several hundred dollars' worth of gilt abbayas, immahs and gifts of every kind that won him genuinely over as it happens, which is the good result of the expedition. M. Sotiro is truly to be congratulated on the wisdom and diplomacy he showed in this instance. Whereas our competitors have been pursued, reviled, pillaged and murdered and by their very disaster been the cause of terrible wars between the tribes, we have established an alliance with the Oughaz and have got ourselves known throughout the Rere Hersi.

Omar Hussein has written to us in Harar and is waiting for us to go down as far as the Wabi with him and all his goums,[94] only a few days distant from our first stopping-place.

That in fact is our objective. One of us, or some energetic native on our behalf, could collect within a few weeks a ton of ivory that could be exported direct through Berbera duty-free. The Habr-Awals, having gone off to the Wabi with a few sodas or Vilayeti tobes on their shoulders, bring back hundreds of dollars' worth of feathers to Boulhar. A few donkeys laden in all with ten or so pieces of <u>sheeting</u> brought back fifteen fraslehs of ivory.

We have therefore decided to create a post on the Wabi, and this post will be roughly at a point named Eimeh, a large permanent village situated on the Ogaden bank of the river a week away from Harar by caravan.

57. *To his family*

Mazeran, Viannay et Bardey.
Lyon-Marseille-Aden.

Aden, 5 May 1884.

My dear friends,

As you know, our company has been totally liquidated, and
the agency in Harar, which I was running, closed down; the
Aden agency is also closed. The Co.'s losses in France are, I'm
told, nearly a million; losses made, however, from dealings
separate from the ones here, which were working quite satis-
factorily. In short, I found myself dismissed at the end of April
and, in accordance with the terms of my contract, I got an
indemnity of three months' salary, up until the end of July. Thus
at present I'm out of work, though still lodged in the Co.'s
former building, which is rented until the end of June. Monsieur
Bardey has gone back to Marseille, ten days ago, to look for
fresh capital to keep the business going here. I wish him success,
but very much fear the opposite. He told me to wait for him
here; but at the end of this month, if the news isn't satisfactory,
I'll look to find employment elsewhere, and different.

There's no work here at the moment, the big firms supplying
the agencies having all gone bust in Marseille. The other thing
is, for anyone who isn't employed, life here is exorbitant, and
existence intolerably tedious, especially once the summer has
begun; and you know that here we have the hottest summer in
the world!

I have no idea where I may find myself in a month's time. I
have from twelve to thirteen thousand francs with me and, since
you can't entrust anything to anyone here, you're obliged to
drag your nest-egg around with you and watch over it constantly. And this money, which might produce a small income
sufficient for me to live on without a job, brings me in nothing,
apart from continual bother!

What a disheartening existence I drag out in these absurd

climes and these senseless conditions! With these savings, I could have an assured small income; I might rest for a bit, after long years of hardship; but not only can I not go for a day without work, I can't enjoy my gains. The Treasury here only takes deposits without interest, and the trading houses are very far from solid!

I can't give you an address for a reply to this, for I don't know personally where I may find myself being dragged off to shortly, by what routes, for where, and for what, and how!

It's possible that the English will shortly occupy Harar; and it may be that I shall go back there. One could trade there in a small way; I could perhaps buy some gardens and a few plantations there and try to live that way. For the climates of Harar and Abyssinia are excellent, better than those in Europe, whose harsh winters they don't get; and life there costs nothing, the food's good, the air delicious; whereas staying on the Red Sea coast enervates the most robust; and a year here ages people like four years anywhere else.

My life here is a real nightmare therefore. Don't imagine that I spend it pleasantly. Far from it; I've always seen even that it's impossible to live more laboriously than I do.

If work can resume here before too long, it'll still be all right: I shan't eat up my wretched capital by running after adventures. In that case, I should still remain as much as possible in this awful Aden dump; for one-man enterprises are too dangerous in Africa, on the other hand.

Forgive me for spelling out my troubles to you. But I can see that I'm about to reach thirty (half a lifetime!) and I'm very weary of knocking about the world, to no effect.

As for you, you don't have these bad dreams; and I like to picture to myself your tranquil life and your peaceable occupations. May they continue that way!

As for me, I'm condemned to live for a long time yet, perhaps for ever, in these parts, where I'm well known at present, and where I shall always find work; whereas in France, I should be a stranger and would find nothing.

Anyway, let's hope for the best.
Greetings and prosperity.

ARTHUR RIMBAUD.
Poste restante, Aden-Camp,
Arabia.

58. To his family

Aden, 29 May 1884.

My dear friends,

I don't yet know whether work is going to resume. I've been telegraphed to stay on, but I'm beginning to find it a drag. Six weeks I've been here without work; and in the heat we've got here, it's absolutely unbearable. But then, it's self-evident that I didn't come here in order to be happy. And yet I can't leave these parts, now that I'm known here and can make a living here – whereas somewhere else I'd only manage to die of hunger.

If work resumes here, therefore, I'll probably be taken on again, for a few years, two or three years, until July '86 or '87. By which date, I'll be 32 or 33. I'll be starting to grow old. That perhaps will be the moment to gather up the twenty thousand francs odd that I'll have been able to put aside here, and come and get married in the village, where I shall be looked on simply as an old man and it'll only be widows who'll accept me!

In short, may the day only come when I'll be able to escape from slavery and have the income to work only as much as I feel like!

But who knows what will happen tomorrow, and what will happen after that!

Is there nothing left of the sums I have sent you in past years, the total of which came to 3600? If there's anything left, let me know.

I have never received your last box of books. How can it have gone astray?

I'd gladly send you the money I have; but, if work doesn't resume, I shall be forced to have some small business here and will have need of my capital, which will perhaps vanish entirely in short order. That's the way things go everywhere, but especially here.

Do I still have to do any military service, past the age of thirty? And, if I return to France, do I still have to do the service I didn't do?

According to the legal requirements, I fancy that in the case of a justified absence, the service is *deferred*, and still remains to be done, in the event of a return.

I wish you good health and prosperity.

RIMBAUD.
Maison Bardey, Aden.

59. *To his family*

Aden, 10 September 1884.

My dear friends,

I haven't had your news in a long time. I like to think, however, that all is well with you, and I wish you good harvests and a long autumn. I think of you as being in good health and at peace, as usual.

The third month of my new six-month contract is just about over. Business is bad; and I fancy that, at the end of December, I shall have to look for another job, which I shall find easily as it happens, or so I hope. I haven't sent you my money because I don't know where to go; I don't know where I shall find myself in the near future, and whether I won't have to use my capital in some lucrative trafficking.

It may be, in the event of my having to leave Aden, that I shall go to Bombay, where I could find somewhere to invest the money I have at high rates of interest in reliable banks, which would almost enable me to live off the income. 6,000 rupees at 6 per cent would yield 360 rupees a year, or 2 francs a day. And I could live on that, while waiting for jobs.

....

Anyone here who's not a big trader provided with funds or

sizeable credit, anyone who only has a small capital, runs a much greater risk of losing than of seeing them bear fruit; for you're surrounded by countless dangers and, if you want to live at all comfortably, life costs you more than you earn. For the employees, in the East, are at present as badly paid as in Europe; their lot is even far more precarious, because of the deadly climate and the enervating existence one leads.

Myself, I am more or less used to all climates, cold or hot, fresh or dry, and I no longer risk catching fevers or other diseases of acclimatization, but I feel I'm getting very old, very quickly, in these idiotic *métiers* and these companies of savages or imbeciles.

Indeed, you'll think as I do, I fancy: given that I'm earning a living here, and since every man is the slave of this miserable fatality, as well in Aden as elsewhere; better even in Aden than elsewhere, where I'm not known, where I've been completely forgotten and where I'd have to start again! For as long as I can make a crust here, therefore, should I not stay? Should I not stay here, for as long as I lack the wherewithal to live in peace? In fact, it's more than likely that I shall never have the wherewithal, and that I shan't live or die in peace. Well, as the Muslims say: It is written! – That's life: it's not so funny!

The summer finishes here at the end of September; from then on, we shan't have more than 25 to 30° centigrade during the day, and 20 to 25 at night. That's what's known as the winter, in Aden.

The whole seaboard of this filthy Red Sea is tormented like this by the heat. There's a French warship in Obock, on which, out of a total complement of 70, 65 are sick with tropical fevers; and the captain died yesterday. Yet at Obock, which is four hours from here by steamer, it's cooler than in Aden, where it's very healthy and enervating only because of the excessive heat.

And is the wonderful Frédéric over his escapades; what are these ridiculous stories you were retailing about him? He's frantic to get married, he is. Give me an account of it all.

Fond regards,

RIMBAUD.

60. *To his family*

Aden, 7 October 1884.

My dear friends,

I have received your letter of 23 7ember, your news saddens me, what you tell me about Frédéric is very tiresome and may do the rest of us great harm.[95] It would be quite awkward for me, for example, if people knew I had a character like him for a brother. It doesn't on the other hand surprise me with Frédéric: he's a complete idiot, we've always known that, but we always admired the hardness of his skull.

You don't need to tell me not to get into correspondence with him. As for giving him something, what I earn is amassed with too much sweat for me to make a present of it to a Bedouin of that kind who, materially speaking, is less worn out than I am, I'm sure. Anyway, I hope meanwhile for your sake and mine that he'll finally put an end to this play-acting.

As for exercising his tongue on my account, my behaviour is well known here as elsewhere. I can send you the testimonial of *exceptional* satisfaction that the liquidated Mazeran Company granted me for *four years' service* from 1880 to '84, and I have a very good reputation here, which will enable me to earn my living decently. If I had unhappy moments earlier on, I have never sought to live at other people's expense or by doing wrong.

We're in winter here at the moment: the average temperature is 25 above zero. All is well. My contract finishing at the end of December will, I hope, be renewed to my advantage. I shall always find a way to live honourably here.

Near by is the unhappy French colony of Obock, where they're currently trying to set up an establishment; but I don't think they'll ever do anything there. It's a forlorn bit of coast, scorched, nothing to live off, no trade, good only for coaling depots, for the warships for China and Madagascar.

The Somali coast and Harar are busy passing out of the hands of poor Egypt into those of the English, who don't, however, have enough manpower to maintain all these colonies. The

English occupation is ruining all the coastal trade, from Suez to Gardafui. England is horribly caught up in the Egyptian business, and it's very likely it will turn out really badly for them.

Fond regards,

RIMBAUD.

61. To his family

Mazeran, Viannay et Bardey
Telegraphic address:
MAVIBA-MARSEILLE

Aden, 30 December 1884.

My dear friends,

I have received your letter of 12 December, and I thank you for wishing me prosperity and good health, which I return likewise for each day of the year ahead.

As you say, my vocation will never lie in tilling the soil, and I have no objections to seeing that land rented out: I hope for your sake that they'll be rented soon and successfully. To keep the house is always a good thing. As for coming to you for a break, that would be most agreeable: I'd be very happy, indeed, to relax; but I can hardly see the opportunity for relaxation taking shape. Up until now, I've managed to survive here: if I leave, what shall I find in exchange? How can I go and bury myself in a countryside where no one knows me, where I can't find any opportunity to earn something? As you say, I can only come there so as to rest; and to rest, you need an income; to get married, you need an income; and I don't have any such thing. So for a long time to come, I'm condemned to follow the trails where I can find a living, until, by dint of wearing myself out, I can scrape together the wherewithal for a moment's respite.

I have thirteen thousand francs in hand at the moment. What do you expect me to do with that in France? What marriage do you expect it to procure me? So far as poor and honest wives are concerned, you can find them all over the world! Shall I come and marry there, and yet be forced to travel in order to live?

In short, I'm past thirty and have had a pretty bad time and I can't see that that is going to end, far from it, or at least that it's going to end by getting any better.

In short, if you can give me a good plan, I'll be very pleased.

Business is very bad here at the moment. I don't know whether I'm going to be taken on again, or, at least, on what terms I'll be taken on. I've had four and a half years here; I don't want to be demoted, yet business is very bad.

The summer will be returning in three or four months' time, and living here will become ghastly once again.

It's in fact the English, with their absurd policy, who are currently ruining trade on all the coasts. They've been trying to rearrange everything, and they've managed to do worse than the Egyptians and Turks that they've ruined. Their Gordon[96] is an idiot, their Wolseley[97] a donkey, and all their undertakings a senseless series of absurdities and depredations. As far as news from the Sudan is concerned, we know no more than in France, no one comes from Africa any more, everything is disorganized and the English administration in Aden is only interested in issuing falsehoods; but it's very likely the Sudan expedition won't succeed.

France too is coming and doing stupid things in these parts; a month ago, they occupied the whole of the Bay of Tajura, so as to occupy the heads of the routes to Harar and Abyssinia. But those coasts are utterly desolate, the expense they're going to there is completely pointless, if you can't quickly advance towards the plateaux of the interior (Harar), which are then good country, very healthy and productive.

We can also see that Madagascar, which is a good colony, is nowhere near being brought under our control;[98] and they're spending hundreds of millions on Tonkin,[99] which, according to all those who come back from there, is a wretched landscape and impossible to defend from invasions.

I don't think any nation has a colonial policy as inept as the French. – England may make mistakes and run up the bills, but at least it has serious concerns and important perspectives. But no power knows how to waste its money, for no gain at all, in impossible places, the way France does.

In a week's time, I'll let you know whether I've been re-engaged, or what I shall have to do.

Fond regards,

RIMBAUD.
Aden-Camp.

62. To his family

Aden, 15 January 1885.

My dear friends,

I have received your letter of 26 Xmber '84. Thank you for your good wishes. May your winter be short and the new year happy!

I'm still well, in this filthy country.

I've signed up again for a year, that's to say until the end of '85; but it's possible that, this time yet again, business will be suspended before that end-date. These countries have become very bad, since the Egyptian business. I remain on the same terms. I get 300 francs net a month, not counting my other expenses, which are paid and which represent another 300 francs a month. The job is thus about 7000 francs a year, of which I have about 3500 to 4000 net left at the end of the year. Don't think I'm a capitalist: my whole capital at the moment is some 13,000 francs, and will be about 17,000 frs at the end of the year. I shall have been working for five years to amass that sum. But what could I do anywhere else? I've done better hanging on somewhere where I could live by working; for what prospects would I have anywhere else? But it's all one; the years go by and I amass nothing, I shall never manage to live off my investments here.

My work here consists of buying coffee. I buy about two hundred thousand francs' worth a month. In 1883, I bought more than 3 million during the year, but my profit on it is no more than my miserable salary, whether three or four thousand francs a year: you can see that jobs are badly paid everywhere. It's true that the old company went bankrupt for nine hundred thousand francs, but not attributable to the Aden business, which, if it didn't leave any profit, at least didn't lose anything. I also buy a lot of other things: gum, incense, ostrich feathers, ivory, dried hides, sunflowers, etc., etc.

I'm not sending you my photograph; I'm careful to avoid all pointless expenditure. I'm in any case always badly dressed; you can only wear very light cotton things here; people who've spent a few years here can no longer spend the winter in Europe, they'd croak straight away from some pneumonia or other. If I come back, it'll only ever be in the summer therefore; and I shall be forced to go back down, in the winter at least, towards the Mediterranean. In any case, don't count on my mood becoming any less vagabond, on the contrary, if I had the means to travel without being forced to stay so as to work and earn my living, I wouldn't be seen in the same place two months running. The world is very big and full of magnificent bits of country that a thousand men's lifetimes wouldn't be enough to visit. On the other hand, I wouldn't want to be a vagabond in poverty, I'd like to have a few thousand francs invested to be able to spend the year in two or three different countries, living modestly and trafficking in a small way to pay my expenses. But I shall always be unhappy living permanently in the same spot. Anyway, the most likely thing is that you'll go instead where you don't want to go, and do instead what you wouldn't want to do, and that you live and die quite otherwise from how you'd ever want, without the hope of any sort of recompense.

As for the Korans, I received them a long time ago, just a year ago, in Harar indeed. The other books must in fact have been sold. I'd very much like to get you to send a few books, but I've already wasted money on that. However, I have no amusements here, where there are no newspapers or libraries and where they live like savages.

[. . .]

Fond regards,

RIMBAUD.

63. To his family

Aden 14 April 1885.

My dear friends,

I have received your letter of 17 March, and I can see that things with you couldn't be better.

If you complain of the cold, I complain of the heat, which has just started again here. We're suffocating already, and it'll go on until the end of September. I'm suffering from a gastric fever, I can't digest anything, my stomach has become very weak here and makes me very unhappy for the whole summer; I don't know how I'm going to get through this summer, I greatly fear being forced to leave the place, my health is much impaired, a year here is the same as five anywhere else. In Africa, on the contrary (in Harar and Abyssinia), the weather's very good, and I'd like it much better than in Europe. But since the English have been on the coast, trade on all those coasts has been completely ruined.

I still have the same salary: I don't spend a *sou*. The 3600 fr I get, I still haven't touched at the end of the year, or more or less, since in 4 years and 4 months, I still have in hand 14,500 fr. The camera I've sold, to my great regret, though not at a loss. When I told you that my job is worth 6000 fr, I'm counting in the costs of food and lodging that are paid for me, because everything's very dear here. I drink absolutely nothing but water, and I need *fifteen francs'* worth a month! I never smoke, I dress in calico: I don't spend 50 fr a year on clothes. One lives horribly badly here, for a lot of money. Every night of the year, you sleep in the open, yet my lodgings cost 40 francs a month! And so on. In fact, one lives the most ghastly life in the world here; and I'm certainly not staying here next year. You wouldn't want to live the life I lead here for anything; one comes thinking one will make something, but a franc somewhere else would be worth 5 here.

We never get any newspapers, there are no libraries at all; as for Europeans, there are only a few idiotic commercial employees who squander their salaries on billiards and then leave the place cursing it.

[. . .]

Business has got very difficult here and I live as meagrely as possible, so as to try and to get out of here with something. I'm busy every day from 7 to 5, and I never have a day off. When will this life end?

Who knows? We shall perhaps be bombarded soon. The English have set the whole of Europe against them.

War has begun in Afghanistan, and the English will only end up giving in temporarily to Russia, and Russia, after a few years, will return to the attack against them.

In the Sudan, the Khartoum expedition has retreated; and, as I know that climate, it must be two-thirds melted away. Over by Suakin, I fancy the English won't advance for now, before knowing how things will turn out in India. Those deserts are uncrossable moreover, from May to September, for armies moving at speed.

In Obock, the small French administration is busy banqueting and boozing away government funds, which will never get a single sou out of that awful colony, only colonized up until now by a dozen pirates.

The Italians have come poking about in Messawa, nobody knows how. It's likely they'll have to evacuate, England not being able to do anything more for them.

In Aden, in the expectation of war, they're rebuilding the whole system of fortifications. It would give me pleasure to see the place reduced to dust – but not while I'm here!

In any case, I certainly hope not to have much more of my existence to spend in this filthy place.

Fond regards,

RIMBAUD.

64. To his family

Aden, 26 May 1885.

Dear friends,

I'm well in spite of everything, and I wish you far better.

We're in our spring steamroom; skins stream, stomachs turn sour, brains are disturbed, business is lousy, the news is bad.

Whatever may have been said lately, it's still greatly feared that the Russo-English war will shortly be declared. The English anyway are continuing to arm in India and, in Europe, are seeking to make it up with the Turks.

The war in the Sudan has ended shamefully for our Englishmen. They're abandoning everything, so as to concentrate their efforts on Egypt proper: there will probably next be a fuss over the Canal.

Poor France is in just as ridiculous a situation in Tonkin, where it's quite possible that, despite the promises of peace, the Chinese will chuck the remainder of the troops back into the sea. And the war in Madagascar seems to have been abandoned too.

I have a new contract here until the end of 1885. It's very possible I shan't finish it; business has got so thin here that it would be better to abandon it. My capital comes to just 15,000 francs at the moment; that would give me 6 per cent in Bombay from any bank, an income of 900 francs which would enable me to live while waiting for a good job. But we shall see until the end of the year.

Waiting to hear from you.

RIMBAUD.
Maison Bardey, Aden.

65. To his family

Aden, 28 September 1885.

My dear friends,

I have received your letter of late August.

I didn't write, because I didn't know if I was going to stay here. That will be decided at the end of this month, as you'll see from the enclosed contract, three months before the expiry of which I have to give notice. I'm sending you this contract, so that you can present it in the event of any demands by the military. If I remain here, my new contract will take effect from 1 October. I shall perhaps still do this six-month contract; but won't be spending next summer here, I hope. The summer finishes here around 15 October. You can't begin to imagine the place. There isn't a single tree here, not even a dried-up one, not a blade of grass, not a patch of earth, not a drop of fresh water. Aden is the crater of an extinct volcano filled in the bottom with sand from the sea. So you see and touch absolutely nothing except lava and sand which can't produce the scantiest vegetation. The surroundings are a desert of absolutely arid sand. But here, the walls of the crater stop the air from entering, and we roast in the bottom of this hole like in a lime-kiln. You need to be forced to work for your daily bread, to be employed in such hellholes! There's no society at all apart from the local Bedouin, so you become a total imbecile in a few years. In short, it would be enough for me to get a sum together here which, invested somewhere else, would pay me more or less enough secure interest to live off.

Unfortunately, the rupee–franc exchange rate is going down in Bombay by the day; *money* is depreciating everywhere; the small capital I have (16,000 francs) is losing value because it's in rupees; this is all abominable: awful countries, business lamentable, it poisons one's existence.

[...]

India is pleasanter than Arabia. I could also go to Tonkin; there must certainly be jobs there at the moment. And if there's nothing there, one can push on as far as the Panama Canal, which is still far from finished.

[...]

If I make a new contract, I will send it to you. Send this one back once you no longer need it.

Fond regards,

RIMBAUD.

66. To his family

Aden, 22 October 1885.

Dear friends,

When you receive this, I shall probably be in Tajura, on the Dankali coast annexed to the colony of Obock.

I've left my job in Aden, after a violent disagreement with those unspeakable skinflints whose aim it was to stupefy me for all eternity. I've done those people a lot of favours; and they've always tried to do me down. Anyway, they can go to the devil! ... They've given me excellent references for my five years.

I have several thousand guns coming from France. I'm going to form a caravan, and carry this merchandise to Menilek, the king of Shewa.[100]

The route to Shewa is very long: two months' march almost as far as Ankobar, the capital, and the country you pass through on the way is a frightful desert. But up there, in Abyssinia, the climate is delightful, the population is Christian and hospitable, and life costs almost nothing. There are only a few Europeans there, a dozen in all, and their occupation is the trade in weapons, which the king buys at a good price. If no accidents befall me, I reckon on getting there, being paid straight away and coming back down with a profit of 25 to 30,000 francs realized in under a year.

Should the affair succeed, you would see me in France, around the autumn of 1886, where I should myself buy fresh merchandise. I hope it will turn out well. Hope it also, for my sake; I have great need of it.

Were I able, after three or four years, to add a hundred thousand francs or so to what I already have, I'd be glad to leave these wretched parts.

I have sent you my contract, by the last mailboat but one, to plead my case with the Army authorities. I hope that from now on it'll be in order. With all of which, you've never managed to tell me what sort of service I have to do; so that, if I present myself to a consul for some certificate, I'm incapable of informing him about my situation, not knowing it myself! It's ridiculous!

Don't write to me at the Bardey outfit any more: those animals would intercept my correspondence. For another three months, or at least two and a half, from the date of this letter, that's to say up until the end of 1885 (including the fortnight from Marseille to here), you can write to me at the address below:

Monsieur Arthur Rimbaud
Tajura
French colony of Obock

Good health, have a good year, rest and prosperity.

Fond regards,

RIMBAUD.

67. To his family

Tajura, 3 December 1885.

My dear friends,

I am here busy forming my caravan for Shewa. It's not going quickly, as per usual, but in the end, I'm reckoning on starting up from here around the end of January 1886.

I'm well. – Send me the dictionary requested, at the address given. All subsequent communications for me to the same address. They'll be forwarded to me from there.

Tajura here has been annexed to the French colony of Obock for the last year. It's a small Dankali village with a few mosques and a few palm trees. There's a fort, built in the old days by the Egyptians, where six French soldiers sleep at present under the orders of a sergeant, in charge of the post. The region has been left with its petty sultan and native administration. It's a protectorate. The local trade is trafficking in slaves.

The Europeans' caravans leave from here for Shewa, it's nothing much; but you have great difficulty getting through, the natives on all these coasts having become enemies of the Europeans, since the English admiral Hewett made the emperor Yohannes of Tigre[101] sign a treaty abolishing the slave trade, the one native commercial activity that was at all healthy. However, under the French protectorate, they're not trying to obstruct the trade, and that's better.

Don't go thinking that I've become a slave trader. The goods we import are guns (old percussion rifles taken out of service forty years ago), which, among the dealers in used weapons, in Liège or in France, are worth 7 or 8 francs each. You sell them for about forty francs to the King of Shewa, Menilek II. But there are enormous overheads, not to mention the dangers of the journey, both there and back. The people along the way are Dankalis, Bedouin herdsmen and fanatical Muslims: they're to be feared. It's true that we travel with firearms and the Bedouin have only spears: but all the caravans come under attack.

Once past the river Awash, you enter the domains of the powerful King Menilek. There, they're Christian farmers; the country is very high up, as much as 3000 metres above sea-level; the climate is excellent; you can live absolutely gratis; all European products grow; you're well thought of by the people. It rains there for six months of the year, like in Harar, which is one of the spurs of the great Ethiopian massif.

I wish you good health and prosperity for 1886.
Fond regards,

A. RIMBAUD.
Hôtel de l'Univers, Aden.

68. To his family

Tajura, 28 February 1886.

My dear friends,

This time, I haven't heard from you in almost two months.

I'm still here, with the prospect of remaining here for another three months. It's very disagreeable; but it has to end sometime, however, and I shall get under way, to arrive, I hope, without hindrance.

My merchandise has all been landed, and I'm waiting for the departure of a large caravan, to join up with it.

I fear you may not have completed the formalities for sending the Amharic dictionary: nothing has reached me up until now. But perhaps it's in Aden; for it's *six months* since I wrote to you about the book, for the first time, and you can see what a talent you have for getting the things I have need of out to me on time: six months to receive a book!

In a month's time, or six weeks, the summer will begin again on these accursed coasts. I hope not to spend a large part of it here but to take refuge, within a few months, among the mountains of Abyssinia, which is the Switzerland of Africa, without winters and without summers: springtime and perpetual greenery, and a life of freedom with nothing to pay!

I'm still reckoning on coming back down at the end of 1886 or beginning of 1887.

Fond regards,

RIMBAUD.

69. Labatut[102] and Rimbaud to the Foreign Ministry

Monsieur le Ministre,

We are French traders established for some ten years past in Shewa, at the court of King Menilek.

In August 1885, the King of Shewa, Ras Govana and several of our connections in Abyssinia placed an order with us for arms and ammunition, tools and various other merchandise. They advanced us certain sums and, assembling in addition all our available capital in Shewa, we went down to the coast at Obock.

There, having requested and obtained from M. the Governor of Obock authorization to disembark in Tajura and to despatch by caravan the precise quantity of arms and ammunition that we wished to purchase, and having also obtained from the government in Aden, through the good offices of M. the French Consul, authorization to have the aforesaid arms transited to Aden for Tajura, we had our purchases made in France by our agents, one of us remaining in Aden for the transit, the other in Tajura, for the preparation of the caravan under French protection.

Towards the end of January 1886, our merchandise having been forwarded to Aden was unloaded in Tajura and we organized our caravan, with the difficulties normal in Tajura we would add. Finally, our departure was to have taken place towards the end of April.

On 12 April, M. the Governor of Obock came to announce that a despatch from the Government had ordered a summary cessation of all arms imports into Shewa! An order was given to the Sultan of Tajura to halt the formation of our caravan!

Thus, with our merchandise sequestrated, our capital dispersed in the overheads of the caravan, our personnel subsisting indefinitely at our expense, and our matériel deteriorating, we await in Tajura the reasons for and consequences of so arbitrary a measure.

Meanwhile, we are certainly in compliance with all the regulations, as the colony's authorities can testify. We have brought in arms only on the order from the government of Shewa, and, equipped with the necessary authorization, we are proceeding to despatch them to their destination as speedily as possible; we can prove that we have never sold, given or even entrusted a single weapon to the natives at any time or place. Our arms are to be delivered to Menilek in the packaging in which they left France, and nothing can ever be subtracted from them, either on the coast or in the interior.

Whatever the eventual decisions of the Ministry may be, we wish it to be understood from the outset that it would be quite impossible for us to liquidate our enterprise legally or normally, 1. because these arms and ammunition were ordered by the Shewa government, 2. because it is impossible for us to recoup the costs incurred.

Nowhere would these weapons realize their value *on return to Tajura*. People well acquainted with these operations know that a capital sum three times the actual value of the weapons is at once absorbed on the coast by the unloading, by the provisioning and wages of a whole population of Abyssinian servants and camel-drivers assembled for the caravan, by the considerable baksheesh in money and presents to notables, by the extortions of the Bedouin in the neighbourhood, wasted advances, hire charges for the camels, recruitment duties and taxes of passage, the costs of housing and feeding the Europeans, the purchase and maintenance of a mass of matériel, foodstuffs and baggage animals for a journey of fifty days in the most arid of deserts! The population of Tajura subsists entirely on the formation of a caravan for the three, six or even ten months one inevitably finds oneself delayed in the place.

[. . .]

It will be understood that one undertakes affairs as slow, dangerous and tedious as this only in the assured prospect of large profits. The prices paid for these weapons in Shewa, where they are anyway few in number up until now, are in fact extraordinarily high, all the more so in that payment is made in merchandise ceded by the King at the Shewa price, leaving a profit of about 50 per cent when one returns in the Aden market. This explains why French traders operate in Shewa with funds borrowed at 50, 75 or 100 per cent annual interest.

[. . .]

Adding 50 per cent on our return, that is to say the profit from the sale in Aden of the merchandise (ivory, musk, gold) given in payment in Shewa by the King, we establish that this operation should produce a net sum of 60,000 dollars within the space of a year to eighteen months, 60,000 dollars, at the average rate of exchange in Aden (francs 4,30) are equal to 258,000 francs.

We consider the Government to be our debtor for this sum for as long as the present embargo lasts and, if it is maintained, that will be the figure of the indemnity that we shall claim from the Government.

We cannot help but make the following observations on a few political motives which may have inspired the measure inflicted on us:

1. It would be absurd to suppose that the Dankali might arm themselves on the occasion of this traffic. The extraordinary fact, which would not be repeated, of a few hundred weapons being looted a long way off at the time of the attack on the Barral caravan,[103] and shared out among a million Bedouin, does not constitute any danger. The Dankali, moreover, like the other peoples of the coast, have so little liking for firearms, that you would never find the smallest outlet for them along the coast;

2. It cannot be said that there is any correlation between the importation of arms and the exportation of slaves. This latter traffic has existed between Abyssinia and the coast since the most ancient times, in unchanging proportions. But our business dealings are wholly independent of the obscure trafficking of the Bedouin. No one would dare to argue that a European has ever sold or bought, transported or helped to transport a single slave, either on the coast or in the interior.

In any case, the fact of the embargo on the importation of arms intended for Shewa will have as its sole, certain and immediate consequence the radical suppression of commercial relations between the colony of Obock and Abyssinia.

While the Assab route will remain open especially to the importation of arms under Italian protection, and the excellent Zeilah route will corner the importation of native fabrics and merchandise under English protection, no Frenchman will dare venture any longer into the Obock-Tajura ambush, and there will no longer be any reason to pay a stipend to the chiefs of Tajura and the ill-omened route linking it to Shewa.

Hoping for better from the Government of the French nation which we have honourably and courageously represented in these regions,

We remain, Monsieur le Ministre, your most respectful and obedient servants.

LABATUT and RIMBAUD.
Tajura, 15 April 1886.

M. le Ministre des Affaires Etrangères,
Paris.

70. *Menilek II to Rimbaud*

Menilek II, King of Shewa, of Kafa and all the surrounding Galla lands.

May this reach Monsieur Rimbaud. How are you? I, God be praised, I am well, as is all my army.

The letter that you sent to me has reached me. I thank you for all the news that you have sent me.

The interest on the price remaining on account is too high. I have sent the order to Dajaz Mekonnen[104] to pay you. Receive this sum from him. If you have news from Europe and from Messawa, send it to me, without delay.

Written the 30 sanié 1879 [June 1887], in the country of Adea Bagoftou.

71. *To M. de Gaspary*

Aden, 30 July 1887.

Monsieur le Consul,

I have the honour to give you an account of the liquidation of the late Labatut's caravan,[105] an operation in which I was an associate in accordance with an agreement made in the consulate in May 1886.

I learnt of Labatut's demise only at the end of '86, at the moment when, all the early costs having been met, the caravan was starting to get under way and could no longer be halted, thus I was unable to come to a new arrangement with the operation's creditors.

In Shewa, the caravan's transactions took place under disastrous conditions: Menilek took possession of all the merchandise and forced me to sell it to him at a reduced price, forbidding me to sell them retail and threatening to send them back to the coast at my expense! He gave me 14,000 thalers for the whole caravan en bloc, subtracting from that total amount a sum of 2500 thalers as payment for the second half of the hire of the camels and other costs of the caravan settled by the *hazage*,[106] and another sum of 3000 thalers, in settlement of an account held with him by Labatut, so he told me, whereas everyone assured me that the King was, rather, Labatut's debtor.

Pursued by the band of Labatut's purported creditors, whose side the King always took, whereas I was never able to recover anything from his debtors, and tormented by his Abyssinian family, which was furiously claiming his succession and refused to recognize my proxy, I was afraid of soon being stripped completely bare and took the decision to leave Shewa, but I was able to obtain from the king an IOU on the governor in Harar, Dajazmach Mekonnen, for the payment of some 9000 thalers, which alone remained due to me, after the theft of 3000 thalers effected by Menilek from my account, and in accordance with the derisory prices he had paid me.

The cashing of Menilek's IOU was not concluded in Harar without considerable expense and difficulty, some of the creditors having come all the way there to renew their attacks on me. In sum, I returned to Aden on 25 July 1887 with banker's drafts for 8000 thalers and about 600 thalers in cash.

[. . .]

All the Europeans in Shewa were witness to the progress of this affair, and I am holding the documents at M. le Consul's disposal.

Please accept, Monsieur le Consul, my loyal respects.

A. RIMBAUD.

Monsieur de Gaspary,
Vice-Consul of France,
Aden.

72. To the Editor-in-Chief of the Bosphore égyptien[107]

Cairo, [20] August 1887.

Monsieur,

Having returned from a journey into Abyssinia and Harar, I take the liberty of addressing the following few remarks on the present state of things in that region. I believe they contain some previously unrecorded information; and as for the opinions expressed therein, they have been prompted by the experience of a seven-year residence down there.

Since what is involved is a round trip between Obock, Shewa, Harar and Zeilah, allow me to explain that I went down to Tajura at the beginning of last year in the intention of forming a caravan destined for Shewa.

My caravan was made up of several thousand percussion rifles and an order of tools and various equipment for King Menilek. It was held up for a whole year in Tajura by the Dankali, who proceed in this same manner with all travellers, opening the route for them only after having stripped them of everything possible. Another caravan, whose merchandise was disembarked in Tajura along with mine, only succeeded in getting going after fifteen months and the one thousand Remingtons brought by the late Soleillet[108] at the same date are still lying after nineteen months under the village's solitary clump of palm trees.

Six short stages from Tajura, or some 60 kilometres, the caravans descend to the salt lake along terrible routes recalling the presumed horror of lunar landscapes. It appears that a French company is currently being set up to exploit this salt.

Certainly, the salt exists, over very extensive areas, and quite deep perhaps, although no soundings have been taken. Analysis is said to have declared it chemically pure, although it lies in unfiltered deposits on the shores of the lake. But it is very much to be doubted whether its sale will cover the costs of laying a Decauville track,[109] between the shore of the lake and that of the gulf of Goubbet-Keratb, or the cost of personnel and manual labour, which would be exceedingly high, all the workers needing to be brought in, because the Dankali Bedouin do not work, and maintaining an armed force to protect the work-site.

[. . .]

Menilek was still campaigning in Harar when I reached Farra, the point of arrival and departure for caravans and the furthest extent of the Dankali race. The news soon reached Ankober of the King's victory and of his entry into Harar, and the announcement of his return, which was effected within some three weeks. He entered Entotto preceded by musicians sounding deafeningly on Egyptian trumpets discovered in Harar and followed by his troops and his booty, amongst it two Krupp cannon each transported by twenty-four men.

Menilek had long had the intention of taking possession of Harar, where he thought he would find a formidable arsenal, and had warned the French and English political agents on the coast. In recent years, the Abyssinian troops had been regularly ransoming the Itous; they ended by installing themselves there. On the other hand, the emir Abdullah, after the departure of Radouan-Pasha with the Egyptian troops, had been organizing a small army and dreamt of becoming the Mahdi of the Muslim tribes in the centre of Harar. He wrote to Menilek laying claim to the Awash frontier and intimating to him that he should convert to Islam. An Abyssinian post having advanced to within a few days of Harar, the emir sent a few cannon and a few Turks who had remained in his service to disperse them: the Abyssinians were beaten, but Menilek was annoyed and set off himself from Entotto, with some thirty thousand warriors. The encounter took place in Chalanko, 60 kilometres to the west of Harar, at the place where Nadi Pasha had, four years earlier, defeated the Galla tribes of the Meta and Oborra.

The engagement lasted a bare quarter of an hour, the emir had only a few hundred Remingtons, the rest of his troops fighting with their bare hands. His three thousand warriors were put to the sword and crushed in the blink of an eye by those of the King of Shewa. Around two hundred Sudanese, Egyptians and Turks, who had remained with Abdullah after the Egyptian evacuation, perished along with the Galla and Somali warriors. Which is what led the Shewan soldiers, who had never killed any whites, to say on their return that they were bringing back the testicles of all the Franguis[110] in Harar.

The emir managed to flee to Harar, from where he left the same night to go and take refuge with the chief of the Guerri tribe, to the east of Harar, in the direction of Berbera. Menilek entered Harar a few days later unopposed, and having posted his troops outside the town, no looting took place. The monarch restricted himself to imposing a tax of 75,000 thalers on the town and district, and confiscating, in accordance with the Abyssinian right of war, the movable and immovable goods of the vanquished who died in the battle and carrying off from the houses of the Europeans and others all the articles that took his fancy. He made them hand over all the weapons and ammunition stored in the town, formerly the property of the Egyptian government, and returned to Shewa, leaving three thousand of his riflemen camped on a height near to the town and entrusting the administration of the town to the uncle of the emir Abdullah, Ali Abu Bekr, whom the English had, at the time of the evacuation, led off prisoner to Aden, only to release him immediately, and whom his nephew had been keeping in slavery in his house.

It turned out, subsequently, that Ali Abu Bekr's administration was not to the liking of Mekonnen, Menilek's agent general, who descended into the town with his troops, billeted them on the houses and mosques, imprisoned Ali and despatched him in chains to Menilek.

Once inside the town, the Abyssinians reduced it to a horrible cesspit, demolished the dwellings, ravaged the plantations, tyrannized the population in the way the blacks know how to among themselves, and, Menilek continuing to send troop reinforcements from Shewa followed by masses of slaves, the number of Abyssinians currently in Harar could be twelve thousand, four thousand of whom are riflemen armed with every sort of gun, from Remingtons to flintlocks.

The tax returns from the surrounding Galla country now come only from raids, in which the villages are set on fire, the livestock stolen and the population borne off into slavery. Whereas the Egyptian government extracted eighty thousand livres from Harar without any effort, the Abyssinian coffers are permanently empty. The revenues from the Gallas, from customs duties, from the postal service, from the market, and the other receipts are rifled by whoever gets to handle them. The townspeople emigrate, the Gallas are no longer growing anything. Within a few months, the Abyssinians devoured the supply of durra left behind by the Egyptians which could have sufficed for several years. Famine and plague are imminent.

[. . .]

Menilek would like to keep Harar in his possession, but he realizes that he's incapable of administering the country in such a way as to derive significant revenues from it, and he knows that the English have taken a poor view of the Abyssinian occupation. It's said, in fact, that the governor in Aden, who has always been very active in expanding British influence on the Somali coast, would do his utmost to get his government to have Harar occupied in the event of an Abyssinian evacuation, which might come about as a result of famine or complications in the war in Tigre.

For their part, the Abyssinians in Harar think every morning that the English troops are going to appear round the mountains. Mekonnen has written to the English political agents in Zeilah and Berbera not to send their soldiers to Harar any more; these agents used to have each caravan escorted by a few native soldiers.

[. . .]

Menilek was greatly vexed by the embargo on the importing of arms on the coasts of Obock and Zeilah. Just as Yohannes dreamt of having his sea-port at Messawa, so Menilek, though tucked away deep in the interior, flatters himself that he will shortly possess a port on the Gulf of Aden. He had written to the Sultan of Tajura, unfortunately, after the advent of the French protectorate, proposing to buy his territory. On his entry into Harar, he declared himself sovereign of all the tribes as far as the coast, and charged his general, Mekonnen, with not missing the opportunity of seizing Zeilah; only the Europeans having talked about artillery and warships, his views on Zeilah have been modified, and he wrote recently to the French government to ask them to cede Ambado.

We know that the coast, from the end of the gulf of Tajura to beyond Berbera, has been shared out between France and England in the following manner: France keeps the whole coastline from Goubbet Keratb to Djibouti, a cape a dozen miles north-east of Zeilah, and a strip of territory I don't know how many kilometres deep in the interior, the boundary of which on the side of the English territory is formed by a line drawn from Djibouti to Ensa, the third staging-post on the route from Zeilah to Harar. We thus have an outlet on to the route for Harar and Abyssinia. Ambado, which Menilek aspires to own, is a cove near Djibouti, where the governor in Obock long ago had a tricolour boundary-plank planted which the English agent in Zeilah stubbornly had dug up again, until the negotiations were concluded. Ambado is without water, but Djibouti has good springs; and of the three stages joining our route to Ensa, two have water.

[. . .]

From Harar to Entotto, Menilek's present residence, is some twenty days' march on the Itou Gallas plateau, at an average altitude of 2500 metres, provisions, means of transport and safety guaranteed. That means a month in all between our coast and the centre of Shewa, but the distance to Harar is only twelve days, and the latter, invasions notwithstanding, is certainly destined to become the exclusive commercial outlet for Shewa itself and all the Gallas. Menilek himself was so struck by the advantages of Harar's position that on his return, calling to mind the ideas about railways that Europeans have frequently sought to get him to adopt, he was looking for someone to give the commission or concession to for a railway-line from Harar to the sea; he then changed his mind, recalling the presence of the English on the coast! It goes without saying that, in the event of it being constructed (and it will be constructed moreover, in a more or less near future), the Shewa government would contribute nothing to the costs of the operation.

Menilek is completely without funds, remaining still in the most complete ignorance (or insouciance) when it comes to exploiting the resources of the regions he has subjected and continues to subject. He thinks only of assembling the guns that will enable him to send his troops to requisition the Gallas. The few European merchants who have been up to Shewa have brought Menilek, in all, ten thousand cartridge rifles and fifteen thousand percussion rifles, over five or six years. That has sufficed for the Amharas to subject all the Gallas round about, and the Dajaz Mekonnen, in Harar, is planning to descend to conquer the Gallas as far as their southern boundary, towards the coast at Zanzibar. He has the order for this from Menilek even, who has been brought to believe that he could open up a route in that direction for the importing of arms. And they can at least expand a very long way from the coasts, the Galla tribes being unarmed.

[. . .]

People are wondering what Menilek's attitude is and will be during the Italo-Abyssinian war. It is clear his attitude will be determined by what Yohannes, his immediate neighbour, wants and not by the diplomatic manoeuvrings of the governments who are far out of his reach, manoeuvrings that he does not understand in any case and which he always mistrusts. It's out of the question for Menilek to go against the wishes of Yohannes, and the latter, who is very well informed about the diplomatic intrigues that involve Menilek, will know very well how to stay out of things whatever the event. He has already ordered him to choose his best soldiers, and Menilek has had to send them to the Emperor's camp in Asmara. In the event of a disaster even, Yohannes would effect his retreat on Menilek.

Shewa, the one Amhara region that Menilek possesses, is not worth the fifteenth part of Tigre. His other domains are all Galla regions precariously subjected and he would have great difficulty in avoiding a general uprising in the event of his compromising himself in one direction or another. It must not be forgotten either that both Shewa and Menilek, ambitious though he be, have a sense of patriotism and it is out of the question that he should see either honour or advantage in heeding the advice of foreigners.

Since these peoples recognize nothing unless it is visible and palpable, he will act only as his nearest neighbour makes him act, and he has no neighbour but Yohannes, who will know how to keep him from temptation. This doesn't mean that he does not hear the diplomats obligingly out; he will pocket what he may be able to make out of them and, at the given moment, Yohannes, having been alerted, will share with Menilek. And once again, the general sentiment of patriotism and the opinion of Menilek's people are certainly good for something in the matter. But, they can't be doing with foreigners, or their interference, or their influence, or their presence, on any pretext, in Shewa any more than in Tigre, or among the Gallas.

Having settled my accounts with Menilek promptly, I asked him for a draft to be paid in Harar, anxious as I was to travel the new route opened by the King through the Itous, a route hitherto unexplored, and where I had attempted in vain to make headway in the days of the Egyptian occupation of Harar. On this occasion, M. Jules Borelli[111] asked the King for permission to make a journey in that direction, and I thus had the honour of travelling in the company of our amiable and courageous compatriot, whose wholly unpublished geodesic work on the region I then had sent on to Aden.

[...]

As for affairs in Shewa, at present there is nothing to be imported there, since the embargo on the arms trade along the coast. But anyone who went up there with a hundred thousand talaris or so might use them within the year for buying ivory and other goods, exporters having missed recent years and currency becoming exceedingly rare. It is an opportunity. The new route is excellent, and the political state of Shewa will not be disturbed during the war, Menilek being anxious, before anything else, to maintain order on his home ground.

I ask you to accept, Monsieur, my hurried compliments.

RIMBAUD.

73. *To his family*

Cairo, 23 August 1887

My dear friends,

My journey to Abyssinia is ended.

I've already explained how, my partner having died, I had great difficulties in Shewa, concerning his estate. I was made to pay his debts twice over and I had terrible trouble saving what I'd invested in the affair. If my partner hadn't died, I would have made some thirty thousand francs; whereas I find myself with the fifteen thousand I had, after having worn myself out in a ghastly fashion for nearly two years. I have no luck!

I've come here because the heat was appalling this year, in the Red Sea: 50 to 60 degrees the whole time; and finding I was much weakened, after seven years of unimaginable trials and the most frightful privations, I thought that two or three months here would set me up again; but it's more expense, because I can't find anything to do here, and the life is a European one and pretty costly.

I've been tortured just recently by rheumatism in the small of the back, which drives me crazy; I've got it in my left thigh also, which paralyses me from time to time, a pain in the joint of my left knee, rheumatism (already old) in my right shoulder; my hair is grey all over. I imagine my existence is under threat.

Imagine the state one must be in, after feats of the following kind: sea-crossings and overland journeys on horseback, by boat, without clothes, without provisions, without water, etc., etc.

I'm exceedingly tired. I have no job at present. I'm afraid of losing the little I have. Imagine, I carry continually in my belt sixteen thousand and a few hundred francs in gold; it weighs eight kilos or so and has landed me with dysentery.

However, I can't go to Europe, for many reasons; first of all, I'd die in the winter; and then, I'm too used to the wandering life and living for free; and anyway, I have no situation.

I must therefore spend the remainder of my days wandering amidst trials and privations, with the sole prospect of a death sentence.

I shan't be staying long here: I have no job and everything's too expensive. Necessarily, I shall have to return in the direction of the Sudan, Abyssinia or Arabia. Perhaps I shall go to Zanzibar, from where you can make long journeys into Africa, and perhaps to China, or Japan, who knows where?

Anyway, send me your news. I wish you peace and happiness. Fond regards,

> Address: ARTHUR RIMBAUD,
> poste restante, Cairo (Egypt).

74. To M. Alfred Bardey

Cairo, 26 August 1887.

My dear Monsieur Bardey,
Knowing that you always take an interest in things African, I take the liberty of sending the few remarks that follow on how things are in Shewa and Harar at present.

From Entotto to Tajura, the Dankali route is wholly impracticable; the Soleillet guns, which reached Tajura in February '86, are still there – the salt in Lake Assal, which a company was to have worked, is inaccessible and would anyway be unsaleable: it's piracy.

My affair has turned out very badly, and for some time I was afraid I would come back down without a thaler; I found myself assailed up there by a gang of Labatut's false creditors, with Menilek at their head, who robbed me, in his name, of 3000 thalers. To avoid being wholly cleaned out, I asked Menilek to get me through Harar, which he had just annexed: he gave me a Shewa-style bill of exchange on his *oukil* in Harar, the dajaz Mekonnen.

It was only when I'd asked Menilek to go by that route that M. Borelli had the idea of joining up with me.

[. . .]

In Harar, the Amhara are proceeding, as we know, by confiscation, extortion and raids: it's the ruination of the country. The town has become a cesspit. The Europeans had been confined to the town up until our arrival! All this from the fear the Abyssinians have of the English. – The Issa route is very good, and the route from Geldessey to the Herer too.

There are two deals to be done in Shewa at present:

1. To bring sixty thousand thalers and buy ivory, musk and gold. – You know that all the traders, except for Brémond,[112] have come down, even the Swiss. – There's not one thaler to be found in Shewa any more. I've left the ivory, retailing at fifty talaris; with the king, at sixty talaris.

Ras Govana alone has more than forty thousand talaris' worth of ivory and wants to sell: no buyers, no funds! He's also got ten thousand okiets[113] of musk. – No one wants it at three talaris for three okiets. – There are a lot of other holders of ivory too that you can buy from, not counting the private individuals who sell under cover. Brémond tried to get them to give him the Ras's ivory, but the latter wants to be paid cash. – Sixty thousand talaris can be used on such purchases for six months, without overheads, via the Zeilah, Harar, Itou route, and leave a profit of twenty thousand talaris; but you need to be quick, I believe Brémond is going to come down to look for funding.

2. To bring two hundred camels with a hundred armed men from Harar to Ambado (the dajaz gives all this for nothing), and, at the same time, land eight thousand Remingtons off some boat or other (without cartridges, the king's not asking for cartridges: he found three million in Harar) and load up instantly for Harar. France has, at present, Djibouti with a way out to Ambos. There are staging-posts from Djibouti to Ambos. – Here

they've been selling and are still selling Remingtons at eight francs. – The one question is the boat; but you'd easily find one to hire in Suez.

As presents for the king: a machine for melting down Remington cartridges. – Plates and chemical products and equipment for making percussion caps.

I came here to see if something could be set up along these lines. But here they think it's too far away; and in Aden, they're sick of them because such undertakings, partly from bad management, partly from bad luck, have never succeeded. – Yet there are things to be done, and those who get a move on and go about it economically will make it.

My affair turned out very badly because I was a partner of that idiot Lebatut, who, to put the lid on it, died, which meant I had his family and all his creditors in Shewa on my back; with the result that I'm coming out of the affair with very little, less than what I'd put in. I can't undertake anything myself, I don't have the funds.

Even here, there wasn't a single French trader for the Sudan! Passing through Suakin I was told that the caravans pass through and go as far as Berbera. The gum's beginning to arrive. When the Sudan opens up again, and it is slowly opening up, there'll be lots doing.

I shan't stay here, but will go back down as soon as the heat, which was excessive this summer, drops in the Red Sea. I'm at your service in the event of your having some undertaking in which I could be of use. – I can't stay here any longer, because I'm used to the free life. Be so good as to keep me in mind.

RIMBAUD.
Poste restante, Cairo.
Until the end of September.

75. To his family

Aden, 8 October 1887.

Dear friends,

Very many thanks. I can see I'm not forgotten. Don't worry. If things aren't brilliant with me at the moment, at least I'm not losing anything; and I very much hope that a less disastrous period is about to open for me.

So, for the past two years, things have gone very badly, I have worn myself out to no avail, I have great difficulty hanging on to the little I have. I'd very much like to have done with these damnable lands; but one always has the hope that things will take a turn for the better, and stays on wasting one's time in the midst of privations and suffering that the rest of you can't imagine.

And then, what could I do in France? It's quite certain that I can no longer live a sedentary life; above all, I'm very afraid of the cold, – then, anyway, I have neither a sufficient income, nor a job, nor anyone behind me, nor acquaintances, nor a profession, nor resources of any kind. To come back would be to bury myself.

The last journey I made in Abyssinia, which did my health no good at all, could have brought me in a sum of thirty thousand francs; but thanks to the death of my partner and for other reasons, the affair went very wrong and I came out of it poorer than before.

I shall stay here for a month, before leaving for Zanzibar. I don't choose that direction cheerfully; I only see people coming back in a deplorable state, although I'm told that you can find things to take on there.

Before leaving, or even if I don't leave, I shall perhaps decide to send you the funds I left on deposit in Egypt; for, in a word, what with the difficulties in Egypt, the blockade of the Sudan, the blockade of Abyssinia, as well as for other reasons, I see that one can only lose by holding on to capital, whether a little or a tidy sum, in these desperate regions.

You can write to me therefore in Aden, at the following address:

Monsieur Arthur Rimbaud, poste restante.

If I leave, I'll tell them there to forward it.

You must see me as another Jeremiah, what with my perpetual lamentations; but my situation really isn't very jolly.

I wish you the opposite, and am your affectionate,

RIMBAUD.

76. *To the French Consul in Beirut*

Aden, 12 October 1887.

Monsieur,

Forgive me for needing to ask you for the following information: to whom can one apply in Beirut or elsewhere on the Syrian coast for the purchase of four standard asses, in prime condition, of the finest stock employed for the procreation of the biggest and strongest pack-mules in Syria. What might the price be, and also the freight charge via the Messageries and insurance, from Beirut to Aden?

The order in question is from King Menilek of Shewa (southern Abyssinia) where there are only donkeys of inferior stock and where they would like to create a superior breed of mules, given the very great quantity and very low price of mares.

Awaiting your reply, I am, Monsieur le Consul,

Your obliged,

A. RIMBAUD,
at the French Consulate,
Aden, English possessions.

77. To Monseigneur Taurin[114]

Aden, 4 November 1887.

Monseigneur,

May this letter find you in peace and in good health. Next, forgive me for coming to ask that you intercede in the following matter.

You will know that King Menilek had sent me to Harar with a draft for payment of Th. 9866. Now a M. Audon, in Ankobar, had in his hands a note for Th. 1,810, underwritten by the late Labatut to M. Deschamps of Aden, and payable to M. Audon, M. Audon's agent[115] in Shewa. In Shewa, having no money, I was unable to pay out anything on this note. Subsequently, after my departure from Shewa, the aforesaid Audon advised the dajaz Walde-Thadik to write to Mekonnen in Harar to have my payment stopped for the sums which I owed him. In order to release myself from this stoppage, I told Mekonnen to keep by 866 thalers, and repeated that he was to pass this sum on as soon as possible to Audon, to him personally, and not to his Abyssinian or European creditors. Mekonnen gave me a receipt for the aforesaid 866 thalers in the name of M. Audon, and even wrote to the Consul in Aden concerning the matter, acknowledging once again the receipt of the said sum on behalf of the said individual in Shewa.

But at present M. Deschamps refuses to discharge me from the Labatut account (which I settled with a reduction) until he has received news that the said 866 thalers have been paid to M. Audon, and he is even writing to MM. Moussaya in Harar, delegating them to themselves draw out the said sum of Th. 866 from the Dajaz in Harar, and remit it to him in Aden, in the event of the Dajaz not having sent the sum to M. Audon.

I fear the Dajaz may have had the idea of crediting one of M. Audon's Abyssinian creditors with this sum; in which case my payment would become void, and that would prevent me from settling my account here. But most likely Mekonnen has allowed the matter to lapse, and is no longer thinking about the

Th. 866, all the more so because, having received a receipt from him for the said Th. 866, to be passed on to M. Audon, I have naturally given him a receipt for the whole of the sum of Th. 9866 that the King had sent me to draw out in Harar and, if he was acting in bad faith, which is always the case with them, the one recourse I would have against him with the King would be to send the receipt for Th. 866, signed by him, which I have here, – because he would present the King with my receipt for the Th. 9866 and say he knew nothing about the rest.

As it is likely that he will consult you on this matter, you will oblige us all by pricking his conscience, by reminding him that he has received this sum from me, or at least that I gave this amount up to him off my account, so that he might have it sent personally to M. Audon in Shewa.

If he has taken it into his head to credit with this sum one of M. Audon's more or less regular (I'm speaking of the Abyssinians) creditors, I shall consider myself as having been *robbed* by the Dajaz of the sum of Th. 866, and he similarly will have *robbed* M. Audon, since I indeed advised him to pass this sum on to M. Audon alone.

In which event, the settlement of my account with M. Deschamps would be stopped, and the one recourse I would have against the Dajaz would be the seizure of his merchandise at the coast by consular means, which is scarcely possible.

I would wish you to give him to understand, however, that he has made himself responsible for the said sum vis-à-vis the consulate, since he wrote to the Consul here, acknowledging receipt of this sum for the purpose indicated.

– If the money has remained with him in Harar, let him do as M. Deschamps asks, let him hand it over to MM. Moussaya. For myself, I am almost certain that he has sent nothing. In any case, he did not have the right to send it to anyone other than M. Audon.

– M. Savouré wrote to us yesterday that he has bought the Soleillet caravan, and will be back in Aden in a month's time.

– M. Tian returns to Aden at the end of November.

– The troops are said to have embarked from Naples, but England is still seeking to settle the Italo-Abyssinian affair, and it seems that the expedition is becoming less and less decided on, or at least that it will not be on the scale earlier projected, it has completely run out of steam. The correspondents of the Italian newspapers are in Messawa, however. Here, they are buying a few mules and horses, but, at this rate, the preparations will take three years, since the Italians in the Red Sea only remain on their feet during the winters!

– As for the Russian religious mission, it's no longer coming.

– We have Monseigneur Touvier here, the bishop of Messawa, leaving for France until events reach a conclusion.

– As for myself, I am looking for an opportunity to go back up into Ethiopia, but not at my own expense, and it's possible that I shall come back with M. Savouré's caravan.

– I do not need to tell you that I cashed your Th. 500 note straight away at M. Riès'.

– Give my greetings, will you, to M. Sacconi. Here he was said to be seriously ill. I am counting on his having recovered.

– I'm being asked also to point out to the Dajaz that Bénin here is very unhappy at the delay that has occurred in his agent's payment in Harar. But these commercial concerns are not yours. – I have only asked you to intercede in my business with M. Audon because it's a matter in that case of pricking the Dajaz's conscience, and preventing him from committing a theft if he has not already done so. For myself also, I am in a hurry to see the affair untangled, and I shall thus obtain acquittal of the last account relating to the Labatut business.

I am, Monseigneur, your servant

RIMBAUD.
Poste restante
Aden-Camp.

Monseigneur Taurin,
Apostolic Vicar of the Gallas
Harar.

78. To Monsieur de Gaspary

Aden, 9 November 1887.

Monsieur,

I have received your letter of the 8th and take note of your observations.

I am sending you the copy of the account of the Labatut caravan's expenses, needing to keep the original in my possession, because the leader of the caravan who signed it subsequently stole part of the funds that the Dajaz had counted out to him as payment for the camels. The *dajaz* insists indeed on never paying the caravan's expenses to the Europeans themselves, who would then settle up without difficulty: the Dankali find it a good opportunity to embroil both the *dajaz* and the Frangui, and every one of the Europeans has thus found 75 per cent or more of the costs of the caravan being snatched away by the Bedouin, the *dajaz* and Menilek himself being in the habit, before the opening of the route to Harar, of invariably finding for the Bedouin against the Frangui.

It was having been forewarned of all this that I had the idea of making my leader sign a caravan account. This did not prevent him, at the moment of my departure, taking me in front of the King claiming some 400 thalers over and above the account he had himself approved! He had for an advocate on this occasion *the redoubtable bandit Mohammed Abu-Bekr*, the enemy of the European traders and travellers in Shewa.[116]

But the King, without taking into consideration the Bedouin's signature (papers mean nothing at all in Shewa), realized he was lying, happened to insult Mohammed, who went beserk against me, and merely condemned me to paying a sum of 30 thalers and one Remington rifle: but I didn't pay anything at all. I learnt subsequently that the leader of the caravan had deducted these 400 thalers from the funds put into his hands by the *dajaz* with which to pay the Bedouin, and that he had employed them on buying slaves, whom he sent with the caravan of MM Savouré, Dmitri, Brémond, and who all died along the way, and he himself went and hid in Djimma Abba-Djifar, where he's said to have died of dysentery. One month after my departure therefore, the *dajaz* had to reimburse these 400 thalers to the Bedouin; but if I had been present, he would have certainly made me pay them.

The Europeans' most dangerous enemies on all these occasions are the Abu-Bekrs, thanks to the easy access they have to the *dajaz* and the King, in order to slander us, denigrate our way of doing things and pervert our intentions. They set a shameless example of theft to the Dankali Bedouin, and advise them to murder and pillage. They're assured of impunity in everything thanks to the Abyssinian authorities and the European authorities on the coast, both of whom have been crudely taken in by them. There are even Frenchmen in Shewa who, having been pillaged along the way by Mohammed, and are still prey to all his schemes even now, will nevertheless tell you: 'Mohammed's a good fellow!', but the few Europeans in Shewa and Harar who know the policies and customs of these people, who are execrated by all the Issa Dankali tribes, by the Gallas and Amharas, shun them like the plague.

The thirty-four Abyssinians in my escort had indeed made me sign in Sajalo before I left an obligation to pay each of them 15 thalers for the journey and two months' back pay, but in Ankobar, irritated by their insolent demands, I grabbed the IOU and tore it up in front of them; there was subsequently a complaint to the *dajaz*, etc. Never, moreover, do you take receipts for the wages paid to servants in Shewa: they would find such an action very strange and would fancy themselves to be at risk from I don't know what.

I wouldn't have paid the *dajaz* the 300 thalers for Labatut had I not myself discovered, in an old notebook found in Mme Labatut's hut, a note in Labatut's handwriting acknowledging receipt from the *dajaz* of five okiets of ivory less a few rotolis.[117] Labatut had in fact been drafting his memoirs: I collected up thirty-four volumes, i.e., thirty-four notebooks, in his widow's home and, despite the latter's imprecations, consigned them to the flames, which was, it was explained to me, a great misfortune, a few title deeds having been slipped in among these

confessions which, skimming through them, seemed to me not
to merit serious examination.

Moreover, that sycophant of a *dajaz*, debouching in Farra
with his asses at the moment when I was debouching with my
camels, had immediately insinuated, after the salutations, that
the Frangui, in whose name I had come, had a huge account
with him, and he seemed to be asking me for the entire caravan
as a pledge. I soothed his ardour, temporarily, by the offer of a
telescope of mine, and several jars of Morton's sugared almonds.
And I subsequently despatched to him, from a distance, what
he seemed actually to be due. He was bitterly disillusioned, and
is still acting in a very hostile manner towards me; among other
things, he stopped the other sycophant, the abuna,[118] from
paying me for a load of dried grapes that I'd brought him for
making cheap communion wine.

As for the various debts I paid on Labatut, this worked in the
following manner:

A Dajaz would arrive for example in my house and sit down
to drink my tedj,[119] vaunting the noble qualities of our *friend*
(the late Labatut) and displaying the hope of discovering the
same virtues in myself. At the sight of a mule grazing the lawn,
they would exclaim: 'That's the mule I gave Labatut!' (no mention was made of the fact that Labatut had given him the
burnous he wore on his back!). 'Moreover,' they added, 'he
remained my debtor for 70 thalers (or 50 or 60, etc.!).' And they
insisted on this claim, with the result that I sent the noble
brigand away by saying: 'Go to the King!' (Which roughly
means 'Go to the devil!'). But the King made me pay part of the
claim, adding hypocritically that he would pay the rest!

But I also paid out on well-founded claims, the wages of the
servants who died en route on Labatut's descent to their wives,
for example; or else it was the reimbursing of some 12, 15,
30 thalers that Labatut had taken from a few peasants when
promising them guns, fabrics, etc. on his return. These poor
people being always in good faith, I allowed myself to be affected
and I paid out. A sum of 20 thalers was also claimed by a
M. Dubois; I could see he had a right and I paid, adding, by way

of interest, a pair of my shoes, the poor devil complaining of going barefoot.

But the news of my virtuous proceedings had spread far and wide; a whole series, a whole band, a whole horde of Labatut's creditors rose up, from this side and that, with a sales pitch to make you go ashen-faced, and that modified my benevolent disposition, and I took the decision to come down from Shewa at an accelerated pace. I recall that on the morning of my departure, already trotting towards the NNE, I saw a delegate of a wife of one of Labatut's friends loom up out of a bush, demanding the sum of 19 thalers from me in the name of the Virgin Mary; and further on, a creature with a sheepskin cloak rushed down from on top of a promontory, asking me if I had paid his brother 12 thalers, borrowed by Labatut, etc. I shouted to them it wasn't time any longer!

On my ascent to Ankober, the widow Labatut had brought a tricky case against me with the *dajaz* with a view to claiming the inheritance. M. Hénon, a French traveller, had appointed himself as her advocate in this noble task, and he it was who had me cited and who dictated the statement of her aspirations to the widow, with the help of two old Amhara women advocates. After odious disagreements of which I sometimes got the better and sometimes not, the *dajaz* empowered me to seize the deceased man's houses. But the widow had already hidden a long way off the few hundred thalers' worth of merchandise, effects and curiosities he had left, and at the seizure, which I carried out not without opposition, I found only some old pairs of drawers which the widow took possession of shedding burning-hot tears, a few bullet moulds and a dozen pregnant slaves whom I left behind.

M. Hénon took the case to appeal on behalf of the widow, and the flabbergasted *dajaz* abandoned the whole affair to the verdict of the Franguis then present in Ankober. M. Brémond then decided that, my business already seeming to be a disaster, I would have to give up to this Fury only the deceased man's land, gardens and livestock, and that, on my departure, the Europeans would chip in for a sum of a hundred talaris to give to the wife. M. Hénon, standing proxy for the plaintiff, took responsibility for the operation and himself remained in Ankobar.

On the eve of my departure from Entotto, going up to the monarch's with M. Ilg to fetch the credit note on the Dajaz in Harar, I caught sight behind me in the mountains of M. Hénon's helmet, who had learnt of my departure and had rapidly covered the 120 kilometres from Ankober to Entotto, and behind him, the burnous of the frantic widow, winding along the precipices. At the King's, I had to do a few hours of antechamber, and *they* made desperate overtures to him. But when I was shown in, M. Ilg told me in so many words that *they* hadn't succeeded. The monarch declared that he had been this Labatut's friend, and that he intended to perpetuate his friendship on his descendants, as proof of which he at once withdrew from the widow the enjoyment of the land he had given Labatut!

M. Hénon's aim was to make me pay the hundred thalers that *he* was due to collect for the widow from the Europeans. I learnt that after I left the subscription didn't take place!

M. Ilg who, by virtue of his knowledge of the languages and his honesty, is usually employed by the King to settle the affairs of the court with the Europeans, gave me to understand that Menilek claimed to be a large creditor of Labatut's. Indeed, on the day when the size of my own stake was quoted, Menilek said that he was owed a great deal, my riposte to which was to ask for proof. It was a Saturday, and the King answered that they would consult the accounts. On the Monday, the King declared that, having had the scrolls that serve as records unrolled, he had rediscovered a sum of around 3500 talaris, and that he was subtracting it from my account, and that what was more, in truth, the whole of Labatut's estate should go to him, and all this in a tone of voice that didn't leave room for any challenge. I invoked the European creditors, finally producing my own claim, and, on M. Ilg's remonstrations, the King agreed hypocritically to give up three-eighths of his claim.

For myself, I am convinced the Negus robbed me, and since his merchandise is circulating on routes I'm still condemned to travel, I hope one day to be able to seize them, to the value of what he owes me, just as I have to seize a sum of 600 talaris from the Ras Govana in the event of his persisting in his demands after the King has told him to shut his mouth, which the King always tells others to do once he's been paid himself.

Such, Monsieur le Consul, is the story of my payment of moneys owing to the natives on the Labatut caravan, forgive me for having told it to you in this style, as a distraction from the nature of the memories the affair has left me with, which are, all in all, most disagreeable.

Yours faithfully,

RIMBAUD.

Monsieur de Gaspary,
French Consul,
Aden.

79. To his family

Aden, 15 December 1887.

My dear friends,
I have received your letter of 20 November. I thank you for thinking of me.

I'm quite well; but I've not yet found anything good to set in train.

I require a small service of you which will not compromise you in any way. It's an experiment I would like to make, if I can obtain ministerial authorization and then raise some capital.

Send the enclosed letter on to the Deputy for the *arrondissement* of Vouziers, adding his name and the name of the *arrondissement* to the letterhead inside the letter. This letter to the Deputy must contain the letter to the Minister. At the end of the letter to the Minister, at the places left blank, be careful simply to write the name of the Deputy I'm requesting to take the necessary steps. Having done that, despatch the whole thing to the Deputy's address, having taken care to leave the envelope of the letter to the Minister unsealed.

If M. Corneau, the iron merchant, were currently the Deputy

for Charleville, it would perhaps be better sent to him, since it concerns a metallurgical enterprise; in that case, it's his name that should appear in the blanks in the letter and at the end of the request to the Minister. If not, and since I'm quite out of touch with the current political wheeler-dealing, apply as soon as possible to the Deputy of your *arrondissement*. You have nothing to do except what I've just told you; and afterwards, nothing will be addressed to you, because you can see that I'm asking the Minister to reply to me at the Deputy's, and to the Deputy to reply to me here, at the Consulate.

I doubt whether this initiative will succeed, because of the current political state of things on this coast of Africa; but this is a start and will cost only the paper.

Be so good therefore as to address as soon as possible, and without any covering note, this letter to the Deputy (containing the request to the Minister). The affair will go ahead of its own accord if it goes ahead at all.

[...]

I've written an account of my journey in Abyssinia for the Société de Géographie. I've sent articles to *Le Temps*, *Le Figaro*, etc. I also intend to send a few interesting stories of my travels in East Africa to the *Courrier des Ardennes*. I don't think that can do me any harm.

Fond regards.

Reply to the following address, and only there:

                                                    A. RIMBAUD.
                                    Poste restante, Aden-Camp, Arabia.

80. To M. *Fagot*

Aden, 15 December 1887.

Monsieur,

I am a native of Charleville (Ardennes), and I have the honour of asking you by way of the present letter to be so good as to transmit, in my name and supporting it with your kind co-operation, the enclosed request to the Minister of the Marine and Colonies.

I have been travelling for some eight years past on the east coast of Africa, in the countries of Abyssinia, Harar, the Dankalis and Somalia, in the service of French commercial undertakings, and M. the French Consul in Aden, where I normally reside, can inform you as to my honourable character and my actions in general.

I am one of the very few French traders to do business with King Menilek, King of Shewa (southern Abyssinia), the friend of all the European and Christian powers, – and it is in his country, some 700 kilometres distant from the coast at Obock, that I have the intention of creating the industry referred to in my request to the Ministry.

But, since the trade in arms and munitions is forbidden on the east coast of Africa owned or protected by France (that is, in the colony of Obock and the coasts dependent on it), I request by the present letter that the Ministry grant me authorization to *transit* the matériel and equipment described, by way of the aforesaid coast at Obock, without my stopping there longer than the time necessary for the formation of my caravan, for this whole cargo has to cross the deserts on camel-back.

Since none of this matériel or equipment is to be delayed on the coasts affected by the embargo, and since nothing of the entire cargo as stated will be removed, either along the way, or on the coast, and since the importation of the said matériel and equipment is intended exclusively for Shewa, a Christian country and friendly to Europeans; and since I must engage to apply, for the said order, exclusively to French capital and French industry, I hope that the Minister will kindly look with favour on my request and send me the authorization on the terms required, that is to say: a *laisser passer* for the whole Obock coast and the adjoining Dankali and Somali coasts protected or administered by France, for the entirety of the said order intended for Shewa.

Allow me, Monsieur, to ask you once more to support my

request to the Minister, whose reply I would be most obliged to have sent on to me.[120]

I remain, Monsieur, yours faithfully,

ARTHUR RIMBAUD.
Address: c/o French Consulate,
Aden (English colonies).

Monsieur Fagot,
Deputy for the Arrondissement of Vouziers,
Département of the Ardennes.

81. To his family

Aden, 25 January 1888.

My dear friends,

I have received the letter in which you announce the sending-off of my long screed addressed to the Minister. I thank you. We shall see what the answer will be. I'm hardly counting on success; but it's still possible that the authorization will be granted, at least after the Italo-Abyssinian war – which doesn't look to be ending.

Moreover, authorization once granted, the capital would remain to be raised; and you don't find that in two shakes of a lamb's tail, or even one shake. As you can imagine, my [forty] thousand and some odd francs aren't going to be enough for the undertaking; but I might have the opportunity to make some small change with the authorization itself, were it granted, and granted *in precise terms*. I'm already certain of the co-operation of a few capitalists, who may be tempted by such affairs.

Anyway, be so kind as to alert me, if something comes back to you following this request; although I told the Deputy to reply to me in my name, here at the French Consulate. – Don't involve yourselves in the affair in any way. It will go ahead of its own accord; or it won't go ahead, which is more likely.

I still haven't landed anything in Aden; and the summer is rapidly approaching, putting me in the necessity of searching out a cooler climate, for this one absolutely exhausts me, and I've more than had my fill of it.

Business has changed a lot in the Red Sea here, it's no longer what it was six or seven years ago.

It's the invasion of the Europeans, on every side, that's done it: the English in Egypt, the Italians in Messawa, the French in Obock, the English in Berbera, etc. And it's said that the Spanish too are going to occupy some port in the vicinity of the straits! All the governments have come and sunk millions (or even several billions in all) on these accursed, desolate coasts, where the natives roam for months without provisions and without water, under the most appalling climate on the globe; and all the millions that have been chucked into the bellies of the Bedouin have brought in nothing except wars and disasters of every kind! All the same, I'll perhaps find some work to do here!

I wish you a good '88, in all its particulars.

Fond regards,

RIMBAUD.

82. To Ilg[121]

Aden, 1 February 1888.

My dear Monsieur Ilg,

I have received your letter of 16 January with pleasure. I assume you are in good health and peace of mind.

The steps you took were fruitless, which I regret, I knew that already, and we indeed foresaw it. The hopes that the gun merchants sought to raise in their memorandums were simply fish-hooks intended to snap up our capital had we been as foolish as them, which isn't permitted here.

I myself got the Deputies of my *département* to take action with the current Minister, who also comes from my home town, but it was all a total failure; I haven't lost anything thereby, however, because I hoped for nothing, and I haven't incurred any expense.

Your predictions concerning the epic of Messawa are those

of everyone here.[122] They're going to achieve the *conquest* of the volcanic mounds strewn as far as thirty kilometres from Messawa, link them by a bargain basement railway line, and having reached these furthermost limits, they'll loose off a few volleys from their howitzers at the vultures, and launch a balloon festooned with heroic slogans. – That'll be the end of it. Then will be the moment to sell off the few hundred that are left of the several thousand burros and camels bought here recently, the planks from the huts, etc., all the fifth-rate matériel for which their military manufactories have toiled so proudly.

But what will happen after this moment of legitimate delirium? It'll still take a lot of people to hang on to the pretty plain of Messawa. The conquest will cost, and preserving it won't be without risk. It's true that their sentries mount guard, each of them armed with a scaled-down machine-gun.

The idiotic Reuter's agency announced to us this morning that the Porte[123] has demanded that England evacuate Zeilah forthwith! What's behind that? – I fancy the Portal Mission[124] must have demanded the Harar region from the Emperor. – Anyway, in the case of Zeilah, England has naturally replied that it would first consult the Khedive[125] since he is the Porte's tenant in Zeilah.

You've known for a long time that Mekonnen has left Harar, it's not known when he'll be back. There are only about 800 men left there with a Choum,[126] so it's said. The route isn't bad.

Bienenfeld[127] is sending a political agent to Harar. These people are very tiresome with their attempts on Ethiopia's virtue. The agent has been in Zeilah for a month not daring to set off.

Stéphane the Armenian (the trader) has been back through here, he has no complaints at all about Menilek, and is ready to go back up, he's gone off to buy merchandise in Egypt.

Stéphane second-class is here dyeing goatskins red and green, it has to be said he's displaying a feverish activity, because the fever never leaves him.

M. Bion has sold Brémond's ivory after you at 215 or 216 r[upees]. – Ivory is going up, the Zebad[128] is at three thalers.

Whatever they may say, I fancy nothing can stop the Soleillet guns from leaving even at present. If the people responsible for the affair could, however, be manifestly prevented, they could maybe profit by it and get themselves an indemnity.

Nothing new otherwise, except that an English officer and some thirty soldiers were murdered the day before yesterday around Berbera.

From Shewa, the news, whatever they may say, is good. Menilek is pulling a few faces, but things are still the way they normally are for everyone.

– I shall leave for the coast in a week or so, I think, it may be that I shall remain in the interior for two or three months. I would like to see if one could undertake to exploit the gum in the Konollas of Harar, in the Gadiboursi, etc.[129] There are a lot of gum trees there, and I have abbans everywhere.

– The Soleillet caravan people are frantic, they're not getting any news, they'll be a long time yet on the coast, if they don't make more effort.

– It's said that they're about to finish drawing up the boundaries on the Issa coasts between France and England. Djibouti would remain with the English. Ambado is an altogether French spot and the governor of Obock couldn't ask for anything better than that it should be opened up to him.

– It's to be feared that the blockade will continue even with the cessation of hostilities in the vicinity of Messawa, and after the troops have returned. All these incursions, searches, requisitions, prohibitions and persecutions are souring and annoying the natives greatly, on the coasts as well as in the interior. It's all ill suited and ill calculated to rehabilitate the European, already greatly despised in the Red Sea, in the eyes of the blacks. – Moral, stay as the blacks' ally, or don't touch them at all, if you're not in a position to crush them utterly right from the start.

– The sensible course for sure is to see how events turn out, and not undertake anything directly in Abyssinia for the time being. – For myself, if I set foot again on African soil, it won't be any further than Harar, because at least there trade is free and you can get away when you want.

– Later on, we'll see. They say that the various merchandise fetches a good price in Shewa at present, and that the merchandise for export there is at very advantageous prices.

– Dimitry sends his greetings: he has recently recovered almost everything that was lost.

– Apropos the Dajaz W. Gabril's ivory, it was sold here by my Dankali abban, who spent all the money, I'm told, on buying various merchandise for the Dajaz and for himself personally. But I've heard tell that M. Hénon also may have thalers with the Dajaz. I don't know whether that's true or false. But anyway the Dankali and the Abyssinian who went down with the ivory are busy tearing each other apart at present.

Keep well, dear Monsieur; till I have the pleasure of seeing you again.

Yours,

RIMBAUD.
Address: Poste restante,
Aden,
Camp

83. To Ilg

Aden, 29 March 1888

My dear Monsieur Ilg,

Back from Harar a fortnight ago I found your friendly letter. Thank you.

I did the journey to Harar in fact, 6 days going, 5 coming back, an 8-day stay up there, and ten days in the dhows and steamers (that's the longest and most tedious), it was a month's campaign.

Up there, good news. Peace and silence on earth and under the heavens. The doctors are doctorizing (and their wives are being raped, at least that's what happened to the good Sig. Traversi, so they say, who's renounced his lawful wife and carried off his kid?). Sig. Alfieri has gone back up to Shewa. Sig. Antonelli to Lit-Marefia. M. Borelli to the Djimma, M. Brémond en route for Harar, Sig. Viscardi en route for Aoussa, M. Bidault with his boxes to Harar, Herr Zimmermann gone back up to Harar at present, with a three-storey helmet-type hat. In Harar, they've begun sweeping up, but it seems they'll be dying of hunger shortly.

You'll know that M. Lagarde[130] has erected huts in Djibouti and is watching the whole coast, in the expectation of M. Savouré, but the route isn't being opened up.

I'm leaving again very shortly for Harar on behalf of traders in Aden. I shall be the only Frenchman in Harar.

Consequently I am your natural associate up there, and I claim the privilege of serving you in anything that may be of use to you up there in your operations.

In Zeilah my associate will be a Greek, M. Sotiro, an upright fellow who knows the country well.

Don't get involved in doing business with the Moussaya lot.

In Aden, Monsieur Tian will be in touch with me, as will Monsieur Bardey.

– Be very careful (that's my advice and forgive me for taking the liberty), the coast is absolutely in a state of siege.

	RIMBAUD
Or else:	Via the French Consulate
C/o Monsieur Tian	Zeilah
Aden	Red Sea

84. To his family

Aden, 4 April 1888.

My dear friends,

I have received your letter of 19 March.

I am back from a journey to Harar: six hundred kilometres, which I did in eleven days on horseback.

I'm leaving again, in three or four days' time, for Zeilah and Harar, where I am going to settle for good. I'm going on behalf of some traders in Aden.

The Minister's response reached me a long time ago, a

negative response as I foresaw. Nothing to be done in that quarter, and anyway, at present, I've found something else.

So I'm going to live in Africa again, and I shan't be seen for a good long time. Let's hope that things work out not too badly.

Starting now, write to me therefore at my associate's in Aden, avoiding anything compromising in your letters.

Fond regards,

Monsieur RIMBAUD
C/o Monsieur César Tian,
Aden,
English Possessions,
Arabia.

85. To Ilg

Aden, 12 April 1888.

My dear Monsieur,

Monsieur Tian will hand you the present letter when you pass through Aden, and will be able to tell you that I am his associate in Harar and the country round about. I'm leaving tomorrow for Zeilah and shall be in Harar around the end of this month, well provided with funds and merchandise.

I'm entirely at your disposal for all your messages, transport, storage, and all the commissions and transactions in which you're good enough to take advantage of my services, in the whole centre of Harar and all the routes leading to it. This offer is quite disinterested, and I'm advising Monsieur Tian of it, who will himself do everything he can for you in Aden. – My associate in Zeilah is a Greek named Sotiro, with whom you can stay, or who at least has been alerted by me to do everything he can for you in Zeilah and for getting you on the move.

Allow me to warn you never to trust the firm of Moussaya, who are a gang of spies simply studying the moves everyone makes and their methods so as then to obstruct them in every way.

I hope that my new business in Harar will expand, insofar as the place and the time allow, and that we shall subsequently, you in Shewa, with your exceptional experience of the people, affairs and languages, and I in Harar, organize something profitable for the two of us.

So if you write to someone in Harar, do me that pleasure, and believe me to be, while I await your successful arrival, your faithful,

RIMBAUD
At Mr. Sotiro's
Zeilah
Red Sea. Gulf of Aden

Monsieur Alfred Ilg,
Engineer.

86. To his family

Harar, 15 May 1888.

My dear friends,

I am now reinstalled here, for a long time to come.

I'm setting up a French trade counter, on the lines of the agency I had in the past, with a few improvements and innovations, however. I am doing quite a significant amount of business, which leaves me with a bit of profit.

Can you give me the names of the biggest cloth manufacturers in Sedan or the *département*? I would like to ask them for small consignments of their fabrics: they would find an outlet in Harar and in Abyssinia.

I'm well. I have a lot to do, and I'm on my own. I'm in the cool and content to rest, or rather to refresh myself, after three summers spent on the coast.

Keep well and prosper.

RIMBAUD.

87. To Ilg

Harar, 25 June 1888.

Dear Monsieur,

I have received here your kind Tritligasse 27 April.[131] I'm surprised not to have more up-to-date news of you.

I'm at work here, I am gradually stocking up with imported merchandise for Abyssinia: my repeat orders for strange and odious articles exasperate my associate in Aden, Monsieur Tian. However, I'm reckoning on setting up something remunerative here.

Le Roy[132] has returned to Entotto and the brilliant court has been reconstituted, Ato Petros being master of ceremonies.

Antonelli is lying in Lit-Marefia with the pox – Travassi is hunting hippopotamus on the Awash – M. Appenzeller is repairing the bridge, so they say – Borelli at the King of Djimma's – M. Zimmermann awaiting you – Antoine Brémond giving suck to his nurslings in Alin Bimba – Bidault peregrinating and photographing in the hills of Harar – Stéphane the dyer of goatskins stretched out in the stream in front of our doors, etc., etc. . . .

All of which is normal. On the coast you will meet our heroes MM. Savouré and Brémond and you'll know what to think.

As for myself this is the third time the French Government has successively given and withdrawn authorization for me to land arms in Obock for Shewa.

The last letter from the ministry temporarily suspended a formal authorization granted in my name in the second note! – That's how things currently stand.

They may still change a dozen times like this up until the end of '88!

This must be M. Savouré's sort of situation, authorization and prohibition alternately filling the sails of the bloody tartane crammed full of the blasted pipes.

Things here will be fairly active till the end of keremt.[133] Ivory is selling here at a parity of Th. 65 per Shewa okiet (in Shewa it's 45), the Zebad at 2 ounces for 1 thaler in Djimma, sells here for Th 1$^{1}/_{2}$ the ounce. Coffee's worth Th. 5. Gum Th. 5$^{1}/_{2}$.

The commercial situation isn't bad in Shewa. – The gun mania is more frantic than ever. – Relations between here and Shewa are pretty active, and the route from here to Zeilah is good.

Remember, please, that I am wholly at your disposal.

RIMBAUD.

French trader in Harar.

88. *To his family*

Harar, 4 August 1888.

My dear friends,

I have received your letter of 27 June. You mustn't be surprised by the delay in correspondence, this spot being separated from the coast by deserts that the couriers take a week to cross; and then the service that links Zeilah to Aden is very irregular, the post only leaves Aden for Europe once a week and it reaches Marseille only in a fortnight. To write to Europe and receive a reply takes at least three months. It's impossible to write directly from Europe to Harar, since beyond Zeilah, which is under English protection, is a desert inhabited by nomadic tribes. Here, it's the mountains, the series of Abyssinian plateaux: the temperature never goes higher than 25 degrees above zero, and never goes down to less than 5 degrees above zero. So no frosts, no sweating.

We are now in the rainy season. It's rather depressing. The government is the Abyssinian government of King Menilek, that's to say a negro-Christian government; but, when all's said and done, we're at peace and in relative safety, and, so far as business goes, it's sometimes good and sometimes bad. One lives without any hopes of soon becoming a millionaire. Anyway, since it's my lot to live this way in these countries . . .

There are scarcely twenty Europeans in the whole of Abyssinia, including these parts. So you can see over what vast areas they are distributed. Harar is still the place where there are the most: ten or so. I'm the only one of French nationality. There's also a Catholic mission with three fathers, one of them French like me, who educate young blackamores.

I get very bored, still; I've never known anyone in fact who gets as bored as me. And is it not wretched anyway, this existence without a family, without any intellectual occupation, lost in the midst of blacks who, for their part, try to exploit you and make it impossible for you to liquidate your business deals at short notice? Forced to speak their gibberish, to eat their filthy dishes, to suffer countless annoyances arising out of their laziness, their treachery, their stupidity!

Even that's not the most depressing thing. That lies in the fear of gradually becoming stupefied yourself, isolated as you are and far removed from any intelligent company.

We import silkstuffs, cotton goods, talaris and a few other articles; we export coffee, gum, perfume, ivory, gold that comes from a long way off, etc., etc. Although the business is sizeable, it's not enough to keep me active and has to be shared out moreover among the handful of Europeans astray in these vast regions.

My sincere greetings. Write to me.

RIMBAUD.

89. To his mother and sister

Harar, 10 January 1889.

My dear mama, my dear sister,

I have received safely your letter dated 10 December 1888. Thank you for your advice and your best wishes. I wish you good health and prosperity for the year 1889.

Why do you always speak of illness, death, and all manner of unpleasant things? Let's leave all those ideas far away from us, and attempt to live as comfortably as possible, to the extent our means allow.

I am well, I am better than my business affairs, which give me a lot of worry for little profit. With the complications I'm involved in, it's improbable that I shall get away from these parts for a long time to come. Yet my capital is hardly increasing; I fancy I'm going backwards rather than advancing.

It's certainly my intention to make the donation you speak of.[134] It doesn't indeed please me, to reflect that the little that I've toiled to amass should serve to enable those who've never even written me a single letter to live it up! Were I one day to find myself seriously ill, I'd do it, and there is, in these parts, a Christian mission to whom I would entrust my will which would then be sent on to the French Consulate in Aden within a few weeks. But what I have would only leave after the liquidation of the business I'm doing here for the César Tian company in Aden. In any case, were I very ill, I would liquidate the agency myself rather from here; and I'd go down to Aden, which is a civilized spot, where you can settle your affairs instantly.

Send me your news, and believe me,

Your devoted

RIMBAUD.
C/o Monsieur César Tian
Aden.

90. To Jules Borelli

Harar, 25 February 1889.

My dear Monsieur Borelli,

How are you?

– I have received with pleasure your letter from Cairo, 12 January.

A thousand thanks for what you've been able to say and do for me in our colony. Unfortunately, for some unknown reason the Issa are still shunning our Djibouti completely: the difficulty of the route from Biokaboba to Djibouti (for you can't go from here to Ambos, too near to Zeilah, to then hug the coast as far as Djibouti!), the lack of commercial installations and even political organization in Djibouti, the lack of maritime connections between Djibouti and Aden and, above all, the following question: how will the products arriving in Djibouti be treated in Aden? (for there's no installation in Obock for handling our merchandise).

From Djibouti for Harar you can find camels easily enough, and that the merchandise is free of duty more than makes up for the excessive costs of hiring these animals. Thus we've received via Djibouti M. Savouré's 250 camels, whose venture has finally succeeded: he entered here a few weeks after you, with the gentleman who is his partner. The dajaz Mekonnen left again from here for Shewa on 9 November 1888, and M. Savouré went up to Ankober via Herer a week after Mekonnen's departure via the Itous. M. Savouré put up here with me; he even deposited about twenty camel-loads of merchandise with me, which I sent on to him in Shewa, a fortnight ago, by the Herer route. I have proxy to receive on his behalf from the treasury in Harar some fifty thousand talaris in payment for his guns, for it seems he didn't get much from King Menilek. In any case, his partner is coming down from Farra for Zeilah at the end of March, with their first return caravan. M. Pino is going to the coast for the occasion.

[. . .]

M. Ilg arrived here, from Zeilah, at the end of December 1888, with some forty camels' worth of appliances intended for the King. He stayed with me for about a month and a half: they didn't find any camels for him, our present administration is very weak and the Gallas far from obedient. In the end, he was able to load up his caravan and left on 5 February for Shewa, via Herer. He must be at the Awash at present. – The other two Swiss are waiting for him.

[. . .]

We've never been so quiet, and we haven't been affected at all by the so-called political convulsions of Abyssinia. – Our garrison has about a thousand Remingtons.

[. . .]

As for what's been going on in Shewa, you must know. The Emperor had dethroned Takla Haymanot of Gojam in order to put Ras Mikael, I believe, in his place. The former king of Gojjam rebelled, chased out his replacement and defeated the Emperor's men; so Ato Yohannes got going and entered Gojam, which he laid waste and where he still is. We don't yet know whether peace has been made with Takla Haymanot.

Ato Yohannes had numerous grievances against Menilek. The latter refused to hand over a certain number of deserters who had sought asylum with him. They even say he had lent the king of Gojjam a thousand guns. The Emperor was also very unhappy about Menilek's scheming, genuine or not, with the Italians. In the end, relations between the two sovereigns had become very acrimonious, and it was feared, and still is feared, that Yohannes may cross the Abbai and fall on the king of Shewa.

Menilek is apprehensive of this invasion and has abandoned all external commands so as to concentrate all the troops in Shewa, and particularly on the route to Gojjam. The ras Govana and the ras Darghi are at present guarding the Abbai crossing; it's even said that they've already had to repel an attempt by the Emperor's troops to cross. As for Mekonnen, he'd gone as far as Djimma, whose unfortunate king had already paid the guibeur[135] to a detachment of Yohannes's troops that had passed by to the West. The abba Cori paid a second guibeur to Menilek.

The aboun Mathios[136] and a whole host of other personages are interceding for peace between the two kings. It's said that Menilek is very annoyed and refuses to make it up. But the dispute, it's believed, will gradually die down. Fear of the Dervishes holds the Emperor back; and as for Menilek, who's hidden all his wealth a long way off, you know that he's too cautious to try such a dangerous trick. He's still in Entotto. The story is, he's quite unconcerned.

[. . .]

Do make use of me for anything you may have need of in these parts, and believe me your faithful,

RIMBAUD.

Care of Monsieur Tian, Aden.

91. *To his mother and sister*

Harar, 18 May 1889

My dear mother, my dear sister,

I have received safely your letter of 2 April. I am pleased to find that, on your side, all is well.

I'm still very busy in this damnable country. What I make bears no relation to the worries I have; for we lead a sad existence in the midst of these blacks.

The one good thing in this region is that it never freezes; we never get less than 10 degrees above zero and never more than 30. But it rains torrents in the present season; and, like you, that prevents us from working, that's to say receiving and sending off caravans.

Whoever comes this way never risks becoming a millionaire, – unless in fleas, if he gets too close to the natives.

You must have read in the papers that the emperor (what an emperor!) Jean [Yohannes] is dead, killed by the Mahdists. We here too, we depended indirectly on this emperor. Only we depend directly on King Menilek of Shewa, who himself paid tribute to the emperor Jean. Our Menilek rebelled last year against the appalling Jean, and they were getting ready to have a go at each other when the above emperor got the idea of going first of all and sorting out the Mahdists, over Matama way. He remained there: Devil take him!

Here we're very quiet. We depend on Abyssinia, but we're divided from it by the river Awash.

We still correspond easily with Zeilah and Aden.

I'm sorry not to be able to make a trip to the Exposition[137] this year, but my profits are far from enabling me to, and anyway I'm entirely on my own here and, were I to leave, my establishment would disappear altogether. It'll be for the next one then; and at the next one I shall perhaps be able to exhibit the local products and, perhaps, exhibit myself, for I fancy one must look exceedingly baroque after a long sojourn in countries such as these.

I wait to hear from you and meanwhile wish you fine weather and a good time.

RIMBAUD.

92. *To Ilg*

Harar, 1 July 89.

Via Tessamma, M. Ilg's servant.

My dear Monsieur Ilg,
Thanks very much for your kind letter of 16 June. I have read and approved. <u>All right</u>. I'm expecting Ato Guabri shortly and I hope he'll sort things out so as to get our merchandise through with his own, without paying duty, because that's the main thing, ivory being subject here to an entry tax of 10, 9, 8, or I don't know how much per cent, which pleases the customs, – and also subject to an exit tax of 8, 7, 6, we don't know either what per cent. I imagine you'll have explained this to Guabri. At all events, in future, don't forget to arrange things accordingly.

I'm sending you by M. Savouré's men the merchandise, the invoice for which is enclosed, value Th. 776. 2 bales each containing 50 bundles blue silk first q[uali]ty and each one bundle thread, one red, the other blue. – 1 bale cont[aini]ng 16 pieces, 350 metres silks – and one box cont[aini]ng 4 brillé samples.[138]

I'm only charging the silk to you at Th. 4, it would have cost me a bit more, but then I've still got 80 bundles here that I'll sell at a better price by retailing them to the mateb[139] merchants for the troops. There's no risk of your losing on it.

[...]

The 4 jugs are a sample of the 6000 I have in the warehouse. There are still at present about 3000 white ones, 400 blue, 400

yellow, 400 green, 400 mauve. (I'm not sending you the mauve.)
Here I sell 4 for one thaler wholesale, 3 for a thaler retail. At
the Guebi[140] they bought 2000 off me for Th. 500, but the Dajaz
returned them saying he'd *find them for nothing* in Italy! These
jugs were executed to my design and my specifications, and
they're not to be found in the trade. The crates are of 100 and
from Zeilah to here we paid for one camel per three crates, but
from here to Shewa the camel would carry only two. Breakages
in the crates I've opened are only about 2 per cent, the packing
being very thorough. The return here is some $4^1/_2$ per talari,
because of the *enormous* costs incurred by glassware at sea and
everywhere. With the fresh overheads to meet from here to
Shewa, I could hardly deliver them to you, *returned to Shewa
at Farra*, except at $2^1/_2$ jugs to the talari. I'm convinced that
you'll sell them very easily at 2 to the talari, white or coloured
– like the first type I brought last year, all of which sold in
Shewa. Breakages will be my responsibility: I put my faith in
your expertise. I know it's minimal. All the overheads as far as
Farra to be my responsibility also.

These jugs are solid and graceful articles, easily marketed,
and those from Messawa, which we don't get here anyway, pose
no competition.

[. . .]

M. Savouré's servants have returned from Djibouti and are
besieging me here. Since I can't change his stock of piastres for
a week or so, I'm going to send the first group off and the second
will leave in ten days with the remainder of the talaris. On that
occasion I shall send you a bit of merchandise if I can find some
camels, without being forced to wait – and I hope also, a little
of your 5,500 –

– And now about your payment of Th. 5,500. The Dajaz has
brought us a multitude of starving beggars, and himself has
need of money for the road, although I'm told he's only taking
the 2000 pounds sterling that had remained in the treasury in
Harar from the time of the massacre of the Porro expedition.
All his creditors have come down on him in any case, and
the demands for money will drive him crazy. Anyway, in that

event he may go and take the cure in a Pasteur establishment.[141]

Adding to which, the town's receipts are weak at the moment.
The rate for the thaler is 18 piastres everywhere. – In fact it's a
more difficult time than ever for the Harari Treasury's creditors.
Let's hope that H[is] H[ighness] will deliver us soon from his
ruinous and tiresome presence and then they'll practise a spot
of economy in the treasury. I hope so for your sake and hope so
for mine.

[...]

M. Brémond has opened a 13-sou bazaar here where you
can find hairbrushes, carved oystershells, julienne for soups,
slippers, macaroni, nickel chains, wallets, boleros, eau de
Cologne, peppermint and a mass of equally practical products,
equally well suited to native consumption!

That's how much he knows about *Abyssinian wares* after
twelve years' residence!

In his shop there are also Remingtons that he's got hold of to
retail, but which aren't being bought, because he wants Th. 30
for them without a single cartridge – and Mekonnen still claims
to be bringing back cargoes of them gratis from the Italian
arsenals, together with a number of batteries of machine-guns,
thousands of bales of silks, a few million in *beur*,[142] and the
homage of Europe prostrate before the shiny boots and silk
socks that the intelligent Count[143] has already requested for him
by special courier!

Poor tota![144] I can see him from here throwing up into his
boots between Alexandria and Naples – and the Djanos from
the Shewan embassy floating on the ship's planking.

M. Brémond is displaying the intention of building a house
here, appropriate to his vast commercial activities and his
elegant habits.

He has already, it seems, constructed something at the place
known as Djibouti, but it was in inadequately petrified sponge,
and in the spring rains along the coast it seems it swelled up,
only then to deflate and roll on to the ground.

He's still aspiring to create a caravan service along the road from here to the aforesaid Djibouti, with a timetable, itineraries and fixed tariffs, – but for him alone.

He's claiming complete freedom from customs duties, and every imaginable privilege in all times and places.

Let's hope for prompt success in this task which he himself describes, and rightly, as *laborious*!

Meanwhile, he's promising himself a trip shortly to Shewa. Perhaps he'll want to *build* there too. – He's turned into a beaver!

Until next time, my sincere salutations.

RIMBAUD.

93. To Ilg

Harar, 26 August 1889

My dear Monsieur Ilg,

Our 24 camels left yesterday and tomorrow Walde-Thadik and the abban Hussein are leaving to rejoin them. I reckon on them being in Herer around 4 September, and at the Awash around the 20 September. – As said, the hire of the camels was fixed at Th. 9, plus Th. 1 for food, i.e., a total of Th. 10. – I advanced the talari for food here and Th. 5 against the hire, so that there remains to be paid in Farra Th. 4 for 24 camels, i.e., Th. 96, which I handed over to Walde-Thadik. As I've also promised the abban 1 thaler per camel, and as I advanced him 14 of that here, there remains Th. 10 to be paid him on arrival in Farra, if his services have been adequate. I gave these Th. 10 also to W. Thadik. In addition, I handed him an extra Th. 14 for eventual costs arising en route and at the Awash. Thus he's received Th. 120 from me which should amply suffice for *all* the costs of the expedition as far as Farra.

[. . .]

My advice would be to take your payment from the king in gold, if you can't take it in ivory. That would be a very good way of *raising funds* by quickly sending it to be sold here.

Because one has in the end to recognize the reality, and your servant will tell you as well as I what getting paid is like here. *They won't and can't pay you*, at present at least, any more than they pay anyone else, for the reason that the King has demanded a new and formidable extraordinary tax from this unhappy land! He has demanded a hundred thousand talaris, which is quite out of the question. How to pay this sum today, and in three months' time pay the regular annual tax? Epizootic has destroyed everything here, the coffee crop is zero, the durra harvest mediocre, the peasants are crushed by the requisitions of every kind by the horde of starving men brought in by the Dajaz on his return! I don't fancy that they can collect more than Th. 20,000, by dint of extortion, – and these extortions are already being practised on ourselves! All the Europeans here have been condemned to pay their share of this *guibeur*. My share is some Th. 200! I paid Th. 100 yesterday, and in a week's time the other 100 will be extorted from me! And I had to pay in talaris, I wasn't allowed to transfer that sum to your credit or that of M. Savouré. And every month I pay around 400 talaris customs dues, and an annual rent of Th. 100! – Before this reaches you I shall write *Abiete*[145] to the King, and the others will do the same, – and I shall inform our consuls in Obock and Aden of the Abyssinian authorities' manner of proceeding towards us, whereas we are foolish enough to open free ports, and to do these highway robbers all sorts of favours and politenesses.

Your servant will tell you (Guabri too), that I've tried every means of snatching away a few shreds of your payment, even by placing the customs dues I've paid to your credit. But at this moment they seem sunk in some frightful madness and our choums will use any dirty trick to scrape talaris from the distraught population! I've never seen such a wretched state of things here. – In the current conditions, to accept in Shewa to be *paid in Harar* would be equivalent to *deferring the payment indefinitely*, indeed I fancy that's what the man who sent you to get paid here had in mind! There isn't a sou to be found here before January, the moment of the annual tribute, and in Shewa not only do they want to receive the whole of the regular tax when it falls due, but they want to keep the country occupied at other times collecting extraordinary taxes, and the whole time they send an endless queue of creditors here to get paid against receipts that they refuse to allot to the payment of these debts! It's a comedy that at the moment has become appalling, even for us here. They're beginning to make us swallow down mouth-fuls of 200 talaris at a time! – We're now turned into Gabares,[146] it's intolerable, and if it gets worse, and the King doesn't exempt us from these corvées, we shan't hold out for long.

In short, it'll always be far quicker and easier to obtain the payment of your debt from the King, in some merchandise or other, ivory or gold, than by sending to draw it out here. I even despair absolutely of having done with the Savouré account, – and there's already been a loss of more than 300 talaris on the exchange of the last 10,000 talaris of piastres!

You'll always have the facility of liquidating the merchandise here and bringing to Shewa funds that you can put to work and send back here, etc., etc.

So have done with the King. – In the meanwhile I shall certainly still find a means here of applying something to your credit.

Yours ever

RIMBAUD.

94. *To Ilg*

By Ibrahim.   Harar, 7 [September] 1889.

My dear Monsieur Ilg,

[. . .]

– Since the Th. 1000 that I sent you via Engadda, I've been absolutely unable to extract anything from the treasury on your account, despite my numerous *démarches* and prot-estations, and reading what follows will soon make you under-stand why.

King Menilek (who gave him this damnable idea!) wrote here

about a month ago to collect for him an extraordinary tax of a *hundred thousand talaris*! – He must have enjoined on them to extort this sum by every means possible, and even added that they should borrow from the Europeans by promising to pay them back from the funds that the D[ajaz] Mekonnen is or is not due to bring. – Since the order arrived, we've been witnessing a spectacle such as the country has never experienced, either in the days of the emirs, or in the days of the Turks, a horrible, hateful tyranny, which must long dishonour the name of the Amhara in general in all these regions and on all the coasts, – a dishonour that will certainly rebound on the name of the King.

For the past month they've been confining illegally, beating, dispossessing, imprisoning the people of the town, so as to extort from them as much as possible of the sum demanded. Each inhabitant has already paid three or four times in the meanwhile. All the Europeans have been treated in the same way as the Muslims and included in the tax. I've been asked for Th. 200, half of which I've paid, and I fear they may extort the other Th. 100, although they've also forced me to lend money, Th. 4000, in the most arbitrary and bandit-like manner, – an incident that forms the subject of the enclosed claim that you'd oblige me infinitely by presenting to the King on my behalf. – I'm always asking you for some favour, and greatly regret not having the opportunity to return it, but you must believe I am your loyal servant here, and in case of need you know you can always call on me.

So towards the end of August, a few days after paying the guibeur of Th. 100, I received from Zeilah a consignment of Th. 10,000 from M. Tian in four boxes. When the camels arrived at the customs, as I was getting ready to take delivery, a calatié[147] from Mekonnen's wife and from Tessamma ordered the customs man to seize the lot. I tried to protest, they refused to see me or speak to the guebi about me, or explain under what guise the money was being seized, whether as a loan or what. It was only thanks to the energetic intervention of Monseigneur Taurin that I was able, the following day, to take delivery of the four boxes. Monseigneur explained to them that such an act of brigandry would probably expose them to reprisals against the person and the property of the D. Mekonnen on the coast or in Europe, because I was already preparing to send a courier to the consulate in Aden, with a request to telegraph to the embassy in Rome, and to take the matter up diplomatically and in the courts.

Meanwhile I was *forced to lend* a sum of four thousand talaris, for which with great difficulty I obtained a receipt with an obligation to reimburse it on the Dajaz's return!

At the same time funds were arriving for various other Europeans, in lesser amounts, and they carried out the same operation on them, *borrowing* from each of them some 500, 600 or 300 talaris, without giving receipts, guarantees or a time-limit for their reimbursement!

The English soldiers who accompany the money as far as here have left again to bear the news of these goings-on to Zeilah and elsewhere, – and the effect will be enormous on the coast, taken together with the account of the extortions practised on the natives. I'm very much afraid this may utterly discourage my employers in Aden, although I haven't painted too black a picture of the incident to them.

The loan was very awkward for me, however, because those Th. 4000 would have exchanged the last piastres and paid back the coffee I got for M. Savouré, to about that value.

I tried to retain the said sum in my coffers by offering IOUs, one of Th. 3000 for Savouré, the other of Th. 1000 for you, but those baying hounds exacted payment in cash from me, – and I paid up.

In this situation you can see it's impossible for me, *for the moment*, to obtain anything on your two accounts. Instead of paying, they steal! – All possible receipts are carried over without exception on to the total of the taxation. The customs' coffee is also sold for cash, so that its value can be sent off in talaris! The situation is abominable! And despite his senseless demands for Th. 100,000, every day the King sends fresh creditors to get paid here! Only recently Mohammed with a bill of exchange from the King for several thousand talaris! And, *instead of paying it, they* BORROWED two parcels of money from him that he had at the customs, where I'd had them impounded, in

the name of my debt, on their arrival here from Djibouti two
months ago!

[. . .]

Someone needs to be able to make the King realize the harm
the behaviour of his people here is doing him. The place is very
near to the coast, the population in touch continually with those
under the administration of the various governments in the Gulf
of Aden and round about, foreign subjects even are numerous
here, there's a number of natives here who are protected or else
French, English, Italian or Ottoman subjects. Everywhere on
the coast at the moment, among the Bedouin, the poor, the
traders, the consuls, the residents, the officers, they're talking
about what's going on in Harar, where they make no bones
about ransacking the cash-boxes of the European traders who
are agents of the firms in Aden, where they're snatching the
inhabitants from their homes at midnight to make them sweat
out a few talaris on pain of death by the Giraf.[148] There's no
fear of a rebellion here, with a wholly unarmed population, and
reduced moreover to impotence by its own self-interest, but the
moral effect both within and without will be more pernicious
for the Amhara than some uprising or other by the natives.

For myself, I shall do all I can so that it's known among our
political agents and traders how we're vilified here, – but I
doubt, however, whether they'll abandon their policy of falling
into line!

What more can I tell you, dear monsieur, in the midst of these
melancholy preoccupations? Do me the – very real, I repeat –
favour of seeing that the enclosed complaint is handed to the
King, and translated, by Gabriel or someone else, in a faithful
manner, – and complete the good work by reminding the King
to come up with a *melleche*, or in other words a response, which,
I hope, will get me respected by the bandits here. You'll see that
my epistle has a PS that concerns you. While we wait to see, I'm
still counting on getting something for you, in goods, or even in
piastres (which I shall accept only in the certainty of exchanging
them without loss). As for M. Savouré's account, I can but close
it, to say the least, you can have no idea of the grimacing, the

shouts, the play-acting I have to go through in order to pick up a few hundred talaris, or rather the semblance of them, for they don't often let me see *real talaris*! When you see Brémond, he'll perhaps play the matador by talking to you about how he's stood up to them here, but rest assured he'll retain the bitterest memories of the treasury and customs officials of Harar, and that he won't be coming back here. Moreover, of the Th. 9000 that the Daj owes him, he hasn't been paid Th. 3000 in four months.

But, for the time being, we have to let the squall of the royal tax blow itself out. Anyway, the question's settled. We can't find more than thirty thousand talaris or thereabouts, and are obliged to abandon the operation. – We're going to send what we've found, and leave the country in peace. – Let them send it, and to hell with it!

– All this is very disheartening and, if it continues, I can't possibly hold out. How to exist here with the prospect of having your cash-box broken into from one day to the next, of being forced to lend money to a govt that owes it to you, etc., etc. I'm asking the King for a letter of protection, enabling me to trade freely, while paying the local dues. But I want to keep myself ready to liquidate, and for the time being, I'm trying to place the little bit of imported merchandise I have left, and to get the credits back in. Be so good therefore as to do all you can to send me back towards the end of the year, or at the latest up until the end of February '90, the value of the merchandise I've sent you. – If I send you something, it'll only be articles for immediate disposal.

Once again, for all the merchandise you send here, follow it up with a laissez-passer from the King, otherwise you'll *have terrible trouble with the customs here*. They'll estimate the duties, without making you pay them at present, but sooner or later you'll see it arriving on your account. So have your merchandise addressed to me *supposedly in transit*, and with the royal pass they'll enter and leave without costs. Otherwise ivory pays Th. 8 on entry, and on leaving (even if immediately) Th. 6 per frasleh. The Zebad pays 10 per cent on entry, and 2 per cent on leaving. Gold never goes through customs, but were it discovered, it wouldn't fail to pay. All this is absolutely absurd, since Harar forms part of Shewa, and is not an independent administration. We've explained a hundred times over that all entry duties should be totally abolished, to be replaced by a general exit duty of 5 per cent, which would produce far more, for no end of reasons.

[. . .]

Till I have the pleasure of reading you.

RIMBAUD.

95. To Ilg

Harar, 7 October 1889.

My dear Monsieur Ilg,

I have received quite safely your two joint letters from Aibamba 10 September and Ankobar 16 September as I've indeed received all the earlier ones. I have confirmed my letter by an 'Akadar'[149] which contained the accounts for the cooking pot caravan, said letter should have been enclosed in the mail from the Dajaz. Then I gave a letter to your two men travelling with the caravan. Finally, three letters by the Dajaz's last mail via 'Ibrahim' and a last letter via Brémond. – I assume all these are in your hands by now.

[. . .]

You ask for jugs, you got more than you bargained for. I hope you'll make a profit. Here I've liquidated every last one of the 6000. I don't have any left at all, they're first-class items and needn't fear any competition.

As for the goods I sent you with Jean, your comments are all right. But from the total sale of all these bits and pieces I dare in spite of everything prophesy some profit for you. The big pearls are good for Lekka, etc., etc. – Any minute now I'll be giving you lessons in Ethiopian commercial geography from here.

I have delivered your letters for Harar, and will send off tomorrow or later those for overseas.

Not yet received any letters from M. Savouré, what on earth's he up to in Aden, but anyway I count on having news of him within a few days, and I'll probably convey it to you by this post, because you'll have noticed from my earlier letters that the post from here to Shewa only leaves long after the announcement of its *immediate* departure, and you have time, in letters, to accumulate the most eccentric paragraphs, *coups de théâtre* and the most contradictory hearsay.

Thus in my latest I announced to you, in energetic terms even, the stagnation in your payment here. There were, alas, serious reasons for this, and I explained them to you. Then there was a final hiccup in the Hararghe[150] treasury: the soldiers' pay at the end of the year! However, from the copy of the receipt enclosed, you'll see that I succeeded in picking up Th. 755 on your account, in coffee at Th. 7, although the market price is only Th. 6.75: but I worked hard at it. I'm counting on getting a few hundred talaris more on your account in two days' time, in coffee naturally, because if I don't resign myself to taking goods at an excessive price or in piastres I lose on, I might just as well take to my bed. To get talaris here in the present conditions, you'd need to strangle the cashiers and break open the cash-boxes, which I hesitate to do.

Anyway by dint of grumbling and grimacing, that account too will be settled for you, I hope, but there are many times also when I despair. – The one cause, as you can well imagine, of all these delays lies in the exasperated requisitions of the King himself.

Enclosed a collection of cuttings concerning the Shewan mission. I shall send you everything else I get of the sort. I assume they've left Italy by now, and en route for Jerusalem, Bethlehem, Sodom and Gomorrah – for I don't imagine they'll miss the opportunity of visiting the Holy Places. It goes on being said that they won't come back through Aden, which they already disdained to visit on the way out. Anyway in a few days' time a few Wotaderes[151] are being sent to the coast to meet them.

My welcome for the Dajaz will be to present him with your

overdue accounts, – and also the draft for the Th. 4000 I've been forced to lend. Let's hope he's got the wherewithal and is disposed to let go of it. There'll be more nasty moments to go through!

[. . .]

You would give me pleasure and render me a service by informing me as best you can about what they're thinking of doing with this region. Everyone is agreed in saying that the D. Mekonnen won't stay, and will at once stage his return. What will happen next here? They say the Gondaris[152] will return to Shewa, that the Daj's men will return with him, who will stay here then? Will the Daj be replaced, and who by? A fortnight ago the emir Abdullah was taken off from here to Shewa, what the devil do they mean to do with him up there? – Here with a thousand soldiers we don't need to worry, but the route to Shewa needs to be properly open, else business here goes badly, and the town's income drops hugely, as we found out last year.

9 October.

The soldiers who are due to receive the Dajaz in Zeilah haven't yet left. A post that got here yesterday from Aden with a telegram from Italy does not announce the departure of the embassy, which was anticipated for the end of September. I believe they've left today, however.

From this latest post I extract a few new cuttings concerning the Shewan mission. Use them to your advantage.

You'll see that the extortions practised on the town of Harar are known about in Europe even. If I weren't established here, I'd take the opportunity of the Shewa mission to send *Le Temps* interesting details about the economic situation of these regions, about the manner in which the D. Mekonnen pays his debts here, and the manner in which King Menilek sends his creditors to run their heads against a brick wall!

But let's draw a veil over these ignominies!

[. . .]

I've been given news from Aden of M. Savouré, but he hasn't written to me, nor replied to my letters. It's possible he's sent his mail from Djibouti, but nothing ever gets to us from there, the route remaining little frequented.

As from today I still stand to get Th. 1932 on his gun account, and the whole account for the cartridges 160 boxes x Th. 30. We've never known the price of these cartridges.

– Yesterday they promised to weigh me out this morning a hundred fraslehs of coffee, half on your account half on the Savouré account, and this morning they announced that they're taking them back to give them to some skinflint or other in payment for nails supplied for the woodwork in their confounded basilica.

Apart from that, I can't extract one talari, because all the revenues, since they finished paying the King's requisition, aren't enough to finish off paying the soldiers' annual wages.

So all one can do is be patient!

[...]

10 October

In expectation of your good news, I remain, believe me, your faithful

RIMBAUD.

96. To Ilg

Post no 11.
Via the Mission. Harar, 16 November 1889.

My dear Monsieur Ilg,

I have today received your letter of 26 October Entotto, and I send back this one, numbered 11, via the Mission. – My last, no 10, was carried by *Mouhé*. It contained *two IOUs*, one *for Th. 755*, the other *for Th. 350*, the value of the coffee received by me at the Harar customs on your account. Enclosed today an IOU *for Th. 50 and 12 piastres* again on your account. Swallow this delightful peach and listen to this:

I have at last *given a receipt for M. Savouré's two accounts*, with the Dajaz, and the King for the 2000 Remingtons. These two accounts have been *paid in full*. All I need to get now is the price (Th. 4800) of the 160 cartridge boxes. – I've asked to close your account before that, and have been promised. Thus within a fortnight I'm reckoning on receiving on your behalf coffee for a thousand talaris, paying a bit more than in the market, – and your account will thus be closed up until December, scrap by scrap, grain by grain. No good demanding talaris or even piastres, the whole currency is exclusively intended to be despatched to Shewa.

They write from Aden (is it certain?) that the D. has concluded a million talari loan from a bank in Italy, with a government guarantee (from Italy, not Shewa!) but we've not yet received notice of the D's departure – He'd better hurry up and come back soon, with the redeeming roundels, – We await him here with invoices unfurled, and a chorus of maledictions.

Sincere thanks for having sent my letter to the King. He has in fact written to me that I should get the forcibly borrowed Th. 4000, – out of the funds that the D. will bring back. – They've protested similarly from here to the D. – Bienenfeld's agent, from whom they *borrowed*, in two instalments, Th. 3000, had Rome telegraphed at once through his consul. That's what I ought to have done, it would have been more effective than my letter to the King, who must himself have ordered the choums here to employ this pretty method of procuring talaris from the traders. (Always the same comedy!)

The fact is that the day before yesterday the D. wrote to leave us alone, and they've apologized to us here. – We'd have preferred being reimbursed. At all events, this brigandry has had a deplorable effect in Aden and elsewhere, and if it's repeated, the King can be sure of receiving strenuous objections from various governments.

He tells you he hasn't a thing? But did they not send him Th. 40,000 from here a month ago? – and they're about to send him another twenty thousand or so, all of it collected in the manner I've recounted – (The jugs he finds too dear at $3^1/_2$ to the talari are selling here at 3 to the thaler at present. The 1400 jugs that Moussaya sent him, of his own make, were invoiced to him at a thaler each and aren't as good as mine. They left before mine, but via the Tchercher scows.)

If it's all right with you, look on my merchandise as an advance on the payment of your account. With this in hand, you can still work. But some advice, *don't send merchandise here without a customs laisser-passer*, I've already warned you several times about this.

[. . .]

Awaiting your news, I remain, believe me, your faithful
RIMBAUD.

97. *To Ilg*

No 13. Harar,   20 December 1889.
Via M. Mikael,
Russian engineer.

My dear Monsieur Ilg,

I confirm my Nos 10 via 'Mouhé', 11 via the Mission or Bado Guebra Selassie, and 12 via Serquis, the latter having left from here on 11 December.

Enclosed a receipt for a sum of another Th. 625 on your account, received at the Harar customs in 100 fraslehs of coffee at Th. 6$^{1}/_{4}$ the frasleh, whereas the market price is only Th. 6 with a strong downward tendency. Therefore all that's left to your credit of Th. 5500 is a residue of about Th. 1800. – Amen!

I had to employ threats to extract these last hundred fraslehs, just as previously I had to use gifts, entreaties, cunning, intimidation, etc., etc. . . . Mark it down in your notebooks, and make the others mark it down in theirs, that one of the dirtiest tricks they can play on you in Shewa is to saddle you with *orders for payment in Harar*! There's an order to send every last talari to Shewa, every last piastre, which they change here into talaris, – and now to crown everything the furies who govern us have had the idea of putting even the coffee at the customs into daboulas[153] and sending it to Zeilah for the meeting with the great D!

A telegram from the ministry 'degli esteri'[154] advises the administration in Harar that this D. must have quit the lovely soil of Italy on 4 December. But he personally has not advised. Anyway if he embarked on that date he must find himself at present in Jerusalem. I refusalem[155] to believe it.

They write to me in Zeilah that the D. had written to Ephtimios Moussaya to come and meet him in Port Said, and the latter in fact caught the Suez mailboat. I hear the Abyssinians here telling that the D. has bought some 'Sost masseria'[156] in Egypt that he wasn't able to procure in Italy, that these guns will then leave via Assab, etc., etc. – More and more it's even said that he'll return via the urinary tract of Assab. But that would be slightly at odds with the request for 1000 camels he's made in Geldessey, and with the plan they seem to have formed here, of sending him rich caravans of rotting coffee to Zeilah as if a millionaire shouldn't greet such expeditions with disgust! In short, let's reckon on seeing noble things!

I've sent you via Serquis a bundle of old Gazettes that should inform you about the most recent events in Europe, – since *plus ça change, plus c'est la même chose*, there as in Africa.

Nothing new here. I don't know whether MM. Bortoli and Pino have gone directly up from Djibouti for Shewa. No letter from M. Savouré, at the moment or earlier! I already told you I've happily settled his account with the King and his account with the D. – There remain only these 160 cartridge boxes, apropos of which:

1. Kindly send me an order from the King to end payment on these 160 cartridge b.

2. Kindly send me an order from the King to close your account.

3. Kindly send me the King's response concerning the Th. 995 they still want to make M. Savouré pay for his last 65 fraslehs of ivory – and also for the Th. 300 on your 17 packages.

Be done then with all these matters, – for me it's all a reason to delay settling the accounts, which I'd like to do as soon as possible, – just as I would ask you to sell off all my merchandise *to my and your best advantage* and send me the product as soon as possible, wishing for the situation to be all clear for March 1890 – the time of our stock-taking.

[. . .]

In your case, I'm looking for absolutely nothing except to *protect myself more or less from losses, if not risk*. But with M. Savouré, it's settled that I shall be reimbursed for the difference in the exchange rate in Harar – the rest being at my own risk. Moreover, I work on a 2 per cent commission, which is anyway very meagre. M. Brémond here gives 5 per cent to a vile Greek he's put in charge of his business, 5 per cent on purchases, sales and outstanding debts! Apropos M. Brémond, the King has given an order here to collect up and send him in Shewa all the rifles he sold retail in the region.

– As for the payment for the goods of mine which the King may have taken off you, it's better to accept merchandise from Shewa whatever the price rather than a payment here, these sorts of payment *here* are a torture, a disaster, a tyranny, an abominable slavery.

When Tessamma Mekbeb was at the treasury, you could still get him to carry out an order from the King, but you'll know that this Tessamma has been demoted quite a long way down (following Dr Nerazzini's complaints to the King) – and at present the treasury's in the hands of the slaves of the D. Mekonnen who sit there like hydrofobic [sic] Gorezzas[157] and don't let a single piastre out of their grasp.

And then what paralyses them is above all *from on high*. A few naggadies[158] who finally came from [uncertain] complain to one in the bitterest fashion of the deplorable things that have gone on in Shewa in connection with the ivory.

– I confirm in all seriousness my request for a very good mule and two slave boys.

Finally, write more often! I wish you good health and good business in 1890.

Kind regards.

                                                                RIMBAUD.

98. To Ilg

No 14.   Harar, 24 February 1890.
Via the 'Hazage'.
Monsieur Ilg,

My dear Monsieur Ilg,

[...]

Since 24 December 1889 we've been, as you must very well
know, completely blockaded here in the direction of Zeilah.
Everyone in Shewa must know of the massacre at Ensa, where
two French missionaries and two Greeks perished. In that caravan there were Th. 25,000 belonging to the Europeans from
here (Th. 10,000 of them to me) which fortunately they managed
to save and send back to Zeilah. But the English then launched
a campaign against the Issas and the Gadiboursis, which set
everything ablaze and cut all the routes, to the great danger even
of our merchandise piled up in Geldessey, – and amongst mine,
all your famous coffee, *the whole of which has been still at
Geldessey since 12 November and hasn't moved an inch since
that date* and won't move for several more weeks, the route
being still quite bad, although the English expedition has been
back (defeated it's true!) in Zeilah since the end of January – so
that one can't as yet risk *one talari in the direction of Zeilah*, or
one daboula in this direction. *Nothing is going up, nothing is
going down, neither money, nor goods. I've been without one
talari since about 15 December 1889*, and all the traders from
here are in the same boat. We don't even have enough to
live on. – However, the mail arriving yesterday from Zeilah
announced that the Issas and other rebel tribes have made their
submission to the English government, and we're advised they're
going to send us our funds very shortly, but I don't *fancy we're
going to get anything before the end of March*, the route not
being safe except in force, and where's force going to come
from?

There'll be the same delay in lifting your coffee, or rather the merchandise that's at Geldessey. – During these two months of war and blockade, *we haven't been able to get the smallest package through to Zeilah*. – It was quite difficult even to send couriers!

So, *dear Monsieur, no good asking for the impossible* and you can see that I'm reduced to complete helplessness. – Take it out on whoever sent you to get paid here!

[. . .]

I await your news, meanwhile I am, believe me, your faithful,
RIMBAUD.

Hasty greetings to M. Zimmermann.

99. *To his mother and sister*

Harar, 25 February 1890.

Dear Mother and Sister,

I have received your letter of 21 January 1890.

Don't be surprised that I hardly ever write: the main reason would be that I never find anything interesting to say. For when you're in countries like these, you have more to ask than to tell! Deserts populated by stupid blacks, without roads, without any postal service, without travellers: what do you expect anyone to write to you from there? That one's bored, that one's having a bad time, that one's becoming an idiot; that one's had enough, but that one can't be done with it, etc., etc.! That's all, all one can say, as a result; and since that's no longer much fun for anyone else, one must remain silent.

They massacre, indeed, and pillage a fair amount in these parts. Luckily I haven't yet found myself at these occasions, and I certainly count on not leaving my bones here – that would be stupid! Anyway, locally and along the road, I enjoy a certain consideration thanks to my humane methods. I've never done anyone any harm. On the contrary, I do a bit of good when I get the opportunity, that's my one pleasure.

I do business with the Monsieur Tian who has written to you

to reassure you on my account. Business, basically, wouldn't be bad here, if, as you read, the routes weren't constantly being closed by wars and rebellions, which endanger our caravans. This Monsieur Tian is a big trader in the town of Aden, and he never travels into these regions.

The people of Harar are neither any more stupid nor any more of a rabble than the white drudges in the so-called civilized countries; they're not of the same order, that's all. They're less malicious even, and can, in certain instances, display gratitude and fidelity. It's a matter of treating them humanely.

The Ras Mekonnen, whose name you must have read in the papers and who led an Abyssinian embassy to Italy, which caused such a stir last year, is the governor of the town of Harar.

Till we get a chance to see one another again. Fond regards,

RIMBAUD.

100. To Ilg.

Harar, 1 March 90

No 15.

My dear Monsieur Ilg,

My No 14 that I thought had left for Shewa has come back into my hands, and I'm adding this to it in the hope of a rapid opportunity and soon.

We're anyway still in the same situation here, the Zeilah route completely cut, nothing comes up and nothing goes down, although the English expedition is over. *I've literally been without a talari since 15 December 1889*, and am heavily in debt locally even! I wanted to go down to Zeilah to bring back myself the funds held up there *these two and a half months* but I can't leave without getting the merchandise that's at Geldessey on its way, and from Geldessey nothing's stirring, absolutely nothing up until now! 300 Amharas are to leave with Ahmed Iera to go and fetch Mekonnen's merchandise at Zeilah. These soldiers have been camping at Geldessey for the last two months, not knowing whether they're going forwards or backwards. They're billeted in our Zerbias[159] in Geldessey, and their presence has done quite a bit to mess things up. This merchandise of the King's won't get here in the next six months, they're talking about 600 camels! There's no sort of authority here, everything's going very badly.

I've asked for reimbursement of the Th. 4000 that were borrowed from me seven months ago, the interest on which I pay to Tian, – I could certainly use them, and I'd be able to advance you something on the price of your blasted coffee out of these Th. 4000 if they gave them back to me! But they've refused to reimburse me, on the pretext that it was written in the receipt: payable on the return of the D. Mekonnen! What destitution! What a filthy trick! So here I am, the slave of these swindlers, they maintain they'll reimburse the amount only when they feel like it, and I can only wait for them.

A fortnight ago I wrote a strong demand to the King (in Amharic and French) for the reimbursement of this sum of Th. 4000 that I so badly need, along with the interest calculated at Th. 40 a month, as I pay it, for why should I have to pay out of my own pocket the interest on the money lent to a King! – That would be too comical! I entrusted the letter to a courier of the Hazage's, but I don't really know if it'll get there! – Meanwhile I'm naturally being debited for the amount by M. Tian, who as it happens does nothing but call for the interest, instead of worrying about the reimbursement!

You can see what an imbroglio the Abyssinians have landed us in! – When I wrote to you to take my merchandise on account, that naturally meant to take on account *what you've already realized*, not what may remain to be realized, for it's money after all! I don't understand why you should think this goes against your interest, it's only mine it goes against!

[...]

For your business has in fact been disastrous for me: *Th. 4000 of coffee paid for on your account and which can't be lifted from Geldessey! And you want Th. 4000 in ready cash when I don't have a sou in my cash-box! And I don't see one talari of my Th. 4500 stock of goods arriving in Shewa!* – That makes me more than 12,000 talaris overdrawn! Impossible to sort it out this way! Even if I'd had any talaris I wouldn't have sent you more than 2000 (while admitting that I hadn't received about Th. 2500 worth on my merchandise). So send me that Th. 2500 worth and I'll pay the balance of your account, for I don't think at the moment I'll be more than 20 days without money. Moreover, Th. 2500 worth of goods sold in Harar doesn't even represent Th. 2000 in Shewa, so I don't think I'm demanding too much.

I'm paying the whole of the rest of M. Savouré's account in Aden, *in Aden* he himself will send his talaris to Shewa when he likes, as for me it's absolutely impossible to get talaris here, even for myself. And I haven't received one talari on the balance of his account.

Sincere greetings.

RIMBAUD.

101. To Ilg

No 18   Harar, 7 April 1890
Via M. Nicholas Kaledji.

My dear Monsieur Ilg,

What the devil are you up to? I confirm my Nos 13 via the Russian Mikaël, my Nos 14, 15 and 16 via the two Greeks, my No 17 via an Abyssinian, Joseph from the Mission.

I wrote to you *to send your men here to receive your talaris, with an order from you,* – because for my part I can't find any opportunity. So send to fetch them as soon as you can, – I'm waiting.

The Zeilah route has finally been reopened, Mekonnen's merchandise will enter Geldessey in a few days' time, along with the Marquises, doctors, etc., of the Italian government.

I've fallen out altogether with M. Tian over the matter of the Th. 4000 I was forced to lend to the Abyssinian govt, and it's likely he'll withdraw his agency from me if restitution is delayed.

So you'll do me a very great service in getting the enclosed

letter handed *to the King in which I demand* THAT SUM
PLUS THE INTEREST, *which I pay every month out of my
own pocket*! – As for the shuftas[160] in Harar, they refuse to
reimburse me!

*Send back as soon as possible the full yield of the merchandise
sold, and liquidate the rest as best you can*, I want to have done
with Tian's account.

M. Savouré arrived on 24 March in Obock: he's expecting
your merchandise as soon as possible. – I've had him paid T.
8833 in Aden, the whole of the balance of his account, so don't
expect anything from here, it's been impossible for me to bring
cash here over the past three months, even for myself.

Yours ever. Write.

RIMBAUD.

Friendly greetings to MM. Zimmermann and Appenzeller.

102. To Menilek

Letter from M. Rimbaud,
trader in Harar,
to His Majesty,
His Majesty King Menilek.

Your Majesty,

How are you? Please to accept my loyal greetings and my
sincere good wishes.

The choums, or rather the shuftas, of Hararghe refuse to give
me back the 4000 talaris that they extracted from my cash-boxes
in your name, on the pretext of a loan, seven months ago now.

I have already written to you three times on this matter.

This money is the property of French merchants on the coast,
they had sent it to me so I could trade here on their account,
and at present, they have for this reason seized all that I have
on the coast, and wish to withdraw their agency from me here.

I estimate at 2000 talaris the *personal* loss this affair is causing
me. – What will you return to me of this loss?

In addition, each month I pay one per cent interest on this

money, that makes 280 talaris already that I have paid out of my own pocket for this sum that you are withholding from me, and each month the interest accrues.

In the name of justice, I ask you to have these 4000 talaris returned to me as soon as possible, in good talaris such as I lent, and also all the interest at 1 per cent a month, from the day of the loan up to the day of reimbursement.

I am writing a report on the matter to our choums in Obock and to our consul in Aden, so that they may know of the way in which we are treated in Harar.

I ask for a response as soon as possible.

Harar, 7 April 1890.

RIMBAUD,
French trader in Harar.

His Majesty
H. R. H. the Emperor Menilek
Entrusted to the good offices of Monsieur Ilg.

103. To his mother

Harar, 21 April 1890.

My dear Mother,

I have received your letter of 26 February.

As for me, alas, I have neither the time to get married, nor to consider getting married. It's quite impossible for me to abandon my business affairs for an indefinite time to come. When you're involved in business in these damnable lands, you never re-emerge.

I'm well, but my hair is going white by the minute. Since that's been happening, I've been afraid of soon having a head like a powdered topknot. It's heartbreaking, to be betrayed by one's scalp; but what can one do?

Fond regards,

RIMBAUD.

104. To Ilg and Zimmermann

30 April 1890

No 20

Dear Messieurs,

Your bl—y servants have returned today, telling me that one of the mules (*one of M. Savouré's agassas*) passed out between Warabeili and Chalanko. They'd probably overloaded it with their stuff. In the end I coughed up another fifteen talaris on your account so that they could buy other animals if need be, and expelled them from my presence.

I must warn you again that M. Tian has paid M. Savouré in Aden the whole balance of his credit with me. I thus no longer have a single piastre of his, and am released altogether from his affairs, kindly take note.

– I have finally received from the Municipal Treasury the Th. 4000 that were extracted from my cash-box in September '89 on the pretext of a loan. No point in mentioning it again to the King therefore.

– Send me as soon as you can the balance on my merchandise please, I am anxious to settle with M. Tian shortly.

Write more often. Kind regards.

RIMBAUD.

MM. Ilg and Zimmermann, Shewa

105. To Savouré

[April 1890?]

I had no need whatsoever of your filthy coffee, bought at the cost of so much trouble with the Abyssinians; I only took it so as to end your payment, in a hurry as you were. And moreover, I repeat, had I not proceeded in that way, you'd *have never had a thing, nothing, not a thing*, and everyone knows that and will tell you so! You know it yourselves, but the air in Djibouti scrambles your wits I can see!

So, having transported *garbage at my own risk* without any profit, I'd have been cretinous enough, idiotic enough, to import here, on behalf of whites, talaris at 2 per cent costs of transport, 2 or 3 per cent loss on the exchange rate, in reimbursement for coffee that I never asked for, which brings me in nothing, etc., etc. Are you seriously capable of believing that?

But people coming out of Shewa really do reason like Abyssinians!

Examine my accounts then, dear Monsieur, get the true picture, and you'll see that I have every right – and you every good fortune to have managed to be done with it as we have!

Be so good then to send me as soon as possible a receipt for *th. 8833 as the whole balance of your account*, – without any more pleasantries; – because, for my own part, I could easily draw up an account for several thousand talaris of losses I've incurred doing business with you, business I should never have got mixed up in.

In the expectation of your receipt, please accept my sincere greetings.

RIMBAUD.

106. To Ilg and Zimmermann

No 21.   Harar, 15 May 1890
By Dinkon.

Messrs Ilg and Zimmermann,

I confirm my letters Nos 19 and 20 via your servants, accompanying a remittance of T. 3000 to you. At the last moment, your servants, in accordance with the laudable Abyssinian custom, found the means of breaking the back of one of M. Savouré's agassas, which came back to me absolutely unserviceable and which I've had to abandon. Ask your men to account for the T. 30 they took from me for the journey, on your account. I'm sure they'll still find a way of complaining about me, and you likewise, perhaps, ingratitude being the fashion among all the inhabitants of Shewa. But it hardly matters.

M. Savouré has at last sent me from Djibouti the receipt for the T. 8833, the value of the *trash* with which I've finally been paid on his account! He made up his mind to draw that sum from Tian's when I let him know about the distraint on Brémond. Just imagine, he'd have wanted me to import talaris here, and keep them in reserve for him, in payment for the ghastly coffee I've been made to swallow here at $^1/_4$, $^3/_4$, 1 and 2 talaris above the going rate! The coffee lost in Aden, and anyway I wasn't claiming from him for the loss, I simply refused to pay another 2 per cent for transporting talaris, after running, and having to run all the risks of every kind! – But let's leave that aside. I'm simply declaring that I no longer have anything whatsoever to do with Savouré's accounts, old or new, just as I have declared to him that never again was I going to get mixed up in any capacity in his affairs.

Anyway he's written to me again asking me to send his servants to Shewa, advancing them their expenses, which is what I'm again having the kindness to do, and I'm sending you them.

In the interim the Brémond who was to have entered here in great haste has, no one knows why (so as not to pay duty on the ivory, I fancy) gone directly from Herer to Djibouti, where he is at present, and where I hope these two personages will be able to reach an agreement. – I'm fortunate not to have had a visit from Brémond, because you tell me you committed the folly of giving a guarantee on what Savouré might get here, where he isn't worth a single piastre. On the contrary, he re-owes me a few thalers. So that I'd have had some bother on Brémond's part. And for having been obliging, I'd have been disobliged again. That's the custom with all the traders in Shewa!

So take care, once again, no longer to address anything to me in M. Savouré's name, not men, nor merchandise, nor correspondence, or anything at all. I should refuse everything, absolutely everything. Involve yourself in those sorts of affairs and it's nothing but weariness and losses.

And now, dear Messieurs, the matter of my merchandise.

I repeat, send what the goods fetch to me here, in Harar, as soon as possible. I will pay the cost of the customs myself, and will claim nothing from you. This is the one matter that keeps me here, because I should long ago have gone down to Aden, where I absolutely must change the way my business affairs are going.

[. . .]

I repeat, I will pay the customs dues here, but send, send as soon as possible everything you can on the account of my merchandise. The delay is very unpleasant for me, you've no idea. Anyway I hope you'll understand, because I can't wait any longer. My sincere greetings to you.

RIMBAUD.

P. S. Enclosed a letter from M. Tian for the empress, it'll no doubt be a waste of time! Look to settle that matter too, please. R.

107. To his mother

Harar, 10 August 1890

It's a long time since I heard anything from you. I like to think you are in good health, as I am myself.
....
Could I come and get married at home, next spring? But I shan't be able to agree to settle at home, or abandon my business affairs here. Do you think I can find someone who will agree to follow me on my travels?

I'd very much like to have an answer to that question, as soon as possible.

My very best wishes.

RIMBAUD.

108. To Ilg

Harar, 20 September 90

B 30/1

My dear Monsieur Ilg,

I have received your letter of 23 August via M. Davico. M. Zimmermann left here on 28 August, I believe, and has long ago reached Djibouti. They've written me that M. Savouré has left for France, I don't know if your compatriot has followed him. M. Zimmermann took 259 talaris on your account from me. As I remained owing you T. 1242, I'm your debtor at present, after what Zimmermann took, and various other expenses, for no more than T. 961 net. I've passed on to the Ras, who entered only a week ago, the various letters in which you claim T. 500 on top of the T. 5500 already paid, as well as the return by the customs of the 17 parcels of ivory and the reimbursement of the excess on the price of the coffee. He told me, as always, that he'd see. I very much doubt that he will reimburse the difference on the coffee and the customs, but he'll give the T. 500, since he knows how to give, if you keep on at him but still trying to get a discount from you. I fancy he's become more and more horribly avaricious! Moreover, he's sunk in increasingly terrible difficulties, which it would take me too long to describe.

[. . .]

– And now, give the most serious attention to what follows, in your own personal interest:

In the last two months, there's been an enormous revolution in the exchange rate of the rupee and the talari. Silver has gone up enormously in value as the result of a certain 'Silver bill' passed in the United States, according to which, to re-establish monetary stability, the US has begun to <u>coin</u> I don't know how many million dollars' worth of silver. And this isn't a question of a momentary crisis, you must believe that silver won't go down again for several years. The rupee has reached F. 2,30, 5 centimes at a time, and must soon reach F. 2,50. The thaler is worth 5 francs at the moment, and will go up more. The guinea is at 11 rupees at the moment, the napoleon at 9. Etc. – Thus all the prices of the goods selling in talaris have gone down enormously. Gold has tumbled to T. 19, 18,50, 18, 17, 16½ and *finally T. 16 in Aden*! Ivory's no longer worth more than *T. 80 to T. 90, the zebad T. 1 or less*, yet it's still very difficult to sell the least thing in Aden, until the rupee rate is finally stable: the rate will finally be fixed, I fancy, at 2fr, 20, and then we'll have a fixed base for buying in talaris. Meanwhile, our merchandise is losing a lot en route, I'm going, or rather we're going, to take a loss of at least 2000 talaris on the caravans that are going down! This year will have been a disaster.

[. . .]

– I think I've done well to alert you! Enclosed six letters for you, and one for M. Appenzeller.

Hasty salutations.

RIMBAUD.

As for the coffee, Moussaya has never mentioned it.

109. To his mother

Harar, 10 November 1890.

My dear Mama,

I have received your letter of 29 September 1890 safely.

In speaking of marriage, I've always meant that I intended to remain free to travel, to live abroad and even to continue living in Africa. I've become unused to the European climate, I'd have difficulty returning to it. I'd probably even need to spend two winters away, while allowing that I may return one day to France. And then how would I re-establish contact with people, what jobs would I find? That's another question. Anyway, there's one thing I find impossible, and that is a sedentary life.

I'd need to find someone who could follow me on my wanderings.

As for my capital, I have it in my own hands, it's free when I want.

Monsieur Tian is a very honourable businessman, established in Aden these thirty years past, and I am his partner in this part of Africa. My association with him dates back two and a half years. I also work on my own account, alone; and I'm free, moreover, to liquidate my affairs as soon as it suits me.

I send to the coast caravans of products from these parts: gold, musk, ivory, coffee, etc., etc. Half the profits from what I do with M. Tian are mine.

For the rest, for information, you need only apply to Monsieur de Gaspary, the French consul in Aden, or his successor.

No one in Aden can speak any ill of me. On the contrary. I'm known for a good man by everyone in the region.

Should anyone be interested!

As for Harar, there's no consul, no post, no road; you get here by camel, you live here exclusively with blacks. But at least you're free, and the climate is good.

That's how things stand.

Au revoir.

A. RIMBAUD.

110. *To Ilg*

Harar, 20 November 90.

Via No. 24
B. 30/1

My dear Monsieur Ilg,

One word more at the last minute.

Find me therefore a very good ASS (not a mule but an ass), young, big, very *saggare*,[161] very strong, good climbing and good coming down, etc., etc., in fact the best you can lay hands on: I'm not concerned by the price, you can go as high as T. 60 for something really good. You may find it among the choums of your acquaintance. Send it to me along with the men I'm waiting for to close our accounts, in six weeks or 2 months.

Make a big effort to get rid of all my merchandise, and send me what it fetches right away. Forgive me for troubling you: I hope you'll still have made something out of my junk. If I haven't sent you back the whole balance of your account in one go, it's so as not to appear too exposed in the bimonthly inventories Tian demands from me. Anyway, with the money you'll get back from my ironmongery, haberdashery, trinketry, etc., you can make something by selling them here, the difference between our prices and those in Aden being hardly more than 6 per cent to 10 per cent.

[. . .]

It's said that the Ras is to come up to Shewa along with Antonelli, who's expected here in a few days' time. These continual absences of the governor are deplorable. We remain at the mercy of the petty choums, who are as voracious as crocodiles, and of the Muslims who seek out every opportunity to do us harm.

– The politicians in Aden foresee complications in Abyssinia. The Italians, unable to obtain Kassala from the English, are going to occupy the line of the Mareb, etc., etc.

Loyal greetings.

RIMBAUD.

111. To Ilg

Harar, 5 February 91.

No 27.

My dear M. Ilg.
Still without news of you and of what's going on up there.

We're told meanwhile that the Ras is returning to us shortly. On this occasion, send me back the yield from the total sale of my goods, which, I hope, you'll have unloaded, having left you the freest of free hands for the sale.

I hope that the yield won't be less than T. 2000. The amount I've had shown on our end of February inventory is the true balance, T. 2328,775.

Awful stagnation in Aden. The rupee dances around 10 per cent every day. The pound sterling is worth $11^{1}/_{2}$ to 13 rupees. Everything depends on the law on the minting of silver in America. The senate has voted through a bill authorizing unlimited coinage; that means a rise. But it's said that the Congress won't ratify the bill; that means a fall. But if the law finally passes, there'll be a serious rise in silver.

[. . .]

In a few months' time we shall have a terrible famine. The durra harvest is nil. The durra caravan, which normally doesn't cost more than 2 piastres at this time, – costs P. 5, i.e., half a talari, and in three months' time it will cost 1 talari. They'll have to import rice.

The celebrated Grazmatch Banti (the protector of dogs)[162] left six weeks ago and has gone to install himself in *Faf El Kebir the other side of the Ogaden* (550 kilometres from here)! It seems that the epizootic hasn't got that far. I can foresee that this year they'll be going to hunt for food as far as the Zanzibar coast.

Hurried salutations.

RIMBAUD.

112. *To his mother*

Harar, 20 February 1891.

My dear Mama,

I have received your letter of 5 January safely.

I can see that all is well at home, except for the cold which, according to what I read in the newspapers, is extreme all over Europe.

I'm not well at the moment. At least, I have varicose veins in my right leg that cause me a lot of pain. That's what you get for toiling away in these miserable lands! And the varicose veins are complicated by rheumatism. It's not cold here, however; but it's the climate that causes it. It's fifteen nights today since I got a minute's sleep, on account of the pain in this accursed leg. I'd gladly leave, and I fancy the great heat in Aden would do me good, but I'm owed a lot of money and I can't leave, because I'd lose it. I've asked in Aden for a stocking for varicose veins, but I doubt whether one can be found.

Do me the following pleasure therefore: buy me a stocking for varicose veins, for a long, dry leg – (shoe size 41). The stocking needs to come up above the knee, because there's a varicose vein above the calf. The stockings are in cotton, or woven silk with elastic threads that hold the swollen veins in. The silk ones are best, the most solid. They don't cost a lot, I don't think. Anyway, I'll reimburse you.

Meanwhile, I keep the leg bandaged.

Wrap it securely and address it by post, to M. Tian, in Aden, who'll send it on at the first opportunity.

These varicose vein stockings can perhaps be found in Vouziers. At all events, your doctor at home can get a good one sent, from somewhere or other.

This infirmity has been brought on by overstraining myself on horseback, as well as by tiring journeys on foot. Because in these regions we have a maze of steep mountains, where you can't even stay on horseback. And all of it without roads or even paths.

Varicose veins aren't any danger to the health, but they prevent any violent exercise. This is a great nuisance, because the veins produce sores if you don't wear a stocking; and then again, nervous legs won't willingly tolerate the stocking, especially at night. Together with which, I've got a rheumatic pain in my accursed right knee, which torments me, taking me only at night! And you have to imagine that at this time of year, which is the winter locally, we never have less than 10 degrees above zero (not below). But the prevailing winds are dry, and very unhealthy for whites in general. Even young Europeans, from twenty-five to thirty, are afflicted with rheumatism, after two or three years residing here!

Bad food, unhealthy housing, too light clothing, anxieties of every kind, boredom, perpetual rage amidst blacks as stupid as they're crooked, it all has profound effects on your morale and your health, in a very short time. A year here's worth five anywhere else. You age very quickly here, as everywhere in the Sudan.

In your reply, settle for me how I stand in relation to military service. Do I have to do any? Make sure, and reply.

RIMBAUD.

113. To Ilg

Harar, 20 February 91.

No. 28.

My dear Monsieur Ilg,

I have received your letter via M. Teillard.

I have paid out to M. Teillard a sum of T. 600 as *the balance of all accounts between myself and MM. Chefneux and Deschamps*, and M. Teillard is sending M. Chefneux by this post the lifting of the distraint on my merchandise.

Once again, liquidate all the merchandise as soon as you can. Thanks to this wretched consignment I'm obliged to remain here where there's nothing to be gained from the manner in which I have to work. Get it over with, get it over with therefore!

Ras Mekonnen *has not reimbursed me the T. 296* customs duty on your 17 parcels of ivory. He can't have understood what you were saying! He hasn't ever mentioned it to me! How can you believe that I wouldn't have let you know! As for the difference in the price of the coffee, I have nothing to pay back on my side. As for the T. 15 loss on the last T. 500, what do you expect me to do! At the moment the Abyssinians *are paying at 11 piastres to the thaler*. You'll realize all this once you're here.

Don't think I'm going to go bankrupt with your T. 941. They're still in the corner of the cash-box. At any other time I'd be buying you some coffee. But it's dearer than in Aden at present, I'm not buying for myself, and I don't want to cause you any loss. As soon as [illegible] are good, I'll buy, despatch and have them sold in Aden for you.

I am losing hugely on the merchandise consigned to you. T. 100 paid for no reason to Labatut's former negress – T. 600 that they've just extracted from me so ingeniously – T. 200 losses on Zimmermann's gold, the costs you announced to me, and another final loss on the liquidation of the remaining merchandise! You've got me into a nice mess! Thank you for the consignments to Shewa!

I have to get it over with. So sell off everything that's left, don't go and play the trick on me again of departing from Shewa leaving my merchandise unsold! That would be a right mess!

Above all let me not hear any more stories of distraint, etc., on things that no longer concern me! It's enough to drive one crazy!

If you want your T. 941 in specie, you can send for them here.

Anyway, let's count on everything being finished when you pass through here.

Sincere greetings.

RIMBAUD.

114. To his mother

Aden, 30 April 1891.

My dear Mama,

I have received your two stockings and your letter safely, and received them in unhappy circumstances. Seeing the swelling in my right knee and the pain in the joint still increasing, and not finding any remedy or any advice, since in Harar we're surrounded by blacks and there are no Europeans there, I decided to come down. I had to abandon my business affairs: which wasn't so easy, because I had money dispersed on all sides; but finally I managed to liquidate more or less totally. For nearly three weeks I was lying in Harar quite unable to make a single movement, suffering appalling pain and never sleeping. I hired sixteen black porters, at a rate of 15 talaris each, from

Harar to Zeilah; I had a stretcher made with a canvas cover, and it's on that that I've just done, in twelve days, the 300 kilometres of desert that separate the highlands of Harar from the port of Zeilah. No need to tell you of the ghastly pain I endured on the way. I wasn't able to take a single step away from my stretcher; my knee was swelling as you watched, and the pain was getting worse the whole time.

Having got here, I entered the European hospital. There's just one room for paying patients; I am occupying it. As soon as I showed him my knee, the English doctor exclaimed that it's a *synovitis that's reached a very dangerous point*, as a consequence of the lack of attention and of strain. He spoke at once of cutting off the leg; then, he decided to wait a few days in order to see if the swelling might go down a bit after the medical attention. It's now been six days, but no improvement, except that, because I'm resting, the pain has decreased a great deal. You'll know that synovitis is a disease of the liquids in the knee joint, it may come from heredity, or accidentally, or from a lot of causes. In my case, it was certainly caused by the strain of travelling on foot or on horseback in Harar. Anyway, in the state I've reached, there's no hope of a cure for at least three months, under the most favourable circumstances. And I'm stretched out, my leg bandaged, tied, retied, chained up, in such a way as to be unable to move it. I've become a skeleton; I scare people. My back is all raw from the bed; I don't sleep for a minute. And the heat has become very great here. The hospital food, which I pay quite a lot for, is very bad. I don't know what to do. For another thing, I haven't yet closed my accounts with my partner, M. Tian. That won't be done for a week or so. I shall get out of the business with about 35,000 francs. I might have had more; but because of my unfortunate departure, I'm losing several thousand francs. I want to have myself carried to a steamer, and to come and be treated in France, the voyage would enable me to pass the time. And, in France, medical treatment and remedies are cheap, and the air is good. So it's very likely that I'll be coming. Steamers for France are unfortunately always full up at the moment, because everyone goes home from the colonies at this time of year. And I'm a poor invalid who has to be *transported* very gently! Anyway, I shall be making up my mind within the week.

Don't be frightened by all this, however. Better days will come. But it's a sorry reward for so much hard work, privation and difficulty! What a wretched life we lead!

Heartfelt greetings.

RIMBAUD.

P.S. – As for the stockings, they're no good. I'll sell them again somewhere.

115. To his mother and sister

Marseille [Thursday, 21 May 1891].

My dear Mama, my dear sister,

After terrible suffering, unable to get treatment in Aden, I caught the Messageries boat to return to France.

I arrived yesterday, after thirteen days of pain. Finding myself far too weak on arrival here, and gripped by the cold, I had to come here into the *Hôpital de la Conception*, where I pay ten frs a day, doctor included.

I'm very bad, very bad, I'm reduced to a skeletal state by this trouble in my left leg,[163] which has become enormous at present and looks like an enormous pumpkin. It's synovitis, hydarthrosis, etc., a disease of the joint and the bones.

It's going to last a very long time, if complications don't oblige them to cut off the leg. At all events, I shall be left a cripple. But I doubt whether I can wait. Life has become impossible. How unfortunate I am! How unfortunate I've become!

I have to cash a bill of exchange here for 36,800 frs on the Comptoir National d'Escompte in Paris. But I have no one to take care of investing the money. As for me, I can't take a single step out of bed. I haven't yet been able to draw out the money. What am I to do. What a dismal life! Can you not help me somehow?

RIMBAUD.
Hôpital de la Conception.
Marseille.

116. *Telegram to his mother*

Marseille [22 May 1891]
Handed in 2.50 p.m.

You or Isobel come Marseille today fast train. Leg being amputated Monday morning. Life in danger. Serious business to settle. Arthur. Hôpital Conception. Answer.

RIMBAUD.

117. *Telegram from Mme Rimbaud*

Attigny, 6.35 p.m.

Am leaving. Will arrive tomorrow evening. Be brave, be patient.

118. *To His Excellency Ras Mekonnen*

Marseille, 30 May 1891.

Excellency,
How are you? I wish you good health and complete prosperity. May God grant you everything you desire. May the course of your existence run peacefully.

I am writing this to you from Marseille, in France. I am in hospital. They cut off my leg six days ago. I am doing well at present and in three weeks I shall be healed.

In a few months' time, I am counting on returning to Harar, to trade there as before, and I thought I would send you my greetings.

Your loyal servant,

RIMBAUD.

119. To his sister Isabelle

Marseille, 17 June 1891.

Isabelle, my dear sister,

I have received your note along with my two letters returned from Harar. In one of these letters I'm told a letter was previously sent back to me at Roche. Have you not received anything else?

I've not yet written to anyone, I've not yet got out of my bed. The doctor says I shall have another month of it, and even then I shall only be able to start walking very slowly. I still have a severe neuralgia in the place where the leg was cut off, that's to say the bit remaining. I don't know how this will end. Anyway I'm resigned to everything, I have no luck!

But what do you mean with your stuff about funerals? Don't be so afraid, you be patient also, look after yourself, bear up. I'd very much like to see you alas, what can be the matter with you then? What illness? All illnesses are cured with time and treatment. At all events, one must resign oneself and not despair.

I was very angry when Mama left me, I couldn't understand the reason. But at present it's better she should be with you to get you looked after. Apologize to her and say hello to her on my behalf.

Till we meet then, but who knows when?

RIMBAUD.
Hôpital de la Conception,
Marseille.

120. To his sister Isabelle

Marseille, 23 June 1891.

My dear sister,

You've not written to me; what has happened? Your letter scared me, I would like to hear from you. Provided it doesn't involve fresh troubles, for, alas, we're being too sorely tested all at once!

As for me, all I do is weep day and night, I'm a dead man, I am crippled for the whole of my life. Within a fortnight, I shall be healed, I believe; but I shall only be able to walk on crutches. As for an artificial leg, the doctor says we shall have to wait a very long time, at least six months! In the meanwhile, what shall I do, where shall I stay? Were I to come home, the cold would drive me out within three months, or even less time; for I shan't be capable of moving from here inside six weeks, the time to practise on the crutches! I wouldn't be at home until the end of July therefore. And I'd have to leave again at the end of September.

I have no idea at all what to do. All these anxieties are driving me crazy: I never sleep for one minute.

In fact, our life is a misery, misery without end! Why do we exist therefore?

Let me hear from you.

My best wishes.

RIMBAUD.
Hôpital de la Conception,
Marseille.

121. To his sister Isabelle

Marseille, 24 June 1891.

My dear sister,

I have received your letter of 21 June. I wrote to you yesterday. I have received nothing from you for 10 June, no letter from you, no letter from Harar. I have received only the two letters of the 14th. I'm very puzzled as to where the letter of the 10th may have gone to.

What new horror are you telling me? What's this story about military service again? On my reaching the age of twenty-six, did I not send you from Aden a certificate proving that I was employed in a French firm, which is an exemption, – and subsequently when I questioned Mama she always answered that everything had been sorted out, that I had nothing to fear.

Scarcely four months ago, I asked you in one of my letters whether there was anything they could require of from me in this connection, because I wished to return to France. But I didn't get a reply. I for my part thought it had all been arranged by you. At present you give me to understand that I'm listed as an absentee, that they're after me, etc., etc. Don't inquire into it unless you're sure you won't draw attention to me. As for myself, there's no risk, in these circumstances, of my coming back! Prison after what I've just been through, death would be preferable!

Yes, death would have been preferable for a long time now as it happens! What can a crippled man do in the world? And at present still reduced to expatriating himself for good! For I certainly shan't come back again with that sort of thing, – lucky if I can escape from here by sea or overland and get abroad.

Today I tried walking with crutches, but was only able to take a few steps. My leg was cut off very high up, and it's difficult for me to keep my balance. I shan't feel easy until I'm able to put on an artificial leg, but amputation causes *neuralgia in what's left of the limb*, and it's impossible to put on a mechanical leg before the neuralgia has completely gone, and there are amputees for whom that lasts four, six, eight, twelve months! I'm told that it hardly ever lasts less than two months. If it only lasts two months I shall be happy! I would spend that time in hospital and would happily leave with two legs. As for leaving on crutches, I can't see what good that would do. You can't go up or down, it's an awful business. You run the risk of falling and crippling yourself even more. I had thought of being able to come home to spend a few months while I wait to get the strength to support the artificial leg, but at present I can see it's impossible.

Well, I shall resign myself to my fate. I shall die wherever my destiny casts me up. I hope to be able to go back where I was, I have friends I've known for ten years there, who will have pity on me, I'll find work with them, I shall live as best I can. I can at least have a life there whereas in France, aside from you, I have neither friends, nor acquaintances, nor anyone. And if I can't see you, I shall return there. I have to return in any case.

If you make inquiries concerning me, never let them know

where I am. *I'm even afraid they may take down my address at the post office. Don't go and give me away.*

All my best wishes.

RIMBAUD.

Mademoiselle Isabelle Rimbaud,
In Roche, Attigny canton,
Ardennes (France).

122. *To his sister Isabelle*

Marseille, 29 June 1891.

My dear sister,

I have received your letter of 26 June. I had already received the day before yesterday the letter from Harar on its own. As for the letter of 10 June, no news: it has disappeared, either in Attigny, or here in the administration, but I presume in Attigny rather. The envelope you sent me made me realize who it was certainly from. It must have been signed Dimitri Righas. He's a Greek residing in Harar whom I'd entrusted with a few business matters. I await news of your inquiries on the subject of military service: but, however it may be, *I fear traps*, and have no wish at all at present to return home, despite the assurances you might be given.

In any case, I'm completely immobile and am unable to take a single step. My leg is healed, that's to say scarred over, which has happened quite quickly moreover, and gives me to think that the amputation could have been avoided. So far as the doctors are concerned I'm healed and tomorrow, if I want, they would sign my authorization to leave the hospital. But what am I to do? I can't take one step! I am all day in the open air, on a chair, but I can't move. I practise on the crutches; but they're bad, and anyway I'm long, my leg was cut off high up, balance is very hard to maintain. I take a few steps and I stop, for fear of falling and crippling myself again!

I'm going to have a wooden leg made to start with, you push the stump (what's left of the leg) into it padded out with cotton, and get about with a stick. After some time practising with the wooden leg, you can, if the stump has been well reinforced, order an articulated leg which grips tightly and with which you can more or less walk. When will that moment come? Perhaps some fresh misfortune will befall me between now and then. But this time, I'll soon know how to rid myself of this miserable existence.

It's not good that you should write to me often and my name be noticed *at the post offices in Roche and Attigny*. That's where the danger lies. Here no one would pay any attention to me. Write to me as little as possible – when it's indispensable. Don't put Arthur, write Rimbaud on its own. And tell me as soon and *as clearly as possible* what the military authorities want with me and, in case of their pursuing me, what the penalty is. – But then I'd waste no time catching the boat.

I wish you good health and prosperity.

RBD.

123. *Isabelle Rimbaud to her brother*

Roche, 30 June 1891.

Dear Arthur,

I am worried at not having had a letter from you, I was expecting one this morning. Can you have got worse? Reassure me if my fears are childish. I was waiting before writing to you myself to have something to tell you about your military service; we still don't know anything precise; we have again seen the person we'd asked to make inquiries for us; the steps he has taken have not got anywhere so far as you are concerned; they've been very strict about military offences since the new law of 1889, but we do not yet know whether you're at fault.

[...]

Now, dear Arthur, you must take heart! I can see a man going past through the window who has also had a leg amputated, but a long time ago now (it was the 1870 war, I fancy).

The man is perched up on a tall basket wagon, he stops at the inn and gets down as nimbly as if he had two legs; I see him at least two or three times a week like that and always nimble and cheerful. He gets up on his wagon again as easily as he gets down; I've heard it said that with his wooden leg he's the most indefatigable dancer at the village festivities. I'm telling you this to make you see that, although deprived of a limb, one can still be good for something, and even get some enjoyment here on earth. One sees men, still young, like you, or even younger, suffering from paralysis or rheumatic pains that confine them to a bed for the whole of their lives, which are no less long; aren't they more to be pitied than the ones who have only lost a leg? You must be brave. What would you? It's no good being in despair, your unhappiness will not set anything right; on the contrary, you may contract some other incurable ailment.

I would like you to let me know which days exactly you receive my letters, and what state they arrive in. I have reasons to be mistrustful and afraid they may be opened. I have had to give up posting them in Roche; I shall take them to the station in Voncq. Did you receive the 24 June one? And the 26th one?

Here, we're in despair because it never stops raining, and the fodder is going to go rotten in the fields. The haymaking has been stopped, they won't be harvesting any corn, and the March standing crops are flat on the ground and in great danger, in short, God have mercy.

I will say *au revoir*, my dear Arthur, and hold you against my heart.

ISABELLE RIMBAUD.

Write to us please.

124. To his sister Isabelle

Marseille, 2 July 1891.

My dear sister,

I received your letters of 24 and 25 June safely and have just received that of the 30th. Only the letter of 10 June has ever been lost, and I've good reason to believe it was misappropriated at the post office in Attigny. Here they don't appear to be in the least concerned about my affairs. It's a good idea to post your letters somewhere other than Roche, and in such a way that they don't go through the Attigny post office. In that way you can write to me as much as you like. As for the military service question, I have absolutely to know where I stand, do what's necessary therefore and give me a definite answer. For my part, I very much fear a trap and would very much hesitate to come home whatever the case. I don't think you'll ever get a certain response, and then it will always be impossible for me to come back home, where I might be caught in a trap.

I've long since healed over, although the neuralgia in the stump is still just as severe, and I'm still out of bed, but now the other leg is proving very weak. It may be the long stay in bed, or the lack of balance, but I can't go more than a few minutes on crutches without the other leg turning purple. Can I have some bone disease, and am I to lose the other leg? I'm much afraid, I fear tiring myself and I abandon the crutches. I've ordered a wooden leg, it only weighs two kilos, it'll be ready in a week. I shall try to walk quite slowly with it, I'll need at least a month to get gradually used to it, but perhaps the doctor, given the neuralgia, won't allow me to walk with it as yet. As for an elastic leg, it's much too heavy for me at present, – the stump could never support it; that can only be for later. In any case a wooden leg is just as beneficial; it costs about fifty francs. With all this, I shall still be in hospital at the end of July. I pay six frs board and lodging a day at present for sixty francs an hour's worth of boredom. I never sleep for more than two hours a night. It's the insomnia that makes me fear I've still got some illness to endure. I'm terrified at the thought of my other leg: it's my one support in the world at present! When the abscess in my knee began in Harar, it started like this with a fortnight's insomnia. Well, perhaps it's my destiny to become a *legless cripple*! At which moment, I assume the army authorities would leave me alone! – Let's hope for the best.

I wish you good health, good weather and everything as you would wish it. *Au revoir*.

RBD.

125. Isabelle Rimbaud to her brother

Roche, 8 July 1891.

Dear Arthur,

We have finally managed to sort out your army business; I am sending you the copy of a letter we have received just today from the Commissariat in Mézières:

'Rimbaud, J.-N. Arthur, has been in Arabia since 16 January 1882; in consequence, his military situation is legal; he need not concern himself with his period of training, his deferment is renewable up until the time of his return to France.'

Mézières, 7 July 1891.

Officer i/c Recruitment: BERTAUX.

As for your final discharge on health grounds, you can only obtain that by going in person to the Commissariat, either in Marseille, if you are to stay there for a certain time still, or in Mézières, if you come back, or even through the gendarmerie in Attigny; you will realize from the copy of the letter above that, in order to get information and put an end to the uncertainty, we have not revealed your presence in France nor your amputation which renders you unfit for all military service; had you returned in a fit state you would have had to fulfil your 28 days on returning to France; you must therefore present yourself to the military authorities, who will confirm your unfortunate situation and give you your medical discharge.

And so, dear Arthur, you are free; before you come back, let us know a bit in advance, whether you want to have your room on the ground floor or on the first floor for your greater convenience; whether we need to prepare some piece of furniture or utensil made necessary by your leg; in fact you must find when you get here everything you may have need of; in return, I ask you to bring us a bit of warmth and good weather, things we are badly in need of. Will you make the journey alone? – I distinctly recommend that you get off at the station in Voncq and not Attigny, for your own sake as much as for ours, and especially to warn us, when you're in Paris, by letter or even by telegram, of what time you will be getting to Voncq, so that I can come and fetch you from the station.

I am overjoyed at the thought of seeing you again; but alas, there is one large shadow cast on my joy, I would like to see you happy and well, and you are neither. But there's nothing we can do about it, the best thing is to resign yourself and take heart. I shall wait impatiently to hear from you, when will you be returning?

Au revoir, dear Arthur, we embrace you from our hearts.

ISABELLE RIMBAUD.

– Do you have your army record-book? If not, say, should anyone ask for it, that you were so unwell in Arabia that you forgot to take it and that it has now been lost. Overall, it would be better, if you're going to come back, as I hope, to regularize your military situation here rather than in Marseille.

126. To his sister Isabelle

Marseille, 10 July 1891.

My dear sister,

I have received your letters of 4 and 8 July safely. I'm glad that my situation has finally been declared clear. As for the record-book, I did indeed lose it on my travels. Once I'm able to get about I shall see if I should get my discharge here or elsewhere. But if it's in Marseille, I fancy I shall need to have the autograph reply from the commissariat in my possession.

It's better therefore that I have that declaration in my own possession, *send it to me*. With it no one will approach me. I'm also keeping the hospital certificate and with these two documents I shall be able to obtain my discharge here.

I'm still out of bed, but I'm not well. So far I still haven't learnt to walk except with crutches, and still find it impossible to go up or down a single step. In which event they're obliged to lift me up or down bodily. I've had a very light wooden leg made, varnished and stuffed, very well made (price 50 francs). I put it on a few days ago and tried to haul myself about while still raising myself on the crutches, but the stump became inflamed and I put the accursed instrument aside. I shall hardly be able to make use of it inside two or three weeks, and still with crutches for a month at least, and not for more than an hour or two a day. The one advantage is having three points of support instead of two.

I'm beginning to go on crutches again therefore. What tedium, what weariness, what sadness when I think of all my old journeys, and how active I was only five months ago! Where are the trips through the highlands, the rides on horseback, the excursions, the deserts, the rivers and the seas? And at present the existence of a *legless cripple*! For I'm beginning to realize that crutches, wooden legs and mechanical legs are so many bad jokes and that all you can manage with it all is to drag yourself miserably about without ever being able to do anything. And I who'd just decided to come back to France this summer to get married! Farewell marriage, farewell family, farewell future! My life is over, I'm no longer anything but an immobile tree-stump.

I'm still a long way from being able to get about even with the wooden leg, which is the lightest there is even so. I'm reckoning on another four months at least to be able to go up a few steps only on the wooden leg with the sole support of a stick. What's so difficult is to go up or down. Only in six months will I be able to try a mechanical leg and with a great deal of pointless difficulty. The big problem is being amputated high up. First of all, the neuralgia subsequent to the amputation is all the more violent and persistent when a limb's been amputated high up. Thus, people who've had a knee disjointed can tolerate the apparatus much quicker. But none of it matters much at present, life itself hardly matters!

It's hardly any cooler here than in Egypt. At midday we get from 30 to 35, and at night from 25 to 30. – So the temperature in Harar is pleasanter, especially at night, which doesn't go above 10 to 15.

I can't tell you what I shall do, I'm still *too low* to know that myself. It's not going well, I repeat. I'm very much afraid of some accident. The end of one leg is much thicker than the other, and full of neuralgia. The doctor of course no longer sees me; because, so far as the doctor's concerned, it's enough that the wound should be scarred over for him to let you go. He tells you you're healed. He only concerns himself with you when abscesses break out etc., etc., or when other complications occur necessitating a few cuts with the knife. They look on patients only as the object of experiments. That's well known. Especially in hospitals, for the doctor there isn't paid. He goes after the job only in order to acquire a reputation and a clientele.

I'd very much like to come home to you, because it's cool there, but I don't fancy there's too much ground there suitable for my acrobatic exercises. And then I'm afraid that it may go from cool to cold. But the main reason is that *I can't move*; I can't, I shan't be able to for a long time to come, – and, to tell you the truth, I don't even think I'm cured inside and am expecting some explosion . . . I'd need to be carried in a cart, lifted down, etc., etc., it's too much trouble, expense and fatigue. My room is paid for until the end of July; I'll think about it and *see what I'm able to do* in the interim.

Until then I'd rather think it'll go better as you kindly give me to believe; – however stupid his existence may be, man still clings to it.

Send me the letter from the commissariat. There is in fact at my table a sick police inspector who was always annoying me with stories about the service and was getting ready to play some trick on me.

Forgive me for troubling you, I thank you, and wish you good fortune and good health.

Write to me.

Fond regards.

RIMBAUD.

Mademoiselle Isabelle Rimbaud,
Roche, Attigny canton
Ardennes (France).

127. *Ras Mekonnen to Rimbaud*

How are you? I, thanks be to God, am well. I have learnt with astonishment and compassion that they had been obliged to cut off your leg. According to what you have told me, the operation was a success. God be praised!

I learn with pleasure that you are proposing to come back to Harar to continue with your business: that gives me pleasure. Yes, come back soon in good health. I am still your friend.

Written in Harar 12 July 1891.

RAS MEKONNEN.

128. *Isabelle Rimbaud to her brother*

Roche, 13 July 1891.

Dear Arthur,

[. . .]

I'm distressed to find you're not in a fit state to come back yet; I was hoping for better. But then what is it exactly, the trouble that's come into your knee, and how did it start? I'd very much like to know, because for a long time now I myself have had a leg that swells up at times. I think you are mistaken in your estimation of doctors; they would be monsters if they tended their patients so as to carry out experiments on them, if they cut off a leg simply to see what there is inside; no, that's impossible; in your case you ought to find out whether the opinion of the doctor in Aden or Zeilah agreed with that of the doctor in Marseille: it would have been better, however, if they had opened up and examined your knee first of all, with a view to cutting off the leg if no cure was possible otherwise.

[. . .]

Here the weather has recovered in the past three or four days. We're mowing, we're putting off the clover and the hay and we're very busy.

Au revoir, Arthur, I embrace you.

ISABELLE RIMBAUD.

129. To his sister Isabelle

Marseille, 15 July 1891.

My dear Isabelle,

I have received your letter of the 13th and take the opportunity of answering it at once. I'm going to see what steps I can take with that note from the commissariat and the certificate from the hospital. It would please me, for sure, to have the matter sorted out, but, alas, I can't find the means of doing so, I who am scarcely capable of putting my slipper on my one leg. Anyway, I shall manage as best I can. At least, with these two documents, I no longer risk going to prison; for the army authorities are capable of imprisoning a cripple, if only in a hospital. Where the declaration of my return to France is concerned, to whom and where to make it? There's no one to hand to give me information; and the day is far off when I shall be able to go into offices, with my wooden legs, to make inquiries.

I pass the nights and days reflecting on the means of getting about: it's a real torment! I'd like to do this and that, to go here and there, to see, to live, to leave: impossible, impossible at least for a long time to come, if not for ever! All I see beside me are the accursed crutches: without these sticks, I can't take a step, I can't exist. I can't even dress myself without the most ghastly acrobatics. I've got as far as running almost with my crutches, but I can't go up or down staircases, and if the ground is uneven, the jolting from one shoulder to the other is very tiring. I have a very severe neuralgic pain in my arm and right shoulder, along with which the crutch cuts into the armpit, – more neuralgia in the left leg, with all of which one has to play the acrobat all day long so as to give the impression one exists.

Here is what, at long last, I've worked out was the cause of my illness. The Harar climate is cold from November to March. I, out of habit, wore almost nothing: a simple pair of linen trousers and a cotton shirt. Along with which journeys on foot of from 15 to 40 kilometres a day, senseless rides on horseback through the steep mountains in the region. I fancy that an arthritic pain must have developed in the knee brought on by fatigue, and the hot and cold. In fact, it began with a hammer blow (so to speak) below the kneecap, a light blow that kept hitting me; a great dryness in the joint and retraction of the nerve in the thigh. Next came the swelling of the veins all round the knee which made me think of varicose veins. I was still walking and working a lot, more than ever, thinking it was a simple chill. Then the pain inside the knee got worse. Every step I took, it was like a nail sticking in sideways. – I could still walk, though with greater difficulty; I rode for the most part and dismounted every time almost crippled. – Then the top of the knee swelled up, the kneecap became puffy, the calf too seized up, getting about became painful, and the pain jarred the nerves as far as the ankle and the small of my back. – I could no longer walk except with a heavy limp and I was getting increasingly bad, but I still had a lot of work on, necessarily. – I then began to keep my leg bandaged from top to bottom, to massage it, bathe it, etc., without result. Meanwhile, my appetite was going. A persistent insomnia was starting. I was getting very weak and thin. – Around 15 March, I decided to take to my bed, or at least maintain a horizontal position. I arranged a bed between my cash-box, my accounts and a window from where I could keep an eye on my scales at the far end of the yard, and I paid people on top to keep the work going, staying stretched out myself, at least the bad leg. But day by day, the swelling in the

knee made it look like a ball, I noticed that the inner face of the
tibia at the top was much fatter than on the other leg: the
kneecap was losing all movement, drowned in the excretion
produced by the swelling in the knee, and I was terrified to see
it become as hard as bone within a few days; at which moment,
the whole leg became stiff, completely stiff, within a week,
I could only go to the lavatories by dragging myself along.
Meanwhile the leg and the top of the thigh were still getting
thinner, the knee and the calf were swelling, petrifying, or rather
ossifying, and I was getting physically and morally weaker.

At the end of March, I made up my mind to leave. Within a
few days, I liquidated everything at a loss. And, since the stiffness
and pain stopped me using a mule or even a camel, I had a
stretcher made for myself covered with a curtain, which sixteen
men carried to Zeilah in a fortnight. On the second day of the
journey, having gone a long way ahead of the caravan, I was
surprised in a desert spot by a rainstorm. I remained lying for
sixteen hours under the rain, without shelter or any possibility
of moving. That did me a lot of harm. En route, I was never
able to get up from my stretcher, they spread the tent over me
at the same spot where they had set me down and, digging a
hole with my hands near the side of the stretcher, I managed
with difficulty to get myself a little bit to one side so as to pass
a motion over the hole, which I filled in with earth. In the
mornings, they removed the tent from over me, and carried me
off. I reached Zeilah utterly exhausted, paralysed. I rested there
for only four hours, a steamer was leaving for Aden. Thrown
on to the deck on my mattress (I had to be hoisted aboard on
my stretcher!) I had to endure three days at sea without eating.
In Aden, another descent in the stretcher. I then spent several
days at M. Tian's to settle our affairs and left for the hospital,
where the English doctor, after a fortnight, advised me to go off
to Europe.

I'm convinced that the pain in the joint, if it had been attended
to in the first few days, would have been easily soothed and
wouldn't have led to anything. But I knew nothing about it.
It's I who ruined everything by my insistence on walking and
working to excess. Why at school don't we learn medicine, the

little at least we each of us need so as not to do such stupid things?

If someone in this condition were to consult me, I'd tell him: you've reached this point: but never let them amputate. Have yourself butchered, ripped apart, chopped in pieces, but don't allow them to amputate. If death comes, it'll still be better than a life minus limbs. Many have done that; and if I had things over again, I'd do it. Suffer the tortures of the damned for a year rather than be amputated.

And here is the lovely result: I'm sitting down, and from time to time I stand up and hop for a hundred paces on my crutches, and sit down again. My hands can't hold anything. When I walk, I can't turn my head away from my one foot and the end of the crutches. My head and shoulders are bent forward, and you arch yourself like a hunchback. You shudder at seeing objects and people moving around you, afraid you may get tipped over, and break your second leg. They snigger watching you hop about. When you sit down again, your hands are numb and your armpit sawn in two, and you have the look of an idiot. Despair takes hold of you again and you stay sitting like someone completely helpless, snivelling and waiting for the night, which will bring back a perpetual insomnia and the morning that's even sadder than the evening before, etc., etc. The rest in the next issue.

All my best wishes.

RBD.

130. Isabelle Rimbaud to her brother

Prés de Fontenille, 18 July 1891.

Dear Arthur,

[. . .]

Why, now the military question's settled, should you not come back to Roche? – I can hear you answering, the problem of transport. Can you not take a sleeping compartment so as to be better off? You could have yourself carried from the hospital to the station, and you hardly change trains except in Paris and Amagne; you could have yourself lifted down, carried and lifted back in again by railway staff. The journey by sleeping compartment would be expensive, but at least you wouldn't have to pay your board and lodging at the hospital. And in Roche you'd always be better off than among strangers; if there are people stupid and spiteful enough to laugh and enjoy your situation, you have enough spirit not to pay any attention to them.

It's warm and fine, you'd be well off here; I'd like you to be with me, you'd see it would take your mind off things.

Some advice from Mama: take good care of your money or your securities if your money's been invested, and if you come home, be very careful, during your journey, not to lose it or get it stolen.

Write to me, dear Arthur, and write at length; you told me the day before yesterday: the rest in the next issue; I noted those words down and wait impatiently to hear from you.

Here the farm servants coming back into the fields with the wagon, we're going to load the dry hay. *Au revoir*, dear Arthur, I am with you and hold you to my heart.

ISABELLE R.

131. To the Officer i/c Recruitment in Marseille

Monsieur the Officer i/c Recruitment in Marseille,

I am a conscript from the class of 1875. I drew lots in Charleville, in the dept of the Ardennes, I was exempted from military service, having an older brother serving in the colours. In 1882, on 16 January, at the time of my 28 days' training, I was in Arabia, employed as a trader in a French firm: I made my declaration as a resident abroad, and sent a certificate to M. the local C[ommandan]t in Mézières, the said certificate confirming my presence in Aden. I was given a renewable deferment up until my return to France.

On 22 May last, I returned to France with the intention of fulfilling my military service: but on landing in Marseille, I was obliged to go into the Hôpital de la Conception and on the 25th following I had my right leg amputated. I hold the certificate from the director of the hospital where I still am available to the recruiting officer, along with that of the doctor who treated me.

I ask the Officer i/c Recruitment to regularize my situation in respect of military service, and to have me granted a final discharge, if, that is, I am no longer fit for any service.

Dated from the Hôpital de la Conception.

132. To his sister Isabelle

Marseille, 20 July 189[1].

My dear sister,

I am writing this under the influence of a violent pain in my right shoulder, it almost prevents me from writing, as you can see.

All this stems from a constitution that's become arthritic as a result of being ill treated. But I've had enough of the hospital, where I'm also exposed, every day, to catching smallpox, typhus and other plagues that live here. I'm leaving, the doctor having told me that I can leave and that it's better for me not to remain in the hospital.

In two or three days' time I shall be coming out therefore and will be looking to haul myself as far as you as best I can; for I can't walk with my wooden leg, and even with the crutches, I can't at present take more than a few steps, so as not to make the condition of my shoulder any worse. As you said, I shall get off at the station in Voncq. As for lodging, I'd rather live upstairs; no point then in writing to me here, I shall very shortly be on my way.

Au revoir.

RIMBAUD.

133. Isabelle Rimbaud to her mother

Marseille, Tuesday 22 September 1891.

My dear Mama,

I have just got your brief note, you are very laconic. Have we become so antipathetic to you that you no longer wish to write to us or answer my questions? Or else are you unwell? That is my greatest concern, what would become of me, dear God, with a dying man and an invalid 600 miles apart! How I would like to divide myself up and be half here and half in Roche! Although it may seem to you a matter of indifference, I have to tell you that Arthur is very ill. I told you in my last letter that I would again question the doctors in detail; I spoke to them in fact and here is their response: Here we have a poor boy (Arthur) who is slowly leaving us, his life is a matter of time, a few months perhaps, unless some devastating complication arises, which might happen from one day to the next; as for a cure there's no point in hoping, he won't get better; his condition must be a propagation through the bone marrow of the cancerous state that necessitated the amputation of the leg. One of the doctors, Doctor Trastoul (an old man with white hair) added: Since you've remained here for a month and he wants you to remain longer, don't leave him; in the state he's in it would be cruel to deny him your presence. – That, dear Mama, is what the doctors told me alone, of course, because they tell him the exact opposite; they promise him he will be radically cured, trying to make him believe he's getting better day by day, and hearing them I'm confused, to the point where I ask myself who they are lying to, whether it's to him or else to me, because they seem as convinced in talking to him of a cure as in putting me on guard against his death. [. . .] Since his reason returned he is always weeping, he doesn't yet believe that he will stay paralysed (that's supposing he lives). [. . .] He wants so much to live and get better that he demands any treatment however painful it may be so long as they cure him and give him back the use of his arms. He wants absolutely to get his jointed leg, so as to try and stand up and walk, when for the past month he's only got up to be set down stark naked on an armchair while they were making the bed! His great concern is anxiety about how he will earn his living, if he isn't given back his right arm completely, and he weeps when he compares the way he was a year ago with what he is today, he weeps to think of the future when he won't be able to work any more, he weeps over the present in which he suffers cruelly, he takes me in his arms sobbing and shouting and begging me not to abandon him.

[The last sheet of this letter is missing.]

134. Notes made by Isabelle Rimbaud

Sunday, 4 October 1891.

[. . .]

He then begins to recount to me improbable things that he imagines have taken place in the hospital during the night; it's the one reminiscence from his delirium remaining to him, but stubborn to the point where, every morning and several times during the day, he recounts the same absurdity and is angry when I don't believe him. So I listen to him and try to dissuade him; he accuses the male nurses and even the nuns of abominable things that cannot exist; I tell him he's no doubt been dreaming, but he won't let go and treats me as an innocent and an imbecile.

[. . .]

I have to rack my brains all day long to stop him from committing countless follies. His one idea is to leave Marseille for a warmer climate, either Algiers, or Aden, or Obock. What keeps him here is the fear that I might not go any further away with him, because he can't do without me.

[. . .]

I am thinking and writing all this while he is deep in a sort of lethargy, which is not sleep but rather weakness.

On waking, he looks out of the window at the sun, which is still shining in a cloudless sky, and begins to weep, saying that never again will he see the sun outside. 'I shall go under the earth,' he says to me, 'and you'll be walking in the sunshine!' And that is how it is all day long, a nameless despair, an everlasting lament.

135. Isabelle Rimbaud to her mother

Marseille, Monday 5 October 1891.

My dear Mama,

[. . .]

I don't believe Arthur will undertake any commercial operation at this moment, he is too bad: at all events I would do everything in my power to dissuade him. He thinks that 30,000 francs are at Roche and I could tell him also that you've invested them; that would always delay things for nearly a month if he wished absolutely to have them back. What torments me rather is that the winter's now upon us and he'll never want to spend it here. Should I go with him, whether to Algiers, or Nice, or even Aden or Obock? If he wants to leave I doubt whether he'll be able to withstand the journey in the state he's in; to let him go alone is to condemn him to dying unassisted and to wasting his money without remission; if he absolutely wants to go what must I do?

[. . .]

It's more than a week now since his bed was made because they can no longer even take him and sit him in the armchair during the time it takes to make it; his right arm is completely inert and becoming swollen, his left arm causes him terrible pain and is three-quarters paralysed and frighteningly wasted; he is in pain everywhere in every part of his body; they think he's going to be paralysed bit by bit until it reaches the heart; no one tells him that but he's guessed and is desperate and despairs every minute of the day. I alone tend to him, touch him, approach him.

The doctors have handed him over to me, I have at my disposal all the medicines from the pharmacy intended for friction rubs, linaments, ointments etc. . . . They've also entrusted me with the electricity and I have to apply it myself; but no matter what I do, nothing can cure him or even bring relief.

[. . .]

Au revoir, dear Mama, take good care of your health, and don't go too long without writing to me.

I hold you against my heart.

ISABELLE.

136. Isabelle Rimbaud to her mother

Wednesday, 28 October 1891.

My dear Mama,

God be blessed a thousand times over! I experienced on Sunday the greatest happiness that I can have in this world. It is no longer a poor unfortunate reprobate who is going to die beside me: it is a just man, a saint, a martyr, one of the elect!

In the course of the past week, the chaplains had twice come to see him; he had received them kindly, but with so great a lassitude and discouragement that they hadn't dared talk to him of death. On Saturday evening, all the nuns prayed for him together that he might make a good death. On Sunday morning, after High Mass, he seemed calmer and fully conscious: one of the chaplains returned and suggested he make his confession; he was willing to! When the priest came out, he said to me, looking at me with a troubled expression, a strange expression: 'Your brother has the faith, my child, so what were you telling us? He has the faith, and never have I seen faith of that quality!'

[. . .]

Death is coming apace. I told you in my last letter, dear Mama, that his stump was very swollen. Now there's an enormous cancer between the hip and the stomach, just above the bone; but the stump, which had been so sensitive and painful hardly gives him any pain any more. Arthur hasn't seen this fatal tumour: he is surprised that everyone comes to look at the poor stump in which he hardly feels anything any more; and all the doctors (a good ten have been already since I drew attention to this terrible affliction) remain speechless and terrified faced by this strange cancer.

[. . .]

When he is awake, he is ending his life in a sort of continual dream: he says weird things very softly, in a voice that would enchant me if it didn't pierce my heart. [. . .] He recognizes everyone. Me he sometimes calls Djami,[164] but I know that that is because he wants him, and that it goes back into his deliberate dream; for the rest, he mixes everything up and . . . with art. We are in Harar, we are always leaving for Aden, and we have to look for camels, to organize the caravan; he is walking very easily with his new articulated leg, we take a few rides on beautiful mules richly caparisoned; then we have to work, keep the books, write letters. Quick, quick, they're waiting for us, let's close the bags and go. Why has he been allowed to sleep? Why did I not help him to get dressed? What will be said if we don't arrive on the appointed day? They'll no longer take him at his word, no longer have confidence in him! And he starts to weep while regretting my clumsiness and negligence: for I am always with him and it's I who am in charge of making all the preparations.

He is taking almost nothing in terms of nourishment, and when he does it's with an extreme repugnance. So he's as thin as a skeleton and has the colour of a corpse! And all his poor paralysed, mutilated, dead limbs around him! God, the pity of it!

[. . .]

Au revoir, dear Mama, I hold you against my heart,
                                                                ISABELLE.

137. To the Managing Director,
Messageries Maritimes Steamship Company

Marseille, 9 November 1891.

ONE LOT: A SINGLE TUSK
ONE LOT: TWO TUSKS
ONE LOT: THREE TUSKS
ONE LOT: FOUR TUSKS
ONE LOT: TWO TUSKS

Monsieur le Directeur,

I have come to ask you whether I may have left anything on account with you. I wish to change today from this service, whose name I do not even know, but at all events let it be the Aphinar[165] service. All these services are everywhere here, and I am helpless and unhappy, I can find nothing, the first dog in the street will tell you that. Send me therefore the prices of the services from Aphinar to Suez. I am completely paralysed: I wish therefore to be on board in good time. Tell me at what time I need to be carried on board . . .

[Rimbaud died on 10 November 1891, the day after dictating this last letter to his sister.]

Notes

POEMS

from POEMS, 1869–71

The Orphans' New Year Gifts

1. *Here, by their mother's bed ... cut in gold*: The closing lines of this poem, as Graham Robb comments (*Rimbaud*, 2001), make their point rather obliquely, and the reader may fail, just as the two children do, to grasp that their mother is dead: the bright images in her bedroom which they mistake for gifts are funeral ornaments.

Blacksmith

1. *circa 10 August 1792*: The date of the incident in the Tuileries on which this poem is based is in fact 20 June 1792. When the palace was stormed, Louis XVI was forced to wear the Phrygian cap. Among the leaders of the revolutionary crowd was Louis Legendre, a butcher, and very likely the model for the blacksmith. The Revolutionary theme is a blunt allusion to the Second Empire, and the Emperor Napoleon III, whom Rimbaud so despised.

2. *sprigs of oak*: In Paris, three days before the fall of the Bastille, those who had no green bonnets – green was proclaimed 'the colour of hope' – wore leaves in their caps.

Ophelia

1. *sallow, courtly prince*: Hamlet.

Venus Rising from the Water

1. This sonnet takes its cue from 'Les Antres malsains', a poem by Albert Glatigny in *Vignes folles* (1860), describing a prostitute whose arm bears the inscription 'PIERRE et LOLOTTE'.

Nina Gets Back to Him

1.   The version of this poem in the 'Douai notebook', which Rimbaud gave to Paul Demeny in October 1870, does not contain the two verses in square brackets. These appear in a version presented to Georges Izambard in the same year.

Set to Music

1.   *a cheap cigarette*: For 'des roses': 'roses' were probably an issue of low-quality cigarettes referred to by the colour of the pack.

Seat-People

1.   *barcarole*: A boatman's song.

The Hands of Jeanne-Marie

1.   The poem is a homage to the militant women in the Paris Commune (18 March–28 May 1871), especially at the barricades during the last days. The most famous of these was Louise Michel. Another, Anne-Marie Menand, known as Jeanne-Marie, may have supplied Rimbaud with the name of his revolutionary heroine.

2.   *Juana*: Here the choice of name may derive from a poem by A. de Musset (1810–57), 'A Juana', or more likely, from the white-handed heroine of his dramatic poem, 'Don Paez'. Gautier's 'Etudes des mains', a poem in octosyllabic quatrains which gave Rimbaud his point of departure, contains a reference to Don Juan.

3.   *Khenghavar*: A variant spelling (Rimbaud's own) of the Persian city Kengawar.

4.   *prostitutes*: For 'cousine', from the Ardennes colloquialism 'macouzine'.

5.   *Kyrie Eleison*: From the Mass, meaning 'Lord have mercy'.

Seven-year-old Poets

1.   *She'd got the blue gaze – the gaze that lies*: Is it the eyes of 'the Mother' that are blue and hypocritical? This would make sense of the boy's surge of well-being in the face of her distress. In another interpretation, however, it is he who turns his deceitful gaze on her (she 'gets' his blue look).

To the Poet on the Matter of Flowers

1.   This superb and difficult poem was dispatched to Théodore de
     Banville a month after composition. It is provocatively dated:
     14 July was the anniversary of the storming of the Bastille. Rim-
     baud had already sent work to Banville (see Letter 1), with a view
     to publication. A year later he was poking fun at Parnassian
     conventions: far too many flowers, and too much exoticism for
     his taste. Often a combination of the two (whence the 'Asoka
     Ode') is disparaged here. Yet the mockery of this poem, appar-
     ently at the expense of the Parnassians, depends for many of its
     effects on Banville's own verses in *Odes funambulesques*: it is a
     homage as much as a clever piece of insolence. Rimbaud's target
     is the preciousness of Parnassian verse. He sets the Parnassian
     view of poetry as a rigorous practice against other disciplines –
     the natural sciences in particular, in which a flower is more than
     a verse-trapping. But he also derides the imperial Enlightenment
     habit of 'discovering' exotic places and flora (salon exoticism
     depended on many such discoveries), only to put them to work for
     gain. Banville would no doubt have enjoyed Rimbaud's parody of
     the no-nonsense, philistine profiteer recommending that poetry
     should speak about 'tobacco' and 'exotic harvests' (v.23). Here
     again, the piece falls short of outright insult. The Parnassians
     were drawn to positivist ideas, but Rimbaud seems briefly to side
     with them against a bustling, vulgarized version of positivism
     that sees the value of nature purely in terms of its practical benefits
     to mankind.
         These witty ambiguities, combined with rapid changes of tone
     and flurries of allusion, make the poem as challenging for the
     modern reader as it would have been for Banville – a protean
     experiment which ends up a good way from where it began.
     The last two stanzas return briefly to the original theme: the
     Parnassians are craven dilettantes, who will have to browse the
     Hachette picture-almanacs for inspiration – like a 'Seven-year-old
     Poet' – and for commercial success. In the meantime, however,
     the poem has gone beyond mockery to more extravagant forms
     of statement which, in vv.29 to 32 (Section IV), anticipate another
     masterpiece, 'The Drunken Boat', written a month or so later.

2.   *Kerdrel*: Vincent Audren de Kerdrel was a royalist member of the
     National Assembly in 1871 – a champion of the Bourbon dynasty,
     whence his association with the symbol of the lily.

3.   *The Sonnet of 1830*: Perhaps an impatient allusion to the fact

that the traditional sonnet form survived, sometimes complete with floral subject-matter, into the first phase of French Romanticism, a phase that ended in 1830 with the July Revolution and the overthrow of the Bourbon monarchy. One modern editor, Jean-Luc Steinmetz, detects an allusion to Lucien de Rubempré, the flower-sonneteer of Balzac's *Les Illusions perdues*.

4. *the pink and the amaranth*: Both were presented to poets competing in the *Jeux floraux*, a troubador-revivalist festival held in Toulouse and attended by many admirers of French Romanticism. The Académie des Jeux floraux exists to this day.

5. *Asoka*: An exotic species of plant named for the Buddhist ruler in India during the third century BC.

6. *Grandville*: The metamorphic drawings and prints of Jean-Ignace-Isodore Gérard, or J. J. Grandville (1803–47), influenced Tenniel and later charmed the Surrealists. Rimbaud has in mind Grandville's *Fleurs animées*, a collection of colour-prints personifying flowers. (See Letter 2.)

7. *warmed-up Wiltshire*: For 'Oises extravagantes'. The Oise is a river in the north-east of France.

8. *Pedro Velasquez of Havana*: Obscure. Perhaps derived from Diego Velásquez, who took part in the Spanish colonization of Cuba; perhaps an echo from José-Maria de Hérédia, the French poet, born in Cuba, whose work had appeared in the first edition of the *Parnasse contemporain*. The gist, in any case, is that the dollar-value of people and things is the only way to reckon their worth.

9. *the Sea of Sorrento*: The blue waters of the Gulf of Naples were a sickly favourite with the Parnassians, including Banville.

10. *The red of perfumed madders ... Army*: Red was the colour of French infantrymen's trousers.

11. *Thyrsuses*: Wands of Bacchus; wreathed wooden staves carried in Bacchic revels.

12. *Renan*: Ernest Renan's *Vie de Jésus* was published in 1863.

13. *Kater Murr*: Tomcat Murr, from E. T. A. Hoffmann's *Life and Opinions of Tomcat Murr*. Kater Murr also crops up in Banville's *Odes funambulesques*.

14. *Tréguier*: Renan's birthplace in Brittany.

15. *Paramaribo*: A town in Guyana.

16. *Monsieur Figuier*: Prolific collaborator with the publisher Hachette on the illustrated series, *Tableaux de la nature*.

17. *Alcide Bava*: Alcides was the birthname of Heracles. 'Bava' is

perhaps an obscure wordplay, or simply a conjugation of the verb *baver*, giving 'Alcides Slobbered'.

First Communion

1. *Adonai*: From the Hebrew for 'Lord'.
2. *Queen of Zion*: The Virgin Mary.

Drunken Boat

1. *Marys-of-the-Sea*: A reference simply to the Virgin Mary as Stella Maris, mistress of the sea, or possibly to the three Marys – including Mary Magdalene – said by local legend to have come ashore in the Camargue, having been cast out of Palestine after the death of Christ.
2. *dorados*: *Coryphaena hippuris*, dolphin fish.
3. *prison ships*: A haunting image at the time of writing: the use of decommissioned ships to hold enemy prisoners during the Napoleonic Wars had been revived to intern defeated Communards in the summer of 1871.

Vowels

1. *the violet gleam of Those Eyes*: Often thought to be the eyes of God at the Last Judgement, and, in early Rimbaud mythography, a reference to the eyes of a Charleville girl who took his fancy.

from ALBUM ZUTIQUE

The *Album Zutique* did not come to light until the 1930s. It is a ragbag of parodies, often obscene, written by members of a small avant-garde circle known as the Zutistes (from the French, *Zut!* – loosely speaking, 'Who gives a damn!'). Rimbaud fell in with the Zutistes in the winter of 1871, shortly before the circle ceased to exist, and made about twenty contributions to the *Album*. The names beneath the poems – François Coppée, Albert Mérat – are those of the poets parodied (both had appeared in the 1866 series of *Le Parnasse contemporain*). The initials are those of Rimbaud – and, in the collaboration, Paul Verlaine.

Idol. Arsehole Sonnet

1. This poem was already known before the *Album Zutique* was rediscovered (it had appeared in 1904 in Verlaine's posthumous *Hombres*). It was republished in the 1920s as one of the *Stupra*, and many modern editors have preferred to stick to that

arrangement. It is nonetheless one of the most striking entries in the *Album*, copied out in Rimbaud's hand. The quatrains are by Verlaine, the tercets by Rimbaud.

State of Siege?

1. *State of Siege?*: A play on words referring both to the state of siege imposed on Paris by Prussian troops in 1870 and to the position of the masturbating conductor on his seat (*siège*) at the back of the omnibus.

Very Old Guard

1. *Very Old Guard*: 'Vieux de la vieille' refers to the veterans of the Imperial Guard.
2. *the emperor*: Napoleon III.
3. *progeny of Mars*: A reference to the birth of the Emperor's son in the month of March (*mars*) 1856; also a sarcastic allusion to the military incompetence of his father in the war with Prussia.
4. *18 March*: In fact, the Imperial Prince was born on 16 March; 18 March was the date on which the Paris Commune came into existence.
5. *Eugénie*: Wife of Napoleon III.

THE STUPRA

The title is from the Latin for 'obscenities'.

'Animals in former times . . .'

1. *Kléber*: Jean-Baptiste Kléber, French Revolutionary general. Perhaps Rimbaud has a statue of Kléber in mind.

from LAST POEMS

'What are they to us . . .'

1. A furious response to the suppression of the Paris Commune.

Memory

1. A sublimated biography, compacted into a child's point of view. But the poet's flight to Paris in 1871 may also be in play; or possibly the disappearance of his father in 1860. Either would enrich the enigmatic 'HE' of v.6 without fully appropriating it. The desperate 'SHE' is a poetic silhouette of Rimbaud's mother

– introduced as 'Madame' in v.5, where she has taken up her characteristically 'stiff' posture. The presence of the water lily – a symbol of conjugal loyalty – seems to point to the father, rather than the son, as the fugitive 'HE'. The blue flower on the water at the end of the poem may stand for a more innocent, non-contractual love. The 'I' of the poem – a sort of 'drunken boat' held fast (vv. 9 and 10) – can have neither.

2. *It slips away*: For 'Elle sombre'. The controversial 'elle' is variously held to refer to the entirety of the child's vision of the world, as set out in these opening stanzas, to the weeds in the water ('l'herbe') and to the water – or the river – itself. The translation here favours the last. In this case, Rimbaud would be using the word 'sombrer', meaning 'to sink', in a figurative way (i.e., to disappear) – or perhaps associating it with the etymologically distinct 'sombre', to give the sense of a darkening.

3. *filaments of toil*: For 'fils du travail'. The 'toil' could well be that of the spider whose threads drift on the air and which are known in French as *fils de la Vierge*, but there may be a visual pun with the word *fils*, or 'son', which thickens this image by associating the (now unusual) sense of *travail* – labour as in childbirth – with the word for 'virgin', to hint at virgin birth. Alternatively – as in this translation – the sense is simply of work in the fields producing a haze of dust. (The phrase 'fils du travail' also occurs in 'Reminiscence of an Aged Cretin', where it presents a different order of difficulty.)

Comedy of Thirst

1. *the Green Inn*: The inn of the earlier sonnet (October 1870).

Good Thought for the Morning

1. *the Hesperidean sun*: In Greek myth, the Hesperides were guardians of the golden apples given to Hera on her marriage to Zeus. The evocation of a summer dawn in v.1 is complicated by the fact that the garden of the Hesperides was in the west.

2. *Queen of the Shepherds*: Venus, by association with the morning star – in French, the 'Shepherd's Star'.

Festivals of Hunger

1. *Anne, Anne*: Some commentators hear an echo of 'Anne, ma sœur, Anne', from Charles Perrault's *Barbe-Bleu*. Scanning the horizon for her brothers, Sister Anne was a watcher from another 'highest tower'.

[Happiness]

1.   The title ('Bonheur') is the one given by Rimbaud in a later version
      which appears in 'Alchemy of the Word' (*A Season in Hell*). In
      the manuscript of the version here, the last six lines are struck
      out. They, and the title, are printed between square brackets.

Shame

1.   The boy-poet rebuked. Rimbaud borrows from the punitive rep-
      ertoire of his mother, and from the tirades of Verlaine, in order
      to restage his humiliation here. Verlaine is almost certainly the
      'He' of the parenthetical second verse – a parenthesis that allows
      the poet his brief counter-attack.

2.   *a Rocky-Mountain cat*: An invention, derived from Roche
      ('rock'), the name of the hamlet outside Charleville where Rim-
      baud's mother kept the family farm.

THE DESERTS OF LOVE

These two dream fragments, probably from 1872, give an indication
of the narrative possibilities that drew Rimbaud to the prose-poem.
The conscious distancing effect of the Foreword is nonetheless an
ungainly device by comparison with the internal recastings and re-
orderings, the skewings and truncations of narrative, that we will find
in *Illuminations*.

Foreword

1.   *man*: André Guyaux, one of Rimbaud's modern editors, sees in
      the italicization of the word 'man' an allusion to the poet's
      homosexual experience, compounded further on by the mention
      of a 'strange, sad waywardness'. In both the 'rustic' and the
      'urban' dreams that follow, the sexual encounter is a disabling
      and frantic affair, which produces deep unhappiness.

2.   *the uninterrupted sleep of the legendary Mohamedans*: These are
      the 'Sleepers of the Cave' in sura 18 of the Koran. Having hidden
      in a cavern to escape the wrath of idolators, they fell asleep and
      woke a century or more later. In Christian mythology, 'the Seven
      Sleepers of Ephesus'.

A SEASON IN HELL

Bad Blood

1. *Declaration of the Rights of Man*: The founding document of the French Revolution, approved by the National Assembly in August 1789, guaranteeing freedom and security, the right to hold property and resist oppression.

2. *De profundis Domine*: Psalm 130. 'Out of the depths have I cried unto Thee, O Lord.'

3. *Ham*: One of Noah's children, mythic ancestor of the so-called Hamitic peoples of the Horn of Africa, which Rimbaud would come to know well.

Delirium I. Foolish Virgin, Infernal Groom

1. In Christ's parable (Matthew 25), ten virgins await the attentions of the Heavenly Bridegroom, but five are ill-prepared and fail to enter the Kingdom of Heaven. There is only one foolish virgin in this counter-parable. She has been accepted by an 'infernal Groom' and condemned to a living hell. Here she laments her misfortunes at his hands. The voice is Verlaine's (Rimbaud himself is cast as the Groom). The theme is the torment to which any couple might descend.

Delirium II. Alchemy of the Word

1. *Kedron*: Stream running through the Kedron Valley to the Dead Sea.

2. *orietur*: From Advent Lauds, 'Super te, Jerusalem, orietur Domine' ('The Lord shall arise upon thee, O Jerusalem').

3. *Cimmeria*: In Ancient cosmology, the fog-bound ends of the earth; close, in Homer, to the kingdom of the dead.

4. *ad matutinum*: 'In the morning'. From Sunday Lauds, often including a Latin hymn by St Ambrose, in which hope dawns with the song of the cockerel ('Gallus'): a preamble to the third couplet of the poem below.

5. *Christus venit*: 'Christ comes'. Also from Sunday Lauds.

Adieu

1. *that horrible stunted tree*: The Tree of Good and Evil, encountered again in 'Morning of Intoxication' (*Illuminations*).

from ILLUMINATIONS

After the Flood

1. *Eucharis*: 'The gracious one', a nymph in Calypso's entourage, from Bishop Fénelon's romance *Telemachus* (1699).

Childhood

1. *superbly black against the grey-green moss*: For 'superbes noires dans la mousse vert-de-gris'. The lack of a comma in the ms. between 'superbes' and 'noires' has led many readers to understand 'superb black women'. This is no less plausible than 'superbly black', but it might be to overstate the exoticism of the passage, with its 'wives of Sultans', to the detriment of a striking visual contrast, achieved by depicting the 'girls and giantesses' as if in negative. The punctuation of the paragraph, and thus the sense, are the subject of controversy.

Morning of Intoxication

1. *Assassins*: The *hashshashin*, a murderous Shi'ite cult (*c.* eleventh–twelfth centuries) whose members were said to eat hashish.

Fragments/12

1. These five brief texts exist on a single, truncated page (p. 12) of the ms. from which the *Illuminations* were assembled for publication. Editors often run them together with another set of fragments on a different page, but it is possible to regard them as a separate group.

Workers

1. *Henrika*: This is not the only name beginning with 'H' in Rimbaud. Elsewhere, the letter seems to denote the 'Habit', in other words, masturbation. Best to settle for an innocent reading of 'Henrika' that does not intrude on the poem.

City

1. *Erinyes*: The Furies. In a later incarnation as Eumenides, or 'Kindly Ones', they became guardians of the law in Athens. That 'Erinyes' – Furies in all their pre-Athenian savagery – are preferred here to 'Eumenides' suggests a dystopian sense of the modern city.

Cities (I)

1. One of a pair of poems which, unlike 'City', revel in vulgarity and contradiction. Much of the extravagant imagery is drawn from Rimbaud's time in London, an industrial-imperial complex *par excellence*. In the early 1870s London would have looked like a sprawling futurist exhibition in comparison to Paris or Brussels.

2. *Nebuchadnezzar*: King of Babylon; conqueror of Jerusalem in 597 BC.

3. *prouder than Brahmas*: I.e. prouder than a God, from Brahma, the Hindu Creator of the Universe. The manuscript (not in Rimbaud's hand but that of his friend Germain Nouveau) has 'nabobs' overscored with what recent editorial consensus takes to be 'Brahmas', even though it is nearly illegible. 'Brahmanes', i.e., Brahmins, has been offered as an alternative.

4. *Sainte-Chapelle*: Louis IX's reliquary chapel on the Ile de la Cité in Paris.

Vigils

1. The last two lines of Section I may be read either as a continuation of the transcendent mood evoked at the outset, or as a return to reality. How to decide? The lucidity of Section II is not the lucidity of disappointment, and Section III is transcendent in another way again. Which lends weight to the first alternative. 'Etait-ce donc ceci?' would then suggest 'So this is what love without enmity is like'. 'Et le rêve fraîchit' might then be understood not as 'the dream goes cold' but as 'the dream comes on', 'fraîchir' here in the sense of growing or getting stronger, as in 'le vent fraîchit': the wind is getting up. The enigma of the 'Amélie' in Section III, like the enigma of Henrika in 'Workers', should not distract the reader unduly. 'Amélie' is, incidentally, an anagram of 'l'aimée', the loved one.

Dawn

1. *wasserfall*: Waterfall (German).

Youth

1. *Psyche*: The lover of Eros, who lost him when she disobeyed his injunction not to look at him.

2. *St Anthony*: The Egyptian hermit tempted by the Devil in a series of hallucinations.

Promontory

1. *Epirus*: Ancient Greek city-state, part of which lay in modern-day Albania.

2. *'Grand'*: According to Graham Robb (*Rimbaud*, 2001, p. 494), 'newspapers known to Rimbaud carried almost daily advertise-ments' for the hotels of Scarborough while he was in England: 'The Grand Hotel, described as "the largest in England", was almost as familiar at one time as the Crystal Palace and Brooklyn Bridge.'

Historic Evening

1. *Tartary*: Central Asian lands east of the Caspian Sea, from which Genghis Khan expanded in the early thirteenth century.

2. *Norns*: The three Fates of Norse mythology, who twine the threads of destiny.

LETTERS

1. *Théodore de Banville*: (1823–91), leader of the so-called 'Parnas-sian school' of poets, who reacted against what they saw as the excesses of Romantic lyricism and whose work appeared in three anthologies under the title of *Le Parnasse contemporain*. Ban-ville's reply to this letter, with which Rimbaud enclosed three of his earliest poems, has been lost. The poems were not published.

2. *I'm seventeen years old*: He was in fact only fifteen and a half.

3. *Ronsard*: Pierre de Ronsard (1524–85), the leader of the group of poets known as the Pléiade.

4. *Anch'io*: An Italian phrase, meaning 'I also'. The painter Correg-gio is supposed to have said, when gazing at a picture of Raphael's, 'I also am a painter.'

5. *Georges Izambard*: A young teacher at Rimbaud's Charleville school with whom he became very friendly.

6. *very different from those under siege in Metz and Strasbourg*: The Franco-Prussian war was still in its early stages, but the French Army was already doing badly.

7. *patriotrolling*: French 'patriouillotisme', a word coined by Rim-baud to combine the senses of 'patrol' and 'patriotic'.

8. *Le Diable à Paris*: A novel by George Sand.

9. *Grandville's drawings*: See note 6 to 'To the Poet on the Matter of Flowers', above.

10. *Fêtes galantes*: Paul Verlaine's (1844–96) collection of poems, *Fêtes galantes*, had been published in 1869.

11. *a nice 120 écu*: I.e. a duodecimo écu, a paper size roughly equivalent to a large post in English paper sizes.

12. *Big liberties . . . d'Hyrcanie*: A liberty because the caesura in this twelve-syllable line occurs in the middle of a word, 'épou/vantable', so infringing the rules of French prosody. The line means 'the frightful Hyrcanian tigress'.

13. *Mazas*: A particularly unpleasant Paris prison of the time.

14. *No siege of Mézières*: Mézières, a short distance from Charleville, was bombarded by the Prussians in December and occupied the following month. Rimbaud made his own inspection of the enemy troops.

15. *girls*: The French word is *fille*, which was then a local word for a jug of wine. Either meaning is possible.

16. *Sta[ba]t mater dolorosa, dum pendet filius*: The opening words of a Latin hymn, misquoted by Rimbaud: 'The dolorous mother stood, as the son hung there'.

17. *when my mad rages . . . even as I write to you*: This was written during the insurrection of the Commune, when many workers were indeed killed by Government troops. It's possible that Rimbaud went to Paris during the Commune, only to return to Charleville before it was put down.

18. *Forgive the play on words*: The play involves the two verbs *penser*, 'to think', and its homophone *panser*, 'to dress, as with a wound'.

19. *It doesn't mean nothing*: Rimbaud had clearly meant to write 'It doesn't not mean anything.'

20. *Paul Demeny*: A poet and an acquaintance of Georges Izambard's.

21. *Ennius*: Quintus Ennius (239–169 BC). Latin poet, author of an epic about the history of Rome, much of which has been lost.

22. *Théroldus*: The name that appears at the end of the great French medieval epic *La Chanson de Roland*, and may be that of its author.

23. *Casimir Delavigne*: (1793–1843), poet and playwright, author of patriotic elegies.

24. *Origins*: Several notable French writers had recently published books with the word 'Origins' in the title. Rimbaud's sardonic view of Racine was shared by Romantic authors such as Victor Hugo.

25. *Jeune France*: Noisy young supporters of Romanticism around 1830.

26. *comprachicos*: In Victor Hugo's novel *L'Homme qui rit*, a band of men who steal and then mutilate children so they can exhibit them for money.

27. *Amants de Paris ... Mort de Paris*: Poems of which nothing is known and which may never have existed.

28. *a dictionary, of any language at all*: A reference to the dictionary produced by the members of the Académie Française.

29. *for in a week's time, I shall be in Paris, perhaps*: Six days after the date of this letter, the '*semaine sanglante*' began in Paris, when the Commune was bloodily suppressed by Government troops.

30. *burn all the verses ... Douai*: The poems survived and included everything Rimbaud had so far written.

31. *Glaneuses*: This collection of Demeny's poems had appeared in 1870.

32. *boyars*: Izambard had been offered a tutoring job in Russia, hence the 'boyars'; he didn't take it.

33. *a family Buffon*: Buffon's great *Histoire naturelle* appeared in thirty-six volumes between 1749 and 1789.

34. *To Paul Verlaine*: This fragment from a lost letter was quoted by Verlaine's widow in her memoirs. Verlaine and Rimbaud having become fast friends, and perhaps lovers. While Rimbaud was stuck in Charleville, Verlaine was trying to sort things out with his wife and in-laws.

35. *Closerie des Lilas*: A Paris café long frequented by writers and artists.

36. *Ariette oubliée*: ('Forgotten Arietta'); this was not Rimbaud's work, but by Charles Simon Favart (1710–92), who wrote songs and something like a hundred sentimental comedies.

37. *Bretagne*: Charles Bretagne was an acquaintance of Izambard's in Charleroi, whom Rimbaud met in 1870; he was homosexual, and an occultist.

38. *our revered Priest*: The 'Priest' is Bretagne.

39. *that way of the cross*: A reference to the journey they had seemingly promised to take together.

40. *Gavroche*: The nickname of Jean-Louis Forain, a poet and close friend of both Verlaine and Rimbaud – Gavroche appears in Victor Hugo's *Les Misérables*, as a typically insolent, vital (and ultimately heroic) Paris street-boy.

41. *Stuff Mérat ... twine himself round you*: Chanal and Périn were

among Rimbaud's schoolteachers, Mérat was a poet, the others are unknown.

42. *someone very big in Madrid's*: Probably a reference to a habitué of the Café de Madrid in Paris, much used by writers.

43. *will spk agn re gd safe lodgings*: Written in a sort of shorthand, to mean 'We'll speak again about good safe lodgings.'

44. *Regnault*: Henri-Alexandre-Georges Régnault (1843–71), a painter and friend of Mallarmé's.

45. *Ernest Delahaye*: One of Rimbaud's earliest friends, who many years later devoted no less than three separate books to the writer and his work.

46. *Parishit, Junphe*: The distortions practised here on the words *Paris* and *juin* are typical of the argot Rimbaud used with his close friends in Paris; cf. '*absomphe*' for 'absinthe'.

47. *La Renaissance*: *La Renaissance littéraire et artistique* was a review started in 1872; it had printed a poem by Rimbaud the previous September.

48. *Pagan Book, or Negro Book*: This was to become *A Season in Hell*.

49. *the Nôress*: The *Nord-est*, a Charleville newspaper for which Rimbaud had already worked.

50. *Boglione*: I.e. Bouillon, the border town with Belgium referred to in the previous letter.

51. *Mais qu'est-ce qu'ils ont donc à dire que c'est laid*: 'But what's the matter with them then, saying it's ugly . . .'

52. *Do not stream by fire and milk*: The line would better go: 'Are they not streaming with tenderness and milk?'

53. *Delatrichine*: Delatrichine, Deléclanche and Delamorue are corruptions of the name Delahaye.

54. *Badingue[t]*: A nickname given to the ex-Emperor, Napoleon III.

55. *orde lette*: Exact sense uncertain, but '*orde*' suggests *ordure*, or filth, and '*lette*' is obviously *lettre*, or letter.

56. *Barrère*: Camille Barrère was one of the many Communard refugees then living in London; he later became an ambassador.

57. *Vermersch*: Eugène Vermersch, a radical journalist under sentence of death in France and living in London.

58. *the letter you sent to Mme Smith*: This letter has not survived; Mrs Smith was their London landlady. The sentence underneath had been crossed out by Rimbaud.

59. *Andrieu*: Jules Andrieu (1838–84), a Communard refugee in London, for whom Rimbaud had a rare affection.

60. *Volunteer Spain . . . if possible*: This hysterical threat to go and

fight in the Carlist wars in Spain was enough to send Rimbaud hastening to Brussels.

61. *Wagner*: Not the composer, but the name of the street in which he had been lodging.

62. *Ein freundliches Zimmer*: A friendly room (German).

63. *I salute the army*: His brother Frédéric was doing his military service; Vitalie and Isabelle were his sisters.

64. *Loyola*: I.e. Verlaine, newly converted to Catholicism and Jesuitical in Rimbaud's eyes.

65. *DREAM*: This the last piece of verse Rimbaud is known to have written.

66. *Lefèbvre*: The son of Mme Rimbaud's landlord, to whom Rimbaud had given German lessons.

67. *Keller*: A Deputy who had campaigned to raise the period of compulsory army service to three years.

68. *the current science 'bachot'*: Delahaye had failed the science part of his '*bachot*', or baccalaureate exam, in March.

69. *Petdeloup*: A character in a book by Nadar whose name was applied to old schoolmasters; it means, literally, wolf-fart. Delahaye was an usher in a school in Soissons, a town famous for its haricot beans.

70. The letter was written in English.

71. *Recently deserted . . . French army*: He had in fact deserted from the Dutch Colonial Army, but gives here the number of the French regiment in which his father had been an officer.

72. *Only today . . . sailing*: The power of attorney had been asked for by his family, who were now settling his dead father's succession.

73. *old Michel . . . Cotaîche*: 'Old Michel' was one of the workers on the family farm and 'Cotaîche' his pronunciation of the name of a mare called Comtesse.

74. *the record-book business*: A reference to the army service he had so far avoided doing.

75. *the building works in Panama*: Work had started on the Panama Canal.

76. *I've picked up an illness*: It is possible, but far from certain, that Rimbaud had contracted syphilis.

77. *a letter for Delahaye*: The letter asked Delahaye to buy him a theodolite and other surveying equipment, mineralogical specimens and yet more technical manuals on geodesy, trigonometry, chemistry, meteorology, etc.

78. *Dubar*: A branch manager working for Alfred Bardey.

79. *Moussayas' agent*: The Moussaya brothers were Greek traders in Harar greatly disliked by Rimbaud.

80. *frasleh*: A frasleh was a unit of weight, equivalent to about 17 kilos.

81. *talaris*: The *talari* was the local name of the Austro-Hungarian thaler or dollar, and the principal trading currency in Harar.

82. *paras*: A Turkish coin, of which there were 40 to the piastre.

83. *M. Sacconi*: Pierre Sacconi, a French trader and explorer.

84. *abbans*: Leaders or guides of caravans.

85. *Sebians*: Camel-drivers.

86. *M. Sotiro*: Constantin Sotiro, a Greek trader in Harar and one of the few Europeans Rimbaud liked there.

87. *the Guerris and Bartris*: Tribes living near Harar.

88. *the Itou will again be invaded ... beginning of 1884*: The Itou plateau was especially fertile and a major source of coffee, hence Rimbaud's interest in it.

89. *Guéset, Kéhas, Kasdir, Kahrab, Abbayas*: These were articles copied from native samples: axe-heads, stakes, fabrics, etc.

90. *Vilayeti*: A raw cotton from British India.

91. *maunds*: A unit of weight equivalent to 28 lbs.

92. *2 corja largest aïtabanes ... tobe*: A corja was a batch of twenty; aitabares may refer to animal skins; the tobe was a raw cotton garment worn by Somalis and Gallas.

93. *Oughaz*: The local chief.

94. *goums*: Clansmen or kinsmen.

95. *what you tell me about Frédéric ... great harm*: Rimbaud's brother, a local bus-driver, seems to have been considering black-mail as a way of raising money on which to get married.

96. *Gordon*: Charles George Gordon (1833–85) had become governor of the Egyptian Sudan for the second time; having rejected an order to evacuate Khartoum, he was besieged there for ten months and killed by the Mahdist army fighting for Sudanese independence two days before the city was relieved.

97. *Wolseley*: Garnet Joseph Wolseley (1833–1913) led the attempt to relieve Khartoum in 1885 and later rose to be Commander-in-Chief of the British army, which he did much to modernize.

98. *We can also see that Madagascar ... under our control*: It became a French protectorate officially in 1885, but native resistance continued for many years after that.

99. *Tonkin*: Then the name of the region subsequently known as North Vietnam; it became a French protectorate in 1884.

100. *Menilek, the king of Shewa*: Menilek II became Emperor of Ethiopia as a client of the Italians in 1889; at this time he was preparing to conquer Harar.

101. *Yohannes of Tigre*: The King of Tigre, nominal Emperor of the country and Menilek's expansionist rival.

102. *Labatut*: Pierre Labatut was a French trader who had lived in Shewa for fifteen years; going into business with him proved disastrous for Rimbaud, as we shall see.

103. *attack on the Barral caravan*: Barral was a Frenchman whose party had been massacred by tribesmen in March 1886.

104. *Dajaz Mekonnen*: A *dajaz* was a local governor; Mekonnen was governor of Harar (and the father of the celebrated Ethiopian Emperor Haile Selassie).

105. *the late Labatut's caravan*: Labatut had suffered a brain tumour and had gone back to Paris to die.

106. *the hazage*: In effect a magistrate: this one was a friend of Labatut's Abyssinian widow.

107. *Bosphore égyptien*: This French-language newspaper in Cairo was edited by the brother of Jules Borelli, whom Rimbaud knew in Harar (see n. 111); it published Rimbaud's article in two parts.

108. *the late Soleillet*: Paul Soleillet was another French trader; he, too, had died suddenly before he was able to set out with his caravan.

109. *a Decauville track*: A Decauville was a narrow-gauge railway invented by an engineer of that name.

110. *Franguis*: The contemptuous local term for Europeans.

111. *Jules Borelli*: An explorer from Marseille, who saw quite a lot of Rimbaud and was later to be a prime source of information about his life in Harar and elsewhere.

112. *Brémond*: There were two Brémonds, uncle and nephew, both French traders in Djibouti and Harar.

113. *okiets*: 'Okiet' or 'waqet' is the standard Amharic word for an ounce.

114. *Monseigneur Taurin*: A Franciscan missionary who had become Bishop of Harar.

115. *M. Audon's agent*: Rimbaud should have written, 'M. Deschamps' agent'.

116. *Mohammed Abu-Bekr ... travellers in Shewa*: The Abu-Bekrs were prominent slave-traders, but it's unlikely Rimbaud had dealings with them.

117. *rotolis*: A 'rotol' was a weight, a bit less than half a kilogram.

118. *the abuna*: A senior cleric in the Coptic Church.

119. *tedj*: A mead-like drink made from water, honey and tree-bark.

120. *Allow me, Monsieur . . . sent on to me*: The request was turned down.

121. *Ilg*: Alfred Ilg (b. 1854) was a Swiss, an engineer by training, who had become King Menilek's most influential and trusted adviser, and was admired especially by Rimbaud for his (rare) honesty.

122. *Your predictions . . . are those of everyone here*: A reference to the increasingly aggressive policy of the Italians, who had occupied Messawa three years before.

123. *the Porte*: The Ottoman Government in Constantinople (now Istanbul).

124. *the Portal Mission*: Gerald Portal, British envoy to the Emperor Yohannes IV, led a mission to try and make peace with the Italians.

125. *the Khedive*: The Viceroy in Egypt.

126. *Choum*: A local chieftain.

127. *Bienenfeld*: The Bienenfeld brothers, Vittorio and Giuseppe, were coffee traders from Trieste.

128. *Zebad*: The Amharic name for the civet, the wild cat from which musk is extracted.

129. *the Konollas of Harar, in the Gadiboursi, etc.*: The reference of Konollas is uncertain, but *kolla* was the Amharic term for the lowlands; the Gadiboursi were a native Abyssinian people.

130. *Lagarde*: Léonce Lagarde, the Governor of Obock.

131. *I have received here your kind Tritligasse 27 April*: Ilg was back in his native Switzerland.

132. *Le Roy*: I.e. the King.

133. *keremt*: The name for the rainy season.

134. *It's certainly my intention to make the donation you speak of*: Presumably a contribution towards his brother's upkeep.

135. *guibeur*: A form of tax or tribute.

136. *The aboun Mathios*: The head of the Amharic clergy.

137. *the Exposition*: There was a large international exhibition or world fair in Paris in 1889, the event for which the Eiffel Tower was built.

138. *brillé samples*: Jugs used to hold the local mead drink.

139. *mateb*: Silk lace worn by Christian soldiers, to ensure that they would be given a Christian burial if they were killed in battle.

140. *the Guebi*: The seat of the government in Harar.

141. *a Pasteur establishment*: I.e. an establishment for the rabid, Pasteur having in 1885 perfected a vaccine against rabies.

142. *beur*: Money.

143. *the intelligent Count*: Count Antonelli, then in Abyssinia trying
     to establish an Italian protectorate.
144. *tota*: A species of small monkey.
145. *Abiete*: Abet ('Master' in Amharic) was a call for justice from the
     King, or else a demand for an appointment with him.
146. *Gabares*: Those natives liable to be taxed.
147. *calatié*: A word meaning both an order and the person bearing it.
148. *Giraf*: A whip used in punishments.
149. *an 'Akadar'*: A local caravan leader.
150. *the Hararghe*: The Harar region.
151. *Wotaderes*: Soldiers.
152. *Gondaris*: A special body of soldiers from Tigre.
153. *daboulas*: A measure of grain roughly equal to a cwt., here
     referring to sacks containing that weight of coffee.
154. *ministry 'degli esteri'*: The Italian Foreign Ministry.
155. *I refusalem*: A joke formed by treating the Je- of Jerusalem as if
     it were the first-person pronoun.
156. *'Sost masseria'*: Meaning unknown, but clearly a reference to
     guns of some sort.
157. *Gorezzas*: A black and white monkey peculiar to Abyssinia.
158. *naggadies*: Itinerant traders.
159. *Zerbias*: Huts.
160. *shuftas*: Brigands.
161. *saggare*: I.e. *sagar*, an Amharic word meaning very fast.
162. *the protector of dogs*: Rimbaud was fined in Harar for poisoning
     dogs that urinated on his drying hides.
163. *my left leg*: Actually, his right leg.
164. *Djami*: Rimbaud's servant-boy in Harar.
165. *Aphinar*: Not a real or even approximate place-name.

Index of Titles and First Lines

FRENCH TITLES

FRENCH FIRST LINES

ENGLISH TITLES

ENGLISH FIRST LINES

Index of Letters